Credits

Authors
Erez Ben-Ari

Ran Dolev

Reviewers
Ben Bernstein

Dennis E. Lee

Dominik Zemp

Acquisition Editor
Stephanie Moss

Development Editors
Rukhsana Khambatta

Mayuri Kokate

Technical Editor
Arani Roy

Indexers
Monica Ajmera Mehta

Rekha Nair

Editorial Team Leader
Gagandeep Singh

Project Team Leader
Ashwin Shetty

Project Coordinator
Poorvi Nair

Proofreaders
Lesley Harrison

Kevin McGowan

Graphics
Geetanjali Sawant

Production Coordinator
Shantanu Zagade

Cover Work
Shantanu Zagade

Microsoft Forefront UAG 2010 Administrator's Handbook

Take full command of Microsoft Forefront Unified Access Gateway to secure your business applications and provide dynamic remote access with DirectAccess

Erez Ben-Ari

Ran Dolev

PUBLISHING

BIRMINGHAM - MUMBAI

Microsoft Forefront UAG 2010 Administrator's Handbook

First published: January 2011

Production Reference: 1170111

Published by Packt Publishing Ltd.
32 Lincoln Road
Olton
Birmingham, B27 6PA, UK.

ISBN 978-1-849681-62-9

www.packtpub.com

Cover Image by Tina Negus (tina_manthorpe@sky.com)

About the Authors

Erez Ben-Ari is a long time technologist and journalist, and has worked in the information technology industry since 1991. During his career, Erez has provided security consulting and analysis services for some of the leading companies and organizations in the world; including Intel, IBM, Amdocs, CA, HP, NDS, Sun Microsystems, Oracle, and many others. His work has gained national fame in Israel, and he has been featured in the press regularly. Having joined Microsoft in 2000, Erez has worked for many years in Microsoft's Development Center in Israel, where Microsoft's ISA Server was developed. Being a part of the release of ISA 2000, ISA 2004, and ISA 2006, he held several roles, including Operation engineering, Software testing, Web-based software design, and testing automation design. Now living in the United States, Erez still works for Microsoft, currently as a senior support engineer for UAG.

As a writer, Erez has been a journalist since 1995, and has written for some of the leading publications in Israel and in the United States. He has been a member of the Israeli National Press Office since 2001, and his personal blogs are read by thousands of visitors per month. Erez has also written, produced, and edited content for TV and radio, working for Israel's TV Channel 2, Ananey Communications, Radio Haifa, and other venues.

Most recently, Erez has completed his work on a courseware book titled *Planning, deploying, and managing Microsoft Forefront Threat Management Gateway 2010*, in collaboration with several other authors.

Ran Dolev is a veteran of network security and SSL VPN industries. Ran has worked with the UAG product for more than twelve years, since the product's inception at the start-up company Whale Communications in 1998, where Ran was the first full-time developer of the product. After several years he moved to a services position as the EMEA Professional Services Manager for the team. In this role he has designed and delivered numerous IAG and UAG training sessions in North America, Europe, Middle East, Asia, and Australia, to customers, partners, and Microsoft employees. Ran also provides consulting and deployment services for many of Microsoft's enterprise UAG customers.

About the Reviewers

Ben Bernstein is a senior program manager with the Microsoft UAG DirectAccess development team. Ben has worked for Microsoft since 2001, and has held several software development and leadership positions. During his time with Microsoft, Ben has been deeply involved with the development of many of Microsoft's security product suites, including ISA 2004, ISA 2006, TMG, and UAG. Ben often speaks at conferences and public events related to information security and holds a BA and MBA degrees from the The Interdisciplinary Center and Technion Institute in Israel.

Dennis E. Lee is a noted network security expert specializing in Microsoft Forefront Security products. His journey in technology began as soon as he was able to take apart his old electronic toys. Self-taught in the art of web design, he used the Internet as a forum to foster discussion on topics such as computer self-help, graphic design, and programming. That led him into network security in which he actively attends community events and contributes to many different forums and blogs. As a consultant for Celestix Networks, Inc., Dennis travels the globe designing security solutions for organizations of all sizes. Whether it's a startup or global organization, he thrives on the opportunity to help the world do its job better. Checking out the local cuisine in all the places he visits is cool too. He wants you to read this book because while he enjoys traveling, it's unlikely that he'll be able to get to everyone in the world and believes that this book will guide you on how to build the most secure remote access solution using UAG.

Thank you to Sally, my colleagues at Celestix Networks and the people at Microsoft for sharing my passion of working with great products.

Dominik Zemp is a technical solutions specialist for Microsoft' security solutions and has worked in the security market since 2004. He is going to graduate in February 2011 from Lucerne University of Applied Sciences and Arts with a Bachelor's degree in Information Technology specialization in Software Systems. He has served as network engineer, system engineer, and security consultant. He uses Microsoft's Forefront and security products on a daily basis and is specialized in Microsoft's Identity and Access Management solutions such as Forefront Unified Access Gateway 2010.

www.PacktPub.com

Support files, eBooks, discount offers and more

You might want to visit www.PacktPub.com for support files and downloads related to your book.

Did you know that Packt offers eBook versions of every book published, with PDF and ePub files available? You can upgrade to the eBook version at www.PacktPub.com and as a print book customer, you are entitled to a discount on the eBook copy. Get in touch with us at service@packtpub.com for more details.

At www.PacktPub.com, you can also read a collection of free technical articles, sign up for a range of free newsletters and receive exclusive discounts and offers on Packt books and eBooks.

http://PacktLib.PacktPub.com

Do you need instant solutions to your IT questions? PacktLib is Packt's online digital book library. Here, you can access, read and search across Packt's entire library of books.

Why Subscribe?

- Fully searchable across every book published by Packt
- Copy and paste, print and bookmark content
- On demand and accessible via web browser

Free Access for Packt account holders

If you have an account with Packt at www.PacktPub.com, you can use this to access PacktLib today and view nine entirely free books. Simply use your login credentials for immediate access.

Instant Updates on New Packt Books

Get notified! Find out when new books are published by following @PacktEnterprise on Twitter, or the *Packt Enterprise* Facebook page.

Dedicated to my wife, Paula, who forgave me for locking myself up in my study for so many months while writing this book, and to my son, Sol, who, despite just being born, kept quiet and let me do this.

— *Erez Ben-Ari*

I dedicate this to the memory of my father, Dan Costescu, writer, novelist, journalist, newspaper founder and editor, who used writing to fight from exile for justice and for a better life for his fellow countrymen. I miss you, Dad!

— *Ran Dolev*

Table of Contents

Preface

The Israeli department of defence has one of the strictest information security guidelines in the world, and a part of these guidelines is the requirement to have complete physical separation between the public and internal networks. A regular firewall just won't do, and this requirement gave birth to the concept of the **Air-Gap**, a revolutionary product for its time. The Air-Gap and **e-Gap** products used a physical switch that enabled the transfer of data from one network to the other, but still kept them physically disconnected. One might think of this like a shuttle transferring passengers from one land-mass to another. Whether this is more secure than advanced software-based firewalls can be debated, but the product did meet the guidelines and became very successful in Israel.

Building on this success, Whale Communications distributed the e-Gap appliance throughout the world, and continued its development. In 2006, Whale Communications was purchased by Microsoft, and the next version, named **Intelligent Application Gateway** or **IAG**, had similar capabilities, but ditched the physical switch and the dual-server design with a software firewall — **Microsoft's ISA 2006 server**.

The success of IAG led, of course, to the next version — **UAG**, short for **Unified Access Gateway**. UAG has some new capabilities although fundamentally it is very similar to its predecessor, IAG. Like IAG, UAG combines two major functions:

- Application publishing (also known as **reverse proxy**)
- **VPN server**

For those who are familiar with proxy servers, a reverse proxy does exactly the opposite. A proxy sits at the edge of an organization's network, and fetches data from the Internet for the employees inside the network. A reverse proxy also sits at the edge, but fetches data from within the internal network, and delivers it to people connecting from outside. This allows employees to be away from the office, at their home or on the road, but still have access to the sensitive organization applications in a way that's easy to use, but secure at the same time.

For those who are not familiar with the concept of a **VPN — Virtual Private Network**, this is a common way to let employees connect to the internal network remotely. Many products on the market provide VPN services including the built-in Windows service **RRAS**. However, using a reverse proxy instead allows quicker and easier access. Using a VPN service requires the end user to create configurations that may be complicated and are often not very secure. For example, an employee that uses his own home computer to connect to the organization's network may be sharing the same computer with his family, and that computer could be home to a virus zoo, or be exposed to external penetration via an unsecured Wi-Fi home network. If the computer is a laptop, it could potentially be stolen or lost, allowing the thief or finder to connect to the internal network and compromise it.

UAG's feature-set offers solutions to these problems using advanced features. The reverse-proxy side of the house allows easy access through most modern web browsers, with no configuration required by the user. The user simply types in the designated URL, waits for the special client-components to be installed automatically, and after a simple log-on, they can run the organization's web-based applications. While almost all firewalls offer the ability to do simple server-publishing, using a reverse-proxy is more secure. The reason is that a firewall, even one that does stateful inspection, is only passing data back-and-forth between the internal server and the client. A reverse proxy, on the other hand, stands-in for the internal server. The client is talking to the proxy, which impersonates the internal server. Even if the proxy is successfully attacked and taken-down, the internal server is never touched, and service is not interrupted.

Unfortunately, the reverse proxy service is only usable for Web-based applications. It's good for things such as Outlook Web Access and SharePoint, but many other applications require more complicated TCP/IP traffic. A good example is RDP, which works on port 3389, and cannot be simply reverse proxied. For that reason, the original e-Gap server included a feature called **SSL-VPN**, which has been expanded to a full range of VPN options with UAG. VPN allows pretty much any networked application to connect to internal servers by simulating a full network connection to the corporate network. Originally, e-Gap and IAG offered a VPN connection which was encrypted using **SSL (Secure Socket Layer)** and offered better security than many of the VPN products that existed in the market at the time. With UAG, SSL-VPN is still included, but also with several other options, most notable of which is **DirectAccess**. DirectAccess was originally developed to be integrated into the Windows Server 2008 R2 and Windows 7 Client platform, but the integration of this technology with UAG adds several additional security mechanisms that make for an easier and more secure deployment.

Using **DirectAccess** (frequently referred to as **DA**) with UAG includes several components that allow for a better integration with networks that are based on the **IPv4 protocol**, and also includes very advanced endpoint security, which has been a strong selling point for IAG and e-Gap for many years. UAG's endpoint security allows an administrator to enforce certain security policies by preventing client computers that do not meet these policies from connecting, or from accessing specific applications. These policies can include, for example, the requirement to have an antivirus product installed on the computer as a condition for allowing a connection. A policy can be even more granular and require a specific AV product, and even when the AV definitions were updated on the client. In fact, an advanced administrator can even write his own policy using VBScript to obtain the utmost granular control, down to the registry-key level.

What this book covers

Chapter 1, Planning Your Deployment, will cover the hardware and software requirements for using UAG, and what needs to be planned before purchasing the product, such as Load Balancers, client-support (PC, Mac, and Linux), and so on.

Chapter 2, Installing UAG, will cover the required steps to prepare and install UAG. We will discuss the critical settings you will need to configure before the installation and how to prepare the server for it, and then we will go through the setup process step-by-step. Finally, we will review how to verify that the installation went successfully and learn how to handle some common issues we might face.

Chapter 3, Trunk Types and Uses, will cover UAG's building blocks—trunks and applications. We will review the various types of each, what they are used for, and how to create them. We will not cover specific application publishing, but we will introduce some of the concepts that make the whole thing tick.

Chapter 4, Publishing Web Applications, will cover web applications and how to publish them, including focusing on the most popular applications types—SharePoint and Exchange.

Chapter 5, Advanced Applications and Services, will review the various applications, how to choose to appropriate templates, and how to configure them. We will also discuss in detail some of the additional built-in applications, and briefly introduce DirectAccess.

Chapter 6, Authenticating and Controlling Access, will explain the various types of authentication that UAG can use with Windows servers and third party servers. The chapter will also talk about managing user access to applications and trunks (authorization).

Chapter 7, Configuring UAG Clients, will cover UAG's client components. The client components are what the end-user sees, and they control the user's access to the portal and applications, so it's very important to understand how they work, and what they can and cannot do.

Chapter 8, Endpoint Policies discusses endpoint policies—how they can be used to provide high security, how to configure them, and how to manage them.

Chapter 9, Server Maintenance and upkeep, will cover ways to keep an eye on the server using built-in tools such as the Web Monitor, the Event Log, and the TMG live monitoring console. It will also discuss keeping the server in top shape by performance monitoring, applying patches, updates and service packs, and performing backups.

Chapter 10, Advanced Configuration, will discuss the Advanced Trunk Configuration, which allows the admin to control various aspects of the portal behavior and special-functions.

Chapter 11, DirectAccess, will introduce the admin to various DA related concepts such as IPv6, Teredo, IPHTTPS, DNS64, and NAT64. It will then detail how to configure DA in various scenarios.

Chapter 12, Troubleshooting, will discuss common problems and how to address them, as well as more generic troubleshooting concepts and technologies such as Netmon, PerfMon. The chapter will also offer a collection of external resources, such as blogs, wikis, and articles.

Appendix A, Introduction to RegEx, introduces us to Regular Expressions and the UAG RegEx syntax.

Appendix B, Introduction to ASP, gives a short introduction to ASP programming. Since UAG has quite a bit of web-based user interface, knowing a little about ASP and how it works will allow you to customize it to some degree.

What you need for this book

You will need Microsoft Forefront **Unified Access Gateway** (UAG) with Update 1 for this book. UAG is offered to the public in two distinct distributions. A company can choose to purchase the product in the form of an appliance, or as a downloadable **ISO** image file, which can be burned to **DVD** or mounted on a virtual DVD drive. UAG is a server product, and can only be installed on a Windows Server 2008 R2 or later, therefore the hardware requirements are combined with those of R2. The primary requirement for R2 is having a 64 bit processor and 32 GB of free disk space. UAG's minimum requirements are that the processor is a dual-core one running at 2.66 GHz or faster, and that the system has 4 GB of memory, and an extra 2.5 GB of disk space.

Who this book for

This book is intended for IT Personnel, Network Engineers, System Engineers, System Administrators, and Security Engineers who are planning to implement UAG in their organization, or have already implemented it and want to discover more about the product's abilities and how to use them effectively. To properly use the book, you should have some understanding of IT and networking technologies and terminology, such as IP, DNS, Ethernet, Web Server, and VPN. Programming knowledge is not required; though it might be of benefit for advanced customization techniques that are supported by UAG, this is not within the scope of this book. The book also requires fundamental understanding of Microsoft technologies and systems, such as Windows and Internet Explorer. For some chapters, understanding of more advanced concepts may be needed, such as SSL, Firewalls, IPv6, Adv. TCP/IP, XML, and HTML.

UAG versus IAG

As mentioned before, the basic functionality of the product from IAG to UAG has not changed much. UAG adds some broader functionality for newer applications, and support for more modern VPN technologies. The application publishing that was a part of IAG is mostly still here, with some updates to the user-interface, and some new application templates like Exchange 2010 and RemoteApp publishing. The SSL Wrapper and Network connector are also still here, but **SSTP (Secure Socket Tunneling Protocol)** and DA (DirectAccess) are now also included. The client components have gone through some improvements as well, and now support Windows 7, Internet Explorer 8, and several 64 bit operating systems. The user interface has gone through a nice face-lift, both on the server side and client-side (the "look and feel" of the portal).

A significant change in UAG compared to the previous generations is the availability of UAG as an installable software. IAG has been traditionally available as a hardware appliance, and recently as a virtual-appliance (a VHD file that can be run on Hyper-Visor or other virtualization products), but with UAG, an administrator can now install the product on any server he wishes to (assuming, of course, it meets the specifications for the minimum hardware support and for running Windows Server 2008 R2). This makes UAG much more readily available, and far easier to integrate into complex enterprise environments, reducing the total-cost of ownership (TCO) for IT resources.

Another improvement added to UAG over IAG is the built-in support for arrays, and integration with Windows **NLB (Network Load Balancing)**. In the past, integration of IAG was only possible with third-party load balancing solutions, and even then, it was somewhat limited, as administrators had to manually mirror the configuration between servers, and repeat the manual sync whenever a change was required. With UAG's built-in array management functionality, an administrator can build a cluster of up to eight UAG servers. If using an array, it can be load balanced using external load balancers, or integrated with Windows NLB.

Another notable addition to the functionality of UAG is the integration with **NAP (Network Access Protection)**, which provides an extensive platform for maintaining endpoint health and sanity that goes beyond even the native endpoint policy management that IAG had. For example, NAP continually monitors the client's health and can respond to changes even during a session. It can also direct a client to an update server or other remediation server, so the client can address the health issues and reconnect, rather than just getting blocked from access.

From the management side of the house, UAG now allows the server administrator more control over logging and monitoring of user activity. This is achieved by enabling logging to SQL, which allows for better performance and easier analysis of logged data, and creating highly customized reports.

What's in the box?

Just like IAG included ISA 2006 as its built-in firewall, UAG similarly includes Forefront **TMG (Threat Management Gateway) 2010**, which is the latest incarnation of Microsoft's highly regarded firewall server. TMG is automatically installed as a part of the UAG setup process, and once in place, protects the server from the outside world using its well known stateful inspection engine. Although it's tempting to think of this as two products in one, in reality, the use of TMG is somewhat limited, because it's controlled by UAG. Whenever the UAG configuration is changed and activated, UAG pushes various configuration elements and rules directly into TMG's configuration containers, and these might override or conflict with manual configuration done by the administrator. This poses some security risk; such manual configuration may unintentionally expose the server to outside threats. The same goes for **IIS (Internet Information Services)**, which are a part of Windows Server. To perform its reverse-proxy functionality, UAG pushes various configurations directly into IIS, and changes to IIS's configuration, puts it at risk of a conflict or vulnerability which could jeopardize the entire server. For this reason, Microsoft recommends against attempting to leverage a UAG server for additional functions within organizations, and does not support this.

Conventions

In this book, you will find a number of styles of text that distinguish between different kinds of information. Here are some examples of these styles, and an explanation of their meaning.

Code words in text are shown as follows: "but you can also use the command `gpudate /force`, which forces the computer to update its group policy right away".

Any command-line input or output is written as follows:

```
auditpol.exe /set /SubCategory:"IPsec Main Mode","IPsec Extended Mode" /
success:enable /failure:enable
```

New terms and **important words** are shown in bold. Words that you see on the screen, in menus or dialog boxes for example, appear in the text like this: "To do so, open **Administrative Tools** and open **Group Policy Management**."

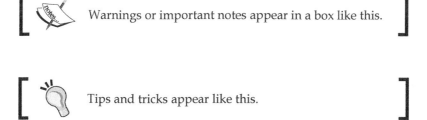

Warnings or important notes appear in a box like this.

Tips and tricks appear like this.

Reader feedback

Feedback from our readers is always welcome. Let us know what you think about this book—what you liked or may have disliked. Reader feedback is important for us to develop titles that you really get the most out of.

To send us general feedback, simply send an e-mail to feedback@packtpub.com, and mention the book title via the subject of your message.

If there is a book that you need and would like to see us publish, please send us a note in the **SUGGEST A TITLE** form on www.packtpub.com or e-mail suggest@packtpub.com.

If there is a topic that you have expertise in and you are interested in either writing or contributing to a book on, see our author guide on www.packtpub.com/authors.

Errata

Although we have taken every care to ensure the accuracy of our content, mistakes do happen. If you find a mistake in one of our books—maybe a mistake in the text or the code—we would be grateful if you would report this to us. By doing so, you can save other readers from frustration and help us improve subsequent versions of this book. If you find any errata, please report them by visiting http://www.packtpub.com/support, selecting your book, clicking on the **let us know** link, and entering the details of your errata. Once your errata are verified, your submission will be accepted and the errata will be uploaded on our website, or added to any list of existing errata, under the Errata section of that title. Any existing errata can be viewed by selecting your title from http://www.packtpub.com/support.

Piracy

Piracy of copyright material on the Internet is an ongoing problem across all media. At Packt, we take the protection of our copyright and licenses very seriously. If you come across any illegal copies of our works, in any form, on the Internet, please provide us with the location address or website name immediately so that we can pursue a remedy.

Please contact us at copyright@packtpub.com with a link to the suspected pirated material.

We appreciate your help in protecting our authors, and our ability to bring you valuable content.

Questions

You can contact us at questions@packtpub.com if you are having a problem with any aspect of the book, and we will do our best to address it.

1
Planning Your Deployment

In this chapter, we will discuss the various environmental issues that need to be planned ahead of deploying **UAG** (**Unified Access Gateway**). We shall look at what makes UAG tick and look at software, hardware, and networking considerations. We will review how UAG interacts with what's around it and discuss where in your network to place the server for optimal usability and ease of deployment, as well as looking at how clients fit into the picture.

Basic principles

Even though installing a UAG server is quite straightforward, it is very important to plan your deployment ahead of time and prepare your hardware, software, and network correctly. Failing to do so might end in an installation failure, or even worse—a situation requiring a lengthy re-planning of the integration, not to mention explaining all of this to "the guys upstairs".

When planning the installation, one must keep in mind that a UAG server is fundamentally a router. It has an external side that would be the access point for connecting clients from the internet, and an internal side through which the server can fetch data from internal corporate servers. While it is theoretically possible to use the server with a single network card, this option is not supported, and will not work for most of UAG's functionality. UAG includes Forefront **TMG** (**Threat Management Gateway**) 2010, Microsoft's well known enterprise-class firewall; therefore it is possible to have the external interface connected directly to the internet. Nonetheless, many organizations choose to play it extra-safe and place the server behind an additional firewall, which can also improve UAG's performance by eliminating junk traffic that might otherwise burden it. This, of course, requires careful planning of the routing, as well as opening the proper ports on the firewall to allow traffic to take its course.

UAG is designed to enable remote access in two primary roles: application publishing and VPN. A regular proxy is a server that resides at the edge of an organization's network, like a guard at the building's reception. The regular proxy fetches data from the outside world for the company's employees, much like a guard would escort a guest to an employee's office. A reverse proxy does the exact opposite—it fetches data from within the internal network, and delivers it to people on the outside. A regular proxy is usually about speeding things up, but also about protecting the network from uncontrolled access, while a reverse proxy is mostly about security. This is especially so for UAG, which might slow things down a bit, but provides a high level of security.

The benefit to an organization is that, using reverse proxy publishing, employees working from home or on-the-go can access the organization's internal applications from wherever they are, while still maintaining the organizational network safely and securely. Those of you who know their firewalls must be thinking "But...any firewall can do this!" That is correct – almost all modern firewalls allow various forms of server publishing, but UAG adds additional levels of security. Firewall server publishing is usually quite simplistic – an administrator specifies the internal IP and port, and the firewall listens and forwards the requests and responses to and from the internal servers. From a security standpoint, this is almost equivalent to allowing the users to interact directly with the internal server, as the firewall inspection usually takes place at the TCP packet level only. Sure, it can recognize and stop some common **Denial of Service (DoS)** and other attacks like Port scan and half scan, but hardly any application-level attacks. UAG, on the other hand, is much cleverer:

- Firstly, UAG includes TMG—a firewall, so it does exactly what was described above.

- UAG also impersonates the internal server, so the end-user is actually interacting only with UAG. If the user is able to mount a successful attack and crash the server, UAG may go down (this has never happened, by the way), but the sensitive internal server will march on, undisturbed.

- Another security layer on top of that is endpoint detection, which boosts security even further. Clients connecting to UAG must undergo a configurable security policy check that can eliminate many threats. For example, it can reject connections from computers that have not gone through a specific "preparation" by the organization, so that potential attackers are turned away even before they try to log in. It can reject connections from computers which are not well protected by an Anti-Virus or a personal firewall, to reduce the risk of a worm infecting the internal network. If this is not enough, the UAG logon process can be customized extensively, to boost security even further. We will not discuss this sort of customization in this book, but just to give you an idea, one example is the ability to include a **CAPTCHA** mechanism, so automated brute-force attacks cannot be executed to try to obtain a login to the server.

The second major functionality of UAG is VPN, which allows remote users to connect to the organization's network in a way that emulates them being connected directly to the network while at the office. This sort of connection can allow them to do anything they could do in the office, and provide the most advanced work environment (pyjamas notwithstanding). This functionality was included with previous versions of UAG under the name Network Connector. **Network connector**, or **NC** for short, was a VPN ability that was based on encrypting the connection with **SSL**, and was a proprietary technology developed by Whale Communications. At the time, Windows Servers also had built-in VPN abilities, but only based on the **PPTP** protocol, which is considered to be not very secure, and **L2TP**, which is quite secure, but difficult to deploy because of its complexity.

Today, with UAG, multiple VPN technologies are included. NC is still there, though it has been renamed to **SSL Network Tunneling**. SSL Network Tunneling is also limited to classic client operating systems like Windows XP and Windows Vista. A new addition is **SSTP**, which is a more modern incarnation of SSL-VPN for Windows 7 users The most important remote-access technology included with UAG is **DirectAccess (DA** for short), which offers a new and unique seamless VPN-like integration. With DA, users are virtually connected to the corporate network as soon as they connect to the internet, with no interaction or any need to configure components and launch diallers. All these will be covered in detail later in the book.

How UAG works

UAG's core functionality is as an **ISAPI** filter and extension, as well as various mechanisms to control other parts of Windows. **ISAPI (Internet Server Application Programming Interface)** is a technology that allows programmers to build add-ons for websites, enriching their functionality. UAG is heavily reliant on ISAPI to do its job, and integrates itself into Internet Information Services (**IIS**), Microsoft's Web server components that ships with Windows. This integration gives UAG its "face" — users logging in see a website that is generated by UAG, and UAG's ISAPI filter and extension are the components that fetch data from internal servers and show it to the user.

To do this, UAG has a mechanism that allows it to manipulate the IIS configuration directly. It creates one or more sites in IIS, and integrates itself into them by registering its ISAPI filter. Since the UAG ISAPI components are integrated into the IIS website, content going to and from the site goes through these, and they can manipulate the data directly and efficiently. To learn more about ISAPI, read the following article: `http://msdn.microsoft.com/en-us/library/at50e70y(VS.80).aspx`

If you take a look at IIS on a fresh UAG installation, you will notice that the Default Website contains some new virtual directories, such as "**InternalSite**", which has been created by UAG. This virtual directory hosts the login screen that users see, as well as other pages like the log-off page, error pages, and others. "InternalSite" also includes the various authentication mechanisms, the client detection and installation system and more. It looks darn good, if you ask us. As you'll start configuring portals on UAG, new virtual directories will appear under the Default Web Site of IIS running on the UAG server, the PortalHomePage virtual directory. This directory hosts, as its name suggests, the web resources that together compose the homepage or landing page of the portal, which end-users reach after successfully authenticating to UAG. This page displays links to all the published applications through this portal, as well as a UAG-specific toolbar.

The building blocks of UAG are **Trunks** and **Applications**. You can think of trunks as an organizational unit that can contain multiple applications. Depending on an organization's needs, the server can publish a single application, several applications within a trunk, or multiple applications within multiple trunks. An application is typically an internal server that is published through UAG, although the term can also be used to describe something that is not a website. For example, UAG has a "SSL-VPN tunneling" application, which creates a VPN connection from the user's computer to the organizational network, and allows direct access to internal resources.

If you have never seen a UAG server at work, the following screenshots offer a quick peek. Home users type into their browser a URL they are given by the networking team, and reach the illustrated login page. Even before reaching this page, their computer is checked to see if it meets the organization's security policy. For example, the organization might require that the computer is running an updated copy of Norton Anti-Virus as one of the conditions for entry:

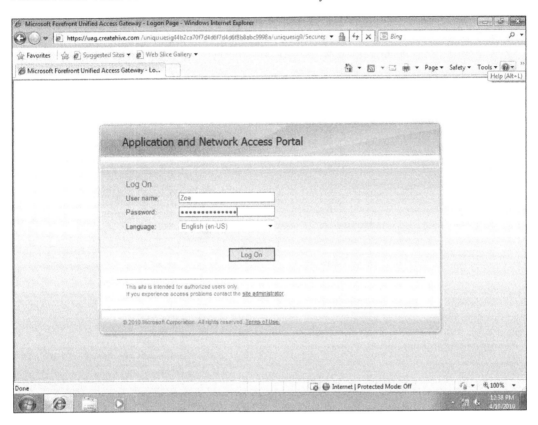

Once users enter their password and it has been successfully verified, they are taken to the "portal" page, which lists the applications that have been published by the networking team. The middle section of the screen shows the icons, and there is also a frame on the left of the screen that shows the same applications. The top of the portal shows additional action buttons:

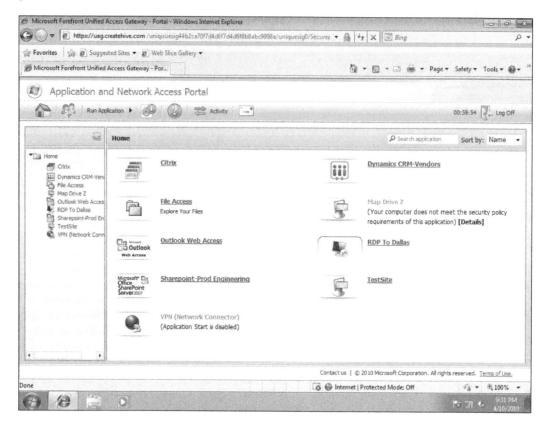

Users may select to launch the **SharePoint** application. This looks like any ordinary SharePoint page, but it's actually being displayed by UAG. Users get to it without having to type in their username and password again, since UAG has performed single-sign on to the SharePoint server, using the credentials that it has already collected from the users. On the left, the application tool bar remains, although it can be collapsed to free up screen real-estate. The top bar also stays there and contains the **Log Off** button, the **Home** button and more:

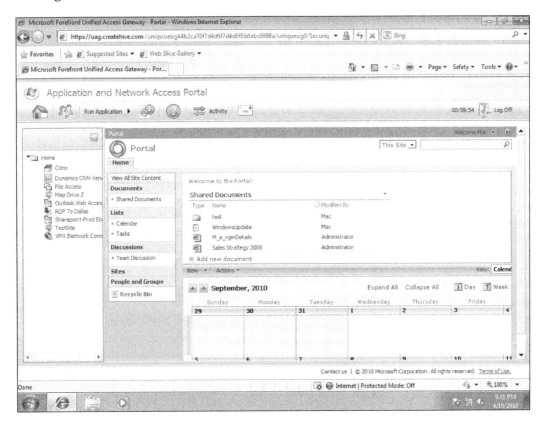

When finished, users click on the **Log Off** button on the right-hand side of the portal bar, and disconnect from the portal. This not only disconnects them, but also wipes clean temporary files that have been downloaded to their computer while working. For example, if they opened Office document attachments from the site, these will be wiped securely, so even if their computer is stolen, that data will not be recoverable by the thief:

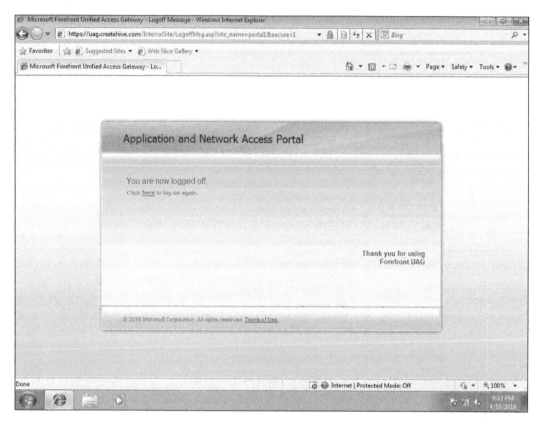

When working with some services, such as OWA and SharePoint, UAG has the ability to manipulate the data stream received from the backend server, and add functionality to it. For example, in the case of SharePoint, as seen above UAG rewrites the functionality behind the **Log Off** button, so that when a user clicks on it, it not only logs off from SharePoint, but also from the UAG portal itself. This is designed for convenience, of course, this way the user does not have to press **Log Off** multiple times. In fact, for SharePoint and OWA, UAG also rewrites the data that comes in from the server and hides the log-off buttons that these servers normally show, so that the user can have only one button to click. This manipulation is called **Application Wrapping**, and it's also customizable by the server's administrator. With a good understanding of **HTML** and other web development technologies, as well as careful planning, an administrator can affect the way anything that goes through UAG looks. For example, the organization's logo can be added to pages, or specific text messages can be shown. Some customers have even used this technique to replace whole pages with others, to "cover up" information that they wanted to keep confidential.

Software requirements

UAG is offered to the public in two distinct distributions. A company can choose to purchase the product in the form of an appliance, or as a downloadable **ISO** image file, which can be burned to **DVD** or mounted as a virtual DVD drive and installed from. If you have elected to go with an appliance, then there's nothing to worry about with regards to requirements, but if you are to install it yourself, there are more things to consider.

UAG is a server product, and can only be installed on a Windows Server 2008 R2 or later. Windows 2008 R2 is only available as a **64 bit** system, so that will affect the hardware requirements that are discussed a little later in this chapter. Since UAG is ultimately just a piece of software running on Windows, this might be tempting for some organizations to try and conserve resources by assigning multiple roles to the UAG server. For example, a company might want to use the TMG included with UAG to publish some internal servers, or try to use TMG's web-caching features to speed up a user's access to the web. Microsoft strongly discourages that notion, and for a very good reason. The reason for this is because UAG is not just a program – it's a service that interacts with many other components. For example, when you publish an application on the server, UAG pushes the configuration directly into TMG, as well as IIS, so any changes the administrator makes to any of these components manually could interfere and conflict with those done by UAG. This could lead to various breaks and interruptions in functionality, and in a worst case scenario, could seriously jeopardize the security of the system. For example, misconfiguring TMG's **Local Address Table (LAT)**, which lets TMG know which IP addresses are within the internal network, and which are not, could lead it to think that a connection attempt from the external network (the internet) is actually coming from the internal one, and trust it falsely. In this case, it could let an attacker sneak in unnoticed. What's even more problematic is that if an administrator makes changes to components that they are not supposed to, it makes it difficult or impossible for Microsoft to support. You can think about this like a warranty sticker. Just like the fact that opening up your stereo's case and fiddling with the wires would void the warranty, messing around with the "wires" of a complex software product can make the product unsupportable.

If you run into a problem, Microsoft's support can't guess what you've done and can't possibly check every setting in the entire system. They can inspect UAG's configuration and Networking configuration, but might not be able to find the real cause, as it's lurking away in some other configuration dialog that is not normally used.

The official guidelines dictate that UAG needs to be installed on a "clean" server, with no other applications installed on it. This might be somewhat over-protective. This doesn't mean you can't have an Anti-Virus running on the server—on the contrary, having an AV product is a great idea. However, to decrease the likelihood of an installation failure, it's best to start with a server that's clean, if possible. "Clean", in our book, doesn't mean a server that was loaded with stuff, and that stuff has been uninstalled. If your organization mandates certain software to be installed on every server, like a remote-management agent or hardware-specific software, these should not be seen as a deal breaker, and installation should still run smoothly. Keep in mind, though, that if it fails, Microsoft Support may request that you retry it with a clean server.

Another requirement for installation of UAG is Administrative rights. This should be a no-brainer for most administrators, though we have seen cases where it has been missed. The computer can be a stand-alone server, or a Domain member, but if it is a domain member, then the installation needs to be done while logged on to the server as a domain user with local administrative permissions.

It's very important to correctly define the computer's Network configuration, computer name and domain membership before starting the installation, as some of these settings are difficult or impossible to change afterwards. You should have two Network cards installed – one for the "external" network, and one for the "internal" one. The external could connect to the **DMZ**, and you can rename the network cards at any point, but the following need to be configured:

- IP addresses for each network interface
- Subnet mask for each network interface
- **DNS for at least one of the network interfaces** (most organizations would use their internal DNS, and so configure that only on the internal NIC)
- Default Gateway on only one of the interfaces, usually the external interface.

If the computer name is some random string generated by your system deployment automation, make sure you set the server name to a permanent one, and if it is to be a domain member, join it to the domain first.

An installation option favoured by many organizations these days is a **virtual-machine based installation**. This has many advantages – it allows easy change control via Snapshots or saved-states, as well as setting up a warm backup server easily. One must keep in mind, though, that this might have an impact on the server performance, as a guest machine is inherently weaker than its host, and this might introduce risks, especially in the Network Performance arena. When considering using a virtual machine, one must keep in mind that not all virtualization platforms are the same. Certain platforms are incompatible with UAG, so you should consult the **Windows Server Virtualization Validation Program** (SVVP) to make sure yours is supported. Don't take this lightly, as using an unsupported platform can cause serious problems. The SVVP validation website is here: `http://www.windowsservercatalog.com/svvp.aspx?svvppage=svvpwizard.htm`

Lastly, many organizations have their server hardware located in remote or secure server rooms, with management being done remotely. If that is the situation in your case, keep in mind that the installation of UAG affects the server's networking, and the installation might sever communications with the computer, since as part of the UAG installation, TMG is installed and launched. You might find yourself thrown off the RDP session and unable to reconnect to the server. We recommend you prepare a plan to gain physical access to the server in that case.

Hardware requirements

Since UAG is installed on top of Windows Server 2008 R2, the hardware requirements are combined with those of R2. The primary requirement for R2 is having a 64 Bit processor and 32 GB of free disk space, and that's easy enough to get these days. UAG's minimal requirements are that the processor is a dual-core one, running at 2.66 GHz or faster, 4 GB of memory, and an extra 2.5 GB of disk space.

In reality, UAG can run on weaker systems, so if you just need to install it temporarily for a proof-of-concept or for training purposes, you could get away with a lot less (though installing it on a Commodore-64 is really taking it too far). For production environments, the stronger the better, especially with memory size, as going with the bare minimum may limit the number of concurrent users the server can handle.

If you were hoping to learn here how many concurrent users the server can support, you're in for a disappointment. While some other server software has a very linear model for client support, UAG's performance varies significantly by the type of applications that are published and the way users use them. For example, RDP applications transfer a lot of data back-and-forth between the client and the target internal server, so that would put more stress on the UAG server compared to a typical intranet, mostly-text web portal. The only way to know with a reasonable amount of certainty how many users your server can support is with a baseline performance analysis. That would include analyzing typical user activity and simulating multiple users in a test-environment, while using the built-in Performance Monitor to see how things are going. Doing performance analysis is not easy, and there's always a risk of miscalculating, but be wary of skipping this just because a sales person claims your server can support "thousands" or "millions" of users. We have seen quite a few deployments where the customer found out too late that they require more servers, and that was not only costly, but also quite frustrating and embarrassing to all parties involved

We already mentioned the Networking requirements earlier, but it's worth repeating. A UAG server is a router, and as such, needs two Network cards. If you are deploying on a virtual machine, this is rather easy, but if it's a physical, make sure you have two real NICs in place. There's no harm in having additional cards, although one must carefully plan the IP, Mask and Gateway settings so as to not arrive at a configuration that will prevent the routing mechanisms of TMG from making the correct decisions as to where to send packets and block dangerous or inappropriate traffic.

Considerations for placing the server

We assume a network administrator does not need this book to learn how to physically secure a server, but there is one hardware aspect that should be kept in mind. Many organizations place their servers in a secure location – a dedicated server room (a.k.a. **The Dungeon**), which is sometimes even isolated from the main company campus. This is not a bad practice, but keep in mind that during installation, remote-desktop connection to the server might be disconnected, so it's worthwhile to keep an option to reach the server physically. Another thing that's good to keep in mind is that UAG is designed to serve clients connecting from outside the organization, and so using it from "inside" is unsupported and will not work for the most part. Some features can be tested from the internal network, and some can even be tested by launching a browser on the server itself, but we strongly recommend that any organization plan for a "real" test client.

Installing the UAG client components on the UAG server itself, by using Internet Explorer on the UAG server and browsing to a UAG portal and allowing the installation of these components, can lead to undesired results. A real test client would be just a regular computer that is physically connected (either permanently or when needed) to an external NIC on the UAG machine, or to the same switch the Server is connected to on the external interface, and dedicated to being used to test the server, if a need arises. This is pretty easy to accomplish if the UAG server is a Virtual Machine, but even if it isn't and it sounds a little dumb to "waste" a computer or a switch port just for that, do it! It could save you hours and hours of frustration if the server experiences a problem. For example, if the organization decides to place an external Load Balancer in front of the server, you might have a tough time knowing to which server your test clients are connecting, but such a standalone client could eliminate that problem easily. If you are able to dedicate a reasonably strong machine for this, it would be even better to run several client Virtual Machine guest OSs on it, and thus be able to quickly test various scenarios.

From a networking perspective, placing is even more important. Most organizations place the server in their DMZ, and have one firewall in front of it, and another behind it. This is not a bad idea, even though UAG does include its own robust firewall – TMG. Regardless, if any additional networking hardware is in the picture, care must be taken to allow the right traffic to flow. The frontend firewall needs to allow traffic to the UAG server's external IP from any IP, and allow ports 443 for Secure portal trunks, and port 80 for non-secure trunks or **HTTP** to **HTTPS** redirection trunk (those are used when the portal is on HTTPS, but you want to avoid forcing your users to type the elusive 'https' prefix to the URL).

The backend firewall needs to be configured to allow UAG to communicate with whatever servers it needs to publish, as well as traffic to its domain controllers, and to the authentication servers used by UAG to authenticate end-users. In some scenarios that require the use of digital certificates, access to a Certificate Authority is also required. Keep in mind that if UAG is used to publish non-HTTP or non-HTTPS servers, additional ports may need to be opened. For example, if **RDP** access to internal servers is required, port 3389 needs to be allowed.

If load balancers are to be part of this dance, it introduces quite a few other considerations. For example, how is stickiness going to be preserved? Different load balancers have different mechanisms, and those need to be accounted for to make sure that once a user has connected to a UAG array member, they will not be handed off to another one, mid-session. UAG's session information is not shared across members of a UAG array, so if that happens, the user will be redirected to login again, and depending on what they were doing, may lose data.

Another important consideration to take into account is DNS. Clients that are connecting to UAG from the public internet will need to connect to the server using a host name, and not an IP address. Depending on an organization's DNS hierarchy and server placement, this may affect the deployment. This is especially true if **SharePoint** servers are to be published, as they require their own additional **DNS mapping** (more about that in *Chapter 4*). The UAG server needs to be able to resolve internal hostnames, so Port 53 needs to be open on the internal firewall, if one exists. If load balancing, either front or back, is done, the effect it has needs to be planned as well, to make sure UAG has access to all the relevant internal servers.

Planning the networking infrastructure

From a networking perspective, one must carefully plan the IP addresses assigned to the server, especially when **NAT** needs to be used on either the external or internal side. During the installation of UAG, the TMG firewall is also installed, and it includes a set of access rules that define the internal and external networks. An administrator should avoid assigning temporary or invalid IP addresses to the server, if possible. If the plan is to have the server hosted in a temporary test environment before deploying it to the production environment, do your best to simulate the real environment as closely as possible. A common bad practice that often leads to problems is configuring the external side of the UAG server so that it's facing into the internal corporate network. This sounds attractive as it would let you do testing with internal corporate computers, but it could lead to impossible routing scenarios, and is strongly discouraged. A good practice would be to dedicate a computer or a virtual machine to be used as a test client, and physically connecting it to the same subnet as the external interface.

As stated before, UAG is, fundamentally, a router, so the Subnet Mask and default gateway are also very important. A default gateway should be assigned to the external interface of UAG only, and the subnet masks and IP addresses need to be carefully planned so that there is no overlap. If the internal network contains additional IP ranges that are outside the IP range assigned to the internal Network Card, these may need to be added to the Server's routing table in the form of static routing rules. All this should be done before the product is installed, so that the TMG server does not end up being inoperational due to network configuration conflicts or blocking traffic it should not be blocking.

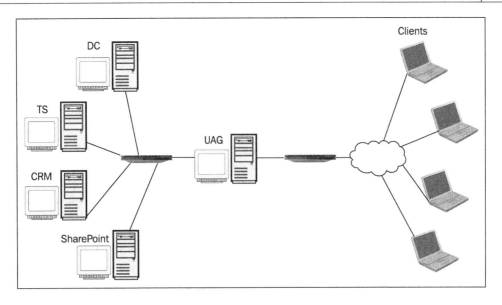

Domain membership

An important consideration for UAG is whether to have the server as a domain member or not. From a security perspective, the less connection the server has to other infrastructure, the better, and so most organizations would prefer to have the server be a stand-alone server (member of a workgroup that is). However, some UAG features and scenarios necessitate domain membership. Also, even when not a domain member, UAG usually needs to provide it's users with access to the published applications based on the user's domain membership. In that case, even though the server does not have to be a member, it does need the type of access a domain member would need in order to authenticate the user. For example, free passage for the **RPC (Remote Procedure Call)** protocol is necessary to let UAG query a user's group membership.

As mentioned before, the following specific scenarios do require explicit domain membership:

- ADFS
- Publishing applications that use Kerberos Constrained Delegation (KCD) to authenticate users
- Publishing the UAG File-Access application
- DirectAccess
- SSTP VPN
- UAG Array

We will discuss these scenarios in further detail in *Chapter 6*, and *Chapter 11*. Please note that if your plan is to use this server for DirectAccess, then you might need to address some additional requirements. In that case, don't start the installation before reading *Chapter 11*.

Planning remote connectivity

UAG supports several types of remote connectivity that are beyond simple application publishing, and these sometimes require additional considerations. The first such scenario is, of course, DirectAccess—a.k.a. the VPN Celebrity of 2010. DirectAccess configuration is pushed out to clients using Group Policy, so this has to be factored in as well. Just having a group policy active is not enough, of course. UAG will create the proper policy, but collateral policies may need to be adjusted. For example, the local Firewall service on each client needs to be on (although the Firewall itself can be off). If your organization's group policy has been defined to set Firewalls to off, you might have to go in and change that.

Another consideration for DirectAccess is to have an elaborate infrastructure of digital certificates, also known as **PKI or Public Key Infrastructure** set up, in order to satisfy the requirements that are imposed by the highly secure IPSec tunnels, which are the fundamental tunnels used by DA. The UAG servers need to have digital certificates with their public hostnames, and the Certificate Authority (CA) that issued those needs to be trusted by the clients. In fact, you will have to have each client computer connect to the corporate network at least once to obtain the DirectAccess Group Policy, so if you were counting on sending out an email with instructions and going home early, think again. We will discuss DirectAccess in more detail in *Chapter 11*.

Another way of providing remote connectivity with UAG is SSL Network Tunneling, formerly known as Network Connector, and its successor, **SSTP (Secure Socket Tunneling Protocol)**. Network Connector has been around for ages, and as such, it has some limitations, the most important being that it is unable to support Windows 7 clients. SSTP can be a suitable solution for some scenarios, because it supports Windows 7. SSL Network Tunneling is not difficult to configure, but it does require careful planning of the IP and Network configuration assignment, as well as the split-tunneling mode. You will have to configure SSL Network Tunneling with an IP pool that does not overlap with your Network's range. You can also assign a specific IP range and Networking configuration so as to control the client's access to various servers. For example, you might feel that connecting clients should have access to RDP to their own corporate computers from home, but not to the corporate servers—or the other way around.

You could also decide to set your NC clients to a non- split tunneling mode, which routes their connection to internet servers through the corporate network instead of directly through their local ISP. The advantages and disadvantages of each of those will be discussed in *Chapter 5*.

SSTP has a configuration that's somewhat similar to NC, although SSTP can be used by Windows 7 clients, which NC cannot. Many companies will have to set up both an NC option and an SSTP one to cover all their clients. SSTP is a little simpler to plan and configure—you simply enable it, and set a range of IP addresses for connecting clients. You can even set it to assign the IPs from **DHCP** in non-array scenarios, which is probably the most convenient for almost everybody.

Chapter 5, which discusses remote connectivity, will also discuss topics that are not categorized as VPN, but are still more related to connectivity than to simple application publishing. Of these technologies, it's worth noting **File Access** and **Drive Mapping**, as these pose additional requirements and considerations. File Access allows connecting clients to browse network shares, retrieve and save files, and more. Drive Mapping maps a server's share as a temporary network drive that allows the user to retrieve data from places like their own folder on the company's file server, or from generally available network shares. These two, however, require that the UAG server has access to the shares itself. This is not about file-level permissions, but more about ports and protocols. File Access and Drive Mapping use **RPC**, which may require special routing and IP configuration if an internal firewall or load balancer is in use.

Load balancing and high availability

Opting to employ several servers for high availability is a prudent step in most modern organizations, and thus, UAG includes built in support for arrays and NLB. Some organizations may still prefer using third party hardware, like **F5 BigIP** or **Citrix Netscaler**. The common scenario for load balancing would be to have several UAG servers running an identical configuration, and using a load balancer on the "external" side to distribute the load between the servers. Another scenario is when an organization has multiple internal servers, like a SharePoint server farm, and uses a **Load-Balancer** between it and UAG. Naturally, some organizations have both.

The most important consideration in a high availability scenario is the routing. With multiple virtual and physical IP addresses, the routing on all devices needs to be carefully planned, so that the data will have a clear path all the way from the client, through UAG, to the backend server and back. Stickiness also needs to be considered, as noted before (see *Considerations for placing the server*).

Another consideration for high availability is the **keep-alive** mechanism. Load balancers need to discern if the servers they are balancing are alive, and they usually do so by initiating some kind of contact with them. A popular way is by issuing a simple **ICMP** packet, like **PING**, but it's usually also possible to configure them to send an HTTP request to the server, or a TCP-SYN request. This needs to be planned carefully, so as to not have the keep-alive check impact the servers' performance, and also so that false-positives will not have bad consequences. We've seen many organizations configure their keep-alive to perform a check every second, which is a significant overkill, and caused the servers' logs to cycle so fast that the administrator was unable to track down real errors.

Another aspect of high availability is session failover, which, unfortunately, is not a part of UAGs functionality. NLB or third party load balancing will provide clients with a response even if one member server comes down, but the session management mechanism of UAG will not allow users with existing sessions to be moved over to another server. If a fail occurs, all users who are connected to the failed server will be redirected, upon their next request, to another array member, but they will be required to login again at that point. If they had SSTP, NC, RDP or SSL-VPN apps running, these sessions will be lost and have to be re-established as well. Some application-level protocols are designed to do this automatically, like RDP, but UAG will not do so on its own.

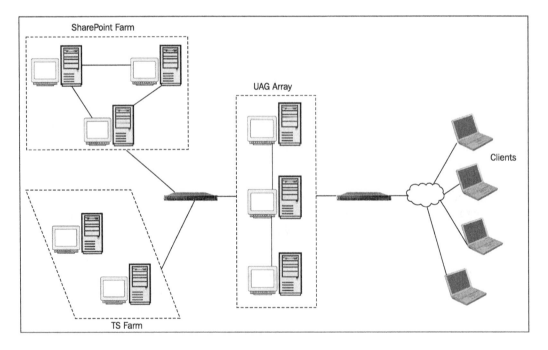

Choosing clients

When considering the implementation of UAG, one must take into account which clients are usable with UAG. Various operating systems have different capabilities and limitations, and not all are supported. At the time of writing, UAG supports the following operating systems as clients:

- Windows XP 32-bit
- Windows XP 64-bit
- Windows Vista 32-bit
- Windows Vista 64-bit
- Windows 7 32-bit
- Windows 7 64-bit
- Windows Server 2003 32-bit
- Windows Server 2003 64-bit
- Windows Server 2008 32-bit
- Windows Server 2008 64-bit
- Mac OX X 10.3+ (PowerPC and Intel) 32-bit only
- Linux (RPM-based Linux distributions: Red Hat Enterprise 4 and 5, Fedora Core 5 and up. Debian Linux distributions; Debian 4 and up, Ubuntu 6.10 and up) 32-bit only
- Windows Mobile 2003
- Windows Mobile 2005
- Windows Mobile 7
- Windows Mobile 6.x
- iPhone version 3.0.x
- Nokia S60 3rd edition, Feature Pack 1—validated on E71, N95
- Nokia S60 3rd edition, Feature Pack 2—validated on E72, E52
- Nokia S60 5th edition—validated on N97

 The above list may change as service packs and updates are introduced for UAG or for various operating systems. For a full list of supported operating systems and browsers, see `http://technet.microsoft.com/en-us/library/dd920232.aspx`.

As stated, not all systems support all functions. For example, using Network Connector is not possible with Windows 7. If your users are running both Windows 7 and Windows XP, the only way to allow all of them to VPN into the corporate network would be to implement both SSTP and NC. Depending on which OS is running, the proper one will be selected automatically.

When clients connect to various UAG services, they might need more than just a browser. For example, Endpoint Detection, Socket Forwarding and Endpoint Session Cleanup are special components that are installed on the client when they are required. These components may not be required, depending on which UAG features you are deploying. With most deployments however, they are necessary, so it's important to keep in mind that they can only be used with certain browsers and operating systems. With Windows and Internet Explorer, everything works nice and dandy. With Linux and Mac, a Java-based version of the client components does a similar job, and almost everything works (see link above). For mobile browsers, including Windows Mobile up to version 7 and Apple iPhone, the "Premium" portal is supported, but the phone cannot perform SSL tunneling, session cleanup or endpoint detection. Nokia phones only support the "Limited" portal. The "Premium" portal is specially designed for the mobile phone view on a small screen. It has fewer graphics, but still looks pretty darn good. The Limited portal is a text-only version that is usable even for phones with limited web capabilities.

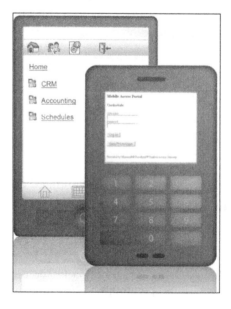

When planning a UAG deployment, it's important to prepare and understand the limitations of client support to make sure the organization's primary target audience will have the right level of access. Discovering in mid-deployment that your number-one app is unusable for most of your users can be embarrassing. This is especially so if the target application or client are not explicitly on the list. Sometimes, even a minor version change can wreak havoc, as in the case of a certain well-known server application that introduced a major change to the way the application handles cookies, and so version 9.5.2 of the application worked perfectly through UAG, but version 9.5.3 failed miserably.

As mentioned before, when a user connects to the UAG portal for the first time, UAG client components are installed on their computer. It's important to keep in mind that the client components' installation process installs some **Active-X** components, and that is considered to be a risky situation. Don't worry—your user's computers aren't going to explode, but if the user is logged on as a non-administrative user, the Active-X registration will be denied and the client components installation will fail. In other words, make sure that when your users log on to the UAG portal for the first time, they will do so while logged on as local administrators, or at least run the browser with elevated privileges. Later, when just launching the portal again, the user no longer needs to be an administrator. If your organization or the user have customized the browser's security settings in some way, it's important to properly test the client component installation, to make sure the security configuration will not cause the computer to end up with a corrupt client installation. One other option that is at the administrator's side is the ability to manually install the client components using a stand-alone installer. The UAG server will have on its hard drive a set of Microsoft-installer files (with the extension of MSI) that can be used to install the client components fully or partially. In fact, if the organization's users take their computers to work regularly, one can even use Active Directory application deployment automation or a logon script to automatically and quietly perform this installation. You can read more about this in *Chapter 7*.

From test to production

For most organizations, a UAG deployment is a lengthy process. Some applications are easy and quick to deploy, but some might take some experimentation and tweaking to get just right. For this reason, most organizations prefer to start by setting up their server in a test or temporary environment, and roll it out to production only at a later point in time. Some organizations even keep a non-production system online on a regular basis as a test platform for new applications, or as a way to verify new service packs or updates to products (incl. UAG itself) before committing them to the scrutiny of their users.

As we mentioned earlier, it is very important to have the test environment simulate the real world as closely as possible. We have seen many deployments where an administrator tried to conserve resources by having the UAG server use only one NIC and connecting it to both the logical "internal" and "external" networks. We have also seen many cases where the administrator connected the UAG's "external" interface to his corporate network, so they can leverage corporate PCs as test clients. Both of these scenarios are invalid, and can cause failure very early on. Even worse, they can lure the administrator into a false sense of security if things appear to be working out, but when the server is finally put in the line of fire, things could go sour in a heartbeat.

A single-NIC scenario (where both internal servers and clients interact with UAG from the same side) can be made to work in some cases, but it's not supported by Microsoft, and so should be avoided. A reversed-side scenario is a problem because UAG's firewall, TMG, defines the external network as "dangerous" and limits connectivity from it. TMG may block access to the domain controllers because of that, and this not only can prevent some applications from working, but it can also cause some of the fundamental services for UAG and TMG to fail, and ruin the party.

Tips for a successful deployment

At this point, UAG does not include the ability to remotely manage the server directly via the use of an MMC add-in, so to manage the server an administrator would have to access it physically via the console, or using Windows Remote-Desktop. Naturally, because the UAG is a gateway into your network, using RDP to connect to it can be risky. If UAG is hacked into, it might compromise your network more than just any regular workstation, so this should be planned carefully. It's also possible to enable remote desktop to the UAG server from outside, as a published application, although we still consider this to be a risky move for the same reasons. The fact of the matter is that most administrators want to have as many ways available to manage their servers, and we need to keep in mind that as we make things easier for ourselves, we usually make it easy for potential attackers as well, often increasing our exposure. For example, you might not allow external access to UAG, but you do publish your own workstation. An attacker breaks into your station this way, and can break into UAG from the "inside". Bottom line: to stay as secure as possible, be a little paranoid, and try to resist temptation to make everything possible remotely. We will discuss Remote Desktop publishing in more detail in *Chapter 5*.

Deployment checklist

When planning your deployment, use the following checklist to make sure you have prepared for everything:

- Software requirements met:
    - ° Virtual Machine or Appliance
    - ° Windows Server 2008 R2
    - ° Clean server
    - ° All available Windows updates installed
    - ° No additional software installed
    - ° You have administrative permissions on the server
- Hardware requirements:
    - ° 64 Bit processor
    - ° 2.66 GHz or higher
    - ° 2 Network Cards
    - ° 4 GB of RAM
    - ° 40 GB of free disk space
- IP assignment to server NICs
- DNS config on server
- Public DNS mapping is configured correctly
- Mapped out applications, URLs, Ports and IPs to be published
- List of clients that will be in use
- Will you be using HTTP or HTTPS?
- Server placement - physical and logical
- Front-end firewall/router config prepared
- Back-end firewall/router config prepared
- Will it be Remote management or Local management?
- Domain membership of the server
- Deployment schedule

Do's and Don'ts for a successful deployment

- Do analyze your client needs and usage statistics
- Do prepare ample time to experiment with the product before going into production

- Do perform baseline performance testing regularly, to avoid surprises at production time
- Do map your applications' properties and prepare a written plan
- Do prepare a support plan for your server, as most support calls may be at night or weekends
- Do consider using an experienced consultant, especially if your deployment involves sensitive material, or is time critical
- Do plan your routing and networking carefully — it's one of the common causes of failure
- Don't try to use your server to host other functions or roles
- Don't fiddle with TMG and IIS configuration before, during, or after installation
- Don't assume that any and all applications can be published with UAG

Summary

In this chapter, we have talked about preparing your environment for the deployment of UAG, and addressed the considerations that are required to pave the path for a successful roll out. For many experienced IT administrators, UAG may seem to be just another server to install and squeeze into their already busy schedule, but UAG is a unique product in its abilities, and also in its requirements. Bringing up a server to host a simple web application can be accomplished quite easily, but that rarely ends there. Most organizations, when discovering how UAG empowers their home and mobile users to accomplish so much remotely, start piling on more and more applications and requirements, and at that point, any cracks in the initial design may show up. For example, setting up a SharePoint server may seem simple. After all, it's just a website, right? Not so fast. We soon discover (and will discuss this in *Chapter 4*) that the advanced code that makes SharePoint's content so dynamic and rich may also cause quite a headache if hostnames were not designed properly. In that case, an organization may find that it needs to reconfigure SharePoint's **AAM** settings, fiddle with DNS and in extreme conditions even reinstall the SharePoint server to allow it to be published perfectly. Will this happen to you? We hope not, so read *Chapter 4* carefully (in fact, reading the entire book carefully won't hurt either) and don't rush into publishing the UAG portal before you have considered the various scenarios that can develop.

In the next chapter, we will learn how to install UAG with the various **SKUs** that are available. We will discuss the prerequisites in more detail and go over the installation procedure step-by-step, as well as tips and suggestions on avoiding the most common mistakes.

2
Installing UAG

In this chapter, we will discuss the required steps to prepare and install UAG. We will discuss the critical settings you will need to configure before the installation and how to prepare the server for it, and then we will go through the setup process step-by-step. Finally, we will review how to verify that the installation went successfully and learn how to handle some common issues you might face.

What the installation contains

Compared to many other software products, installing UAG is a simple process. It does not require a lot of of pre-requisite components to be installed or dozens of decisions to be made in the middle of the process. It does, however, require proper planning. We have already discussed how to plan your deployment and we will delve into more detail shortly.

The installation procedure is almost completely automatic. Once run, it will install and configure TMG, the firewall that is the forefront protection for UAG, and then install UAG itself. The installation also installs and configures other components and roles, such as **AJAX**, **Remote Desktop Gateway**, **Network Load Balancing**, **Active Directory Lightweight Directory Services** (also known as **ADLDS**), **Network Policy Server**, and a few others. The installation itself rarely fails, though it does take a significant amount of time—typically half an hour, but in some cases, as much as two full hours. Once it has completed, the next step is running the **Getting Started Wizard**, which is also pretty simple in itself. The **Getting Started Wizard** will configure some basic options that UAG needs, such as the networking and routing configuration and the server topology.

Service Packs and updates

At the time of writing, two updates and one service pack have been issued for UAG, but further updates or Service Packs may be available later on. If you have purchased the product recently, it is likely that the **ISO** image file or **DVD** that you have already contains the service pack 'streamlined' into the installation, so there's little to worry about. If you purchased your server as an appliance, then it's also likely that it already is updated, but in either case, it's a good idea to verify this. In case a later update or Service Pack has been released, you may need to apply them after the installation. In this case, we recommend not waiting, but performing the update as soon as you can, following completion of the installation itself, or after completing the **Getting Started Wizard.** The reason for this is because updates sometimes affect the process of published application generation and templates, so it would be preferable to have the latest settings available while you publish those applications. Otherwise, you might find later that you need to recreate some applications after applying updates. Another good idea is to backup the server before applying any updates or service packs, or take a Virtual Machine Snapshot, if you are using a VM. We will discuss the process of applying updates or service packs later in this chapter.

Preparing your server

Before starting the installation, some tasks need to be completed to prepare the server. First, make sure you have installed the **Network Cards** and configured their settings. Even if your network has a **DHCP** server, it is imperative that the server is assigned a static IP address manually. You should verify that the server has Internet connectivity from the external side, even though keeping the server connected to the public internet is not required for the installation itself. In fact, from a security perspective, it's best to disconnect the server from the internet after having verified that it can connect and reconnect it only after the installation has completed, and the Getting Started Wizard has completed. In case the server is to be domain-joined, verify that you have full connectivity to your domain controller as well. We recommend not trusting **PING** as a way of assuring this connectivity, but using something more reliable, like trying to access a file-share or simply running **NET USE** or **NET VIEW** against the domain controller.

```
Administrator: Command Prompt                                      _ |8| X|
C:\>ipconfig /all

Windows IP Configuration

    Host Name . . . . . . . . . . . . . : WIN-7IDDR1DLTG9
    Primary Dns Suffix  . . . . . . . . :
    Node Type . . . . . . . . . . . . . : Hybrid
    IP Routing Enabled. . . . . . . . . : No
    WINS Proxy Enabled. . . . . . . . . : No

Ethernet adapter Internet:

    Connection-specific DNS Suffix  . :
    Description . . . . . . . . . . . : Microsoft Virtual Machine Bus Network Ada
pter #2
    Physical Address. . . . . . . . . : 00-15-5D-89-4D-20
    DHCP Enabled. . . . . . . . . . . : No
    Autoconfiguration Enabled . . . . : Yes
    IPv4 Address. . . . . . . . . . . : 199.8.7.5(Preferred)
    Subnet Mask . . . . . . . . . . . : 255.255.0.0
    Default Gateway . . . . . . . . . : 199.8.7.1
    NetBIOS over Tcpip. . . . . . . . : Enabled

Ethernet adapter Corpnet:

    Connection-specific DNS Suffix  . :
    Description . . . . . . . . . . . : Microsoft Virtual Machine Bus Network Ada
pter
    Physical Address. . . . . . . . . : 00-15-5D-89-4D-1F
    DHCP Enabled. . . . . . . . . . . : No
    Autoconfiguration Enabled . . . . : Yes
    IPv4 Address. . . . . . . . . . . : 10.0.0.213(Preferred)
    Subnet Mask . . . . . . . . . . . : 255.0.0.0
    Default Gateway . . . . . . . . . :
    DNS Servers . . . . . . . . . . . : 10.0.2.11
    NetBIOS over Tcpip. . . . . . . . : Enabled

Tunnel adapter isatap.{8254E9A2-1AAF-428B-B15D-D3430F0979DF}:

    Media State . . . . . . . . . . . : Media disconnected
    Connection-specific DNS Suffix  . :
    Description . . . . . . . . . . . : Microsoft ISATAP Adapter
    Physical Address. . . . . . . . . : 00-00-00-00-00-00-00-E0
    DHCP Enabled. . . . . . . . . . . : No
    Autoconfiguration Enabled . . . . : Yes

Tunnel adapter 6TO4 Adapter:

    Connection-specific DNS Suffix  . :
    Description . . . . . . . . . . . : Microsoft 6to4 Adapter
    Physical Address. . . . . . . . . : 00-00-00-00-00-00-00-E0
    DHCP Enabled. . . . . . . . . . . : No
    Autoconfiguration Enabled . . . . : Yes
    IPv6 Address. . . . . . . . . . . : 2002:c708:705::c708:705(Preferred)
    Default Gateway . . . . . . . . . :
    NetBIOS over Tcpip. . . . . . . . : Disabled
```

Do you see anything wrong with the configuration above? Right at the top, you can see the computer name as **WIN-7IDDR1DLTG9**, which was created by the **SysPrep** process, as the above server was built from an image. In case you missed that part earlier, changing the computer name after the installation of UAG is unsupported, contradictory, surely you should leave the name as is so leaving that name as is would not be a good idea.

If you are performing the installation on a server that is a **Virtual Machine**, use the **Virtual Network Manager** to create and configure the network. To do so, follow these steps:

1. Open the **Hyper-V** management console.

2. Right-click on your computer name, and choose **Virtual Network Manager**.

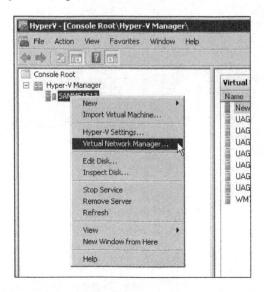

3. Click on **New virtual network** on the left.

4. Make sure that **External** is selected in the list of available network types.

5. Click on the **Add** button.

6. Give a descriptive name to your network (for example *Internal, External, DMZ, Internet*, and so on).

7. Make sure the **External** radio button is selected.

8. From the drop-down menu, select the physical network card that this network will go through.

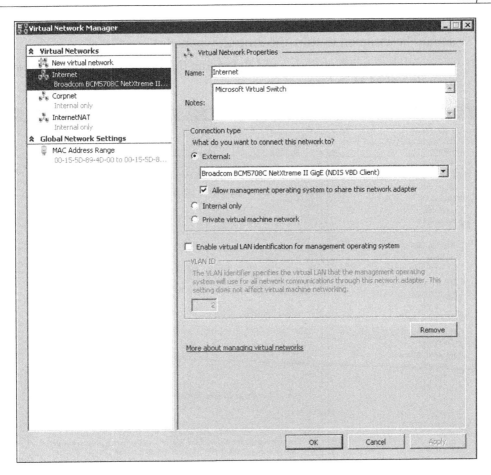

If your server is a virtual machine, edit the Virtual Machine settings to assign the networks to it. To do so, follow these steps:

1. Make sure your virtual machine is off

2. Right-click on your virtual machine, and select **Settings**

3. If the list of hardware on the left contains less than two Network Adapters, add as many as needed using the **Add Hardware** button:

    a. Click on **Add Hardware**.

    b. Select **Network Adapter** from the list of available hardware.

    c. Click **Add**.

    d. Repeat, if necessary.

4.   Click on each of the **Network Adapters**, and select the **Virtual Network** (it should be assigned to from the drop-down menu).

5.   If you plan to use **Network Load Balancing** (**NLB**), check the option **Enable spoofing of MAC addresses**

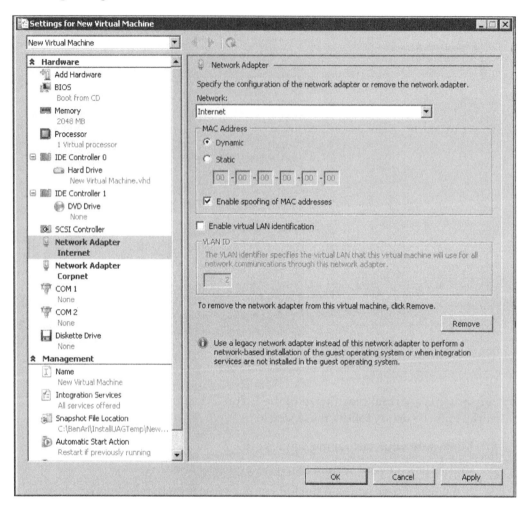

When you turn on the Virtual Machine, you will need to check which of the virtual Network Cards in it are connected to which of the networks, and then rename and configure each card appropriately.

Once the networking is working as expected, the next step is to update your server with all the current updates. It's likely that the update process will require a restart after installing various updates, and possibly even multiple restarts. As we mentioned in the previous chapter, no other software should be installed on the computer. If you have hardware that necessitates installing additional programs, such as Network Card installable drivers, installing them should not cause any problems, but with other things, it is better to avoid, or at least delay until a successful installation of UAG.

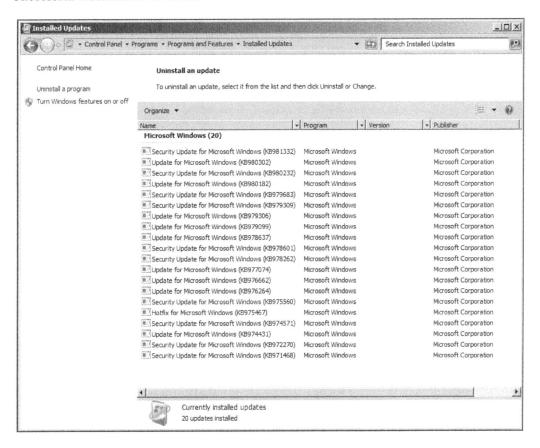

Even though it has been a while since **Windows Server 2008 R2** was released, this might be a good opportunity to make sure it is the full, or **RTM (Released To Manufacturing)** version. You can find that out by running the command **WINVER** from Start/Run. UAG must not be installed on a **pre-release** version of Windows, as this is not a supported configuration. Also, the last thing you would want to handle is to have to reinstall everything from scratch because your server is about to expire.

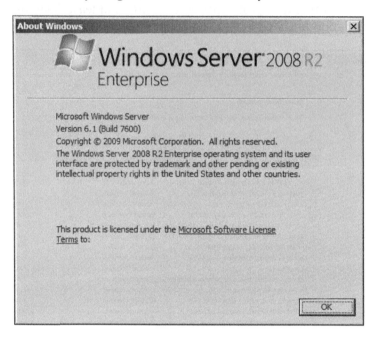

At this point, another decision you need to have reached is whether to have the server be a **domain member** or not. Being a domain member is required for certain scenarios we have mentioned in the previous chapter, but if you have no plan to implement them, you might prefer to keep the server as a standalone server, as some consider this to be more secure. There are good arguments to both sides, but it's ultimately up to you to decide what's best for your organization. If the decision is to have the server be a part of the domain, it's important to perform the UAG installation itself while logged on to the domain, and by a user who has been granted administrative permissions on the UAG server. Trying to perform the installation by a user who does not have the required permissions could cause a failure, and in some cases, serious corruption of the server's configuration. Additionally, the server must **not** be a **domain controller** — that is a major deal breaker for UAG. Lastly, make sure the server's **Computer Name** has been set to something that is acceptable and conforms to the organization's guidelines. Changing the computer name after the installation will require a complete re-install, so better not be stuck with some random and meaningless name.

Another thing that needs to be checked is that no **previous** version of UAG or TMG is installed on the computer. This could be checked easily using the **Add/Remove Programs** control panel. UAG does not allow you to upgrade from another version, like the Trial edition or a pre-released one. Also, the installation is not supported if one of the installed components is already installed. This refers to TMG itself, but also to **SQL Server 2008** which is installed with it. If any of these has been installed, then trying to uninstall will probably be a waste of time, and you should better invest your time in reimaging the server from scratch. Because of the complexity of the components, an uninstall may leave behind bits and pieces that will cause the re-installation to fail. This is a good motive to opt for a Virtual Machine based server, as these allow you to use snapshots and thus go between states quickly.

Another thing that requires changing before starting the setup is the **Windows Firewall.** Something that is confusing to many about the Windows Firewall is that it is actually two things—there's a Windows Firewall service, and the Firewall itself. The firewall service can be on or off, and when it is on, the firewall can be either on or off. For UAG to work, the firewall service *must* be on, but the Windows Firewall itself can be either on or off. To verify the Windows Firewall service is on, open the Services administrative tool and scroll down to **Windows Firewall**. Make sure the service is **running**, and is set to **Automatic**. If the server has been joined to the domain, you might find (or suddenly remember) that your organization enforces this as part of **Group Policy**. If that is the case, this would be a good time to take care of that. This would typically be solved by creating an **Organizational Unit (OU)** that will be subject to laxer policies, adding the server to it, and then creating a more lax policy and assigning it to that OU.

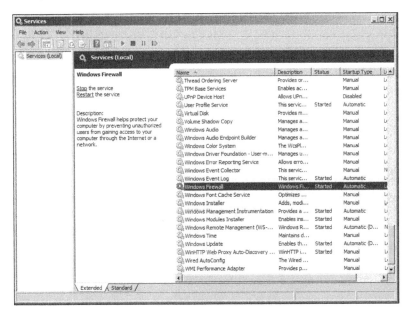

Finally, remember that if you plan to perform the installation remotely, do make sure you have an option to physically access the server, if needed. The reason for this is that during setup, the TMG Firewall may block your connectivity either temporarily or permanently. When you install UAG remotely, a special access rule is created to allow access to the computer you installed from, but when installing locally, this does not happen. In this case, after the TMG service starts, you will not be able to connect to your UAG server using remote desktop. To allow your computer access at this point and going forward, you need to add your computer to the list of Remote Management Computers on TMG.

Pre-installation checklist

Here are the things that you should check and verify before moving on to the next step:

- Networking has been configured correctly
- Static IPs assigned to all Network Cards
- Connectivity to the internet works
- Connectivity to the internal network works
- All available Windows updates installed
- The server is clean, with no additional software installed
- The server is of the appropriate version (Windows Server 2008 R2, Standard or Enterprise)
- Server has been named
- Server has been joined to the domain, if needed
- No previous versions of SQL, TMG, or UAG are installed
- The Windows Firewall service is started, and set to start automatically
- If the computer is a domain member, the installation is being performed by a domain user logged on to the server
- The installation is being performed by a user that has administrative permissions on the server

Preparing the installation files

Assuming you purchased UAG from Microsoft, it would typically be in the form of a **DVD disc**, or an **ISO file**. Depending on your server, you may need to burn the ISO onto a DVD or extract it to an installation folder on your hard drive. Detailing these operations is beyond the scope of this book, but if you are not sure, please refer to this online resource for information: `http://blogs.technet.com/ben/archive/2010/03/02/how-to-use-the-uag-iso-image-file-to-install-uag.aspx`.

Do keep in mind, though, that an ISO file uses the **Joliet file system**, and if you are extracting the image to a folder, do make sure the long file names are preserved, and not truncated to **DOS 8.3** filenames, since truncated file names will undoubtedly lead to a failed installation. Also, do not attempt to perform the installation from a network share on another server, as the connectivity disruption that may occur during the installation of TMG may corrupt the entire installation process.

The last thing to do before starting the installation is to verify you do indeed have the final and official version of UAG, and not a pre-release or trial version. To do so, open the installation folder, and navigate to the **UAG** folder. Right-click on the file **setup.exe** and choose **Properties**. Switch to the **Details** tab and look at the **product version**. If it is **4.0.1101.0,** this means you have the "gold" (pre-SP1) version. A lower number means that this could be a pre-release version (hmmm, torrents, anybody?), though a higher number may mean that this is an installation with a higher-level **Service Pack** included. Naturally, you should strive to obtain the latest version, with SP1 included. This would have a version number 4.0.1752.10000 or similar. This build number IS the final number for SP1.

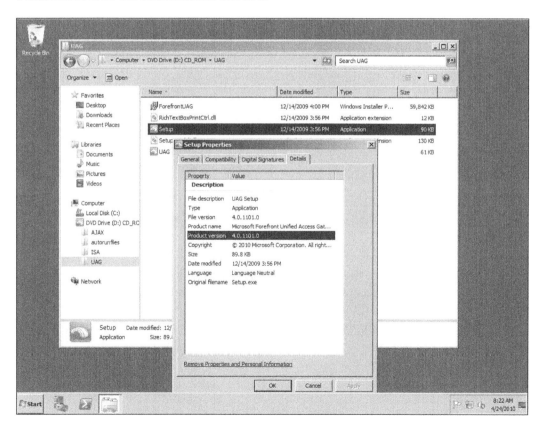

Installation

You are now ready to launch the installation. To do so, insert the installation disc, which should launch the welcome page (`splash.hta`). This is a good chance to review the information offered, such as the **system requirements**, the **deployment checklist,** and the **release notes**. Well, who are we kidding, nobody really does that, so when ready, click on **Install Forefront UAG.**

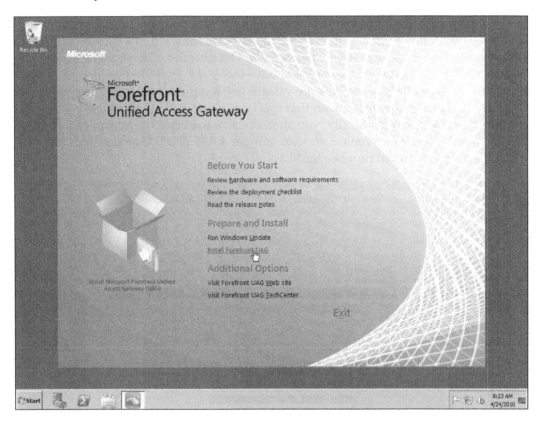

Once the installation starts, the **software license terms** (a.k.a. **EULA**) will be shown, and you will be asked to accept it. The next step is the installation location selection, which by default will install the product under the folder `Microsoft Forefront Unified Access Gateway` in the system's `Program Files` folder.

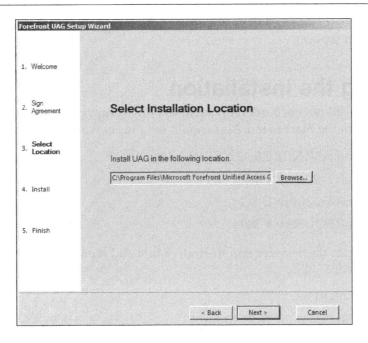

After that stage, the rest of the installation requires no intervention. It will install **Roles and Features**, then **AJAX**, which takes around 1-2 minutes altogether. Then, TMG will be installed, which takes about 15-20 minutes. Lastly, UAG itself will be installed, and that will keep you on the edge of your seat for an additional 5-10 minutes. Once this is done, you will be asked if you want to restart the computer. You don't have to, but don't expect to be able to do anything useful with the server at this stage before the reboot has been done. The following screenshots show the installation progress (left) and the final screen, prompting you to reboot the server:

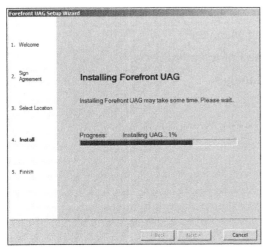
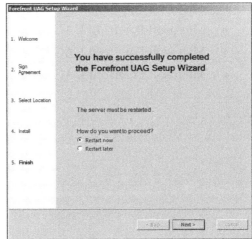

After a reboot, you are ready to launch the UAG management console and the **Getting Started Wizard.**

Verifying the installation

Assuming you did not encounter any errors during setup, you can easily check your installation from the **Start** menu. You should see four new items:

- Microsoft ASP.NET 2.0 AJAX Extensions
- Microsoft Forefront TMG
- Microsoft Forefront UAG
- Microsoft SQL Server 2008

You can also open the Services administrative tool and see the new services which have been added:

- ISASTGCTRL
- Microsoft Forefront TMG Control
- Microsoft Forefront TMG Firewall
- Microsoft Forefront TMG Job Scheduler
- Microsoft Forefront TMG Managed Control
- Microsoft Forefront TMG Storage
- Microsoft Forefront UAG Configuration Manager
- Microsoft Forefront UAG DNS64 Service
- Microsoft Forefront UAG File Sharing
- Microsoft Forefront UAG Log Server
- Microsoft Forefront UAG Monitoring Manager
- Microsoft Forefront UAG Quarantine Enforcement Server
- Microsoft Forefront UAG Session Manager

- Microsoft Forefront UAG SSL Network Tunneling Server
- Microsoft Forefront UAG Terminal Services RDP Data
- Microsoft Forefront UAG User Manager
- Microsoft Forefront UAG Watch Dog Service
- Net. Tcp Port Sharing Service
- Network Policy Server
- Remote Access Quarantine Agent
- Remote Desktop Gateway
- RPC/HTTP Load Balancing Service
- SQL Active Directory Helper Service
- SQL Server (ISARS)
- SQL Server (MSFW)
- SQL Server Agent (ISARS)
- SQL Server Agent (MSFW)
- SQL Server Browser
- SQL Server Reporting Services (ISARS)
- SQL Server VSS Writer
- Windows CardSpace
- Windows Presentation Foundation Font Cache 3.0.0.0

As you can guess, not all of them directly belong to UAG, but they are necessary. For example, the **Network Policy Server** is a service that allows for health checking of client computers which connect to the UAG server. This check allows the organization to block access to computers which do not meet the organization's security standards, thereby protecting the entire network from computers which may contain harmful software such as **back-doors** or **worms**.

Running the Getting Started Wizard

Before you can start publishing applications on the server, you need to configure some basic settings, and that is done with the **Getting Started Wizard**. It will launch automatically once you start the **Forefront UAG Management** console, which you can find under **Microsoft Forefront UAG** on the computer's **Start** menu:

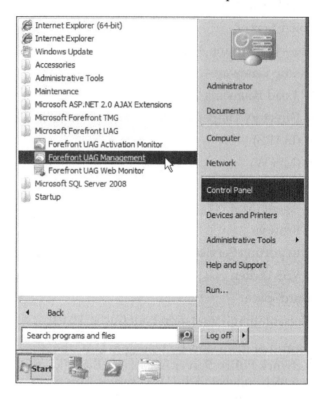

When you launch the wizard, you will see a notification about the application being configured for the first time, and that typically takes about a minute or two. Then, the **Getting Started Wizard** appears, with 3 steps:

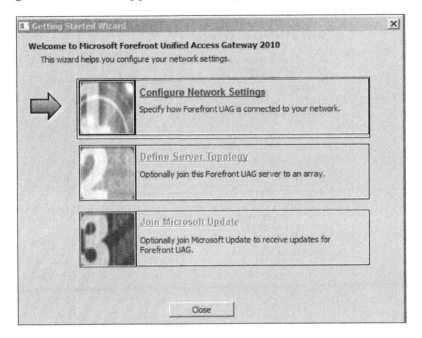

The first step is configuring the network settings. This wizard will show you a table with the network cards that are configured on the server. If you are installing a version of UAG that precedes SP1, you will also see an additional card named **SSL Network Tunneling**, which you should ignore. On this page, click on the appropriate table cell to choose which of the adapters will be **Internal** and which **External**, shown in the following screenshot. If you had not taken the time to rename your Network Cards earlier, this might get a bit confusing. If that's the case, you can either open the **Network management** console or check which is which, but you could also close the wizard by clicking **Cancel**, and then rename the cards.

When you launch the UAG configuration console again, it will launch the wizard again.

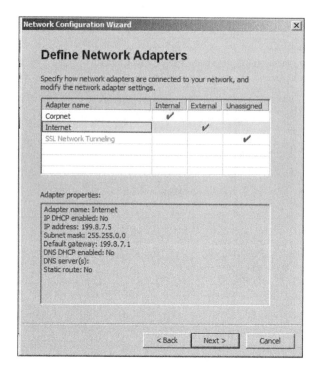

If the **SSL Network Tunneling** adapter is present, it is supposed to remain **Unassigned**, so leave it at the default, and click **Next.** If you have left one or more of the Network Cards with a dynamically assigned (**DHCP**) configuration, you will be warned by the wizard at this stage. You can continue despite this, but again, we strongly recommend against that, even on a temporary basis.

The next page is where you can define the exact IP ranges of the **internal network**. This is one of the most *critical* steps in the installation, as a mistake here can cause the server to go berserk. For example, if you forget to include the range which your Domain Controller belongs to, this will cause TMG to block access to it, thinking it is "External", and then, you won't even be able to open the UAG management console again. If you have configured your networking correctly, UAG should be able to detect the appropriate ranges on its own, and suggest them on this page. Are you using a virtual machine? If so, this would be a good time to pause and take a **Snapshot** of the server. We can't stress enough the importance of setting the correct internal ranges, so if you feel that your **TCP/IP** or **Subnetting** skills are rusty or not up to speed, you might consider involving a senior Network engineer, or refreshing yourself on that topic before continuing.

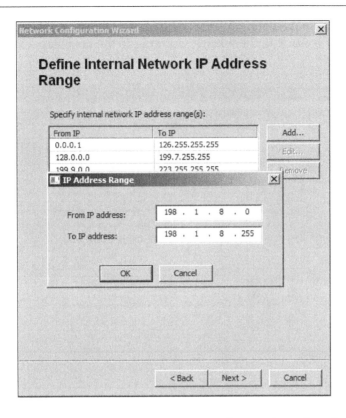

The next wizard page summarizes the settings you have selected, and also reminds you that finishing the wizard might cause a network disruption that would terminate a remote session and may force you to physically go to the server to continue. This would typically happen if you had not included the range of IPs from which you are accessing the server in the internal IP range. Take that into account before clicking **Finish**.

The server will apply the configuration, which should take no more than a few seconds, and go back to the wizard, pointing to the next step—**Define Server Topology**.

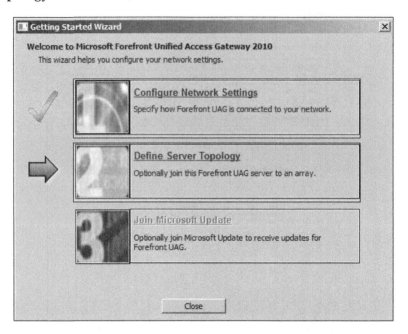

This stage is where you might choose to include this server as part of an **Array** of UAG servers, for **load balancing** purposes. You do not have to make this decision now. You can always start by using this UAG server as a stand-alone server, and join it to an array later. If the computer is not a domain member, then the option of joining an array will be greyed out, since domain membership is a prerequisite for UAG array functionality. Unfortunately, if you do intend to use this UAG as part of an array but have not yet joined the machine to the domain up to this stage, doing it now might be too late, since, as we mentioned earlier in this chapter, this should be performed before UAG installation. If you are planning on creating or joining an array, please refer to *Chapter 10*.

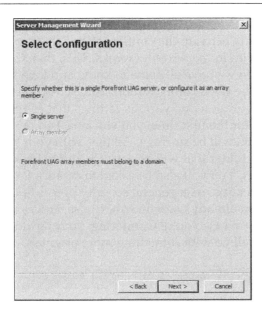

Lastly, the wizard will ask you if you want to use **Microsoft Update** to update the
server when future updates are released. You may choose to **skip** this and install
updates manually, though it's usually a pretty good idea to let this be taken care of
automatically. However, some organizations do prefer to have total control over
updates, in case the update involves downtime for the server.

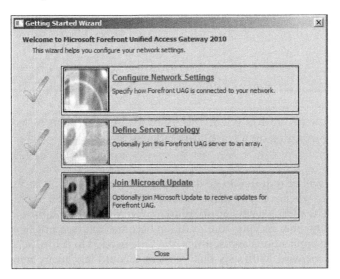

Having completed these three configuration steps, you may click **Close**, at which point you will be asked to **activate the configuration**. That's a term you are about to become very familiar with in the next few weeks. This, thankfully, is not related to the **Windows Activation** we have all come to know and love in the past ten years, but to an activation of the UAG configuration. The Activation process translates the UAG server's configuration into various settings that are pushed into **IIS** and TMG. Upon doing this for the first time, you will be asked to select a default location for **backups**, where UAG will be storing CAB files with your configuration. We recommend choosing a folder that will be easy for you to backup to more secure media on a regular basis. You will also be asked to create a **Password**, which will be used to protect your backups. As a general security precaution, we urge you to avoid re-using a password you already use somewhere else, and as always, do choose one that's not easy to guess (in case you're wondering, your birthday is not that hard to find, so you might as well go with something more original).

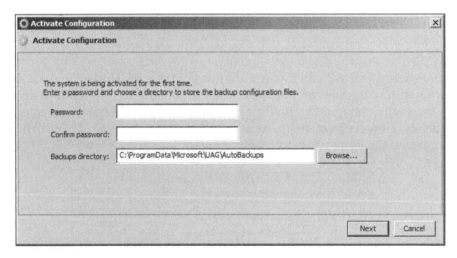

Once you finish the activation wizard, UAG will start the process, which typically takes about three minutes on a freshly installed server.

 You will be required to go through a similar activation process in the future whenever you make a change to the UAG server's configuration, such as adding a new application or changing the configuration of an existing one. As your configuration becomes more complicated, with more applications and settings, the time needed to complete the activation may increase. With very busy servers, it could take many minutes.

Congratulations! Your server is finally ready to publish its first application. Be aware, though, that at this point, there are no **trunks** or **applications** configured on the server, so connecting to it using a browser will not get you anywhere. Creating trunks and applications will be discussed in the next chapter and then you will have something to show for all your efforts thus far.

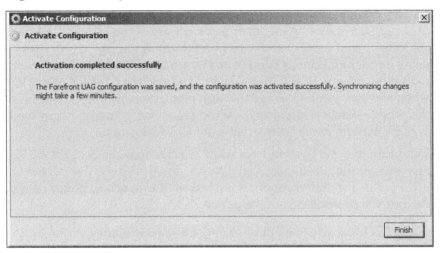

Applying updates or Service Packs

If updates or Service Packs for UAG have been issued, and were not already included with your ISO Image or DVD disc installer, we recommend applying them at this point. Updating UAG is pretty simple, and the only complication is that they require a re-activation of the server (similarly to what we just did, after completing the Getting Started Wizard). Normally, an update is cumulative, meaning it will include all updates that were issued before it, so it is sufficient to install Update 2, and there's no need to install Update 1 before it. Updates, however, are incremental between Service Packs, so in the future, after a Service Pack is released, and an Update is released after it, you will need to install the Service Pack prior to installing the update. This is quite similar to how things are with all other Microsoft products, so that should not come as a surprise or too much of a distraction. In fact, if you are used to installing several Windows updates a month, you will probably be relieved to hear that UAG will most likely have no more than two or three per year.

Common issues during installation

The installation process itself is pretty simple, and very difficult to botch up. Here are some issues that have been observed since the product's introduction into the market and instructions about how to resolve them.

- **File not found** errors during installation may indicate a problem with the original installation media or incorrect use of the ISO disc image. This could happen if the ISO image has been burned improperly, or extracted using a program such as **WinIso** or **WinImage**. There's nothing wrong with these programs and they are very suitable for this type of work, but when accessing an ISO image through them, one must be careful to select the proper extract session, as the wrong one may generate a truncated file-system, with filenames converted to a DOS 8.3 format.

- **Exception of type 'System.Exception' was thrown** can occur if the Windows Firewall is configured incorrectly. Make sure the Firewall service is **ON** prior to the installation, and if it is controlled by a group policy of some sort, exclude the computer from the policy.

The following **TechNet** article mentions a few more possibilities:
`http://technet.microsoft.com/en-us/library/ff607359.aspx`.

Most other installation failures could occur if the server is "dirty" from installation of other products or from a corrupt uninstall of UAG, TMG, or SQL, but that's easily resolvable by simply installing on a fresh and clean server. If you get an unexplained failure that does not meet any of the above, the best place to troubleshoot it would be the installation log. UAG's install logs can be found under `%ProgramData%\`
`Microsoft\UAG\Logs` and if the failure is of the TMG portion of the installation, then those can be found under `%windir%\Temp`. Reading installation logs is a tough job, so don't expect any easy answers, but if push comes to shove, Microsoft's customer support group will surely be able to help.

Post installation issues

Some of the post installation issues are mentioned in this section:

- As we mentioned earlier, if you install UAG on the server locally (as opposed to using remote desktop), you will not be able to access it using a remote desktop unless you specifically configure TMG for this. We already mentioned earlier that adjusting the configuration of TMG is bad, but this is one exception to that rule. To configure TMG to allow remote computer access, follow these steps:

1. Open the TMG configuration console.

2. Click on **Firewall Policy**.

3. On the **Toolbox** tab, click **Network Objects**.

4. Expand **Computer Sets**, and then double-click **Remote Management Computers**.

5. Click **Add**, and then select **Computer**.

6. Type the name and IP of your computer.

7. Click **OK** and apply the changes.

- Another issue that is quite common, is getting the following error when trying to open the UAG management console:

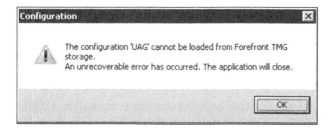

This error could appear upon re-launching the UAG console after having finished the Getting Started Wizard and having closed the console. This error actually means that the server is unable to communicate with its Domain Controller, probably because of incorrect network settings. If, for example, the "internal network" IP ranges were defined during the first stage of the Getting Started Wizard, but the Domain Controller's IP belongs to another range, then TMG will not allow network traffic to it. This is a security mechanism, as any IP outside the range that is defined as "internal" is considered to be "external", and thus tightly controlled. By default, TMG will initially block access to the external network. To resolve this, launch the TMG console and go to the **Network** tab. Switch to **Networks** and inspect **IP ranges** defined there. If the Domain Controller is on a subnet that does not belong to any of the ranges specified, change it, and click **Apply**.

- A variation of the same issue is if the TMG service itself is **stopped**.

  This service is supposed to be started automatically, so if it is failing to do so or stopping on its own, this would be highly unusual. It would be a good idea, in general, to observe the services after the installation has completed, and seeing if any that have been configured to start automatically have not started. Some services may stop without it being a problem. For example, it is perfectly normal for the UAG Watchdog service to be stopped, even though it's set to start automatically. If a service is stopped, the reason will typically be listed in the system's event log, which you can view using the **Event Viewer** in **Administrative** tools. You can also view a service's dependencies, to see if it stops because of another service. A common cause for service issues is when a domain group policy enforces some configuration for the service that causes a problem. For example, many organizations have a policy to prevent the RRAS service from starting, which could cause many problems with UAG and TMG. Another cause for service issues may be an unsupported platform, such as certain versions of VM software. If there are no apparent causes for the service issue, you may need to contact Microsoft support.

- Another variation of this problem can be encountered if the UAG server is connected to the backend network through some **router**, **load balancer** or any other networking device, which has not been configured to properly route data between the networks.

  In that case, the server may be able to send data **to** the backend network (and its Domain Controller), but data may not be able to return. To resolve this, perform basic network analysis, possibly using a network diagram or a network troubleshooting tool to verify that traffic can go back-and-forth on all the appropriate TCP/IP ports.

- If you have decided to change the default installation folder for UAG, and used a folder that has a **double-byte character**, such as often used in some Asian languages.

  This could also occur if the computer itself has some system folders named using Double-Byte characters. If you suspect this to be the problem, simply try to reinstall, specifying a folder on your drive that does not include a double-byte character and is not part of a system folder that has a double byte character.

- Failure to start the **TMG reporting service** following the installation or a reboot of the server.

This issue may occur because of a failure to install or to configure the **SQL Server software**, which is normally part of the TMG installation. Such a failure could happen on a machine that had SQL installed and then removed in a way that left some leftovers behind. We have seen such issues mainly in cases where a server had a pre-release version of UAG or TMG installed on it, and then removed. Essentially, if you are able to perform a complete removal of UAG and all other components, including SQL Server 2008, this should allow a re-install to succeed, but it might also land the machine in a state that's virtually unrecoverable. In other words, if you have stumbled into this error, your time would usually be best invested in formatting the server and re-installing everything from scratch. That's another one of those situations where a Virtual Machine snapshot can become very time-saving.

Summary

In this chapter, we have covered the steps required to prepare the server for the installation of UAG, and completed the installation procedure and the Getting Started Wizard as well. If you have much experience as an administrator or system engineer, you would probably agree, at this stage, that UAG is one of the easiest products to install and configure. With some solid planning, this entire task can be accomplished in just over an hour, including the Windows update. Before proceeding to the next chapter, we recommend documenting the steps you have taken, and parameters you have used, in case the server needs to be reinstalled. Performing a backup of your server is also a good idea.

The next chapter will introduce you to the first building block of UAG publishing — **Trunks**. We will discuss the various types of trunks and what type of publishing they are suitable for, as well as other related considerations, such as HTTPS vs. HTTP and **SSL Certificates.**

3
UAG Building Blocks

In this chapter, we will discuss UAG's building blocks—**trunks** and **applications**. We will review the various types of each, what they are used for, and how to create them. We will not cover specific application publishing as this will be described in depth in *Chapter 4*, but we will introduce some of the concepts that make the whole thing tick.

What are trunks and applications?

Just as we like to organize everything in life into containers, UAG also does the same. As a user of Microsoft products, you are probably used to files or programs that are grouped together within folders and which are stored on hard drives (or hard drive partitions). With UAG, there's one little difference, the primary organizational units are called "trunks", and in those we create (or "publish") applications, and we can also group them in folders too. The reason for this difference in naming goes back into the distant past, but it doesn't really matter.

The first step when starting to publish applications with UAG is to create a trunk, and then, add applications to it, as needed. A UAG server can contain multiple trunks, depending on how many IP addresses are assigned to its external interface. Some organizations need only a single application on a single trunk, while others publish multiple trunks, with dozens of applications on each of them. If many applications need to be published on a single trunk, the administrator can also organize them into folders, which can make it easier for users to find.

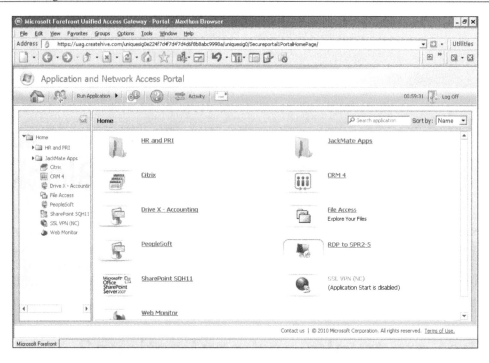

An "application" for UAG is a collection of settings and rules that determine how UAG publishes a certain internal website or application. These settings include, among others, the name or IP address of the internal server that will be published, what files and folders are accessible by the end users, and which users have access to what. We will discuss the various properties and rules specific to application publishing in *Chapter 4*.

At any point, an administrator can add IP addresses to the external NIC of the UAG server, add public **DNS mappings** to these addresses, and add more trunks. This is also an alternative way to organize the various applications—some organizations publish several Portals with different addresses, and provide the public URLs to groups of employees based on their needs. That is done, of course, in addition to defining the *authorization* on the trunks themselves.

Types of trunks

When creating a trunk, you can create trunks of two distinct types—**HTTP** (where traffic between the client and UAG is sent unencrypted as "clear-text") trunks and **HTTPS** (or "secure") trunks. The difference between these is simple—HTTP trunks are accessible by users over the HTTP protocol, while HTTPS trunks require the browser to communicate with encryption. Some UAG customers are perfectly fine with using HTTP trunks, but most customers prefer the more secure HTTPS trunks, because their users will be sending and receiving sensitive data over the link. From a technical perspective, a trunk is a website running on the IIS server that is active on the UAG server, and just like any other website in the world, it has an IP address and a TCP/IP port. If you have a single IP address assigned to the external NIC, you can choose to publish a single HTTP or HTTPS trunk on it. Naturally, you can choose to publish zero trunks, but for that, you don't need this book, or any book, really.

For those of you familiar with previous products, such as e-Gap and IAG, you might be familiar with several types of trunks, such as **Basic** and **Webmail**, but UAG no longer has these. UAG does not support publishing trunks on ports other than 80 and 443 either. It does, however, support **Redirect** trunks. A redirect trunk is meant to make it easier for an organization's users to connect to their server easily when the UAG portal is published as an HTTPS trunk. This is useful, because most users are used to typing HTTP URLs into their browsers, and if they forget to type the **HTTPS://** prefix to the URL, the browser will assume it is HTTP, and receive no response on port 80. The Redirect Trunk will listen on port 80, receive the request and reply with a "redirect" **HTTP 302** response code, asking the user's browser to request the same web address, but with the HTTPS prefix. It is important to note that a redirect trunk is only available to redirect users from HTTP to HTTPS, and not the other way around. Therefore, on the UAG configuration console, the option for a Redirect Trunk is only available in the HTTP trunk wizard.

A redirect trunk can only be created after the HTTPS trunk it needs to redirect to, has been created.

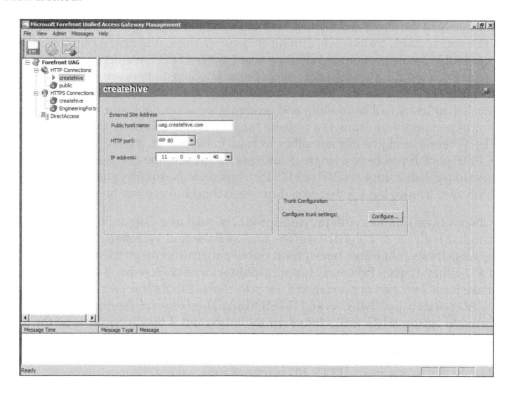

A Basic trunk used to be available in IAG and e-Gap as a means of publishing a single web application on a single trunk, without going through a portal. Even though UAG does not offer a Basic trunk, there is still a way to achieve the same functionality, and we shall discuss this further along the way. A Webmail trunk was used with the previous versions of the product to publish, as the name indicates, webmail types of applications, such as different versions of **Outlook Web Access** (**OWA**), or Lotus Notes, as well as the now out-dated Outlook Mobile Access for Exchange 2003, and the Exchange ActiveSync Service, which allows Mobile phones running Windows Mobile to sync over the internet with Exchange servers. This trunk type is no longer available either, but you can still get the same functionality via the use of the Exchange publishing wizard on a UAG Portal trunk, which we will discuss in *Chapter 4*.

Following the demise of the Basic and Webmail trunks, the remaining options when creating new trunks are **Portal** trunks, and **ADFS** trunks. A portal trunk is the home page of UAG—it will be the home for all the applications you will be publishing on your UAG server. Users who log in to the trunk remotely will see these applications as a list of icons and links referred to as the **Portal Home Page**, and clicking on any of these will launch the specific application, whatever they may be.

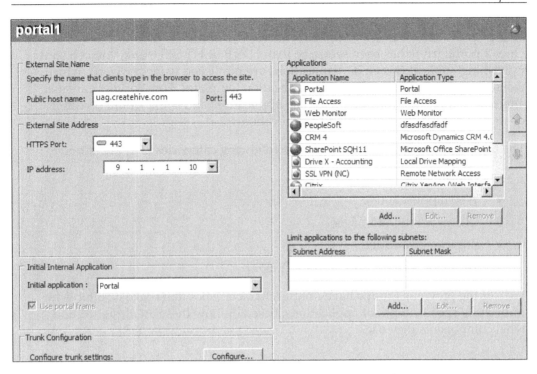

Another type of trunk that exists with UAG is the **ADFS** trunk. ADFS, or **Active Directory Federation Services**, is a technology that allows organizations to provide **Single Sign-On (SSO)** for users from different Active Directory forests. ADFS (sometimes written as "AD FS") has been a part of the Windows Server world since the release of **Windows Server 2003 R2**, and it is used primarily by large organizations. Such organizations can use ADFS to allow users which belong to one forest to access resources in another forest without requiring the need to sign on again. This nice trick can benefit an organization that has multiple forests, or an organization that needs to cooperate tightly with another organization, such as a business partner. This also means that the two organizations do not need to have a shared user database of any kind.

For UAG, this means that users can log on to the portal, and access published applications on servers that belong to another organization quickly and easily. We will discuss ADFS in more detail in *Chapter 6*.

Types of applications

Once a portal trunk has been setup, be it an HTTP or HTTPS trunk, you can start publishing applications on it. Applications are published using a wizard, which includes approximately 40 types of application templates. Some of these are just alternative ways of publishing the same application, and some would be better described as **services** rather than as applications.

The top-level type list is divided into the following categories of applications:

- Built-in services
- Web (applications)
- Client/Server and Legacy
- Browser-embedded
- Terminal Services and Remote Desktop

Each of the previous groups have unique characteristics that make it suitable for publishing specific types of applications, based on how these are designed and what components they use.

Built-in services

Built-in services are the Portal application itself, **File-Access** and the **Web-Monitor**. The portal application is automatically added to a trunk when you create a portal trunk, so you do not need to use it unless you delete the portal application for some reason and need to recreate it. The File-Access service allows users to download or upload files directly from internal file servers. The Web-Monitor is a built-in website that's automatically created when you install UAG, and publishing it on the portal allows an administrator to view and manage aspects of the portal remotely. We will discuss these services in more detail later in the book.

Web applications

The "Web" family of application templates is probably your main focus, as it contains templates for the most important Microsoft Servers—SharePoint and Exchange. It also contains templates for **Forefront Identity Manager 2010**, **Microsoft Dynamics CRM 4**, **Office Communicator Web Access 2007**, **Rights Management Services**, **Active Directory Federation Services 2.0** and most importantly—**Other Web Application**. The "other" web application is the most generic template, and will be your best bet for most applications that do not have a specific template assigned for them. That doesn't mean it **can** be used for everything else, but it is extremely flexible and it will work flawlessly for thousands of web applications.

Client/Server and Legacy

The third group, **Client/Server and Legacy**, which is also extremely useful, is designed for applications that go beyond being a simple website by integrating external components. These applications cannot be published like regular ones, because they run outside the browser.

In the case of applications that are Client/Server TCP/IP based, the user will be running something other than a web browser, and the internal server may be something other than a web-server. For example, the client component may be a CRM application, and the backend server may be a *database* server. To handle such applications, UAG contains **tunneling** components. These are part of the UAG's client components, which are installed on a client machine automatically when required. When a Client/Server based application is launched, the client components launch a special listener that listens for communication attempts from the client application, encrypts them using SSL, and sends them to the backend server through the UAG. At the other end of the tunnel, UAG listens to responses from the backend server, and these are sent back to the client through the UAG client components. All of this is done silently, in the background, although the user can observe that something is happening in the form of a special icon that appears in their System-Tray:

The tunneling technique described previously is extremely versatile and using the templates that are in that group allows incredible types of connectivity to happen. Using the **enhanced generic client application** template, for example, allows you to do pretty much anything.

Another important application in the Client/Server and Legacy group is **Remote Network Access**. If you are familiar with IAG, you might recognize that as "Network Connector". Remote Network Access is an application that creates a fully fledged **VPN** connection to the corporate network, including IP assignment, DNS, and, of course, full SSL encryption of the traffic. We will discuss Remote Network Access in more detail later on, but it's considered by many to be one of the most important and useful abilities of UAG.

Browser-embedded applications

The fourth group of application templates is **Browser-embedded**, which are somewhat similar to Client/Server applications. In this case, the software used by the users to do their work is not a browser, but a piece of standalone code that is embedded in the browser. You can think of it as a middle ground between a standalone "client" application and a browser. This group, for veteran IAG users, used to contain many applications in IAG, but with UAG, it contains but two items. One is **Citrix XenApp**, and the other is simply a generic browser-embedded application template. Citrix is a classic browser embedded application, in which a link on a webpage causes an **ActiveX** version of the Citrix Client. The ActiveX runs within the browser, but it's also a standalone executable, so it requires a tunnel to be able to communicate to the back-end Citrix server. The Citrix XenApp UAG application template creates a tunnel in a way that's identical to the way Client/Server application templates do.

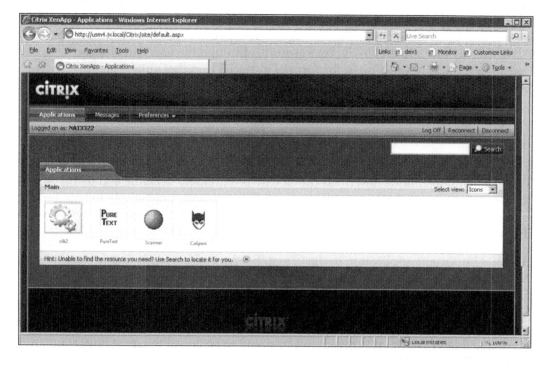

Many customers are not very happy about the fact that UAG misses so many of the Browser-embedded templates they grew to appreciate with IAG, but the fact of the matter is that the generic browser-embedded application template is actually capable of publishing almost all of these applications quite easily. It requires the UAG administrator to know the properties of the applications, like the TCP/IP ports that they use, but other than that, it's all pretty smooth.

Terminal Services (TS) / Remote Desktop Services (RDS)

The final group is **Terminal Services (TS)/Remote Desktop Services (RDS)**, which is a collection of five templates used to provide access to internal servers via the **RDP** protocol. This is pretty straightforward, although the various templates each serve slightly different purposes. Some organizations use these to allow the organization's network administrators to connect to their servers from home and manage them, while others let users use an internal terminal sever to do routine work. Using Terminal Servers in this manner provides a smooth and secure work environment, because the Terminal Server that the user connects to is already configured with various applications that the user may require. Also, these servers are actually **inside** the organizational network, so the environment is a very close match to what the user is used to from working at the office.

What is URL signing and how does it work?

An important part of the way UAG handles applications is the process of **URL signing,** also known as **Host Address Translation (HAT)**. The URL signing mechanism is what allows the UAG server to publish multiple servers from within the organization, all on a single IP and port.

To understand how HAT works, and why it's needed, let's consider a regular website. The user types in a URL into his browser, which retrieves it from the server. The web page typically contains links. These can be images, which the browser automatically retrieves from the server, or actionable items, such as 'blue' links to other pages or various types of action buttons. These links can point to resources on the same server or another.

When a page is visited through UAG, we have a challenge. The back-end server has a certain name, which is often part of the links. For example, the page `http://accounting01/home.htm` may have a link to `http://accounting01/tax/calc.htm`. If the accounting server is published through a UAG portal named `https://uag.createhive.com`, and the user clicks on the `calc.htm` link, his browser will try to contact the server `accounting01`, which is not reachable directly from the Internet. This is what HAT solves for us.

When UAG delivers a page to the user, it has a special engine that goes through all the links on the page and rewrites them. If it finds a link to an internal server name, it changes it to point to UAG's own portal hostname, so that when the link is "activated", it will reach the UAG server. When that happens, UAG also needs to know to which of the applications that it is publishing this relates to (in other words, from which of the many internal servers that the organization has is UAG supposed to retrieve the actual resource). To this end, UAG adds a unique alphanumeric string to each link. For example: `https://ap.createhive.com/uniquesig48cb675c4745e7d473e210fdf4f89f67/uniquesig0/tax/calc.htm`

Then, when a request arrives for this link, UAG decodes back the string (also called 'Signature') and knows that this request is for the `accounting01` server, and proceeds to retrieve the requested file from it.

To the end-user, all of this is transparent—he just sees pages delivered, and all is great. If, however, you view the source of pages delivered by UAG, you will find that every link on the page that normally points to an internal server is "signed", similarly to the previous example. The signature strings are unique to each server that UAG is publishing, and if an application is configured to use multiple servers, we might find multiple signatures in one file.

One challenge that UAG sometimes has a problem handling is that not all web pages are the same. Sometimes, the application's creators build the pages using dynamic scripts that confuse UAG. For example, a JavaScript may be building a link on the client machine, from several variables, which prevent UAG from identifying the link at all. If it misses signing the link, it may not work, either partially, or at all. For example, it may point to an "internal" server that the client won't be able to access, or to the wrong folder on the server. Sometimes, such issues can be fixed by creative ways to publish applications, or by customizing UAG to manually alter the links. These techniques are very complex, and will not be discussed in this book.

For some applications, the link parsing is so difficult that we don't even bother trying. One such example is SharePoint. SharePoint pages are so complex, that the SharePoint development team actually had to write a special component called **Alternate Access Mappings (AAM)**, which helps UAG and other publishing products to handle it. This means that when publishing SharePoint servers, HAT is not done at all, and we will discuss this in more detail in *Chapter 4*, as well as some other applications that bypass the HAT process.

Designing your trunks, applications, and nesting

When publishing applications, the number of applications is not limited beyond the hardware capabilities of the server, though one should consider general User-Interface design considerations. Creating a huge page with dozens of buttons is cool, in some people's opinion, but a general approach says that having no more than eight items on any menu is a good practice. This number is not set in stone, and you can always create some folders and divide the applications logically between them. Another thing to keep in mind is that the applications you define on a trunk will be displayed on-screen arranged from left to right, and from top to bottom, alphabetically. If it's important to you to have the applications appear in a certain order, the only means of controlling that is by naming them in a way that will force UAG to sort them to your liking. For example, you could name all RDP related applications with the prefix RDP ("RDP Exchange", "RDP SQL", and so on), so these will be grouped together, or have each application name start with a number. Another thing you can do to make things easier for users is to assign specific icons that differ from the default, to an application. This book is not about usability or user interface design, however, so let's go on.

Technically, you should be aware of one important fact. UAG has a security mechanism for web publishing that inspects the HTTP requests sent by clients to UAG and decides if these should be sent to backend web applications. This is very useful for several reasons:

- It allows you to block access to parts of the applications that you don't want people to use, such as the part that manages settings, or the part that controls the applications' permissions and authorization.

- It allows you to block specific commands or parameters that might be undesirable or dangerous. For example, certain URL parameters can be blocked in a way that prevents **OWA (Outlook Web Access)** users from uploading or downloading attachments.

- It allows you to block URL and parameter combinations that pose a risk, such as cross-site scripting or attacks that exploit faulty input validations in applications.

The access rules mechanism is controlled using the Trunk Configuration **URL Set** tab, which will be discussed in *Chapter 10*.

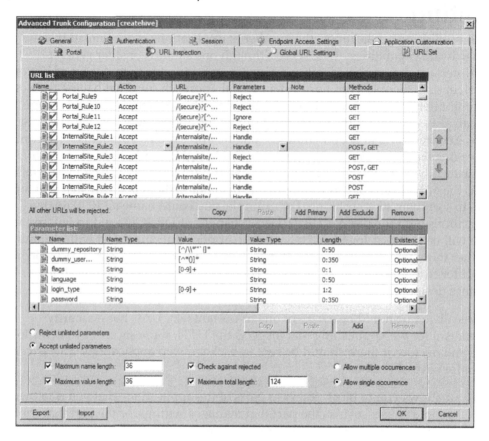

What you do need to realize now, though, is that the rules are named and applied according to an application's **type**, which is determined by the template you select. Most templates have a fixed type, but the generic templates allow you to enter anything you want as the type. What's important to remember here is that if you publish multiple applications with the same type, the same access rules will apply to all of them. This could be a good idea and a time saver if you do indeed need all these applications to have the same level of access but, if not, you must keep this trinket of information in mind.

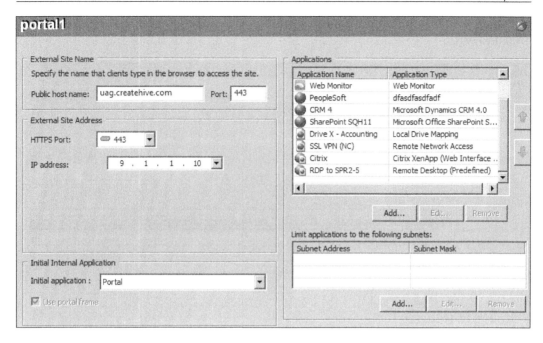

Some common applications and the appropriate templates

At this point, you might be thinking to yourself something along the lines of "Hmmm...I bought this product, which is supposed to publish everything, to publish my fabulous and unique _____ server. Now you're saying I am the one who's supposed to pick and choose?!?!" Well, in short, **yes**. The long answer, though, is that UAG is certainly not "supposed" to publish "everything". It's extremely versatile and flexible, but each application and service has its own characteristics, and some can be difficult, or even impossible to publish.

Some applications will require careful analysis and planning and, occasionally, some trial and error.

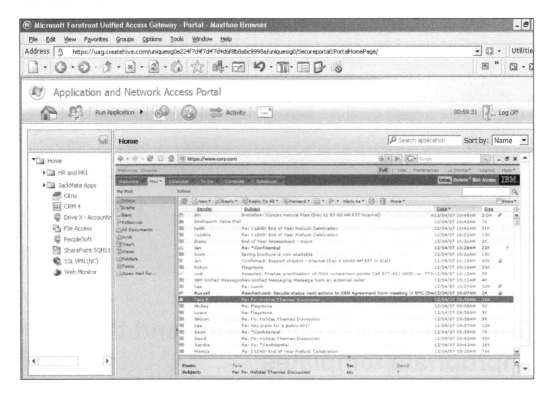

DNS name resolution

For most organizations, the UAG portal and applications are there for employees or partners to use from the public Internet, from home, or while travelling. UAG is designed to be accessed using a host-name that is typed into the browser on a user's computer. This means that the client computers need a way to perform name resolution for the server, and for that, you will have to create a host entry on your public DNS server. For some organizations, this can be tricky, if the DNS is hosted by an **ISP**, or if such change requires assistance from another team within the company. Some companies have very strict change-control procedures, and some hoops will have to be jumped through to get this done. If that is the case, it would be a good idea to get to that early, so it doesn't hamper the production schedule. As an option, you can also use an alternative, such as adding a static entry to the **HOSTS** file on your client computers, though that could be quite a hassle for a large organization. As a temporary means of testing the server, though, it could work well.

Another thing to keep in mind is that the UAG server itself needs to have the ability to perform name resolution of internal hostnames of servers it is publishing. It may also need to be able to do so for public URLs. For example, if you plan on publishing internal servers that use HTTPS, the UAG server will have to be able to accept their server certificates. If those certificates have a **CDP** (**CRL** Distribution Point, where CRL stands for Certificate Revocation List) URL embedded in them, like most certificates do, then UAG will need to be able to resolve the CDP URL. If those certificates have been issued by a public CA (Certificate Authority) like *VeriSign* or *Thawte*, then UAG will need to be able to resolve and contact the public CRLs of those providers. Whether UAG uses internal DNS servers, external ones, or both, the proper routing and access-control needs to be thoughtout.

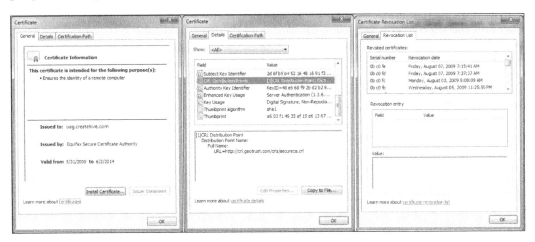

This is a good opportunity to mention a new behaviour in Windows Server 2008, which is different to older versions of Windows Server. The new TCP/IP stack in Windows uses a new model when choosing the IP address it uses as a "source" (this refers only to systems that have more than one IP address assigned to a Network Card). You can think of this like choosing which exit you use when you leave your town to get on the highway. Some people choose the closest one, while others prefer the one that has a drive-through coffee stand or one with a gas station. In previous versions of Windows, the system would always use the primary host, but with **Windows Server 2008** (as well as **Vista**), the source IP is selected based on a set of rules that may cause it to use another IP. This could cause a bit of confusion in case you have some traffic-control mechanism to govern traffic coming out of the server, such as a *firewall* or *load balancer*. For example, if you have set your external firewall to allow access only on certain ports/IP combinations, you may find that some traffic is inexplicitly blocked. To read more about the new TCP/IP stack in Windows Server 2008, read the following articles:

- `http://support.microsoft.com/default.aspx?scid=kb;EN-US;969029`

- `http://www.rfc-editor.org/rfc/rfc3484.txt`
- `http://blogs.technet.com/networking/archive/2009/04/24/source-ip-address-selection-on-a-multi-homed-windows-computer.aspx`

Preparing for an HTTPS trunk

We have chosen to talk about HTTPS first, because these trunks are the most used by UAG customers and because, well, HTTP trunks are as easy as pie. Creating an HTTPS trunk is not difficult but, before going there, you need to have a certificate, and this can make your whole day rainy.

The HTTPS protocol provides better security as it encrypts the traffic between the user and the server. This is an age old protocol that has stood the test of time well, but it may still be a bit challenging to use, because just like real-life certificates, digital ones can't just be handed out by anyone. Many books have been written about **PKI (public key infrastructure)**, so we won't go into much detail about it, but it's important to understand the basics, so here goes.

Encryption is based on a simple concept. You want to send data to someone without anyone else being able to read it. You take the data, and change it in a way that only you and the future recipient know. If that data falls into the wrong hands, it will look like meaningless garbage. The intended recipient, though, knows how to reverse the process and read it.

Encryption is done by taking a **key**, which is a very long and unique number, and using it to perform a mathematical function on the data, resulting in encrypted data that appears to be meaningless. To decrypt the data, you do the opposite, with the same number, and obtain the original data. Let's do a simple example:

Suppose you want to encrypt the word **RIDDLE**:

1. First, you convert each letter to a number. If we start with A=1, B=2, we get 18, 9, 4, 4, 12, and 5.

2. Second, we "encrypt" the data with our key. Let's say our key is "50", so we just add the key to each number, and end up with 68, 59, 54, 54, 62, and 55.

3. Now, when it's time to decrypt this sequence, we just subtract the same number back, and convert font to letters.

Naturally, that level of secrecy wouldn't be too hard to break, but real key-based digital encryption is much more complicated – trust me!

The previous process is known as "symmetric" encryption, because the same key is used to encrypt and decrypt. In old-school espionage, the recipient would be equipped in advance with the knowledge or means to do the decryption. The problem with the internet is that the sender and recipient hardly ever meet, so we need to come up with a way to provide the recipient with the know-how, without it being intercepted along the way, because that will allow anyone who's smart enough to intercept internet traffic (which isn't very hard, really) to decrypt anything and listen in. To our help comes **ASSYMETRIC encryption**, and **digital certificates**.

Asymmetric encryption

Asymmetric encryption uses a special mathematical formula that generates *two different* keys, instead of one. We then use a special encryption formula that cannot be reversed with the same key. If you encrypt using the first key, you need the second to decrypt, and vice-versa. It's really quite a headache, but computers can do this sort of thing almost instantly. What happens when computers need to encrypt data is that the server (this could be your web server, for that matter) creates these two keys randomly. One is called the **public key**, and the other one the **private key**. Now, when that server wants to communicate securely with some other computer (say, your client), it sends it its public key (which is not secret—anyone is free to have it at any time), and then the client creates a unique and random **regular** key (like the one we discussed earlier). The client then encrypts the regular key using the server's public key, and sends it to the server. If you recall, the encrypted regular key stays secret, because even if someone intercepts that message, he can't decrypt it because, to do so, they would need the server's PRIVATE Key, which is kept really private and secret.

So, the encrypted regular key is received by the server, which decrypts it, and now both sides have a regular key that no one else knows, and they can start using it to encrypt and decrypt messages back-and-forth. Fantastic. One thing, though, still needs to be taken care of is—trust. Say you are a client, and a server sends you this nice encrypted key, how do you know it's really a genuine partner, and not some other server that impersonates it? Well, for that, we have **digital certificates**.

Digital certificates

A digital certificate, like a real-world certificate, is a way to prove one's identity. When you want to get on a plane, you convince the security guard that you really are who you say you are by showing him a certificate given to you by the government— a passport or ID card, usually. It would have some unique seal or mark to prevent you from photo-shopping someone else's ID, and that allows the guard to trust you because he trusts the body that gave you that certificate. After all, the government (at least ours) won't hand out a passport randomly, right?

Well, a digital certificate is given out by special companies who give them out only after verifying the recipient's identity properly, and so everyone trusts them. Even if you have never heard of *VeriSign*, *Thawte*, *Valicert*, or *Entrust*, your computer has heard of them. If you open your local certificate store, you can see them, as well as several others. To do so, open the **Internet Control Panel**, and switch to **Content**. Click on **Publishers**, and switch to **Trusted Root Certificate Authorities**, and voila:

Once you have a digital certificate, you install it on the server it was intended for, and then, your server can present it to clients which attempt to connect to it. These clients check if the certificate is a match to the server by comparing the server's URL to the Common Name listed in the certificate. They also check if the certificate has not expired, if the certificate's issuer is a trustworthy one, and if that issuer hasn't revoked that certificate. If that is good and well, the whole encryption process discussed previously can continue. If something fails, the browser will alert you to that fact, and you can then decide if you want to take a risk and go ahead anyway, or walk away.

If you look at the previous screenshot, or your own computer's **Trusted Root Certification Authorities**, you will notice that your browser comes with a pre-populated list of all major Certificate companies, but some companies don't want to buy a certificate from them because it can cost a lot of money, hundreds of dollars in some cases. Instead, they set up their own Certificate Authorities within the organization. Anyone can do that really. In fact, all versions of Windows Server come with a built-in Certificate Authority server that can be enabled for free.

The challenge here is that such a server, by default, is not trusted by other computers unless they are configured to do so. This is done by installing the company's Certificate Authority's own certificate into each computer that needs to trust it. That could be a tedious process but, sometimes, it is inevitable.

So, going back to our HTTPS trunks, to enable computers on the internet to communicate with it securely, it has to be able to prove its identity to these computers by having a digital certificate. The rest of the encryption process is done automatically and there's no need to worry about it. Getting the certificate, though, requires some planning. We already said that the client checks four things:

1. The certificate is issued by a trusted authority
2. The certificate's URL matches the one it's assigned to
3. The certificate has not expired (calendar-wise)
4. The certificate has not been revoked by the publisher

Getting a certificate from a trusted publisher is not a problem—just pick one of the names on the list, or do a web search for it. If you're good at that sort of thing, you might land yourself a nice deal (word on the street is that you can find certificates for less than $20 a year). The URL is where it gets complicated. You probably already made up your mind about the public URL your portal will be accessible through, so you need to make sure that the certificate is for that URL. You can always change your mind, but that might require buying a new certificate, unless you have a **wildcard** or **star** certificate. This is a nice thing to have, because it allows you to publish multiple servers using the same certificate, though it does cost more than a regular one, of course.

For example, if you want to publish your UAG portal as `https://uag.createhive.com`, you can buy a certificate for `*.createhive.com` instead of the explicit `uag.createhive.com`. This way, if you later decide you want to change your portal to `portal.createhive.com`, there will be no need to mess around with the certificate. There's another advantage— publishing some applications with UAG requires the use of multiple public hostnames. SharePoint, for example, is such an application, and so is publishing Exchange Outlook Anywhere. Getting a wildcard certificate can make these go much smoother. Another option is getting a **Subject Alternative Name (SAN)** certificate, which is cheaper than a wildcard certificate, and can contain several (usually four) names within a single certificate.

After having bought the certificate, which could take a few days to finalize, all you have to do is install it on your server. The Certificate Authority will provide you with instructions on creating the certificate request, and then how to install the certificate file that they will send you. Once this is done, you are ready to create your first HTTPS trunk. Take note of the *expiration date* of your certificate – once it expires, you will need to renew, and it's better to do so a few days before it actually expires. Your server will **not** remind you of this, until you start getting those angry phone calls about clients receiving weird errors, so you might as well mark your calendar.

If your plan is to skip buying a certificate completely, you have two other options. One is using a **self-signed certificate**, and another is installing a corporate Certificate Authority server. These tasks are beyond the scope of this book, but you can read about them here:

- http://technet.microsoft.com/en-us/library/cc753127(WS.10).aspx
- http://technet.microsoft.com/en-us/library/cc731183.aspx

If you choose to go down this path, keep in mind that you should establish trust by installing the appropriate root certificates on the client computers. If you don't, you will be prompted about the site's invalid certificate when you try to access it, and it may stop some components from working. For example, Remote-Desktop applications as well as SSTP are sensitive to invalid certificates, and will not work.

Creating an HTTPS trunk

To create an HTTPS trunk, open the Forefront UAG Management console on your
server, right-click on the **HTTPS Connections** branch and select **New Trunk**. On the
wizard, select **Portal Trunk**, but **don't** check the option **Publish Exchange applications
via the portal**, even if you plan on doing so. You will be able to launch the Exchange
publishing wizard at any point, and we will discuss that in depth in *Chapter 4*.

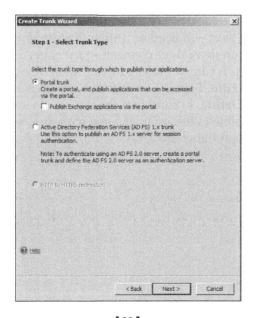

On the next page, type in a name for the trunk, and the **Public hostname** you selected earlier. The public hostname should **not** include the HTTPS:// prefix. Select the **public IP address** that will be assigned to it, or one of them, if there's more than one. Leave the **port** selection fields as they are, and don't worry about the "**80**" one – that does not mean it will be non-secure. Be careful about selecting the trunk name – it's not visible onscreen to the end-user, but it is part of the URL that the user might notice, so make sure it's something respectable and reasonable.

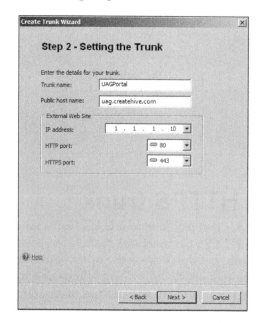

On the next wizard step, you will need an authentication repository, which will allow UAG to check the credentials of connecting users in Active Directory, or other authentication providers. To do so, click **Add**, and then fill out the details of your authentication infrastructure. Type a **Server name**, which is just a name for the repository and click on **Define**, to configure the names of your servers. Keep in mind that the Repository is visible to the users in some scenarios, so the name should make sense or, at least, not be anything embarrassing.

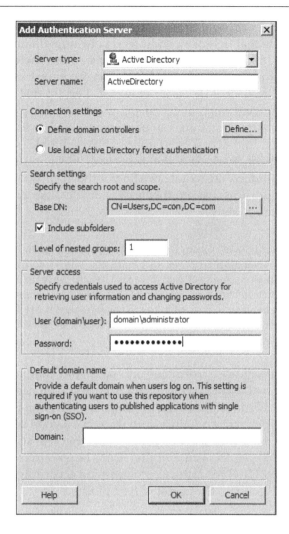

Fill in the name of your AD Server and, optionally, a secondary one. If the UAG server is domain joined, this is not needed, and you can simply use the **Use local AD forest authentication** option. You can also select that the server uses **SSL/TLS**. If you are not the primary network engineer of your company, you might need some help obtaining these parameters.

Back to the **Repository add** page, click on the three dots next to **Base DN** to automatically populate that field. Depending on your domain infrastructure, you may need to edit it manually. You also have the option **Include subfolders**. Including subfolders means that when UAG checks the permissions for a user that is logging in, it can also check if the user belongs to a group that has permissions. For example, you may want to grant access permissions to an application, or to the portal, to a group named `Accounting Department`, rather than for individual users or for "everyone". In that case, you must enable subfolder search, and set the appropriate **nesting level**. By default, that is set to **0**, which means that even if you checked **Include subfolders**, no actual crawling of the groups will be done. If the target users are inside groups that are themselves inside other groups, you should set a nesting level appropriately.

> The "nesting level" settings tempt some to set it to a high number, in order to cover all their bases, but that's actually a bad idea. If you set the number to a high setting, it forces UAG to perform multiple queries against Active Directory, and that takes time. The result could be a big delay on logging in and, in extreme cases, even a nasty timeout. We recommend setting the nesting number as low as possible. For most companies, 1 or 2 would be sufficient.

The **Server Access** settings are a username and password combination of a user that will be impersonated by UAG to retrieve data from AD. You need to make sure that the user you choose will indeed have the appropriate permissions for this. Some organizations use the primary domain admin user, but a good security practice is to use a user that has the lowest level of permissions that will still suffice. Another thing to keep in mind about this is that if that user's password expires, and is reset, you need to update the UAG repository configuration accordingly, or authentication attempts will fail and access to the portal will be blocked.

Lastly, you might want to set a **default domain** name for your users. This is not mandatory, but, by setting it correctly you can make things easier for your users. If you specify a default domain, your users will not be required to enter their domain name when logging in.

It's important to keep in mind that this repository wizard also allows you to create other types of repositories, and not just ones that authenticate against Active Directory. This will be discussed in more detail in *Chapter 10*.

Once done with the repository, close the wizard and return to the Trunk creation wizard by selecting the repository you just created and clicking **Select**. The next page requires you to select the certificate that will be used for this trunk and, assuming you have already taken care of buying and installing it, it should appear in the drop-down.

The next page in the wizard asks you to select if you want to use the standard UAG endpoint policies to control access to the portal, or use a NAP server. **NAP (Network Access Protection)** is a Microsoft technology used to check the health state of computers by checking that said computers meet certain, preset, requirements. For example, the company may wish that only computers that have all current Windows Updates installed to be allowed access to the network. If your network has NAP deployed, you can configure it here, although this is beyond the scope of this book.

If you selected **Use Forefront UAG access policies**, you will now be presented with two drop-down menus, which allow you to select the policies which will be enforced on connecting clients. We shall discuss Endpoint policies in more detail in *Chapter 8*, so, for now, leave the settings at their default and move on.

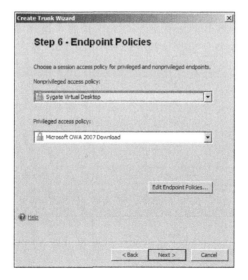

The last wizard page summarizes your settings, and you can click **Finish**. Remember that Activation we talked about earlier? Yup, it's time to do that again. You can do it by clicking on the Cog-Wheel icon that's on the top-left of the screen, or choose **Activate** from the **File** menu. The simplest way, though, is to press *Ctrl+G*. The Activation wizard will offer to backup your configuration before activation. There is not so much to backup at this point, but backing up often is certainly a good idea, and a good habit to make from day one. You will probably notice that the activation process takes even longer than it took before, and don't forget to track it with the **Activation Monitor** to make sure it's really over, despite hearing no singing. The activation monitor is a separate application that you can find next to the UAG management console on your **Start** menu. It shows the activation status for your server, and once the activation is really finished, it will show a long output that describes some of the work the server has been doing during the activation. Once done, you can fire up a browser on your test client, and connect to the portal. Take a few minutes to enjoy and appreciate the fruit of your hard work!

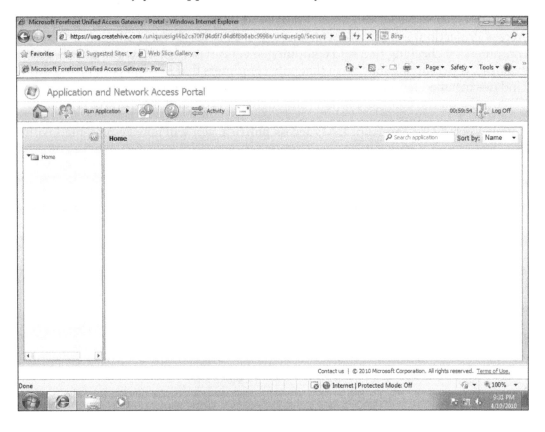

Publishing an HTTP trunk

The HTTP trunk publishing wizard is virtually identical to the HTTPS one, except for the Certificate selection page, which you won't see. Another difference is the option to select a **Redirect Trunk**.

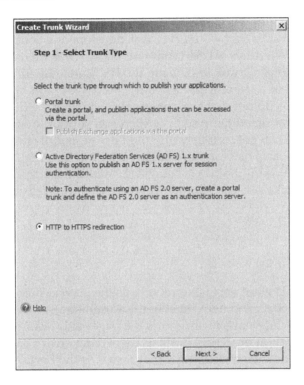

If you have selected the **HTTP to HTTPS redirection** trunk, then the next page of the wizard will ask you to select to which trunk you want the redirection to be done.

Note that if you have not yet created an HTTPS trunk, you will not be able to continue this wizard. Also, you can only create one redirect trunk per HTTPS Trunk. As always, once the wizard has completed, you will need to activate the configuration to make your changes come to life. We hope that by now, you might be mumbling the word "activation" in your sleep.

What happens when you add a trunk?

When you create a trunk, whether it is HTTP or HTTPS, several things occur that you might want to be aware of.

The activation process automatically creates a new website within **IIS**, the built-in Web Server that is included with every version of Windows Server since the dark ages (actually, Microsoft's first web server was developed in Scotland and released as a free add-on for Windows NT 3.51, but you know what we mean). If you inspect your server after adding a trunk to it, using the **IIS Management console**, you will discover that it has several websites on it. Before we go on, we need to make this clear once again—**do not** make any manual changes to the IIS configuration, unless specifically instructed to do so by a Microsoft support document or official representative. UAG can get seriously offended if you meddle in its romantic relationship with IIS, and blow up on you. In fact, even keeping the IIS management console open while a configuration is being activated is risky. Assuming you haven't created multiple trunks yet, you should find three existing websites:

- The Default Website
- A website for your trunk
- The Web Monitor website

The Default website is what we like to refer to as the *internal* site. It is bound to ports 443, 6001, and 6002, and does most of the administrative work for UAG in the background. The Internal Site also hosts the pages and resources that are used during the authentication process, as well as displaying error pages and the logoff mechanism. It also contains a virtual site that serves as the Portal homepage. The portal home includes the various pages and resources that are used to build the portal homepage with its applications.

The trunk website is named according to the name you selected when running the wizard earlier, and should contain three folders: `InternalSite`, `Scripts`, and `WhlServerProxy`.

The **Web Monitor** site is typically bound to port 50002, and will allow you to monitor the activity on the portal. It can show you how many users are connected and what they are doing, as well as show warnings about problems in the configuration. We will discuss the Web Monitor in more detail in *Chapter 9*.

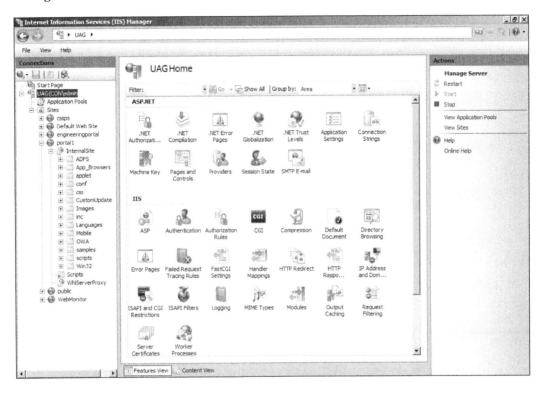

If you click on your Trunk's website, and then click on the **ISAPI Filter** icon (it's under the IIS group of icons, around the middle), you will see an item named **<your portal name>-WhlFilter**. This item is where the magic really happens. It's linked to the `WhlFilter.dll` file, and that **DLL (Dynamic Link Library)** is how UAG does its work. The filter can interact with data that IIS receives and sends, and manipulate it, and that's how UAG can parse and react to URLs the user types or clicks, and modify the content delivered to them.

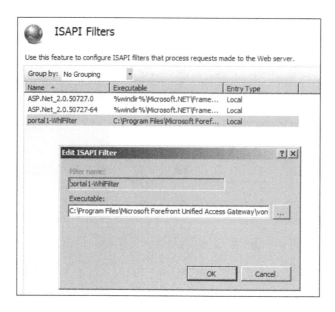

In addition to IIS, UAG also configures TMG with rules that will allow it to communicate with users from the outside, and with servers on the inside. At this point, you can already find over 20 access rules that have been created by UAG. Most of these rules will be named **publishing rule::custom#<some number>,** and you should be able to see that they allow traffic from "**localhost**" (meaning, from the UAG itself) to **Internal**. These rules allow UAG to contact important internal servers, like the Active Directory servers. You will also find two rules, from **All Network** to **PublishingRule::Server#001** and **PublishingRule::Server#002**. One of these rules is for port 80 (your redirect trunk) and another for 443 (your portal trunk).

Another interesting rule you will see is the last **Deny** rule, which is common to pretty much all firewalls. It basically says that anything not specifically allowed in any of the previous rules it will be denied.

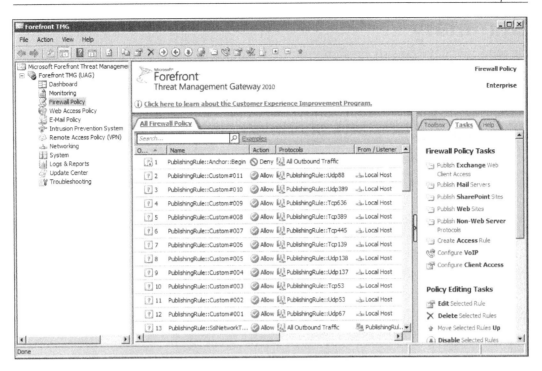

In case we haven't said that enough times already, do not attempt to modify any of the existing rules or configurations in TMG, or add any others, unless specifically instructed by a Microsoft support document or official representative. This is even more dangerous than fiddling with IIS, because you might unknowingly create a rule that is too permissive, thereby exposing your server to hostile parties. Keep in mind that baddies are not only out there, on the web, but can also lurk inside your own company. We've heard of plenty of cases where a company's employee dug around various servers and collected information or implanted back-doors for a rainy day.

You might be asking yourself what to do in case you want to manage your server remotely from the comfort of your desk using Remote Desktop. By default, UAG does not configure TMG for this, although TMG will configure itself if you have used Remote Desktop to install the server. We discussed this in the previous chapter, in the section titled *Post-install issues*, so review it if you plan on using Remote Desktop to install or administer the server.

Summary

By now, you have already created your first trunk, and should have a server that you can connect to and see the empty portal. You are now merely minutes away from publishing your first application, which will be discussed in detail in the next chapter. Getting all your applications to work perfectly will take a while, but if you got over the Certificates issue successfully, you are probably equipped to tackle any obstacle that comes in your way. Congratulations on a job well done!

4

Publishing Web Applications

In this chapter, we will learn about publishing applications using templates from the **Web Applications** category. We will discuss the process of adding an application using the **Add Application Wizard** and understand the significance of the various template properties. Later, we will discuss some of the special considerations for publishing **Exchange** and **SharePoint Servers**.

The four steps to application publishing

In the previous chapter you learned how to create a portal trunk. Now, publishing a new application on it is just a four step process:

1. From the list of trunks on the left, select the portal trunk on which you want to publish the new application. On the right-hand side pane under the **Applications** section, click **Add...** to launch the **Add Application Wizard**. Click on **Next** and on the next screen, select the specific application template that is appropriate for the application you intend to publish.

2. Follow the wizard and fill in the required details.

3. If required, make changes to the **Application Properties**.

4. Activate the configuration and you are done!

Selecting the right application type is usually pretty much straightforward, and you are already very familiar with the activation process by now. However, didn't we just skip a lot of stuff in our Steps 2 and 3? You bet! These are the steps which require some detailed discussion and which will be dealt with throughout the rest of this chapter. Before that, though, there are some additional things that are more general in nature.

Once an application is added to the trunk, you can right-click on it to disable/enable it, edit it, remove it, and duplicate it, as shown in the following screenshot:

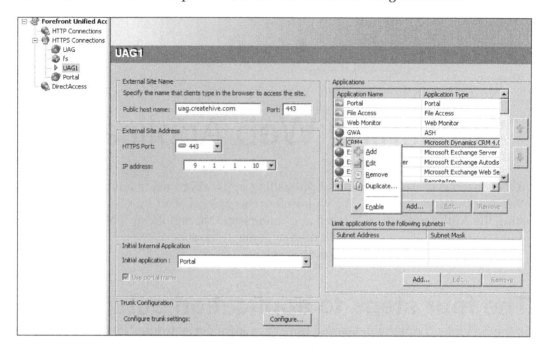

Another important option is the ability to move an application up or down in the list using the up/down arrow on the right-hand side of the list. Why does it matter? It does, of course, and we will discuss it shortly. By clicking on **Edit**, you get the **Application Properties** dialog box. Here you can review or edit the various application settings, some of which were defined while adding the application using the *Add Application Wizard*. As always, any changes to the applications, including removing, disabling, enabling, and editing require you to go through activation once again.

Application specific hostname applications versus Portal hostname applications

In the UAG world, the terms **Application specific hostname applications** (also known as **AAM-like applications**) and **Portal hostname applications** (also known as **Non-AAM** applications) are often used to describe two different categories of Web application templates. Originally, **AAM (Alternate Access Mapping)** was a very powerful feature of SharePoint which we will cover in a later section of this chapter. In the UAG world, this categorization is based on what public host name(s) can be used by users to access a UAG web application. If an application can be configured using its own specific public host name, which usually differs from the trunk's public host name, then this is referred to as an Application specific hostname application (or AAM application). On the other hand, if an application can't be configured with its own public host name and the only way to access it is by using the portal trunk's public host name, this is referred to as a Portal Hostname Application (or non-AAM application).

Let's consider an example of a company that is publishing a trunk with a public host name of `portal.createhive.com`.

This trunk publishes a group of web applications such as Finance, HR, Sales, and so on.

Users from the HR department only need to access their HR application and don't want to go through the hassle of looking for their application on the portal homepage to launch it.

If the HR application is published using the Application specific hostname template, then they can just directly use that application's specific public URL (for example, `hr.createhive.com`) and after a successful login they will be directly taken to the HR application, thus bypassing the portal home page or the trunk's Initial Internal Application.

However, for this to work, the application's public host name must be publicly resolvable to the same IP to which the trunk's public host name resolves. If the application is configured on an HTTPS trunk, then the SSL certificate used on the trunk should also include the application's public host name, otherwise browser clients will display a warning message and non-browser clients may even fail to work.

For the certificate requirements, either a **SAN (Subject Alternative Name)** certificate or a **wildcard certificate** can be used. Applications published using the portal hostname template use the portal trunk's host name and therefore rely upon the **HAT** mechanism (or **Host Address Translation**) which was discussed in *Chapter 3*. Since an Application specific hostname application doesn't rely on HAT, in some cases it is preferable, as some web content or applications do not handle the HAT process gracefully. For publishing a generic web application, we can either choose **Other Web Application (application specific hostname)**, or **Other Web Application (portal hostname)**. For those of you familiar with UAG's predecessors, **IAG** and **e-Gap**, the **Other Web Application (portal hostname)** template is similar to the *Generic Web App* template that was used in IAG and e-Gap.

In addition, with these older products, it was possible to publish applications that are accessible directly by using a "**Basic**" trunk. Basic trunks have been deprecated in UAG, but the *Other Web Application (application specific hostname)* template fulfils a similar function. If you are familiar with ISA or TMG Web Publishing rules, then you can also think of this template as using the Link Translation functionality of ISA/TMG instead of HAT. Examples of some of the other UAG application templates that use the same "application specific hostname" logic are **Microsoft Office Communicator Web Access 2007, Microsoft Forefront Identity Manager 2010, Microsoft Exchange Server, Microsoft SharePoint Server 2010,** and **Microsoft Office SharePoint Server 2007**. Portal hostname templates include all of the Built-in services applications, as well as **Microsoft Dynamics CRM 4.0, Microsoft Office SharePoint Portal Server 2003.** In addition, the web-services part of the **Exchange Server 2003** template is also an application-specific hostname.

The Add Application Wizard

While working through this section and looking at the screenshots, don't be alarmed if the step numbers differ from what you actually see on your own UAG server. The numbers may change based on the selections you make on each page, and that's perfectly normal. The focus should be on the title of the step or page (for example, step 1 is **Select Application**) and understanding the information that needs to be entered in that step, as well as some extra or different information that might be required sometimes.

On the **Select Application** page, select the appropriate application template which you would like to publish and then click **Next**. The **Select Exchange Services** page will only appear if the **Microsoft Exchange Server (all versions)** template was selected on the **Select Application** page.

Select the Exchange version and the services which should be published and click on **Next** to continue.

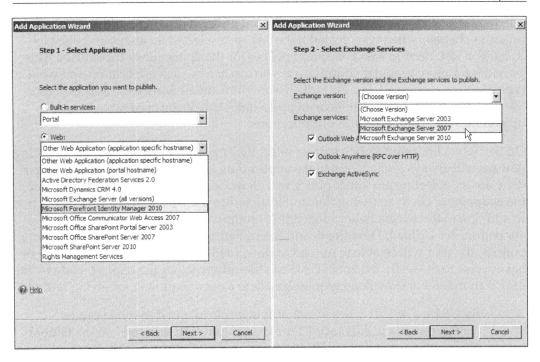

On the **Configure Application** page, specify the **Application name** and the
Application type. This is the name which will appear on the trunk's application list
on UAG Server, and by default, this is also the name that the user will see when
accessing the portal. The Application type is fixed for most application types, but for
the **Other Web Application** templates, you are required to type it. When choosing
the type for **Other Web Applications**, it is important to know that UAG applies the
URL Set (which is also known as the **rule set** or **security rules** that UAG applies
to incoming requests) based on the type, so think about it carefully. If you publish
multiple applications with the same type, the URL Set will apply to all applications,
which might be less secure than you would like. On the other hand, if you do want
several applications to use an identical URL set, make sure you do use the same type
for all of them, to save yourself the trouble of creating many rules. Also, keep in
mind that the type *cannot* be changed after the Add Application wizard completed.

The next step allows you to select the **endpoint policies**. If you recall from the previous chapter, when you created the trunk, you selected an endpoint policy for it, but you also need to select endpoint polices for the applications themselves. This provides for more granular control over who can access each application and what type of access is allowed. For example, we might want all users to be able to access the portal, but only users that have an up-to-date Anti-Virus product to be able to upload files using more sensitive applications.

On the **Select Endpoint Policies** page, select the appropriate **Access policy**. Selecting **Always** will always grant access to the application, and selecting **Never** will always deny access. Selecting any other policy will allow or deny access based on whether the endpoint or client accessing this application meets the policy requirements or not. In addition to the Access Policy, depending on the category of the application, there are policies for **Upload**, **Download**, and **Restricted zone**. If an endpoint meets these policies, the user will be able to upload or download files to the published server, or have access to the restricted zone. UAG can identify whether the request made by the user is an upload or download request based on a combination of following settings:

1. **By URLs**: The URL rules for identifying upload and download can be configured on the **Advanced Trunk Configuration window**, on the **Global URL Settings** tab, in the **URL Settings** section. For some of the applications such as **Exchange**, **SharePoint**, **FIM (Forefront Identity Manager)**, **CRM**, **Web Monitor,** and **File Access**, these URL rules are automatically configured when the applications are added to the trunk. For other applications, you can configure these URL patterns or rules manually. We will discuss this in *Chapter 10* in more detail.

2. **By the file extension**, as it appears in the requested URL.

3. **By the amount of data transferred**. HTTP **GET** requests are treated as downloads whereas **POST** and **PUT** requests are treated as uploads.

4. By default, UAG is not set to identify uploads or downloads by the file extension, but it does identify POST and PUT for files larger than 1024 bytes as upload. These two settings can be configured per application on the **Download/Upload** tab of the Application Properties.

More details about endpoint policies will be covered in *Chapter 8,* but don't worry—endpoint policy settings selected during this wizard page can be viewed or changed at any time from the Endpoint Policies Settings tab of the Application Properties dialog.

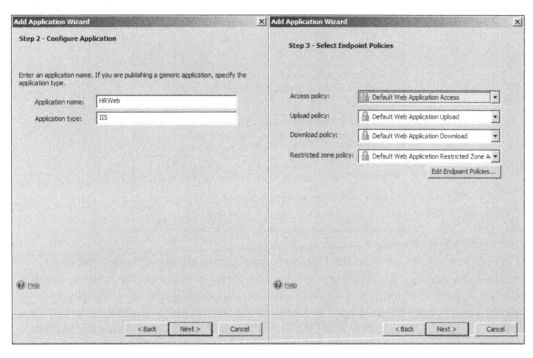

Sometimes organizations deploy their internal applications using a **farm** of web servers with **mirrored** websites to make the applications highly available and/or to distribute load amongst the farm members. Depending upon the scenario, the traffic hitting this sort of farm can be load balanced amongst farm members using either Windows **NLB** or using a third party load balancer. **Web Farm Load Balancing (WFLB)** is a feature in UAG which allows you to load balance the client traffic reaching a single UAG server among several backend farm members, using a **round-robin** mechanism, thus avoiding the need for a third party load balancer or for using NLB on the web farm itself. On the **Deploying an Application** page, select whether WFLB will be used or not. For load balancing a farm of web servers using WFLB, select the option **Configure a farm of application servers**.

Keep in mind, though, that if you are publishing a single web server or a web farm whose members are already load balanced using a third party load balancer or NLB, you should choose the option **Configure an application server**.

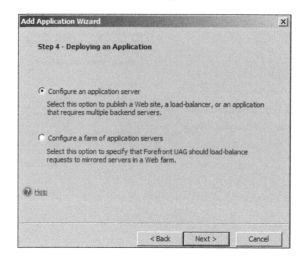

If WFLB was not selected on the **Deploying an Application** page, the next page will be **Web Servers**. The Web Servers page is where you define the internal servers that are hosting the published application. You can specify one or more servers, and you can specify them using their **host name** (also known as **short name**), their **Fully-Qualified Domain Name (FQDN)** or their IP address. It is recommended to define a name wherever possible, rather than an IP address as IP addresses may not work in some of the scenarios (such as Exchange Outlook Anywhere publishing). If UAG is unable to resolve the name of one or more of the servers, it will display a warning **The address is not valid** when you click on **Next**. In case that happens, use standard network troubleshooting techniques to find the cause and fix it. Make sure UAG can resolve the name using either **DNS** or a **Hosts file** entry. The name you enter here should be the same name that your users use to access the website internally (when not accessing through UAG). It is always a good idea to test the website and connectivity from the UAG server itself (as a client), which provides a good indication if the application will work when accessed by other clients through the UAG server. For most browser based applications this testing can be easily done by using **Internet Explorer** on the UAG server. However, for non-browser based applications, perform a test from an internal client wherever possible.

A helpful feature is the ability to define the web servers as a **subnet** or using a **Regular Expression (RegEx)**. This is particularly useful if the application uses a large group of servers that share a similar name, so instead of typing *server1*, *server2*, *server3*, and so on, you could just type "*server.*", in which the dot means "any character" (refer to Appendix B for an introduction to Regular Expressions). Keep in mind, though, that some of the application templates, like Exchange and SharePoint, do not support these address types and therefore the options are grayed out for them. On the Web Servers page you also define whether the internal web server is listening on **HTTP** or **HTTPS**. If it is HTTPS then make sure that the **SSL certificate** used by the backend server is valid and is trusted by UAG. UAG pre-populates the Paths field with default paths for most of the applications like Exchange, **FIM (Forefront Identity Manager)** and **CWA (Communicator Web Access)** based on preset settings in these templates. Thus for these applications, only the required paths are allowed and not everything. For other templates, like **SharePoint** and **Other Web Application**, the default allowed path is "/" (slash), which means that the root folder and everything below it will be accessible. For tighter security, you can modify the allowed path "/" (slash) for the **Other Web Application** templates, but you have to find a way to be sure that you have really included ALL the paths that the application actually needs. This requires a good understanding of how the application works and should be considered an advanced task.

The two following screenshots show the AAM-like template (hence the **Public host name** textbox) on the left and the non-AAM template (notice the **Public host name** textbox does not exist here) on the right.

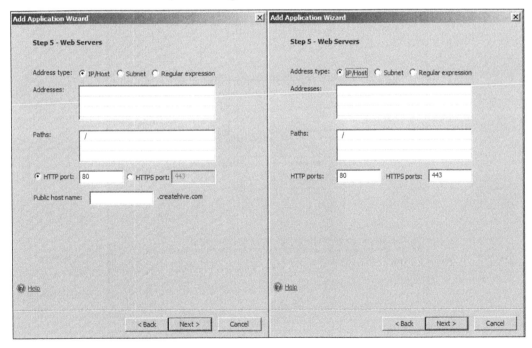

If an AAM application's public host name is the same as its trunk public hostname, then the application path cannot contain a forward slash "/", as a path of "/" used in combination with the trunk's public host name represents to UAG a request to the portal home page. If the application being created is an AAM-like application, then you should define a specific Public hostname for it. Note that the DNS suffix for this hostname must be the *same* as the DNS suffix of the trunk's public hostname. This is required since all applications defined on the same trunk need to share the same UAG **session cookie** (cookies are an important part of how UAG keeps track of user activity, and will be discussed in detail in *Chapter 10*), therefore UAG will generate and send the browser a **domain cookie**, which will then be sent back by the browser with each and every request to any one of these applications.

If you are publishing a SharePoint 2007 or a SharePoint 2010 web application, then your Web Servers page will look like the following screenshot.

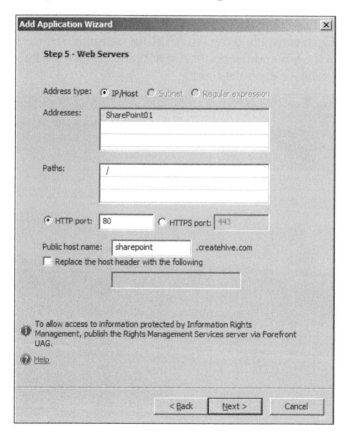

When publishing SharePoint Servers, we also need to configure specific AAM settings on the SharePoint Server with the Public hostname defined here and with the value defined under **Replace the host header with the following** option. The replace host header option is only used in some scenarios. This is not trivial and confuses many users. We will discuss the nuances of publishing SharePoint Servers later on.

If WFLB was selected on the **Deploying an Application** page earlier, the next two pages will have specific settings related to configuring web servers with WFLB. The first page will be **Load-Balanced Web Servers** and the next one will be **Configure Connectivity Verifiers**.

WFLB provides a choice of two **affinity** methods. Affinity determines which backend server a client will reach, attempting to have a specific client connect to the same backend server whenever it reconnects to the farm within a certain amount of time. To control this, WFLB identifies to which server the client had connected recently using either **Cookie-based** affinity (a.k.a. **Session affinity**) or **IP-based affinity**. When using Cookie-based affinity, the UAG server inserts a cookie in the response to the client requests. The cookie is sent back to UAG by the client's browser in subsequent requests and indicates to the UAG server which server in the farm to connect to. On the other hand, IP-based affinity uses the source IP address of the request to determine which server in the farm will handle the request. If many or most of your users are connecting from behind a **NAT** device, then IP-based affinity may not be able to correctly identify them, because UAG will see traffic from different clients as originating from the same source IP (the external IP of the NAT device). Cookie-based affinity comes in handy for such scenarios, and is also the default option for all the application templates except for the Exchange server template (when used with the Outlook Anywhere service). The Outlook client doesn't support the use of cookies and therefore cannot use Cookie-based affinity.

If required, enable the **Use the farm name in the HTTP host header** option and define the **Farm host name**. This may be required by the internal application itself. Other settings are the same as the settings on the regular (non-WFLB) Web Servers page which we discussed earlier. Here too, we would recommend testing the backend website using **IE** on the UAG server. We recommend testing all the individual farm member names, one by one, or if a farm host name is configured, test using that name.

The following screenshots show the **Load Balanced Web Servers** page for an AAM-like application on the left, and a non-AAM application on the right:

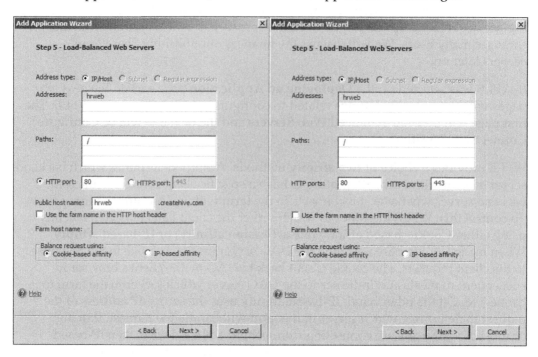

With a WFLB enabled application, the next wizard page will be **Configure Connectivity Verifiers**. WFLB uses connectivity verifiers to detect the state of each web farm member. Connectivity verifiers poll each of the servers defined in a web farm at regular intervals using one of three **Verification Methods**: HTTP GET, a **Ping** request, or simply by establishing a TCP connection. This **polling** is performed in order to determine whether all the servers are available or not. As soon as a connectivity verifier determines that a server in the web farm is unavailable, it stops forwarding user requests to that specific server in the farm, taking it out of the **load balancing pool rotation**. Since the polling is always on for all the farm members, once the server becomes available again, the connectivity verifier discovers that and starts forwarding user requests to that server, bringing it back into the load balancing pool rotation.

If you have chosen the HTTP GET method, note that, by default, this method accesses the **root folder** of the servers, but depending on the application, you may need to modify the Request path in order to be able to poll the appropriate application resource. There are certain threshold values, which determine when a server is considered to have failed or "back in business". These are:

1. **Timeout response threshold** is the time for which the connectivity verifier waits for a response from a web farm member. It is set in milliseconds and defaults to **5000** (which equals to 5 seconds).

2. **Successful response threshold** is the number of consecutive successful responses before a server is considered available again and brought back into rotation.

3. **Failed response threshold** is the number of consecutive failed responses before a server is considered unavailable and taken out of the rotation.

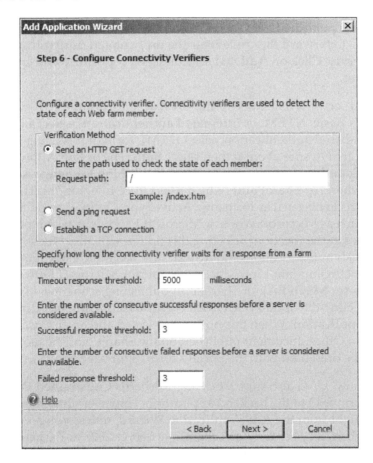

The status of farm members can also be monitored and controlled using the **Farm Monitor**, which is part of the **Web Monitor**. This tool will be discussed in *Chapter 9*.

Keep in mind that an incorrect Web Server address or Public hostname (for AAM applications) or **Replace host header** (for SharePoint applications) are the most common causes of publishing problems, so have another look and make sure these are correctly defined. However, don't worry too much, as these settings can also be viewed or modified later using the **Application Properties | Web Server** tab. If WFLB is enabled, then its settings defined on the **Load Balanced Web Servers** page and the **Configure Connectivity Verifiers** pages are also present on the same **Web Servers** tab.

The **Authentication** page defines how UAG performs **SSO (Single Sign On)** for the application to the published web server. Select the option **Use SSO** to enable it. This will allow UAG to forward the credentials the user entered during trunk login to the internal web server. Click on **Add** and select the **AD repository** you created in the previous chapter.

If the published server is using one of the **401 Authentication** HTTP-based schemes (which includes **Basic, NTLM,** or **Integrated authentication**), select **401 request**. If it is using form-based authentication, select **HTML form**. If it is using both 401 and form, or if you are not sure about it then select **Both**. The option **Allow rich clients to bypass trunk authentication** appears when publishing **Exchange ActiveSync, Outlook Anywhere**, or **SharePoint** (which uses Office Integration). These services use rich clients such as Exchange ActiveSync, Outlook, and Office Client Applications such as Microsoft Word or Microsoft Excel, which cannot authenticate using the trunk's authentication. Selecting this option will allow these rich clients to bypass the trunk's authentication, and instead, use Basic authentication or NTLM authentication. UAG update 1 introduced support for **Microsoft Office Forms Based Authentication** (or **MSOFBA**) for SharePoint publishing scenarios. MSOFBA can be enabled by selecting the option **Use Office Forms Based Authentication for Office Client Based application**. When this option is selected and an end user attempts to directly open an Office document published on the SharePoint site (accessible using UAG), he will be presented with the portal's form login page to authenticate.

As you may know, UAG also supports using **Kerberos Constrained Delegation (KCD)** to perform SSO to the backend application. However, this cannot be configured straight from the **Add Application Wizard**, unless you are configuring Outlook Anywhere services for either Exchange Server 2007 or Exchange Server 2010. If you are using a **smartcard** or **client certificate based authentication** on the trunk, or any other scenario which requires authentication protocol transition to KCD, you must first complete the wizard and then use the **Authentication** tab of the Application Properties dialog in order to configure KCD. We will discuss Authentication and KCD in more detail in *Chapter 6*.

In addition to KCD, the authentication settings defined on this page can be viewed or modified on the **Authentication** tab of the **Application Properties** dialog.

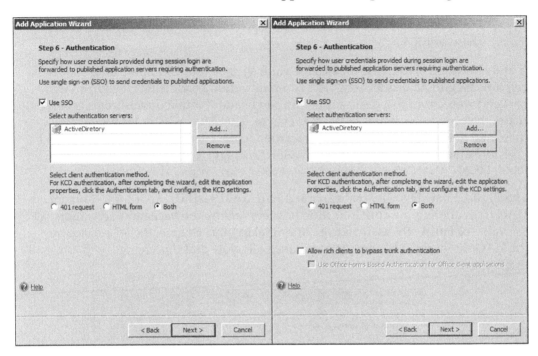

If you are publishing either Exchange Server 2007 or Exchange 2010 using the Exchange template and the Outlook Anywhere service, then the next wizard step will be **Outlook Anywhere**. This step requires you to configure the authentication settings for the Outlook Anywhere and **Autodiscover** services using one of the following options:

- No Authentication: If you don't want UAG to reply to the Exchange Server authentication requests then select this option.

- Use Basic Authentication: This option configures UAG to use Basic authentication to authenticate Outlook clients, as well as to use Basic authentication to reply to the backend Exchange CAS (**Client Access Server**) server's request for credentials. The credentials received by UAG from the Outlook clients are verified using the repository that you have selected on the Authentication page earlier. It is important to remember that in order for this SSO process to work, both the Outlook client and the backend Exchange CAS need to be configured accordingly to use Basic Authentication.

- Using Kerberos constrained delegation: When using this option, Outlook clients authenticate to the UAG server using NTLM and then UAG delegates the credentials to the backend server using KCD. Here too, it is important to ensure that Outlook clients and the Exchange CAS are configured to match these settings.

If authentication is disabled on a UAG trunk application, you may notice that UAG converts **Negotiate headers** or NTLM authentication headers received from the backend web server to a basic authentication header (with a dynamically generated **realm**) before forwarding it to the UAG client. This is normal, but if you want these authentication headers to be forwarded to the client unaltered, you can add a registry value which controls this behavior. Navigate to the following registry key:
`HKEY_LOCAL_MACHINE\SOFTWARE\WhaleCom\e-Gap\von\UrlFilter`

There, add a new DWORD value named **FullAuthPassthru**. In order to prevent UAG from altering the authentication headers sent by the backend application, set the value of **FullAuthPassthru** to **1**. After making this change, the IIS service on the UAG server must be restarted and once set. Note that this change will affect all existing trunks.

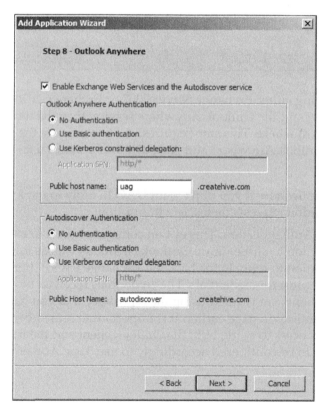

You've now reached the **Portal Link** page of the **Add Application Wizard**. The most important part here is the *Application URL*. The path in this URL is built based on details set during the wizard. Typically, this URL would be identical to the URL your users use to access this application internally. If an application has its own public hostname, then the Application URL should be based on it, instead of on the internal web server address or name. Also make sure the URL includes the correct protocol (HTTP or HTTPS) and port number, if a non-standard port is being used by the backend server.

You can optionally define a folder or a subfolder, which can be useful in organizing applications on the portal home page and on the portal's toolbar. There's no need to "create" a folder—just type a name to your liking, and UAG will know what to do. If you want to have just one level of folders, type the folder name without any slashes. If you would like a deeper folder hierarchy, you can use forward slashes "/" to define it. For example, if you specify **Europe/Engineering**, UAG will place the application inside a folder named `Engineering`, which will reside inside a folder named `Europe`.

Another useful feature is the **Open in a new window** option. If it is disabled, the application is launched in the portal's "main" frame, and this will work well for most applications. Some applications, though, may have issues when running within a frame because of the way they are written. A good example is Exchange 2010 OWA. Its application template has the **Open in a new window** option enabled by default and OWA for Exchange 2010 doesn't work correctly when you disable this option. However, this particular behavior of Exchange 2010 may change with a future update or service pack for Exchange. If your application is exhibiting issues that you suspect could be related to this, you can check the option to open it in a new window.

Sometimes, you might prefer that users do not see the application on the portal home page. This might be useful, for example, if there is an application which is added to the trunk just as a **helper** application. Helper applications are used to let UAG know of the existence of some internal server that is referred to by other applications. If you want this application to be invisible to users, uncheck the option **Add a portal and toolbar link**.

This is a good opportunity to remind you that if you are wondering about the apparent disorder in step numbers ignore them as our focus was on discussing all the possible screens. The step numbers that are shown for the same type of application change dynamically, based on what is selected on the previous page.

The next page is the **Authorization** page. By default, all users are authorized to access the application, but this setting can be changed if your organization's security policy requires it. Uncheck A**uthorize all users** and click **Add** to add users or groups from different authentication repositories and set their authorization permissions (**Allow**, **View,** or **Deny**). We will discuss these options further in *Chapter 6*.

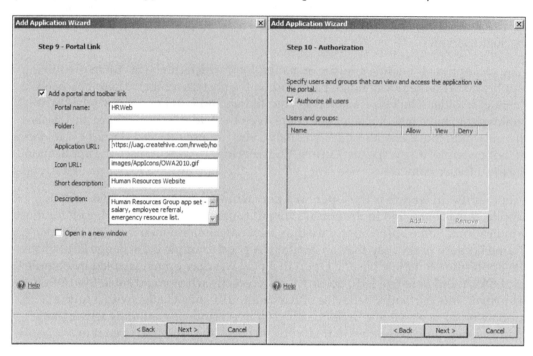

This last screen is just for informational purposes and there are no settings to be configured here. Once you click on **Finish**, your application will be added to the list of applications on this trunk. However, it won't be available to users until you go through the regular activation process.

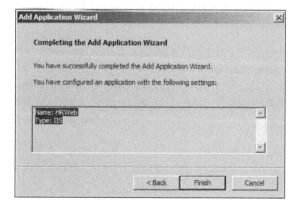

Application order

Remember how the arrow buttons on the main trunk configuration used to move the applications up and down on the list? Normally we don't need to move the applications. One situation where this may be needed is when there is an application conflict because of two applications that use the same internal web server.

When UAG receives a request from a client, UAG tries to match it against the list of applications, from top to bottom. If a match is found (based on the web server name, path, and port number defined in application properties), it is processed (based on that particular application's properties and its related advanced trunk configuration), and UAG does not continue down the list, even if there are additional applications that are configured with the same web server, path, and port number.

To understand the importance of this, consider an example in which you are trying to publish SharePoint and Exchange OWA, which are hosted on the same internal server. Although it's not a very common configuration in the real world, it is ideal to illustrate the problem we are about to discuss. The SharePoint and Exchange OWA applications are configured on the UAG trunk so that SharePoint is listed *above* OWA. When a user tries to access OWA via UAG, their request may fail in some situations. That's because by default, the SharePoint application allows access to the root path and everything below it (the application path is defined as "/"). With the SharePoint application listed above the OWA application, all the requests are matched with it and no request for OWA will ever hit the OWA Application. Failure may occur in some situation where the trunk URL Set (usually referred to as **URL rule set** and discussed in detail in *Chapter 10*) for SharePoint does not allow some specific OWA requests.

To address this type of a problem, you can change the order of the applications on the list, but this is not always simple. To make an informed decision (as opposed to guesswork that could result in applications being blocked or applications being less secure than they should be), consider the *paths* and *URL rule set* of your applications, and make sure there is no conflict in any scenario.

For our example, the fix is to move the SharePoint application below the Exchange OWA application. Now, requests for the OWA application will match the OWA application because it allows specific paths like /OWA or /Exchange. Since these paths are not used by SharePoint, when the user accesses the SharePoint application, the root path or path for a particular site collection will match the SharePoint Application, and both will *live together happily*. Keep in mind that Exchange and SharePoint are just examples and there is no cheat-sheet for deciding which application types should be listed above others. In case you have to troubleshoot a similar issue and you are not able to figure out the correct order because of a long list of applications, the **UAG Web Monitor** comes in handy.

The UAG events will show which request matches which Application Type and in most cases, it will also indicate if there is a failure because of the URL rule set not allowing a specific request. These events are viewable using either the Web Monitor or **Windows Event Viewer** (in the *Application Log* with a source of *Microsoft Forefront UAG*). Monitoring the UAG server will be discussed in more detail in *Chapter 9*.

Considerations for Exchange publishing

Like its predecessors, UAG can publish Exchange Server 2003 and 2007, but is also capable of publishing the new Exchange 2010. Publishing Exchange through UAG supports the following services:

- **Outlook Web Access (OWA)**, also referred to as **Outlook Web App** in Exchange 2010 lets users read their corporate email using a browser-based interface that mimics the thick Outlook client to a high degree

- **Outlook Anywhere** (also known as **RPC-over-HTTP**) allows the thick Outlook client access to a back-end Exchange server over HTTP or HTTPS

- **Exchange ActiveSync**, which allows mobile devices to push synchronize with an Exchange server for real-time email, contacts, calendars, and tasks

Exchange Server publishing can be configured at any point, but also directly during the process of creating a trunk. This is done by selecting the **Publish Exchange application** using the portal option on the **Select Trunk Type** page of the **Create Trunk Wizard**. After you select this option and define the trunk properties on the remainder of the wizard pages, the **Add Application Wizard** starts automatically and you are taken directly to the **Select Exchange Services** page. The rest of the steps are the same as described above in the *The Add Application Wizard* section.

Once the wizard completes, there are a few changes that should be noted. The **Initial application** on the trunk is automatically set to the **Exchange application**. Additionally, the wizard automatically enables the **Apply an Outlook Web Access look and feel** option on the **Advanced Trunk Configuration**, **Authentication** tab. This sets the trunk's login and log-off pages to a graphic theme that mimics that of default OWA pages and gives the user the same experience as if they are accessing OWA directly. You can disable these changes manually, or, if you wish to publish Exchange later, add them manually. We will also discuss these *Advanced Trunk Configuration* settings in *Chapter 10*.

When adding the Exchange Server 2007 or 2010 application, you might also need to add the **Outlook Anywhere** service. In that case, there are two more applications added to the trunk in addition to the regular Exchange application: **Microsoft Exchange Autodiscover** and **Microsoft Exchange Web Services**. The Autodiscover service configures and maintains server settings for the Outlook clients and certain mobile devices. When Autodiscover is set up, users are not required to manually enter server details during the initial Outlook setup but just enter their *email address* and *password* in Outlook and all the rest gets configured automatically. For more information about this Exchange feature refer to the Exchange 2007 Autodiscover Service white paper: `http://technet.microsoft.com/en-us/library/bb332063(EXCHG.80).aspx`.

Exchange Web Services (EWS) is a collection of Web services enabling client applications to communicate with the Exchange server via an **XML** messaging interface. For more information, visit the following URL which provides an introduction to Exchange Web Services: `http://msdn.microsoft.com/library/aa579187.aspx`.

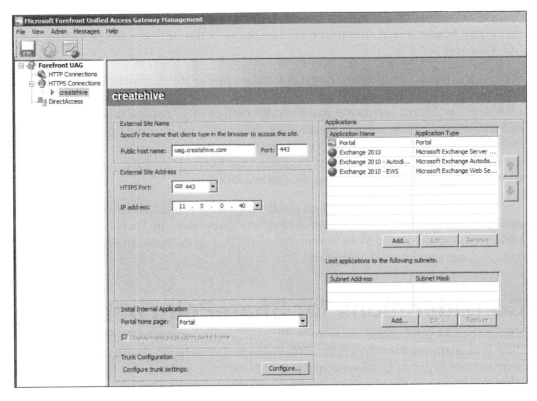

Both Autodiscover and EWS are available only with Exchange version 2007 and onwards, so don't be surprised if these two applications are not added to the trunk when publishing Exchange Server 2003.

It is also important to note that although the Autodiscover and EWS applications are added automatically to the trunk when publishing Exchange 2007 or 2010, there is no linking between these two *helper* applications and the primary exchange application. For example, if you add or remove a *CAS server* on the **Web Servers** tab of the primary application, the other two applications must be manually updated as well, and vice versa.

Another important difference between the application template for Exchange Server 2003 and the templates used for Exchange Server 2007 and 2010 is that while the first is using the portal host name, the latter templates are "**application specific hostname**". By default, the public host name used for the primary and the EWS applications is same as the trunks public host name. However, the public host name of the Autodiscover application is `autodiscover.createhive.com`, where `createhive.com` is derived from the **DNS suffix** set for the trunk. This is because `autodiscover.createhive.com` is one of the few names that the Outlook client searches for when attempting to auto-discover the CAS server hosting the Autodiscover service.

Because the trunk's public host name is not the same as the Autodiscover application's public host name, the SSL certificate used for the trunk must be either a **SAN** or a **wildcard certificate** that includes both of these names. If you plan to add more "application specific hostname" applications to the same trunk later, it is recommended to use a wildcard certificate. As was discussed earlier, these public names should also be resolvable by clients on the Internet, so make sure they are added to the *public DNS server* used by the organization.

Another thing to keep in mind when publishing Exchange is that when you configure the Outlook Anywhere or ActiveSync templates, the Exchange CAS server addresses defined on the **Web Servers** tab must be FQDN (fully qualified domain names) names and not IP addresses.

Considerations for SharePoint publishing

UAG supports publishing of the three different versions of SharePoint Server—2003, 2007, and 2010. We introduced the term AAM earlier to highlight the difference between two types of UAG web application templates, and now it's time to see what this means in the SharePoint world and how we configure this on the SharePoint server.

Similar to UAG, SharePoint also uses the term **Web application** and each of these SharePoint Web Applications has a set of **AAM rules** or **mappings**. These AAM rules are configured using the **SharePoint Central Administration tool**, and must be configured correctly in order for Share Point publishing to work through UAG. When a user accesses a SharePoint Web Application via a UAG server, AAM maps the requests to the correct Web Application and site on the SharePoint server. These mappings allow the SharePoint server to provide content that has been properly "prepared" for external access. The preparation process makes changes to URLs in the delivered pages so that UAG doesn't have to perform any URL *rewriting* (which is otherwise done by the HAT process). An exception to this is SharePoint 2003, which does not have the AAM feature and therefore the relevant UAG template is a non-AAM template.

For the SharePoint 2007 and 2010 application templates, it is *imperative* to make sure the public host name is defined correctly. The public host name of the application cannot be the same as the trunk's public host name because SharePoint applications require a slash ("/") to be included in the application's path definitions. As with all other application-specific hostname templates, the application's public host name must use the same DNS suffix as the trunk's hostname suffix.

The task of properly configuring AAM on the SharePoint server can be confusing at first. We will provide an overview of it here, but you might want to perform this with the person who is in charge of the SharePoint server in your organization, or do some more reading on the topic.

On SharePoint 2010 servers, the AAM settings can be configured using the **SharePoint 2010 Central Administration** tool. To do so, open the tool and go to **System Settings**, and click on **Configure alternate access mappings**. For SharePoint 2007, this is done using the **SharePoint 3.0 Central Administration** tool. To configure this, open the tool and click on the **Operations tab**, and then under **Global Configuration**, click **Alternate access mappings**. Whichever SharePoint server version you are working with, make sure that only AAM settings related to the required web applications are modified. To stay on the safe side, we recommend changing your view to show only the AAM settings for your *specific* SharePoint Web Application, so as to reduce the risk of making changes to other applications by mistake.

To do this, click on the **Alternate Access Mapping Collection** list, **Change Alternate Access Mapping Collection**, and then, on the **Select an Alternate Access Mapping Collection** dialog box, select the application that you want to edit the AAM settings for.

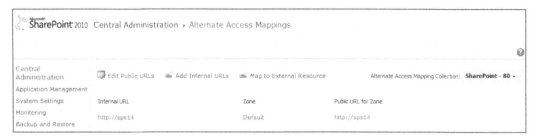

The AAM settings that we configure on the SharePoint server should be in accordance with the settings configured on the UAG server's **Add Application Wizard**, **Web Server** page (or **Load Balanced Web Servers** page). If the SharePoint application is already added, then the same settings can be modified from the **Application Properties** dialog box, **Web Servers** tab. The settings that we are particularly interested in here are: **web server's Address**, **HTTP** or **HTTPS Port**, **host header** (under **Replace the host header with the following**) and **Public host name**.

When publishing a SharePoint server, there are several scenarios, each requiring somewhat different settings. Let's see these settings for the three most common ones:

Different internal and external names

In this scenario, the SharePoint server is hosting a single web application with an internal URL such as `http://sharepoint` and an external FQDN URL such as `https://sharepoint.createhiveextranet.com`.

We are publishing the SharePoint server on an *HTTPS* trunk, and so the external URL starts with HTTPS. For this scenario, the **Web Servers** tab of the UAG SharePoint application should have following settings:

- Addresses: The internal server name. For example: SPS2010
- Public **host name**: The external URL FQDN. For example: `sharepoint.createhive.com`
- Replace **the host header with the following**: This option is not required for this scenario
- HTTP **Port** option should be selected and its value should be set according to the port used by SharePoint internally, 80 in our example

Then, the AAM settings for this scenario would be set by following these steps:

1. On the SharePoint servers **Alternate Access Mappings** page, click **Edit Public URLs**.

2. Pick a zone which is not in use already (**Extranet**, **Internet**, or **Custom**), enter the Public URL **https://sharepoint.createhive.com** and click on **Save**.

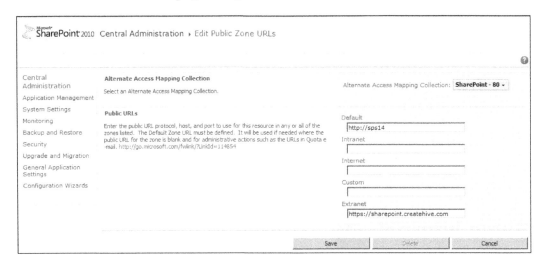

3. Click on **Add Internal URL**. In the **URL protocol, host and port** box, enter the same FQDN specified in the previous UAG configuration (**sharepoint. createhiveextranet.com**), but type **http://** at the beginning and the port number at the end of this FQDN. For this scenario, it should be **http:// sharepoint.createhiveextranet.com:80**. Select the same zone for which you specified the Public URL in the previous step. Click on **Save**.

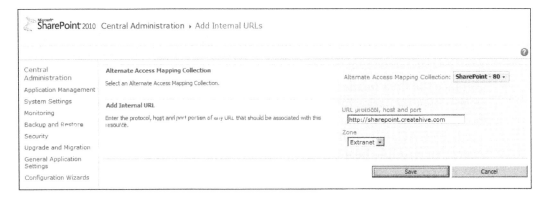

> **Note**: This step is only required when the external URL is HTTPS and the internal URL is HTTP.

If the same SharePoint server is hosting other web applications using different ports, then the same steps can be used to publish them, as well as using the same or a different UAG trunk.

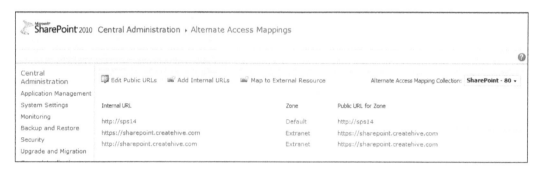

Same internal and external FQDN names but different protocols

In this scenario, the SharePoint server is hosting a single web application with an internal URL such as `http://sharepoint.createhive.com` and an external URL such as `https://sharepoint.createhive.com`.

We are publishing the SharePoint server on an *HTTPS trunk*, and so the external URL starts with *HTTPS*. For this scenario, the **Web Servers** tab of the UAG SharePoint application should have following settings:

- Addresses: The internal server name. For example: SPS2010

- Public host name: The FQDN of the external URL. In our example: `sharepoint.createhive.com`.

- **Replace the host header with the following**: This option is not used for most of the other scenarios but for this one it is required. The host name we define here will be used by the SharePoint server to distinguish between requests made by UAG on behalf of external users versus requests made by internal users. An example host header that can be used here is *sharepointuag*

- The HTTP Port: This option should be selected and its value should be set according to the port used by SharePoint internally, **80** in our example.

Then, the AAM settings for this scenario would be set by following these steps:

1. On the SharePoint servers **Alternate Access Mappings** page, click **Edit Public URLs**.

2. Pick a zone which is not in use already (**Extranet, Internet**, or **Custom**), enter the Public URL `https://sharepoint.createhive.com` and click on **Save**.

3. Click on **Add Internal URLs**. In the **URL protocol, host** and **port** box, enter the same FQDN specified in the UAG configuration above. Type **http://** at the beginning and the port number at the end of this FQDN. In our example, this should be `http://sharepointuag:80`. Select the same zone for which you specified the Public URL in the previous step. Click on **Save**.

Same internal and external names and protocols

In this scenario, the SharePoint server is hosting a single web application with the *same* internal and external URL and the same protocol. For example: `https://sharepoint.createhive.com`.

We are publishing the SharePoint server on an *HTTPS* Trunk, and so the external URL starts with *HTTPS*. For this scenario, the **Web Servers** tab of the UAG SharePoint application should have following settings:

- Addresses: the internal server name. For example: SPS2010.

- **Public host name**: The FQDN of the external URL, which is *sharepoint. createhive.com*

- Replace the host header with the following: This option is *not* required for this scenario.

- With **HTTPS Port** selected, set the port number used by SharePoint internally, 443 in this case.

Since the internal and external URL are the same, no additional configuration is required on the SharePoint server. There is no need for any URL translation, so *AAM is not used*.

Sharepoint and IE security enhancements

Windows Vista and **IE 7** introduced two new security enhancements, **Integrity Levels (IL)** and **Protected Mode**. These security enhancements affect the way we access certain SharePoint features when published through UAG. Let's take a couple of minutes to understand the what and the how of it. In Vista and Windows 7, by default, Internet Explorer runs in Protected Mode and thus has a *Low IL* (Integrity Level), whereas Office has a *Medium IL*. For more details about the IE protected mode and these Integrity Levels refer to the article on `http://msdn.microsoft.com/en-us/library/bb250462.aspx`.

When publishing SharePoint, UAG sets a **persistent cookie** for *Office Integration* and *Explorer View* to work. The cookie is set by an **ASP** page (`SharePointRedirector.asp`). When IE runs in Protected Mode, the cookie is written in the LOW storage and therefore Office, which runs at MEDIUM IL, cannot read this cookie. There are two possible solutions to this problem:

- Make sure the *Endpoint Session Cleanup* component is running. Other than deleting leftovers, this component can also pass the persistent cookie from LOW to MEDIUM storage.
- Alternatively, add the UAG trunk's public host name and SharePoint application's public host name to an IE security zone that disables IE Protected Mode (by default that would be the *Trusted Sites* zone)

We will discuss the **Endpoint Session Cleanup component** and other client components in *Chapter 8*.

What is the Active Directory Federation Services 2.0 application?

Service Pack 1 for UAG 2010 adds a new application template to the *Web* category of applications—the **Active Directory Federation Services 2.0** template. This application template is closely related to the newly added support for AD FS 2.0, also introduced in SP1, and to the different scenarios that the AD FS 2.0 feature in UAG enables. We will discuss the new AD FS 2.0 solution in detail in *Chapter 6*, and this is where we will also cover the Active Directory Federation Services 2.0 application template.

Note: In certain circumstances, depending on the authentication repositories you configure and use for trunk authentication or application-level authentication for your trunk, an Active Directory Federation Services 2.0 application may be automatically added to the list of applications published through your portal trunk. This should not surprise you, as this is the normal behavior when your trunk or one of its published applications are configured to use an AD FS 2.0 repository. More about this in *Chapter 6*!

Certificate validation for published web servers

When the backend web server which is published via UAG requires an SSL connection, UAG validates the certificate bound to the internal website, just like any normal **SSL handshake** process.

This validation requires the certificate used by the backend server to be valid and trusted by UAG. The common name of the certificate also needs to match the name which UAG uses to connect to that server. Additionally, at least one of the **CRL Distribution Points (CDPs)** defined on that certificate and on the other certificates in the **trust chain** should be accessible by UAG. This is in order for UAG to be able to verify that the certificate is not **revoked**. If any of these conditions are not met, the SSL handshake process will fail. Depending upon which conditions are not met, make appropriate configuration changes to resolve such an issue. For example, if the certificate is not trusted by UAG, install the **issuer certificate** in the **Trusted Root CA** folder of the UAG server's computer **certificate store**. For limited testing purposes the certificate validation could be disabled, though this may pose a security risk and should not be done in a production environment. To disable the certificate validation, set the following registry values to *0*:

```
HKEY_LOCAL_MACHINE\SOFTWARE\WhaleCom\e-Gap\Von\URLFilter\Comm\SSL\
ValidateRwsCert
```

```
HKEY_LOCAL_MACHINE\SOFTWARE\WhaleCom\e-Gap\Von\URLFilter\Comm\SSL\
ValidateRwsCertCRL
```

Once set, the **IIS service** on the UAG server must be restarted for these changes to take effect. Once the original certificate validation issue has been resolved, set these registry values *back to 1*.

Did you remember to activate?

Over this chapter, we discussed creating several types of applications. You are probably aware of the importance of activating the configuration, but if not, this is a good opportunity to remind you once again.

When you make any change to UAG's configuration, including adding an application, changing it or removing it, activation is required. Once the activation completes and is reported successful by the Activation Monitor, you should be ready to test it.

From an external client machine, log into the trunk using the portal public host name and access the application. You may also test using the application's public host name if the application you published is an AAM application.

For non-browser based applications like *Outlook Anywhere* or *Exchange ActiveSync*, use their respective clients to test, of course.

Summary

In this chapter we have covered the steps required to publish web applications. We have emphasized the importance of configuring the correct web server address, public host name, port and protocol used by published applications. We have also discussed the specifics required for publishing, Exchange, SharePoint, and using the AAM feature correctly on the SharePoint server. UAG has several additional web application templates that we did not cover in detail, but which follow the same concepts and principals we discussed above. UAG also has many more application publishing options such as client/server applications, remote desktop applications, and many others, which will be covered in the next chapter. The publishing fun continues.

5
Advanced Applications and Services

While UAG can do a fantastic job with publishing the classic applications discussed in the previous chapter, its real power is revealed with the way it publishes advanced applications. In this chapter, we will review the various applications, how to choose to appropriate templates, and how to configure them. We will also discuss in detail some of the additional built-in applications, and briefly introduce DirectAccess, which will be the main topic of *Chapter 11*, Troubleshooting clients and servers.

Advanced application types

Advanced application types allow UAG to provide access to applications which are not classic "web" applications, and were not designed to be published. As you've seen in *Chapter 4*, UAG has **Host Address Translation** (**HAT**), a clever mechanism that parses web-based content, such as **ASP** and **HTML** pages, and translates the links found in them in real time. If this process were performed, the links that show up on the user's browser would all point to URLs that have the internal server name, and the browser would not be able to resolve them. The translation changes the link to point to the UAG server's public hostname, and the added unique signature helps UAG understand the request and send it to the appropriate internal server.

With some applications, this is not possible. For example, if the application uses complicated code to access the internal server, UAG may not be able (fully or partially) to parse the links, and as a result, the client will try to directly access internal servers even when accessed through UAG. When this happens, a good-case scenario is that some images or links would not work, and in worse cases, the application in its entirety may completely fail. We haven't seen a case where the entire universe imploded, but application failures can be quite daunting, especially when this is discovered when the server is already in production.

Another situation where link parsing and signing cannot be done is where the application itself is pre-compiled. For example, some applications use **ActiveX** controls, Flash, Silverlight, and Java, which are usually compiled applications. UAG cannot decode the compiled code, so it cannot find and sign the links in such an application. The way this looks to the user is that the application appears to be working, because the HTML based part does, but at some point, the ActiveX launches on the client side, fails to connect to its server, and reports an error. Sometimes, the ActiveX is visible, and at other times, it's hidden within the browser, which makes it a bit hard to be sure. Sometimes it would take someone who really knows the application to understand the cause of an error or a failure. A well known example of such an application is **Citrix XenApp**, which has its own template under the **browser embedded applications** family.

A similar situation affects applications that are completely browser independent, such as **Citrix Program Neighborhood**. These applications connect to their servers using the TCP/IP protocol, but the traffic is not going through the browser. In such a case, there's no link signing, or links at all, for that matter, and we need to have another way to let the application contact its server through UAG and back.

The solution to all of these is **SSL Tunneling**, which has been available in UAG's predecessors for many years. SSL Tunneling is based on a special component that runs on the user's computer, and helps things along by listening to communication attempts by the client application. When the listener "hears" an attempt by a client application to contact its server, it encrypts that traffic with SSL and routes it to the UAG server over port 443. The UAG server decrypts it, and then sends it to the internal server. When the server responds, UAG routes the traffic back to the client application. Naturally, that traffic may be sensitive, so everything that leaves the client and is sent to the UAG server is encrypted using the SSL protocol, which is considered to be a very secure encryption mechanism.

The tunneling component is a part of the **UAG client components**, and is called **SSL Application Tunneling**. The name comes from the fact that it tunnels the application's communication within SSL encrypted traffic. When a published application is configured properly, this is almost completely transparent to the end-user. Once the user clicks the application's link from the portal homepage, the SSL tunneling component is launched, and appears to the user as an icon in the System Tray. If the application is browser-embedded, the user is taken to the application's initial URL, and when the time comes for the browser-independent component to be launched, it runs, and its traffic is automatically intercepted by the SSL tunneling component and sent to UAG. Later, when the user logs off from the UAG portal, the SSL tunnel is closed.

If the application is completely browser-independent, then the client application will be launched directly by the SSL tunneling component, after the tunnel is established.

The SSL tunneling component is capable of listening on any TCP/IP Port, or a combination of them. For security purposes, it is advisable to limit it to only the ports that are actually required. When SSL-tunneling based applications are configured, two key parameters need to be configured—**the Port** or ports that need to be listened on, as well as **the server**, or servers, that the client needs to talk to in the back-end. This is also a security precaution, because we don't want just any traffic passed on into the internal network. The actual application publishing configuration is still a bit more complicated than that, and we will talk about the specifics later on.

Remote connectivity

Some applications are designed in a way that makes even the SSL tunneling component unsuitable, and so UAG includes three additional types of Remote Connectivity solutions:

- **Network Connector (NC)**
- **Secure Socket Tunneling Protocol (SSTP)**
- **DirectAccess (DA)**

Fans of the previous products, **e-Gap** and **IAG**, are probably familiar with **NC**, but will be glad to hear about the advantages that SSTP and DA bring to the table. The Network Connector is somewhat similar to the SSL tunneling component, with the main difference being that it listens and tunnels ALL traffic into the internal network, unless the administrator specifically sets limits on that. In addition, it creates a virtual Network Card on the user's computer, and assigns it an IP address and other network configuration options. Essentially, it behaves like most **VPN** technologies, which is why it's often referred to as **SSL-VPN**.

SSTP is another VPN technology that accompanies NC and shares a lot of traits with it. It is also SSL based, like NC, but instead of using the SSL tunneling component on the client, and UAG itself on the server, it uses components that are built-in into Windows. In fact, SSTP is a Windows Server feature that is new to **Windows Server 2008**, and joins the previous VPN technologies, **PPTP** and **L2TP**. On the client side, the SSTP "client" is also built-in to **Windows 7** and **Windows Vista SP1**, so essentially, an organization can enjoy the benefits of SSTP without UAG at all, but as we said before, UAG brings some benefits into the game.

When using UAG for SSTP, the main advantage is that there's no need to configure anything on the client side, which makes it very convenient from a supportability perspective. If you have previously implemented VPN in your organization, you are probably aware of the frequent need to guide users through setting up the VPN dialler at users' homes, and many large organizations are forced to dedicate entire teams to handling the constant issues that come up routinely. When UAG is in the picture, it actually has automation that makes the manual configuration obsolete. All that users have to do is click the **Remote Connectivity** (or any other name the administrator chooses to give it, preferably while feeling cheerful) icon and they are immediately connected, with no further configuration. There's one caveat to this, however, with Vista SP1. While Vista SP1 has native support for SSTP, this does not cooperate with UAG, as the UAG application is unable to create the automatic dialler required, and so connecting to UAG SSTP with Vista is not supported, nor any older platforms.

Another thing that's good to keep in mind for SSTP is that it is not supported with Macintosh, Linux, Phones or any other exotic operating system that you might be thinking of now (talking about you, **ZX-Spectrum** fans). This is not unique to UAG – the system just doesn't have an SSTP dialler.

DirectAccess (**DA**) is the latest remote access technology from Microsoft, and it was part of Windows Server 2008 R2 even before UAG was introduced. DirectAccess is based on **IPSec** tunneling, and is built in a way that makes it easier to use, as there's no visible "dialler" at all. When a computer is configured to use DA, it will initiate a connection as soon as it is connected to the internet, whether it is at the user's home, or on some other internet connection or random **Wi-Fi hotspot**. Within seconds of being connected, the tunnels will be established, and the user will be transparently connected to the corporate network. The computer will then have full and uninterrupted access to all internal resources, and all that without the user lifting a finger. If you have ever tried to configure DirectAccess with Windows Server 2008 R2, you will definitely find the UAG experience much smoother.

For the IT Administrator, DA is also great, because the entire configuration is handled with **Group Policy**. Once it is configured correctly, every user that belongs to the appropriate group and connects to the corporate network is automatically assigned the policy. When that user goes home and plugs into his home network, he's back on the corporate network, with no need for any configuration or intervention.

Another advantage of DA with UAG is the integrated array features, which allow you to extend the functionality to multiple servers with very little effort. There's no need to manually configure multiple servers, as UAG pushes the configuration to all array members automatically.

DirectAccess requires extensive planning and configuration, so it will be covered in detail in *Chapter 11*.

Configuring browser embedded applications

Configuring a browser embedded application is pretty simple, and requires three things:

- The name of the server, or servers that the application communicates with on the internal network
- The TCP/IP port or ports that the application communicates on
- The initial URL of the application

If your intention is to publish Citrix, then this is easy, as the built-in template includes the standard ports used by Citrix: 1494, 2598 and 3389. Otherwise, if you are well versed in the application you intend to publish, you should already know these parameters. If not, the application's administrator or owner should know this. Sometimes, no one has a clue, and in that case, it should be possible to contact the application developer or vendor and find that information. If all else fails, it's also possible to simply set up a **Network Monitor capture** (a.k.a. **Network Sniff**) with an application like the free Microsoft Network Monitor or **WireShark**. A quick recording on a client will quickly reveal the server names and TCP/IP ports. The **initial URL** is normally the same URL users type into their browsers when accessing the application from within the organization's network.

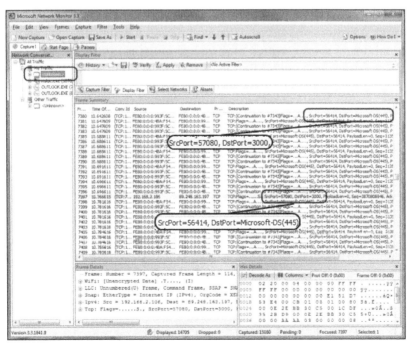

The Browser Embedded Application wizard starts by asking for an **application name**. Next, it asks you to configure the **access policy**, which is configured similarly to any other app you have configured before.

The next step involves choosing whether the application uses a single server, or a server farm. As discussed in *Chapter 4*, a server farm is slightly different, as it applies to a group of servers that are front-ended by a load balancer.

Next, it asks you for the name of the server, which is actually the server on which the **initial URL** launches. It could be the same as the application's server, which the client application actually talks to, but that is not always the case. Additionally, you need to configure the TCP/IP port for that initial URL, and select whether it is **HTTP** or **HTTPS**. Again, this refers to the initial URL, which is usually just a regular web page, and most of these are published on port 80 or 443.

For example, imagine an organizational hiring management application. This imaginary application is built like many standard applications in that it has a "front" server – some website which users go to when they want to use it. They go to this "front" by typing some URL into their browser on their office computer. This "front" website may be running on a Windows Server running IIS, or perhaps a **Unix** server running **Apache**, or any other web server technology that you are partial to. When these users type that URL into their browser, a web page welcomes them, perhaps asking for credentials, or simply logging them into the application automatically. Then, their browser launches a browser-based component, like an ActiveX control, which may be embedded into the page or sometimes runs as a stand-alone application. That browser-based component initiates a connection to some other organizational "back" server, which may be listening on a different TCP/IP port. Sometimes, the "front" server and the "back" server are the same, but not always. How would you know? It's not always easy, but typically the person who is in charge of this specific application would know this.

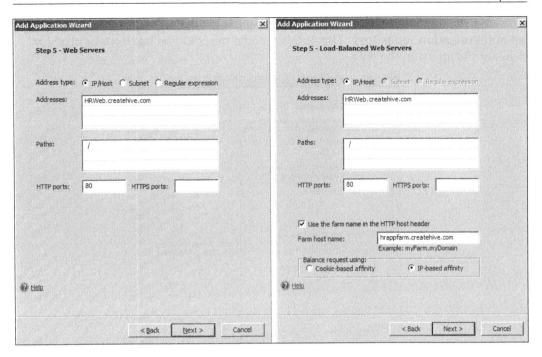

When you click **Next** on the **Web Servers** page, UAG checks if these servers are responding, and will warn you if they are not. You can choose to continue, and the error won't stop you from completing the wizard, but it is an indication that something is wrong, so it would be wise to check connectivity properly before proceeding. Keep in mind that if UAG is unable to connect to the web server, your users will not be able to either.

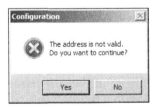

The next step offers you the option of enabling **Single Sign-On** (SSO) by specifying an **authentication repository**. This is exactly like the SSO you have configured for other applications in the past.

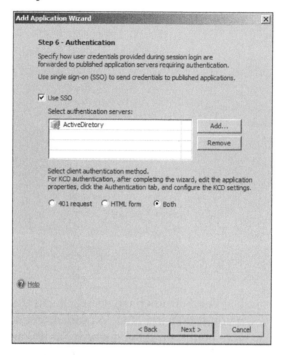

Next, you will need to provide the actual back-end server **names** and **ports**. These settings will determine what traffic passes through the tunnel, and what doesn't, so it is very important to get all the relevant server names or IP addresses right. You can manually specify all the servers, or, if they share a similar name, you can use RegEx (Regular Expression). For example, If your application uses the servers `app1`, `app2`, and `app3`, you can simply specify `app*`, instead of all three servers (read Appendix A for more information about RegEx). If the application talks to the server on multiple ports, you should specify all of them, separated by commas. If a port range is required, you could specify it with a hyphen (see the example in the following screenshot). When you click next, UAG will check if these servers are responding, and will issue a warning if not, similarly to Step 5. The actual warning message in this step is somewhat confusing – it will say **Server cannot be empty and requires a valid IP/DNS name**, even if you did fill out the information and did not leave the field empty. What this means is that the IP/DNS name is not valid, because UAG was unable to resolve or contact it.

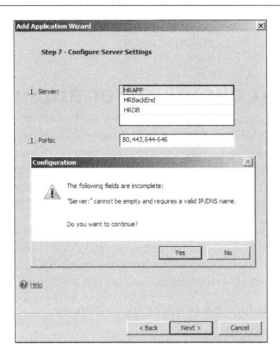

The final page of the wizard is similar to other applications, and asks you to specify details about the application's link on the portal.

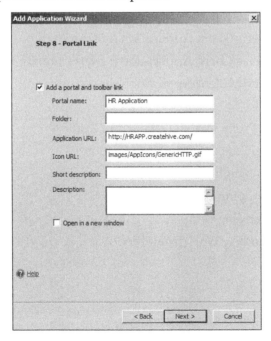

Having completed the wizard, you need to **activate** the configuration, as always, and it should be available in the portal right away.

Configuring client/server applications

Client/server applications are a bit more complicated, and not only because there are more templates. These wonderful applications are closer in nature to Browser-embedded applications than to web apps, in that they are based on standalone client software that runs outside of a browser. A client/server application connects to a back-end server on a TCP/IP port, and therefore, requires a **tunnel** to pass along the data. For example, publishing Telnet or SSH would be done using these templates.

The various client/server application templates are somewhat similar, although they are exceptionally flexible. All of them launch an **SSL-VPN** tunnel using the UAG client components, and then launch a program or script on the client computer to run the client-side application that connects through the tunnel.

The templates available for Client/Server applications are:

- Generic Client Application
- Generic Client Application (Multiple Servers)
- Generic Silent Client Application
- Enhanced Generic Client Application (Multiple Servers)
- Enhanced Generic Client Application (hosts required)
- Enhanced Generic Client Application (hosts optional)
- Enhanced Generic Client Application (hosts disabled)
- Enhanced HAT
- Generic HTTP Proxy Enabled Client Application
- Generic SOCKS Enabled Client Application
- Citrix Program Neighborhood (Direct)
- Local Drive Mapping
- Local Drive Mapping Setup
- Outlook (Corporate/Workgroup Mode)
- Remote Network Access

The most useful of these are the top three. The difference between them is that the first one, **Generic Client Application**, is designed to be used with a single back-end server, while **Generic Client Application (Multiple Servers)** allows configuring an application that connects to more than one backend server. To be clear, this does not refer to a situation where the backend server is a load-balanced "farm" of many computers represented by a single URL or IP, but to an application that may use several different servers. A multiple server application also allows you to configure multiple ports (whether multiple servers are indeed used or not).

Under the hood, the difference between the two is that the Generic Client Application template is using only the SSL tunneling component in order to achieve protocol tunneling between the client and the UAG server, while the Generic Client Application (Multiple Servers) template is using UAG's Socket Forwarding component for the same purpose. You can see this difference between the two templates after you add applications of these types to your portal trunk, and then open their Application Properties window and take a look at the Client Settings tab. The "silent" version of the single-server app differs from the others by the fact that when it is run on the client, it shows no prompt or message. The other two, in contrast, show a message that alerts the user that the tunnel has been established and that the SSL tunneling component is ready to launch the client application.

Some people are not big fans of that little pop-up which the non-silent templates show, and want it tucked away. The good news is that you can customize the default set of templates, and create a copy of one of the non-silent applications, but sentence it to eternal silence. As we said before, customizations are beyond the scope of this book, but the procedure is detailed here:

```
http://blogs.technet.com/b/ben/archive/2009/12/16/creating-a-custom-
application-template.aspx
```

Enhanced Generic Client Applications

The "Enhanced" family of Generic Client Applications provide an enhanced level of access for non-web applications that run in a console environment. Such applications are executables that are installed on the client computer, and cannot be launched by other application types. To understand the meaning of the **Hosts** options, we need to go a little deeper into the way the SSL Application Tunneling component works. The SSL Application Tunneling component is actually a relay, which makes changes on the client machine to cause traffic to flow through it. To do so, the SSL Application Tunneling component may change an application's configuration file, or the registry, or the system's **HOSTS** file. For example, if the client application needs to communicate with a server named "Server1" on the organization's network, the SSL Application Tunneling component may add an entry to the client's HOSTS file to resolve the name "Server1" to a **localhost IP address** (an address in the range 127.0.0.0-127.0.0.255), which is the IP address on which the SSL Application Tunneling component established its listener.

Each variation of the "Enhanced" applications determines how the hosts file change is applied:

- **Hosts Required**:

   When the Hosts Required template is in use, the SSL Application Tunneling component will attempt to edit the HOSTS files, and if it fails to do so (for example, if the user is a Guest user, and does not have the required access permissions for editing system files), it will terminate itself and shut down the tunnel.

- **Hosts Optional**:

   When the Hosts Optional template is in use, the SSL Application Tunneling component will be more forgiving, and won't terminate if it cannot change the HOSTS file. The Tunnel will stay open, and the user can launch the application manually, although it may not work.

- **Hosts Disabled**:

   When the Hosts Disabled template is in use, the SSL Application Tunneling component will not even try to edit the HOSTS file, and will initiate the tunnel directly and run the application.

So, which to choose? Well, it depends on whether you have to make a modification to the HOSTS file in order to make the client application connect to the SSL Application Tunneling component, in which case you would most probably go with the "Hosts required" template, or if you can get the client application to use the SSL tunneling component listener IP address via some other means, like, for example, through some command line arguments. Note that all the "enhanced" templates have two additional configuration fields: "Executable" and "Arguments", which you can use for exactly this purpose. For example, think of using the "Enhanced Generic Client (hosts disabled)" template in order to allow access to the Telnet client. The "Executable" would be, well, you guessed it: **Telnet**, and in the "Arguments" field you would enter: **host %localip%**. **%localip%** is a variable that is dynamically replaced, at runtime, with the actual loopback address on the client machine that the SSL Application Tunneling component listens on.

Enhanced HAT

The Enhanced HAT template is a unique template, because it mixes up tunneling and the Host Address Translation (which we also referred to earlier as "URL Encryption" or "URL Signing"). This template is suitable for publishing websites that have embedded content that is not in "standard" web page format (like **ASP**, **HTML** or **JS**) and which contains some links that UAG cannot rewrite using its Host Address Translation (HAT) engine. For example, these might be links embedded in a **PDF** document downloaded from a web site. Since UAG's HAT engine cannot rewrite the PDF document, such links would get to the client browser pointing to internal server names, which, of course, cannot be resolved correctly and cannot be reached from the client machine over the internet. Enhanced HAT comes to the rescue: in order to solve the issues of un-HAT-ed links on the client browser, when an Enhanced HAT application is launched on the client, it establishes an SSL tunnel and then it intercepts the browser's connection attempt to that unreachable internal server. Once intercepted, the browser's HTTP request is tunnelled over to the UAG server, and an **HTTP 302 Redirect** status is generated in response by the UAG itself. The Location header in the redirect response contains the HAT-manipulated internal server name, which means that it now points to the UAG trunk public hostname. This response is sent back to the browser through the SSL tunnel, and once the browser receives it, it acts upon the redirect, sending the request to the portal listener. Since this request points to the portal hostname and not to the internal server name, the request does not need to be intercepted and tunnelled anymore, and from here on all the subsequent HTTP responses and requests will be HAT-ed normally (that is, until such time when another un-HAT-able content is downloaded, at which point the SSL tunnel will kick in again).

Generic HTTP Proxy Enabled Client Application

The Generic HTTP Proxy Enabled Client Application template, as its name implies, sets up the SSL Application Tunneling component relay as an HTTP Proxy, which allows applications that are proxy-enabled to communicate through it directly, without making changes to the system's HOSTS file. Once the user launches the application from the portal, it will launch the SSL tunnel, and notify the user to configure the application's Proxy settings, and inform the user which IP and Port to use. By default, the loopback address that the SSL Application Tunneling is using when configured to function as an HTTP proxy is **127.0.01** and the port it listens on is port **10081**.

Naturally, not all applications are designed to work with an HTTP Proxy, so this template is only useful for some applications. Web browsers are classic applications that are proxy-enabled, though, of course, these don't need the SSL Application Tunneling component in the first place. Email applications, on the other hand, are often a good fit for this.

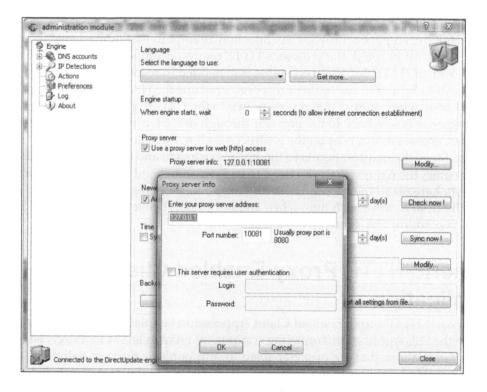

Generic SOCKS Enabled Client Application

The Generic SOCKS Enabled Client Application template is similar to the HTTP Proxy one described previously, but, as its name implies, sets up the SSL Application Tunneling component relay as a SOCKS Proxy, rather than an HTTP Proxy.

Going into details about the SOCKS proxy protocol is beyond the scope of this book, so suffice to say that some applications are not HTTP-Proxy aware, but are SOCKS-Proxy aware, and this template can be the easiest way to allow these applications to connect through UAG. Similarly to HTTP Proxy applications, once the SOCKS proxy application is launched, it will show a pop-up that informs the user that they need to configure the application to use a SOCKS proxy, and will tell the user which IP and Port to use. By default, the loopback address that the SSL Application Tunneling is using when configured to function as a SOCKS proxy is 127.0.01 and the port it listens on is port 1081.

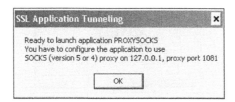

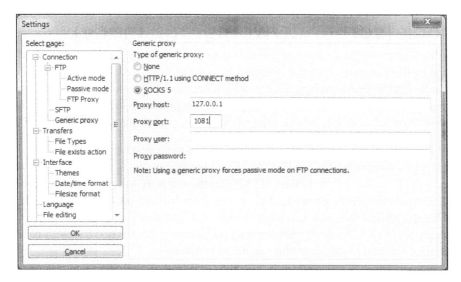

Citrix Program Neighborhood (Direct)

Citrix Program Neighborhood is an alternative way to access Citrix applications. Normally, Citrix applications are accessed through a special webpage that initiates the Citrix client. These are typically published using the Citrix template under "Browser-embedded applications". When Citrix Program Neighborhood is used, the applications are launched through shortcuts in the user's Start menu. Since the application is not launched through the browser, the configuration is different.

When configuring the Citrix Program Neighborhood template, you need to specify the Citrix server names and ports, but also the **XML** Service server name and port. The XML Service usually runs on port 80, while the Citrix servers are often on ports 1494 and 2598. The template contains these ports as the default.

When the client launches the Citrix Program Neighborhood link on the portal, the SSL tunnel will launch, and then the Citrix client will launch. From then onwards, launching the Citrix applications works the same as it would when connecting to the server directly.

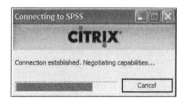

Outlook (corporate/workgroup mode)

The Outlook template may be confusing if you have followed the guide to publishing Exchange in the previous chapter. While UAG includes new functionality to support the fantastic **Outlook Anywhere** (a.k.a. RPC-Over-HTTP) mechanism, this template is a classic template that was included with UAG's predecessors, and allowed the use of Outlook through the SSL Application Tunneling component.

Outlook Anywhere allows Outlook to connect to Exchange servers through simple publishing by encapsulating the RPC protocol traditionally used by Outlook over standard HTTP traffic on port 80 or HTTPS traffic on port 443. This makes it much easier for organizations to provide their users with full access to "push" corporate email. Organizations that still use older Outlook clients or Exchange servers (which do not support the Outlook Anywhere mechanism), or prefer not to use it for other considerations, can use this template as an alternative.

When this template is in use, it launches a standard SSL Application Tunneling component tunnel, and the wrapper is used as the RPC proxy. Then, Outlook is automatically launched on the computer, and will communicate with the internal Exchange server through the relay.

To configure this application, simply provide the internal address of your **Domain** and **Exchange** servers, and leave the other settings as their defaults.

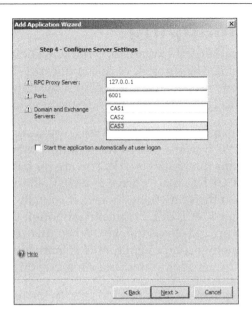

SSL Application Tunneling component automatic disconnection

When a client/server or browser-embedded application launches the SSL Application Tunneling component tunnel, it is important to keep in mind that SSL tunnels have an impact on the resources of the UAG server. This means that keeping idle tunnels running is wasteful, and so the component will keep track of user activity via mouse movements and keyboard activity. If the user is inactive for a long time, the tunnel will be automatically shut down, and a notification will be displayed on the screen.

The maximum idle time is derived from a session timeout setting for the trunk, and coincides with the general timeout period for the session, so when the tunnel is closed, the session itself expires, and the user will have to logon to the portal again, and re-launch the tunnel. We will discuss configuration of the session parameters in *Chapter 10*.

Local Drive Mapping

Local Drive Mapping is rather self-explanatory, but you should understand how it works to make the best of it. The purpose of this application is to simulate a popular feature many organizations use, and that is to map some network share to a drive letter on the user's system. This allows the user easy access to a network location.

The Local Drive Mapping application uses the SSL Application Tunneling component to pass the **RPC traffic** required for standard Network Drive mapping that you would use on your internal network. You are probably familiar with using the command **NET USE** to map a drive to a **UNC share**, and this application template does pretty much the same thing. In fact, it actually launches a small Batch file that performs a standard NET USE command, although the user sees only a black DOS window that opens up and closes quickly. When this application is launched, the SSL Application Tunneling component tunnel is launched, and then a temporary batch file is created on the client computer, and runs, creating the drive mapping.

When configuring this application, you need to specify the name of the server, the name of the share, and the drive letter that will be used in the mapping. You can also specify *, which means that the first available letter will be used.

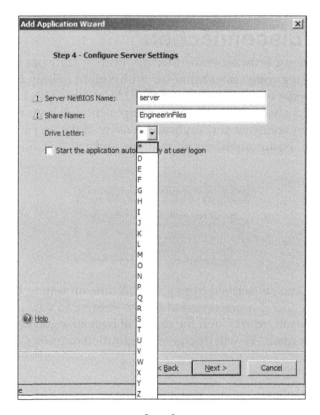

Unfortunately, the Drive Mapping application is limited. It only works on Windows XP and older systems, so if you are using Vista or Windows 7, your users will not be able to use it. An additional important fact about Local Drive Mapping is that for it to work on Windows XP and Windows Server 2003 (as a client), it requires a registry change on the client computer. This is what the "Local Drive Mapping Application Setup" template exists for. When this application is run on the client, it disables **SMB (server message block)** over TCP/IP, and this allows drive mapping to work on these systems. It's important to keep in mind that making this change can affect other applications that might require SMB over TCP/IP to be available, so it might not be suitable for everyone.

Once the "setup" application runs, it modifies the registry key `HKEY_LOCAL_MACHINE\System\CurrentControlSet\Services\NetBT\Parameters\SmbDeviceEnabled` to a value of `0`, and asks the user to reboot their computer. The application is not smart enough to check if the value is already set to this value, so it's important to avoid setting this application to run automatically, as it may confuse your users. If you do, they will see a message that asks them to reboot their computer repeatedly, and that is not really required, of course.

Remote Network Access

The **Remote Network Access** template is a unique application too, as it actually represents two distinct technologies in one. When you add this application to the portal, there's nothing to configure, other than its name and endpoint policy settings. When clicked in the portal homepage, it will launch either the **Network Connector (NC)** or the **Secure Socket Tunneling Protocol (SSTP)**, which are available depending on the user's operating system.

Although the **Add Application Wizard** asks you for some technical details, there is actually nothing to configure—just leave the defaults as they are, and configure the appearance of the application, if you so desire. However, adding the Remote Network Access application to the portal applications list is not enough, in order for any of these two applications—NC and SSTP—to be available to your end users, you also need to configure their server side settings.

The next sections discuss these two connectivity technologies in detail.

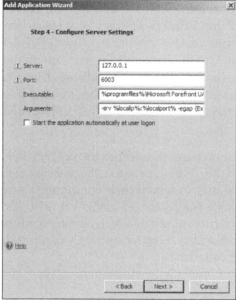

SSL Network Tunneling (Network Connector)

The SSL Network Tunneling service, formerly known as "The Network connector", is the classic remote connectivity technology that has been part of the UAG family for many years. It is based on the **SSL Application Tunneling component** technology we have discussed before, but extends it for full network connectivity that acts similarly to how other VPN technologies work. Once the user connects to the UAG portal and launches the Network Connector application, a virtual Network Card is created on the user's system, and that card is assigned an IP Address and a subnet mask. Depending on the server's configuration, it might also be assigned a **Default Gateway**, a **DNS Server**, a **WINS Server**, and various **ROUTES** are created as well.

Using this virtual NIC and the newly configured routes, the operating system is the one that actually routes traffic into the tunnel listener and the SSL Application Tunneling component then encrypts the traffic and sends it to the UAG server over port 443.

From a technical perspective, NC has the same functionality as any other VPN service, but from an administrative perspective, it makes life easier for the System Administrators and the Information Technology group. The big improvement is that the administrator only needs to define NC on the UAG server once, and when the clients want to connect, all they have to do is login to the UAG portal, and click the link. In contrast, most major VPN technologies require some sort of preparation. Some require a software installation, others require a manual configuration of the VPN dialler on the client.

If this is fantastic, you might be asking, then why do we even need anything else? Well, unfortunately, NC has some limitations too. One limitation is the fact that it does not work with Windows 7 computers, and for that reason, UAG also includes support for Secure Socket Tunneling Protocol, which will be discussed a little later.

Planning for Network Connector

To successfully implement Network Connector, you are going to have to plan and design its integration into the corporate network. This is not dissimilar to other VPN technologies, but it requires a configuration that is somewhat more manual and elaborate than what you might be familiar with.

Here are some aspects that you will have to decide on:

- Will NC clients be assigned IP addresses from the corporate range or from a private range?
- Will NC clients be allowed access to the entire organizational network, just to specific servers or just to other NC clients?
- Will NC clients be forced to connect to (public) internet resources through the VPN tunnel when connected?
- Will NC clients be allowed to pass all traffic, or will there be limits on it, like the blocking of certain protocols?

Some of the previous considerations are more of a practical nature, and others have security repercussions. For example, forcing NC clients to connect to internet resources through the VPN tunnel when connected (also known as **non-split tunneling**) provides for better security, but may put additional load on the bandwidth use of the organizational internet connection. Allowing access to NC clients for all internal resources may also reduce security, but blocking some of it may prevent users from doing their work.

Another thing you need to plan out is the IP address range that will be assigned to NC clients. Unfortunately, you cannot use your trusty DHCP server for this, and so you will have to define the exact range on the UAG server, and take steps to make sure the same addresses are not assigned to other resources.

If your internal network is **subnetted**, additional planning may be required to be sure that traffic can flow in both directions. Connecting clients would typically be sending data onto the "internal" network, via the internal Network Card on the UAG server. If the data is destined for resources that are on other networks, that are behind a router or firewall, that device will be the "gateway" for these clients, but the same device will also need to be aware of their existence, to be able to route traffic back to them. Consider the following diagram:

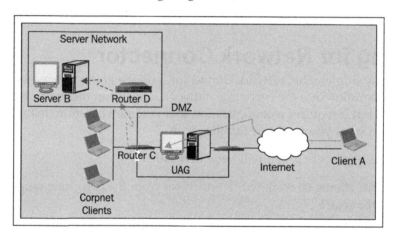

When traffic is being sent from NC client A to internal server B, it is actually being sent by UAG to router C, which forwards it to Router D, which forwards it to Server B. When Server B responds back to NC Client A, it sends the traffic to its own default gateway (Router D), which needs to know that the route to the NC Clients IP range has to go through Router C, and forward the traffic that way. On the same note, Router C needs to know that the NC Clients IP range has to go through UAG's internal network card, and forward the traffic there. Naturally, if the routers also have firewall (or **traffic filtering**) capabilities, make sure the appropriate ports are open. We strongly recommend drawing out your own network using graphics software, and planning out the routes carefully. Then, configure all the relevant routers and/or devices and test them well.

Adding Network Connector to the portal

To add NC to the portal, follow this procedure:

1. On your trunk, click **ADD** to add a new application.

2. From the Client/Server and legacy applications, select **Remote Network Access**

3. Type a descriptive name for the application

4. Define the access policy for this application

5. Leave the settings in Step 4 at their defaults*

There is one scenario in which you need to change the settings in Step 4. The default settings of the Network Connector application include the "external IP", which tell the client to which IP address to connect when establishing the tunnel. The actual value is `-srv %localip%:%localport% -egap {External IP}`, and it populates the Arguments field in Step 4. The string `{External IP}` is dynamically updated at runtime to the UAG Trunk's defined public IP Address, and if the UAG Server is behind a NAT device, this causes a problem, as the client cannot connect to a NAT IP. To the user, this manifests itself as a connection being established, and disconnected within a few seconds. If your server is indeed using a NAT IP address as it's a public IP, then in step 4, you need to edit the Argument, and replace `{External IP}` (including the curly brackets!) with the actual external IP that is configured on the NAT device to forward traffic to UAG. The resulting argument would be something like:
`-srv %localip%:%localport% -egap 174.123.82.2`

Another scenario where this type of change may be required is if UAG is load balanced by an external load balancer. In this case, UAG is not really aware of the virtual IP, so we have to tell it to tell the clients to connect to it.

6. Complete the wizard, but do not activate the configuration until you complete the next step

Having completed this procedure, you need to enable and configure the Network Connector or SSTP before activating the configuration.

Configuring the Network Connector server

To configure the Network Connector server, open the Admin menu, and select the **Remote Network Access** sub-menu. Select **SSL Network Tunneling.**

The first step in configuring the Network Connector is to actually enable it. To do so, check **Activate Network Connector** at the bottom of the page. Next, configure the complementary data. This refers to the Networking configuration that will be pushed to connecting clients besides the IP, such as DNS, WINS, Default Gateway, and DNS suffix.

First, select the Network interface which represents the internal network. This will show, on the left side of the configuration page, the current network settings that the UAG server itself is configured with (you configured these when you configured the Network Cards on the server). On the right-side of the page, you have the option of selecting to have the complementary data sent over only if they are missing, or to force them regardless. Typically, your UAG will have an IP and Subnet and DNS already configured, so you can leave all of those settings blank, except the **Default Gateway**. Since normally, the internal NIC of the UAG does not have a default gateway configured, you will have to provide a gateway address. The function of the Default Gateway is to provide clients that need to send data to resources other than other NC clients a gateway to forward this data to.

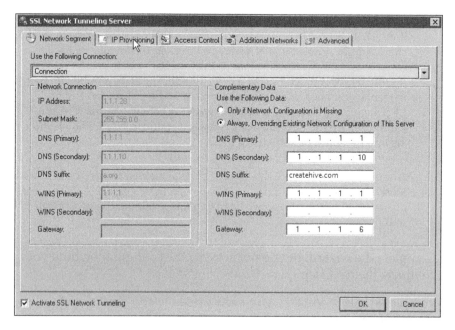

It's important to know that the screenshots in this chapter represent the Network Connector configuration on a **single UAG server**. If you have a few servers in an NLB cluster, the user interface will be somewhat different, although with similar options.

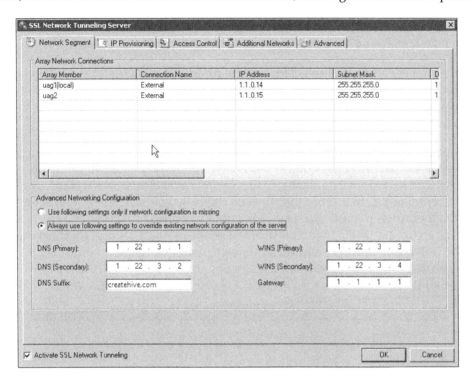

The second step is configuring the IP address assignment. If the IP range you have chosen is on the same subnet as the «internal» IP subnet, set the configuration to **Corporate IP Addresses**, and click **Add** to configure the range you have selected. If the IP range is outside the corporate range, select **Private IP Addresses**, and specify the IP range. We should mention one more time that UAG has no mechanism for checking these addresses, so do make sure they do not conflict with machines that are already preset with these IPs, or any DHCP scope that has been configured somewhere. It's important to know that from any pool you specify, some addresses will not be available. IP addresses that end with zero or 255 are excluded, as well as one additional address that will be assigned to the UAG's virtual Network Card. You will be reminded of this by UAG when you complete this step.

It is also important to keep in mind that a corporate IP range would be a range that is within the IP subnet that is defined for the "internal" network card. If you wish to use a range that is different, then it will still be considered to be a "private" range, from a configuration perspective.

For example, let's say that the "internal" subnet is 10.0.0.0-10.0.255.255 (subnet mask of 255.255.0.0, or 16 bit). Your organization really uses the larger range of 10.0.0.0-10.255.255.255 (subnet mask of 255.0.0.0, or 8 bit), so you want NC clients to use the range 10.1.0.0-10.1.255.255. From your perspective, this is a "corporate IP range", but UAG sees only the smaller range, to which it belongs, so you would have to define your range as "private".

Whatever the IP ranges you selected, keep in mind the way computers know how to route traffic by using the **Subnet calculation** and **Default gateway**. Think of the subnets you have configured, and make sure that all parties have the correct routes so that traffic can go from NC clients to its destination and back.

For example, let's say that the "internal" subnet is 192.168.0.0-192.168.0.255 (subnet mask of 255.255.255.0, or 24 bit). You have set the private IP range of 172.16.0.0-172.16.0.64 for NC clients. Your organizational servers see traffic coming from a client like 172.16.0.7, but that IP is on their own subnet. They send their replies to their own Default Gateway. That gateway needs to know that the range of IPs 172.16.0.0-172.16.0.64 is actually being serviced by UAG, and forward that traffic to it. For this to work, you would have to configure a static route rule on the organizational router to forward all traffic going to 172.16.0.0-172.16.0.64 towards the internal IP address of the UAG server. UAG will take care of the rest.

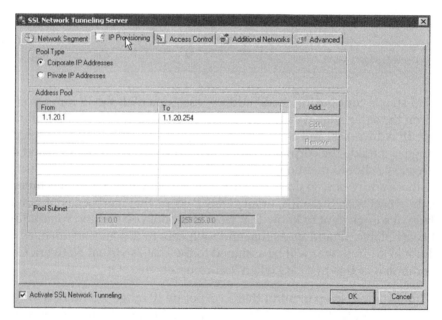

The third step is to set up access control, which controls the Tunneling mode and filtering. Split tunneling is the popular choice, but if you have selected to use non-split, keep in mind that your users will only be able to access the internet through the organizational network while connected to NC. For this to work, you will need to take extra care in setting up the routing, and if your organization's internet access is restricted in any way (for example, **Skype** is blocked, URL filtering is done, or access has to go through a proxy server), make sure your users are prepared for this (or sneak into the office early to avoid the crowds with the pitchforks). You can also choose to have no internet access at all, of course, but if you think this will get you the perfect security for your network, keep in mind that the user can always manually edit the routing on his computer, and bypass it.

You can also choose to block TCP traffic, UDP traffic, or ICMP traffic through the Network Connector. Blocking UDP may be useful for preventing use of certain streaming-based applications, thereby reducing the bandwidth use of the tunnel. However, this should not be considered to be a perfect solution to achieve this goal, as many applications can generate a lot of traffic with TCP as well.

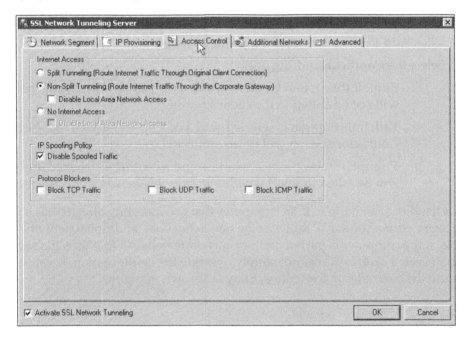

If you have selected to use **Split Tunneling**, in which clients connect to internet public resources through their regular internet connection, and only connections to organizational servers are routed through the SSL tunnel, you may also need to configure **Additional Networks**. In this scenario, you will have to use the **Additional Networks** tab to let UAG know of any additional IP ranges that are part of the organizational network. This option will basically add route rules to connecting clients that will route traffic to these additional ranges through the tunnel. If this is not configured correctly, the clients will try to access these IP ranges through their internet connection.

This also applies if you have selected to disallow all internet access to NC clients. In this case, NC clients will need additional routes to help them "know" that traffic to the additional IP ranges is considered "internal". Otherwise, it will be considered to be traffic to the public internet, and disallowed.

To configure additional networks:

1. Switch to the **Additional Networks** tab.
2. Check **Enable Access To The Following Additional Networks**.
3. Click **Add** to add a range, and type the IP range.
4. Select the **Conflict Handling** option:
   - **Skip**: If this option is selected, and a conflict is detected, the network will not be added to the client's routing
   - **Fail**: If this option is selected, and a conflict is detected, the Network Connector session will be disconnected
   - **Prompt**: If this option is selected, and a conflict is detected, the user will be asked to select whether to skip this network or disconnect

Conflict handling can happen if the computer that is connecting already has a route to a network with a similar IP range as the one defined as "additional network". For example, if the computer is part of another corporate network that uses the same subnet. In such a case, UAG cannot simply override the configuration, because it may cause the computer to lose connectivity to its own network.

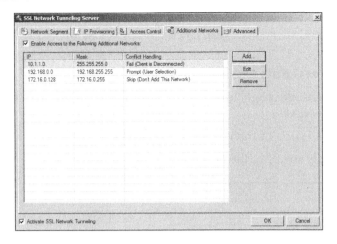

The last step is to add a manual policy rule to TMG, to allow traffic from NC clients. Remember how we said a few times that you should not configure TMG manually? Well, this is one of the rare exceptions to that rule.

To configure TMG to allow access to NC clients, follow these steps:

1. Open the TMG Management console, and navigate to the **Firewall Policy** node.

2. On the Tasks tab, click **Create Access Rule**.

3. On the Welcome page of the **New Access Rule Wizard**, type a name to your liking for the rule, and then click **Next**.

4. On the Rule Action page, select **Allow**.

5. On the **Protocols** page, in the **This rule applies to** list, select **All Outbound Traffic**.

6. On the **Access Rule Sources** page, click **Add**.

7. On the **Add Network Entities** dialog box, click the **New** menu, and then click **Address Range**.

8. On the **New Address Range Rule Element** dialog box, type a name for the range to your liking.

9. Specify the **Start Address** and **End Address** of the IP address pool for NC clients. Then click **OK**.

10. Expand the **Address Ranges** tree, and select the new range you just created. Then click **Add** and **Close.**

11. In the **Access Rule Sources** page, click **Next**.

12. On the **Access Rule Destinations** page, click **Add**.

13. On the **Add Network Entities** dialog box, expand the **Network** branch. Select **Internal**, and then click **Add**. Click **Close** to close the **Add Network Entities** dialog box.

14. On the **Access Rule Destinations** page, click **Next**.

15. On the **User Sets** page, leave the default settings to allow access to all users. Then click **Next**.

16. On the final page of the wizard, click **Finish**.

17. Click **Apply** to apply the new TMG configuration

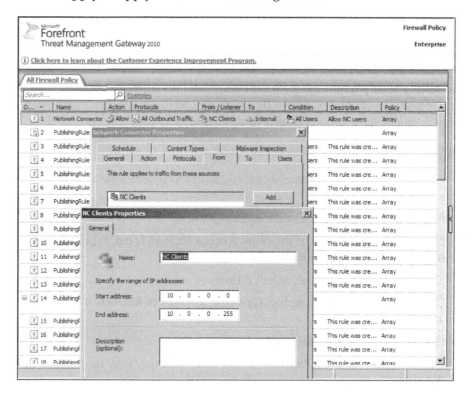

It's important to note, though, that you cannot control access to users and groups for NC access in TMG. You can limit traffic by IP, although that is not very useful for anything.

Activating and testing the Network Connector

Having configured everything, go ahead and **activate** the UAG configuration, and then test this with a client. Keep in mind that the Network Connector is only available to Vista clients or older. Once you have successfully connected, you should see that the client has a new virtual Network Card with an IP address from the pool you configured, as well as the various complementary data. Check if you can connect to internal resources, your gateway and, if relevant, resources behind the organizational router.

Network Connector disconnecting?

Although the Network Connector has been in use with great success over the years, some users have experienced inexplicable disconnects while using it. The symptoms are typically a drop of the connection for no apparent reason, sometimes immediately, and sometimes only after a prolonged session of 20-30 minutes.

Possible reasons for this are numerous. In many cases, this has been traced back to issues with the corporate infrastructure, mostly load-balancers and high-end routers. Some of these devices are pre-configured by default to keep tabs on sessions, and forcibly reset sessions that are "too long". This can be easily seen with a network tracing tool, visible as a "reset" packet being sent by the network device. In other cases, this has been traced back to intermittent network failures. When a network failure occurs, the Network Connector client is designed to disconnect the session, and sometimes, the network failure could be too minor to be visible to the naked eye. This is most common with users who use wireless networks, which are very susceptible to interference. Sometimes, simply moving the laptop around, or turning on a high powered appliance like a microwave oven can cause a minute drop.

If you are running into similar issues, you should first rule out that the problem is with the server. To do so, connect a client directly to it, bypassing all other infrastructure. Ideally, this could be done by connecting some computer with a cross-over cable to the external interface of the UAG server. If the server is running on a virtual machine, then setting up a second virtual machine as a client is also quite easy to do, usually. Another, less favourable option would be to hook up a client to the same switch that the UAG is connected to. This may not provide a clear indication, as some switches perform speed renegotiations on their ports that could cause seemingly random disconnections. Once confirmed that a direct connection can hold, move the client further steps away, until you can determine the source of the interruptions.

SSTP

As said before, the Secure Socket Tunneling Protocol integration with UAG is designed to complement the Network Connector. Since NC is only usable on Vista and older operating systems, SSTP provides a similar experience for Windows 7 users. For usability, UAG integrates both into a single application icon on the portal, so by adding "Remote Network Access" earlier, you are covering both. Even if you are using just SSTP, without the Network Connector, you still need the icon on the portal, so go back to *Adding Network Connector to the portal* and perform the steps detailed there.

The way UAG configures SSTP is complicated, but easy to do. When you configure the SSTP settings in UAG and activate the configuration, UAG pushes the SSTP configuration to TMG, which in turn, pushes it to the **Routing and Remote Access Service (RRAS)**, which is a part of Windows. RRAS itself configures several additional options and services. This is a good opportunity to remind you once again that to use SSTP, the UAG server needs to be a member of your domain, so we are hopeful you took care of that way back in *Chapter 1*.

Now, go to the SSTP configuration page:

1. Open the UAG Management Console.
2. Click on **Admin** and select **Remote Network Access.**
3. Select **SSL Network Tunneling (SSTP).**
4. On the SSTP configuration, check **Enable remote client VPN access.**

The first thing to configure is the number of concurrent SSTP connections that the server will allow. Once that number of concurrent connections has been reached, the server will not allow any more clients to connect, but do not be tempted to specify an unrealistic number here. SSTP requires the server to encrypt and decrypt traffic, and over-working the server's processor may allow more users, but they might not be very happy with the performance. There are no official guidelines as to how many users a server can support, because the performance is affected by too many factors to allow a reliable scale to be set. If you plan on hosting a significant number of users, the best approach, as discussed in Chapter 1, would be to start with a pilot group of users, and measure the server performance to determine the load it can carry for your specific needs.

Next, select the trunk on which you have selected to publish SSTP. Even though you can only select one trunk, you can actually add the application itself on other trunks as well. The downside to this is that the SSTP configuration is universal to all trunks. If you need to have different SSTP configurations, like a different IP range, then you will have to use separate UAG servers.

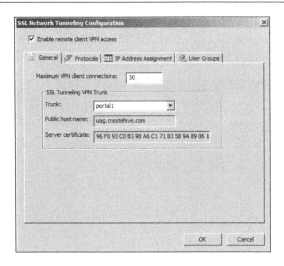

Now, switch to the **Protocols** tab, and check **Secure Socket Tunneling Protocol (SSTP)**. If the other options on that tab seem fun and cool, you will have to find another toy, as these are not supported. It was originally planned to allow you to configure **PPTP** and **L2TP** from the same place, but this dhas not materialized yet.

Now, switch to the **IP Address Assignment** tab and configure the IP options. You can choose to have the addresses assigned via **DHCP**, or manually specify a pool. Note, though, that DHCP is only available in a single-server scenario, and if you have an array, this is not an option. You can also define the **advanced** options, which relate to the DNS and WINS configuration applied to clients. Most customers find it easier to simply use DHCP, but if you have selected to use a static pool, do make sure that it does not overlap with other ranges (including ranges you have set in the Network Connector configuration) that are in use. Also, if the static IP range you selected is part of the IP range defined as the "internal" network, you will have to cancel the wizard and exclude the IP, and only then run the configuration again. To exclude a range from the internal network, follow these steps:

1. Open the UAG Management Console.
2. Open the **Admin** menu, and select **Network Interfaces**.
3. On the wizard, click **Next** twice, to reach the IP range page.
4. Modify the ranges so that there is no overlap—you can **Edit/Remove/Add** ranges until an appropriate configuration has been reached.
5. Click **Next**, and then **Finish**. There's no need to activate the configuration.

For example, if your original internal IP range was 10.0.0.0-10.255.255.255, and you want SSTP to use the range 10.1.0.0-10.1.255.255, edit the original range to be from 10.0.0.0 to 10.0.255.255, and then add a range from 10.2.0.0 to 10.255.255.255.

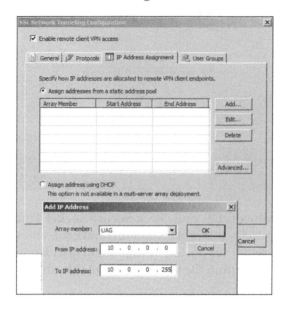

The last step is to configure user and group access. This is not a mandatory step, though you may want to have a finer control over who can do what. By enabling the user group control, you can define user groups from your repositories, as well as single IP addresses or IP Address ranges.

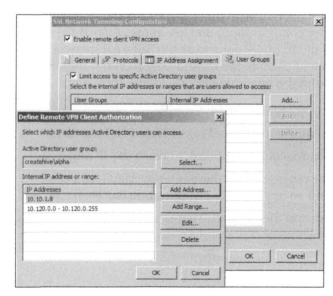

Now that everything has been configured correctly, activate the UAG configuration, and you are ready to connect SSTP clients! Once your users access the portal, they will only see a single icon for Remote Network Access, and it will either launch the Network Connector or SSTP depending on the operating system they are running.

At this point, you can go into the TMG management console, and create access rules to limit access for specific users, groups, and networks. This is also one of the rare things that are OK to do with TMG on a UAG server. Configuring TMG is beyond the scope of this book, but you can learn more about this here: `http://technet.microsoft.com/en-us/library/dd441031.aspx`.

Remote Desktop applications

The last group of applications UAG offers are Remote Desktop applications. There are two types of remote desktop applications—one of them is the applications that are based on SSL-VPN tunneling and the second uses the Remote Desktop Gateway service on UAG. We like to refer to the SSL-VPN based templates as "legacy", because they have been a part of UAG's predecessors, IAG and e-Gap, and they haven't changed since. To the RDG-based templates we refer to as **Remote Desktop Services (RDS)** publishing. The RDS publishing templates rely on a service that is included with Windows 2008 R2, which provide new functionality for publishing **RemoteApps**.

The purpose of these templates, of course, is to let you launch a remote desktop session to an internal server, and that's no small feat, as the remote desktop protocol is not a web-based protocol. With UAG's predecessors, this could be done by tunneling the traffic, and that's what the legacy templates are about—they establish an SSL-VPN tunnel and tunnel the RDP traffic (over port 3389) directly into the corporate network. The two templates used for this were:

- TS Client Tunneling (Windows Vista/Windows XP)
- TS Web Client Tunneling (Windows Server 2003 multiple servers)

The difference between these two is the purpose, as can be deduced from the name. The first one was designed to allow users to remote desktop directly into computers (Servers or workstations) inside the corporate network, and it has certain specific parameters you can configure in accordance with this sort of use. The second one is of a legacy nature, as it designed to be used with the **Active-**X version of the remote desktop client, through a special website running on IIS. This has been useful in the past, when the Remote Desktop client was not available on every computer. These days, using the first template is pretty much ubiquitous.

TS-Web websites, also known as "Remote Desktop Web Connection ", are a special type of website template that IIS servers can publish, unrelated to UAG or its predecessors. A TS-Web website would be published by an organization as a way of letting users connect to organizational servers easily. Instead of users launching the remote desktop client manually and typing in details, they can launch the TS-Web website from their browser, type in a server's name, select the resolution from the drop-down menu and connect. An organization can also customize the default HTML to make things even easier (for example, by having a preconfigured list of servers to choose from).

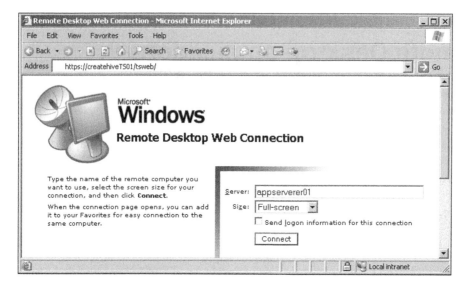

The way the "TS Web Client Tunneling (Windows server 2003 multiple servers)" template works is this:

1. An organization publishes a TS-Web website on some internal IIS server.

2. The application is published on UAG, naming that server as the "web server", and listing permissible internal servers as "servers"

3. The user launches the application on their client

4. The application launches the SSL-VPN tunnel on the client

5. The user sees the TS-Web page (like the previous screenshot)

6. If the TS-Web website has not been customized, the user types in a server name, and clicks **Connect**.

7. The RDP client launches, and connects to the server, if that server has been listed within the application's server list.

Installing and configuring TS-Web on your server is outside the scope of this book, but you can find more information about it here: `http://www.petri.co.il/ install_remote_desktp_web_connection_on_windows_server_2003.htm`.

The application publishing wizard is quite straightforward. You start by selecting the application type, then define a name for it. You then select the endpoint policies and choose if you are defining a single web server, or a web farm. Keep in mind that a "single web server" doesn't mean you can Remote Desktop to only one server, just that the TS-Web website is running on a single server as opposed to a cluster of several servers. On the Web Servers page, you can see how the TSWEB path was already included. It is the default path for Windows 2003-based TSWEB servers, so edit it, if necessary. As always, be careful to select the protocol and port correctly, depending on how the TS-Web server is configured.

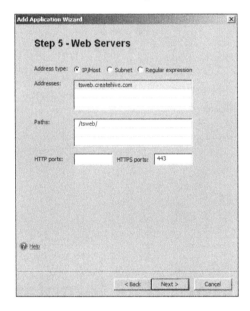

The last wizard pages are about selecting an authentication repository for Single-Sign-On, and defining the portal link. Once you finish and activate the configuration, it should be really easy to use (keep in mind, though, that it can be used only from clients that support SSL-VPN tunneling, as we said earlier).

The TS Client Tunneling (Windows Vista/Windows XP) template is even simpler, because you don't have to configure any web servers (as with the other template). Simply start the wizard, and on the fourth step, specify the target server or servers that you will allow clients to connect to. You can also specify ports other than the default RDP port of 3389, and specify a display resolution to your liking.

One important thing to note is that unless you specify an **Initial Server**, the client will be shown the Remote Desktop Connection software, and will have to type in the name of the server they want to connect to. This depends, of course, on your needs. If the purpose is to allow users to connect to one specific computer, you would add just that one in the **Terminal Servers** list, and specify it also on the **Initial Server**. If the purpose is to let users connect to various computers (for example, every user to his own personal computer), you would specify all their computer names in the **Terminal Servers** list, but leave **Initial Server** empty. Here are these two options:

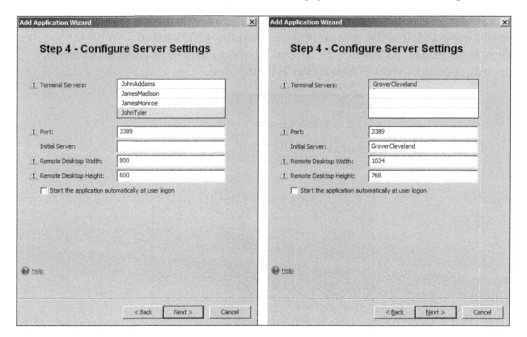

Remote Desktop RDG templates

RDG is a new feature of Windows Server 2008, which can work independently of UAG, but with UAG, it is easier to use, because the user just launches the RDP application from the portal, and there's no need to configure the client with the server's address or move around the RDP configuration files. When you install UAG, it automatically configures the RDG service, and then publishes it using one of the following templates:

- RemoteApp
- Remote Desktop (Predefined)
- Remote Desktop (User Defined)

RemoteApp is a new feature of Windows 2008 as well, which allows the user to connect to a single application using the remote desktop protocol. Instead of having a full connection to the desktop, only the application is running in a window. To the user, it looks as if the application is running on their own computer, but in fact, it's running on the remote computer, and only its display is sent to the client machine. For example, a customer can use his office Email program, with all his folders that exist on his work computer, but still have the same experience as if it's running on his home computer. To learn more about RemoteApp and how to configure it, visit the following links:

- `http://technet.microsoft.com/en-us/library/cc753844(WS.10).aspx`
- `http://technet.microsoft.com/en-us/library/cc730673(WS.10).aspx`

Once you have configured RemoteApp on your Terminal Server, you need to export the RemoteApp configuration as a TSPUB file, and copy it to the UAG server (or put it on a network share that's readable from UAG). This file will provide UAG with a list of applications it can publish as RemoteApps.

To publish RemoteApp applications, select the RemoteApp template, type a name for them and select the endpoint policies. On step 4 of the wizard, import the TSPUB file. The TSPUB file would usually include the details of a Remote Desktop Session Host or Remote Desktop Connection Broker (a.k.a. Terminal Services Session Broker), but if it does not, add them in the appropriate place.

An **RD Connection Broker** is a Windows Server 2008 R2 role that is used to provide users with access to RemoteApp and Desktop Connection. A Remote Desktop Session Host is a server that hosts Windows-based programs or the full Windows desktop for Remote Desktop Services clients. To read more about these roles, visit the following links:

- `http://technet.microsoft.com/en-us/library/dd560675(WS.10).aspx`
- `http://technet.microsoft.com/en-us/library/cc742806.aspx`

When you import the TSPUB file, you need to select the applications that you want UAG to publish among those that the TSPUB file includes, and then configure the screen resolution and color depth for them:

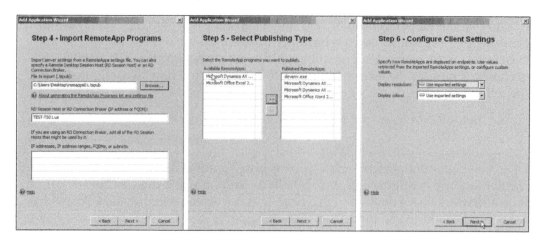

After you complete the wizard and activate the configuration, the independent applications will appear on the UAG portal separately.

Remote Desktop—predefined and user defined

The other two remote desktop applications are also quite straightforward, and similar to each other. The difference is that the predefined application template publishes servers that you, the administrator, determine, while the user defined template allows the end-user to type in whichever server he wishes to connect to. With both applications you define a name, select the endpoint policy, configure the server settings, select the display properties, configure the portal link, and you're done. The difference is in **Step 4 - Configuring Server Settings**. The image on the left is from the predefined template, and the one on the right is from the user-defined template:

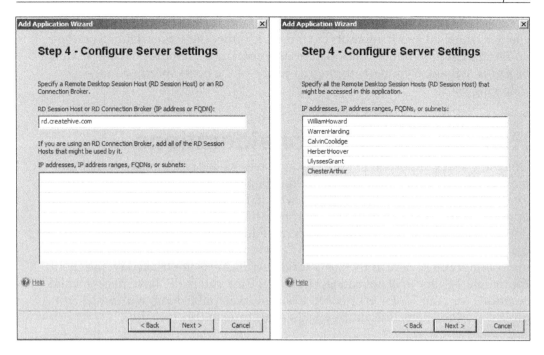

When a user launches the user-defined remote desktop app, he is presented with a pop-up that lets him type in a hostname or IP of an internal server. Naturally, end users will gain access only to computers that have been listed in the server settings tab of the application.

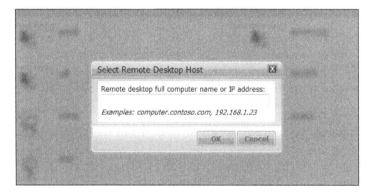

If, however, the user launches a predefined remote desktop app, the remote desktop client is launched and it attempts to connect to either the server defined on the application (if it's a remote desktop session host) or, if a remote desktop session broker is defined, it connects through it to one of the hosts specified in the following list.

Remote Desktop considerations

One thing that's important to know about the RDG-based templates is that they require the client to run version 6.1 of the remote desktop connection software, or higher. Windows 7 comes preinstalled with it, but older systems may require an upgrade. If you try to launch such an application with an incompatible client, a pop-up window will be presented with remediation steps — these are discussed in *Chapter 12*. Another important thing to keep in mind is that certificates are of the utmost importance here. If the UAG server certificate is not trusted by the client, the remote desktop will not connect (which means you really have to get a valid certificate for your UAG, as opposed to simple web publishing, with which you can get around an invalid cert by clicking **continue to this website**).

File Access

The File Access application can be added to the UAG portal from the "Built-in services" group of applications, but we felt it is more closely related to the "advanced" group of applications, so it is covered here.

The purpose of File Access is to provide users with access to file servers within the organizational network directly. We have already talked about **Drive Mapping**, which provides access to a single file share on a single server (though you can publish multiple shares and assign them to different drive letters), but this application provides a more generic interface for accessing all of the organization's file servers from a single graphics user interface.

When a user launches the File Access application from the portal, he is presented with an explorer-like interface, which allows him to view servers and shares that have been configured by the UAG administrator. The user can download or upload files, create folders and much more.

From a technical perspective, the File Access application does not require an SSL tunnel to operate, but it does require the administrator to configure which file servers and shares need to be available to the users.

Preparing to Publish File Access

Before starting to configure File Access, you need to make sure that the UAG server is a **domain member**, and also has NETBIOS access to domain servers. If you have a router or firewall behind the UAG server, it needs to allow traffic on ports 137, 138, and 139 for both TCP and UDP, and in both directions. Essentially, the UAG server has to be able to "browse" the network and enumerate (discover) servers that have file shares. To test if this is working, simply browse the network from the UAG server:

1. On the UAG server, click **Start**, and select **Network**.

2. If you receive a message that states that **Network Discovery** is **off**, enable it.

3. If no servers appear, this means that something is preventing network browsing, and that will prevent you from configuring File Access on UAG.

Some organizations have disabled network discovery for their entire network, often because it uses the **NETBIOS** protocol, which is considered to be undesirable. NETBIOS uses broadcasts for Network Discovery, and that could have a negative effect on network performance, especially with large networks. If that is the case, you will have to choose to either enable Network Discovery, or forget about the UAG File Access service.

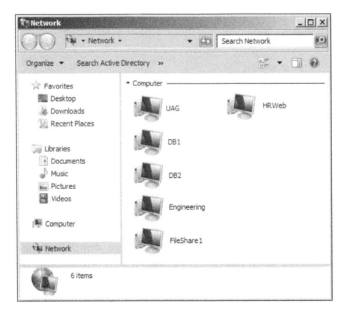

Configuring File Access Domains, Servers, and Shares

Configuring File Access is about defining which **Domains**, **Servers**, and **Shares** will be published within the application. During this process, the administrator chooses the domain or domains, then the servers from these domains, and then the shares themselves. Access to these is actually based on the shares **access-control list** (**ACL**), just like in normal file sharing, but if a Domain/Server/Share was not selected in the configuration, it will not be shown to the users at all, even if they have access. On the same note, if the share is configured, but the ACL does not allow access to the user, they will still see the share, but will be unable to access it from the File Access application. This needs to be configured only once, though the administrator can always reconfigure the application if needed.

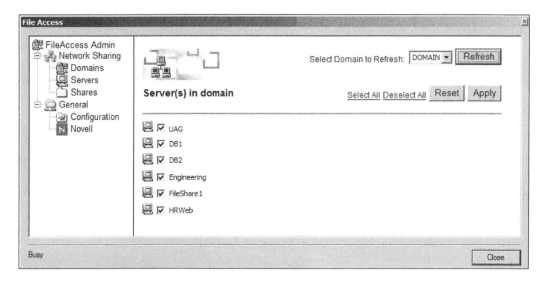

To configure File Access, follow these steps:

1. Open the UAG Management console.

2. From the **Admin** menu, select **File Access**

3. Type in the username and password of a user which has the appropriate permissions to browse the network. The username should be in the format `domain\username`

4. Select the domain you want to enable sharing files from (if none appear, read the previous section again) and click **Apply**.

5. Under **FileAccess Admin | Network Sharing**, click **Servers**

6. Click **Refresh**, and wait for the list of servers to appear (if nothing happens, note the status **busy** or **ready** on the bottom left).

7. Check the servers you want to be available to users, and click Apply.

8. Under **FileAccess Admin | Network Sharing**, click **Shares**

9. Click **Refresh**, and wait for the list of shares to appear (if nothing happens, note the status "**busy**" or "**ready**" on the bottom left).

10. Check the shares you want to be available to users, and click **Apply**.

11. Click **Close.** There's no need to activate the configuration.

Using File Access

Having configured File Access, the next step is to add it to the portal, and start using it. To add File Access to the portal, follow these steps:

1. Open the UAG Management console.

2. Start the wizard for adding a new application.

3. From the Build-In group, select **File Access**

4. Modify the authorization, if required.

5. Finish the wizard, and activate the configuration

The File Access application itself is quite self explanatory, and most users are able to figure it out on their own. Once launched, the application shows a folder tree of the available servers and shares. The user can navigate the folders and perform various file operations—rename, delete, copy, and of course—download or upload files. The user can even create folders and perform searches for files.

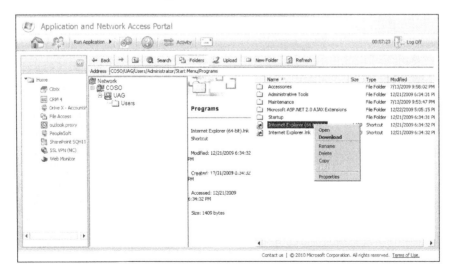

More fun with File Access

To make things easy for users, the File Access application has some more tricks to offer:

- It can automatically show the users' home folder, based on their profile settings in the domain

- It can run a script to map standard drives that users require access to

- It can interact with Novell servers, and allow access to the Novell server shares

- It can display only those shares that the current logged on user is permitted to access, based on the ACL permissions on the share itself

The settings for the above are controlled from the File Access configuration application—the same one you used earlier to select the servers and shares. The Configuration page defaults to not defining user's home directories, but has the option of showing users' directories using either the Domain Controller settings or a template set by you manually.

To configure access to **Novell servers**, you need to install the Novell Client on the UAG server, and then define a Novell authentication repository. These options and the preceeding advanced settings for File Access are beyond the scope of this book, but you can find additional details about them here: `http://technet.microsoft.com/en-us/library/dd897154.aspx`.

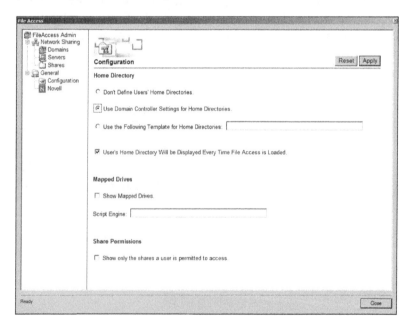

Summary

Having gone through *Chapters 4* and *5*, you are now able to design and publish applications using all of UAG's built in templates. We have also talked about some of the additional magic UAG has to offer, like Virtual Private Networking and file access. Using all of these, you should now be able to publish virtually any web application, as well as many other enhanced applications, and take advantage of many of UAG's abilities. In the next chapter we will examine the issue of user authentication in more detail, and learn about working with different authentication environments beyond active directory.

6
Authenticating and Controlling Access

So far in this book we have discussed several methods of using UAG in order to publish backend applications to end-users on the Internet, or to give these users full network access to a corporate LAN. However there is little chance that in real life, you would allow "free passage" to anyone out there, on the world wide web, to your organization resources. You also wouldn't allow just about anyone to walk into your corporate offices without requiring them to present some credentials before they can get into the elevator, not to mention into your data centre. There is also at least one, if not several, layers of authentication, both at the virtual gate to your corporate network (which is represented by the **UAG portal**), and possibly also at the entrance to different more restricted areas, like, for example, specific applications or even parts of applications published through a UAG portal trunk. In this chapter we will discuss the features built into UAG which, together, add some very strong authentication and authorization capabilities to this product.

UAG session and authentication concepts

The vast majority of user interactions between an end-user and a UAG server are performed within the context of a UAG session. This includes access to all kinds and types of applications that we covered so far in this book—**web**, **client/server**, **browser-embedded**, **Remote Desktop Services**, **Remote Network Access** (both when using **Network Connector** and when using **SSTP**), and so on. In most cases, these sessions are *authenticated* sessions, meaning that the user's identity is verified at the very beginning of the session. In reality, only a very small number of real world scenarios require or allow anonymous access through UAG, so the authentication mechanism is an important part of the entire UAG solution.

So what is a UAG session? A UAG session is a logical grouping of client requests and of server responses, whether issued by the UAG server itself of by a backend application. The common denominator is that all of these are sent by (or to) the same client, and mainly, by (or to) the same user. In most cases, UAG sessions are maintained via the use of an **HTTP cookie**. Every time UAG receives a client request that does not present a valid UAG session cookie, it creates a new session and a new session cookie is assigned to it, and UAG sends this cookie back to the client. From here on, the client will return this cookie to UAG with each and every request, as dictated by **HTTP protocol**. If you're wondering what happens with the cookie and how are sessions maintained when the protocol is non-HTTP, keep in mind that on the client side there are different UAG client components in charge of intercepting those non-HTTP protocols, encrypting them with SSL and encapsulating them within an HTTP tunnel through which they are then sent to the UAG server. During that encapsulation process, the UAG session cookie is added to the traffic, thus allowing UAG to recognize and associate the traffic with a specific session, representing a specific user.

UAG distinguishes between two types of sessions: **authenticated** and **unauthenticated**. The difference between the two is pretty obvious, so we'll just say this: all sessions start as unauthenticated sessions. When a new session begins, as mentioned above, the user is not yet identified, and therefore, at that point, the session cannot be deemed "authenticated". Only once UAG has successfully verified the user's identity through the authentication process, the session status changes from "unauthenticated" to "authenticated", and it will remain that way until it terminates. We will describe different session related settings later in this chapter.

The basic authentication flow

Now that we've (hopefully) answered the question of "What is a UAG session?", we'll discuss the authentication flow in UAG. If you've read the previous chapters and have already configured and used a UAG trunk at least once, then it will probably come as no surprise to you that, at least in one of the authentication scenarios supported by UAG, it presents the user with a logon page, where the user is asked to provide a set of credentials and then submit them for verification. You are also probably aware of the need to configure at least one authentication repository (also known as 'authentication server') and assign it to the trunk, so that UAG can verify the submitted credentials against it. Now it's time to elaborate a bit.

In the most common scenario, a user opens his browser and types (or launches from his browser's Favorites or Bookmarks) a URL that points to a UAG trunk. When UAG receives that request, since this is a new session, it will reply with the logon page (in reality there is another page first— `InstallAndDetect.asp`, but we'll discuss this one in *Chapter 8*). This is `Login.asp`. Once the user fills in the credentials and clicks on the **Log On** button, the next request sent by the browser is an HTTP POST, sent to `Validate.asp`. This server-side ASP script is responsible for gathering the credentials submitted and validating them. The validation itself is performed by a UAG component running on the server, known as the **(Microsoft Forefront) User Manager**. This component, which is actually a service running on every UAG server, communicates with the authentication servers specified for the trunk, passes the submitted credentials for validation and receives the authentication server's response. If the credentials have been successfully validated, then the next ASP script executed is `PostValidate.asp`. This script is in charge of some post-authentication housekeeping tasks, one of them is switching the session's status from "unauthenticated" to "authenticated".

All of these ASP scripts are located on the UAG server, in the `InternalSite` folder. `InternalSite` is not only a file system folder, but it is also a virtual directory defined on the **Default Web Site** running on IIS on the UAG server.

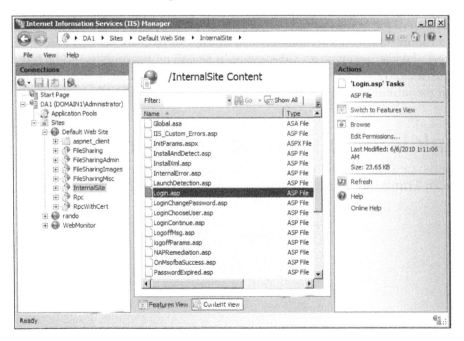

As you can see, there are many other resources in this folder other than just the three ASP scripts we mentioned. Whenever UAG needs to send a page that is related to the authentication process to the browser, like the logon or the logoff pages, as well as some other information pages, UAG fetches these from the `InternalSite` virtual directory of the `Default Web Site`.

A word of wisdom: do not be fooled by the simplicity of the flow described previously! These are just the main building blocks of the authentication flow, and we have only described here the most simplistic authentication process. UAG is extremely powerful in its authentication capabilities, both those supported out-of-the-box, as well as those that can be achieved by using UAG's extensibility options. Out-of-the-box, UAG supports authentication against the following servers: **Active Directory, RADIUS, RSA SecurID, Netscape LDAP, Notes Directory, Novell Directory, TACACS**, and a few others. An important addition in Service Pack 1 for UAG is support for **Active Directory Federation Services version 2.0 (AD FS 2.0)**. As for customizing the authentication process, the possibilities are practically unlimited. Some organizations have used anything from a text file on the UAG server itself, as well as authenticating against different databases, and using mainframe, and so on. Not just the authentication server can be customized, but also the flow of the authentication itself. Some real world deployments include virtual keyboards displayed on the logon page, multi-step authentication with one time passwords sent via text messages to users mobile phones, CAPTCHA mechanisms, and even sound-based authentication where, after submitting a username and password, the user receives an automatic phone call on his mobile and he has to place the device next to his computer's microphone, so that the sounds arriving through the mobile phone can be "heard" by UAG and validated.

Trunk level authentication settings

Most of the settings that define how a UAG trunk authenticates users appear in the **Advanced Trunk Configuration** window, on the **Authentication** tab.

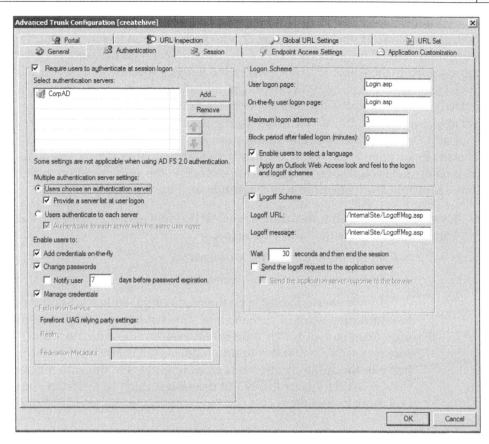

If you just finished configuring a trunk, you can now access this tab and then uncheck the **Require users to authenticate at session logon** checkbox, for those rare occasions where you need to have a trunk that does not require authentication. In case you were wondering, when creating a trunk, the **Create New Trunk** wizard does not allow you to configure an unauthenticated trunk and requires you to assign an authentication server to it, but you can always change this setting later.

As we mentioned already, most deployments will require some form of authentication for the trunk, so you'll probably leave that checkbox checked, as it is by default. The authentication method or methods used for the trunk depend on the authentication servers assigned to the trunk, which appear in the **Select authentication servers** list. As you can see, this being a *list*, you can assign multiple authentication servers to a single trunk, and you can change their order in the list, by using the up and down arrows to the right of the list. If your trunk configuration contains more than one authentication server in the **Select authentication servers** list, then the way UAG presents the logon page to users and the way it validates the submitted credentials depends on the next couple of settings that appear below the authentication servers list, in the **Multiple authentication server settings** section.

- **Users choose an authentication server** – when this option is selected, the logon form displays the following fields:
    - A field for users to type their username.
    - A field for users to type their password.
    - A field where users must type the name of the authentication server to which they want to authenticate. This field is only displayed if more than one authentication server exists in the authentication servers list. Note that this option requires the users to know the name of the authentication server, as it appears in the authentication servers list. This is probably not the easiest thing to ask from your end users to be able to do.

- Provide a server list at user logon: If you selected this option, your users are provided with a drop-down list on the logon page which displays the names of the authentication servers assigned for the trunk, so they can choose which server they wish to authenticate.

- Users authenticate to each server: When using this option, the logon page will display several pairs of "username" and "password" fields, one pair for each authentication server appearing in the list of authentication servers.

- Authenticate to each server with the same username: and finally, if this is your authentication method of choice, then the logon page will contain just one field for the users to type in the username, but multiple "password" fields, one for each authentication server appearing in the list of authentication servers.

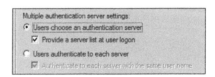

The next group of settings enables several additional UAG capabilities related to authentication and authorization.

The term **on-the-fly** logon is used in the UAG world to describe a scenario in which users have already authenticated to the trunk against a specific authentication server, and later, as they browse through the different applications published through the portal, they are required to provide another set of credentials to authenticate against a different authentication server. This is also sometimes referred to as **step-up authentication**. For example, a user has provided his Active Directory credentials upon initial logon to the trunk but, in order to access a more sensitive application, he is required to provide his **RSA SecurID** credentials as an additional means of security. We will discuss this scenario further when we cover the topic of authorization.

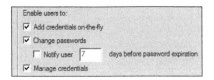

When the **Enable users to manage credentials** setting is selected, the UAG portal toolbar displays a button through which users access the **Credentials Management** window.

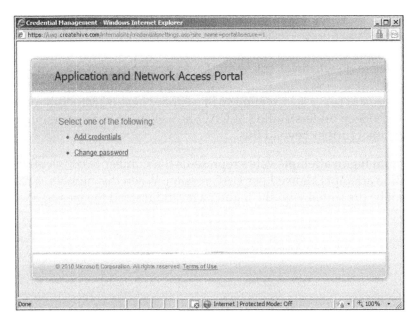

On the **Credentials Management** window, users have the option to add additional sets of credentials besides those they've already provided at trunk logon. The reason for that would be to allow the user to gain access to additional portal applications which otherwise would be blocked for them, due to authorization settings. Another option offered through this window is for users to change their password. Note that this option allows users to initiate a **password change**, while the setting **Enable users to change password** and **Notify user __ days before password expiration** is related to a situation where a user's password is about to expire or expires, and the server can notify the user of this.

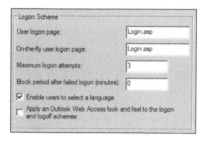

The next group of settings—**Logon Scheme**—includes the **User logon page**, which is the forms-based authentication logon page displayed at the start of a UAG session. Another setting is the **On-the-fly user logon page**, which is displayed when users need to authenticate to another authentication server in mid-session in order to gain access to one or more specific applications. Both of these are by default the same ASP resource—Login.asp—residing in the InternalSite folder. It is worth noting that UAG allows you to specify any URL here, and this allows you to customize the logoff page to do whatever you want. To do this, you create the ASP file, and place it in the ...\InternalSite\CustomUpdate folder, and then specify the path as CustomUpdate/<file>.asp. Creating such custom pages is incredibly powerful, but requires a very deep understanding of UAG, as well as ASP programming, so we will not discuss it further beyond this.

The **Maximum logon attempts** value represents the number of consecutive failed authentication attempts allowed per UAG session. When this number is reached, the user will not be presented with the logon page, and instead the message will be this:

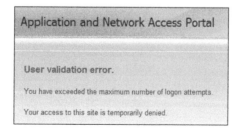

When this happens, the amount of time for which a user will not be allowed to attempt to log on again is controlled by the value in the **Block period after failed logon attempts** field, expressed in minutes. The default value of **0** means that users will not be blocked if they reach the maximum amount of failed authentication attempts.

We have covered authentication settings, meaning those actions that occur when a session starts. What goes up, must come down, and so UAG also has an elaborate mechanism for terminating a session. Let's see what this means.

Normally, logoff is triggered by clicking the 'log-off' button on the UAG toolbar, but this field can be used to trigger the logoff mechanism from some other link on the page. For example, you could set it so that when users click an exit button on a web page that your application has, it will trigger a log-off. The **Logoff URL** field holds the string that, once received by UAG within an HTTP request from a client, will trigger the logoff process. Even though the text next to this field refers to a "URL", actually the way UAG functions is that it treats the value found in this field as a string, and as long as this string appears even as a sub-string within the full requested URL, it is sufficient for UAG to recognize that request as a request to log off. For example, if you configure the value in the **Logoff URL** field to be "=logout", a request such as /some_folder/some_resource.asp?uid=43872&action=logout would trigger UAG's logoff mechanism. The default value that appears in this field does not normally need to be changed, since this is the URL requested by the browser when the user clicks on the UAG **Logoff** button found in the portal toolbar. To use this feature, you must first decide what action, within your application, should trigger a log-off, and observe the URL that is requested when that action is performed (for example, a form-submit button has a URL that you can extract). Then, you would try to identify a part of that URL that is unique to this action, but identical to all users. Then, you would type that URL part into the log-off URL setting in UAG. When the logoff process has been triggered, UAG will execute the resource pointed to by the **Logoff message** field.

As you can see, the default is the same resource requested by the browser when clicking on the portal **Logoff** button but, here as well, you have the option of changing that to something else like, for example, /InternalSite/CustomUpdate/MyLogoff.asp. You might want to change the default page to have it show some graphics design that is unique to your organization, or want it to perform some action after log-off. For example, one organization implemented an automation script that redirected the user after log-off to an extranet site in a way that made it easier to log in to it. Once a logoff request has been identified by UAG, the session status changes from authenticated to unauthenticated, but the session is still maintained "alive" for an additional short period of time, as configured in the **Wait __ seconds and then end the session** field. The last two settings in this group, if enabled, will change the default behaviour of UAG when logging off sessions.

Normally, the log off request sent by the browser "terminates" at UAG and is not forwarded to any backend application. If you enable the **Send the logoff request to the application server** option, and if the logoff request points to one of the backend applications (that means, not to `InternalSite` or to the `Portal Homepage`), then this request is not terminated at UAG, instead UAG sends it, like any other request, all the way to the backend application server. However, the response sent back by that server would be ignored by UAG, and the actual response sent to the browser would be whatever is configured in the **Logoff message** field.

If you want UAG not to ignore the backend server's response to the logoff request, and to return this response to the browser, then you also need to enable **Send the application server response to the browser**. For example if you are publishing an e-banking application, or some other transactional application, you may be interested in displaying to your users, at the end of their session, a recap of the actions they performed during this session.

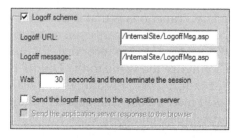

Authentication servers

In *Chapter 3*, as part of configuring the first UAG trunk, we described the necessary steps to define an Active Directory authentication server. But what is actually an authentication server, in the UAG context? First and foremost, as you already witnessed, an authentication server, or repository—as they are called in UAG jargon, is a group of settings that define for UAG against which server it should validate the credentials it receives from the browser. Since there are several types of authentication servers that UAG recognizes, the type of configured authentication server also indicates to UAG what protocol to use in its communication with this server. There is, however, more to an authentication server than this. An authentication server could also be regarded as storage of submitted credentials, for the duration of each session (this is why we also refer to it as a "repository"). Yes, once a set of credentials is successfully validated, UAG will store these credentials in its memory, in order to be able to reuse them later, at any point during the session, when and if the user accesses a backend application for which UAG has been configured to perform SSO using those specific credentials. Note that we said:

"for the duration of a session" once the UAG session is terminated, for to whatever reason, UAG "forgets" all stored credentials it has collected during the session.

In the next paragraphs we'll take a look at some of the most common authentication servers supported by UAG, besides Active Directory. Keep in mind that you are not required to configure authentication servers only when creating a new trunk. You can, at any point, configure new or edit the settings of existing authentication server by accessing the **Admin** menu and selecting the **Authentication and Authorization Servers...** option.

RADIUS

Configuring an authentication server of type RADIUS for UAG is an easy task –just fill in the required fields of the **Add Authentication Server** dialog box. Besides choosing a **Server name** for this authentication server, you also need to supply at least one RADIUS server hostname or IP address. The default port used by the RADIUS protocol, 1645, is already filled. In case you have more than one RADIUS server you can provide an additional hostname or IP address in the **Alternate IP/host** field, otherwise, if you have just one single RADIUS server, leave the "Alternate" fields blank. The RADIUS protocol encrypts credentials when transmitting them over the network, using an **encryption seed** referred to as "the secret". This is a string of your choice, and it needs to be configured on both the **RADIUS server** as well as on the UAG server, which acts as the **RADIUS client**. Pay special attention and make sure you type in the **Secret key** field a string that is identical to what has been entered on the RADIUS server, or else all authentication attempts to this server will fail. Finally, if you want to take advantage of some additional replies that RADIUS can return besides a simple "yea" or "nay", for example, the request to change the user's PIN, then you need to turn on these options on the RADIUS server and to select the setting **Support challenge-response mode** on the UAG authentication server definition.

We will discuss the setting **Use a different server for portal authorization** a bit later in this chapter, when we will cover **Kerberos constrained delegation**, as well as in the *Application-level authentication* settings section.

RSA SecurID

The steps required for configuring a repository of type RSA SecurID are very similar to those described for RADIUS. However, when getting ready to use such an authentication method, your focus should be on correctly setting up the RSA SecurID server and "getting it acquainted" to the UAG server, in order to accept authentication requests from it as a valid RSA client. Contrary to what you might expect if you are already versed with how RSA clients and servers function, you do not need to install any specific RSA client on the UAG server, since this has been taken care of as part of the UAG software installation. We will not cover here in great depth the necessary steps on the RSA server, but we'll just mention that you need to remember to set up the UAG server as an **RSA Agent Host** in the RSA Authentication Manager. Once you've done that, do also remember to generate and then copy the `sdconf.rec` file from your RSA server onto the UAG server, placing it in the `%Windir%\System32` folder. This file is needed in order to ensure correct communication between an RSA client and its server.

You might also want to review a short guide published by RSA. Unfortunately, RSA has not updated their guide for UAG as of now, and so it is targeted at users of UAG's predecessor, IAG, but many of the points are very similar: `http://www.rsa.com/rsasecured/guides/imp_pdfs/IAG_AuthMan6.1_7.1.pdf`.

WinHTTP

If we were to tell you that there is a "WinHTTP authentication server" out there, you would probably raise an eyebrow in scepticism, and you would be right! So what is this WinHTTP "thingy" that UAG tries to pass as a method of authenticating user credentials? **WinHTTP**, or **Microsoft Windows HTTP Services**, is a built-in system component that "provides developers a server-supported, high-level interface to the HTTP/1.1 Internet protocol" (`http://msdn.microsoft.com/en-us/library/aa382925(VS.85).aspx`). UAG utilizes this component in order to allow you to validate user credentials against a website, instead of against a typical authentication server (such as an AD, LDAP, RADIUS, and so on.). This is intended to solve those situations where you might have a web site which performs some kind of user validation, maybe implementing some proprietary user database, which you do not control or cannot change. Think of it as a kind of a "black box". As long as this web site utilizes the standard HTTP RFC authentication method by returning an HTTP "401 Unauthorized" response to the clients attempting to access it (in this case—UAG), the UAG WinHTTP repository can handle this, by taking the credentials submitted by the user via the UAG login page and sending these credentials to this web site. The address to which UAG will send the credentials must be configured in the **URL** field of the WinHTTP authentication server. The **Domain** field is optional—if filled with a value, then this value will be used if the user did not specify a domain as part of his username. If, after receiving the credentials submitted by UAG, the web site responds back to UAG with an HTTP status 2XX or 3XX, the credentials are considered valid. If any other HTTP status is returned to UAG, they are considered not valid and the user's logon attempt is denied by UAG.

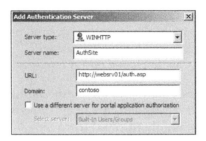

Authentication server of the type "Other"

The authentication server of the type "Other" is just a place holder for implementing your own kind of authentication. Don't be misled by the simplicity of the user interface used to set up such an authentication server! Behind this set of settings lies one of the most powerful customizations that UAG can do! By using an "Other" type of authentication server you have full control of the validation of credentials—you can implement your own logic (for example, collect a set of four credentials per user: username, password, employee ID and one-time password issued by a **One Type Password** device of your choice), you can have an authentication database as simple as a plain text file on the UAG server, or an SQL DB, or a mainframe. You can decide that users are authenticated only on specific days of the week, or between specific hours, and so on. The possibilities are endless.

In the **Add Authentication Server** dialog, the only additional setting you need to specify, besides selecting the **Server type** as **Other**, is the **Server name** you wish to use for this authentication server. Like with all other UAG authentication servers, remember that this name can be visible to your end-users in some circumstances. Therefore, choose a name that is suitable.

The next configuration steps are not UI-based. You need to access the ...\ `InternalSite\samples` folder on the UAG server, locate the file `repository.inc` and copy it to the ...\`InternalSite\inc\CustomUpdate` folder. Then, rename the file with the same name you assigned to the "Other" authentication server, such as `<RepositoryName>.inc`. For example, if you named your "Other" repository **MyCorporateAuthentication**, then the `repository.inc` file should be renamed `MyCorporateAuthentication.inc`.

From here on you will need to dust off your **VBScript** skills. The file you copied from the `samples` folder contains a few function skeletons, which you need to fill with meaningful content in order to implement your desired authentication requirements and logic, mainly the `AuthenticateRepositoryUser()` function. We will not cover the functions of this file here, as this is beyond the scope of this book.

A word of caution: make sure you do not utilize the sample `repository.inc` file "as is", since *the sample file accepts all and any credentials submitted*, effectively rendering your trunk equivalent to an unauthenticated trunk!

Smart card/client certificate authentication

Many organizations are basing their UAG trunk authentication on **client certificates** presented by the users accessing the trunk, whether these are smart cards or regular certificates (also known as "soft certificates") that are stored on a user's computer, rather than using form based authentication. In UAG, this kind of authentication requires some special configuration steps, which are not performed from within the UAG Management console. The basic flow of the client certificate authentication in UAG is as follows:

1. User sends a request to UAG.

2. Where UAG would normally reply with the login page, in this scenario it redirects the browser to a different `InternalSite` resource (`cert.asp`).

3. As a result of this redirect, the browser requests this resource, which requires a certificate in order to be accessed.

4. The browser presents a pop-up to the user, asking the user to select which certificate he wants to provide.

5. Once UAG receives the certificate, it checks its validity (this includes verifying that the dates on the certificate are valid, that the certificate is not revoked by a Certificate Revocation List and it that it is issued by a trusted Certificate Authority).

6. If the certificate is deemed valid, UAG extracts a few details from it and then compares them to the information about the user that it retrieves from Active Directory. If these match, then the user is considered authenticated.

From the preceding steps, you understand that an Active Directory authentication server is needed when configuring UAG for client certificate authentication. You already know how to configure this. The remaining steps are sample files that need to be copied from the `InternalSite\samples` folder to `InternalSite\inc\CustomUpdate` and renamed in order to match usual UAG naming conventions for custom files. These configuration steps are covered on the relevant TechNet UAG documentation (`http://technet.microsoft.com/en-us/library/ee861163.aspx`). In addition to this, though, you will also need some editing of these custom files. The amount of editing required ranges from just a couple of entries to quite a lot of changes to the sample files, depending on your Active Directory format and on your client certificate template. This is required due to the sixth authentication step mentioned above. Every organization has its own specific fields that it wishes UAG to extract from the client certificate and compare with fields in Active Directory — these can be the email address, the UPN, and so on. This determines the amount of effort required to perform this task.

We cannot discuss here all the different script ASP customization required to achieve such tasks, firstly because we cannot anticipate the requirements of such customization, and secondly because this book is about UAG configuration and not an ASP guide. But we're confident that you can find quite a few articles, blog posts and other guidance through an Internet search, at least to get you started. From there on, it's just a matter of changing those to match your exact needs.

Special handling for MS Office Rich Clients

Not all UAG sessions begin with a browser sending a request to a UAG trunk, which then replies with its logon form in order to collect credentials. Some special handling is required for those sessions where the initial (and subsequent) requests are sent by one of the Microsoft Office client applications, such as Word, Excel, PowerPoint, Outlook, and others. Take, for example, a scenario in which, during the course of a previous UAG session which started normally, from a browser, you access a SharePoint site and from within it, you click on an Office document to open it. Next, you close your Office application and log off in the browser from the UAG trunk. You now open the same Office application and, from its Recent Documents list, you open the same file that you have just accessed through the UAG session. The location of this file is a URL that actually points to a UAG trunk. Since at this stage you have not already logged on to UAG, this attempt of the Office client application to fetch the Office document from the backend SharePoint server through UAG represents a new session to UAG and therefore authentication needs to take place. If UAG were to respond with its regular logon page process, this could not be handled by the Office client and therefore the attempt to open that document would fail.

UAG handles the authentication of such non-browser clients, to which it refers as "rich clients", by presenting them with a different authentication challenge from the one used for browsers. In the UAG 2010 version, prior to Update 1, the authentication method used for these was **Basic** or **NTLM authentication**, which is a standard, based on the HTTP protocol RFC. By the way, do not be confused by the label used in the UAG user interface, as it appears both in the **Add Application Wizard** and in the **Application Properties** window: **Allow rich clients to bypass trunk authentication**. Selecting this option does not mean that these clients will not be authenticated at all by UAG and will be granted free passage to your LAN. The label is just trying to say, perhaps without too much success, that these clients will not go through the normal trunk authentication, and instead, they will be handled differently.

Starting with Update 1 for UAG 2010, an additional method of authenticating these clients has been added, besides Basic and NTLM authentication. This additional method is based on the Microsoft Office feature named **Office Forms Based Authentication** (or **MS-OFBA**) which has been introduced in Service Pack 2 of Office 2007. When MS-OFBA is used, when a rich client attempts to open a resource that is published via UAG, UAG responds with its regular login form (although the underlying protocol between that client and UAG is different than that of a browser). The user experience is that, when the rich client application is launched, a separate window will open up presenting UAG's login page, and after successful authentication that window closes and the requested resource is displayed in the main rich client application window.

In order to configure either one of the rich client authentication methods above, you need to select the relevant option, either when adding the application to the trunk or at a later time, by launching the **Application Properties** window and accessing the **Portal Link** tab.

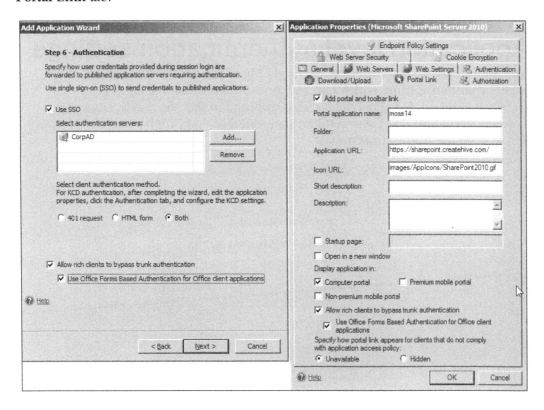

When you select one or both of the MS-OFBA related settings in the **Add Application Wizard**, as shown in the previous screenshot, a pop-up message will be displayed, informing you that rich clients will be authenticated using Basic or NTLM, and asking you to confirm.

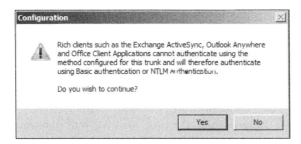

This message is correct if you only select the **Allow rich clients to bypass trunk authentication**, but, as we have just explained, not if you have selected the **Use Office Forms Based Authentication for Office client applications** option. This will probably be fixed in one of the future releases of UAG.

Application level authentication settings

Application level authentication, or **Single Sign On**, can also be referred to as **backend authentication**, which refers to the authentication that UAG performs, on behalf of the user, against the backend application that the user is attempting to access through UAG. These settings are located on each application's properties window, on the **Authentication** tab.

The first setting here is whether you want to enable UAG's single sign-on feature. We're assuming that you do, since you want to make your end-users' lives a bit easier by not requiring them to provide the same credentials again and again, when accessing various applications. Then you need to inform UAG whether the backend application, to which SSO will be performed, expects UAG to provide the actual credentials or whether the backend application can consume Kerberos tickets—**Use Kerberos constrained delegation for single sign-on**—which we will discuss later in this chapter. If you chose **Use credentials for SSO** then you need to **Select authentication servers**. Here you need to decide which set of credentials will UAG use when performing this backend authentication. There are several aspects that you should consider when making this selection, and we will discuss them next.

First, in the most common usage scenario for the single-sign on feature, you will probably want to select the same repository that you have used for the trunk authentication. If you do that, then this means that a set of credentials, as submitted by the user on the trunk's Login form, have already been collected, verified against the actual authentication server, deemed valid and stored in UAG's memory. Remember that we have established a bit earlier in this chapter that a UAG repository is not only an authentication server but also a storage of submitted credentials, for the duration of a session? Well, this is exactly the place where this "storage facility" comes into play. If you have configured UAG to perform SSO and you use the credentials stored for the user (which is equivalent to "session") as part of a specific repository, then UAG can simply retrieve those credentials and submit them to the backend application.

However, what happens if you have configured your trunk's front end authentication to allow the user to select to which repository he wishes to authenticate? No worries! UAG can handle this easily. You simply need to select here, on the **Authentication** tab of your **Application Properties** window, all the repositories that you have assigned for trunk authentication. When such a configuration exists for SSO, UAG goes through all the repositories defined in the **Select authentication servers** list and looks for a set of credentials stored for the user. If it finds a set of credentials, in any one of these repositories, then it will use those credentials to perform SSO. This way, regardless of what repository has the user authenticated to when logging on to the trunk, UAG can still provide a seamless SSO experience.

You could also have a situation where, when UAG prepares to perform SSO, it finds more than one set of credentials for the same user. For example, a user has already authenticated to one repository at trunk logon, and then used the **Credentials Management** button on the portal toolbar in order to provide an additional set of credentials to another repository. When this happens, if the user launches an application for which UAG should perform SSO, UAG prompts the user to select which set of credentials should be used for SSO.

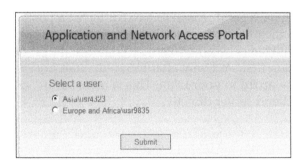

Another scenario could be one in which UAG does not yet have any credentials for this user, when it's time to perform SSO. This is when the setting **Enable users to add credentials on-the-fly**, that we mentioned earlier in this chapter, is relevant. If this option is disabled, then users will receive a message in their browser saying **You are not authorized to access the application**, when attempting to access an application for which UAG is configured to perform SSO and does not have any credentials it can use to do so. However, if the option **Enable users to add credentials on the fly**, found on the **Advanced Trunk Configuration** window, on the **Authentication** tab, is enabled (which is so by default), then UAG will present the user with the *on-the-fly* login page, requesting him to provide his credentials to one of the configured repositories which UAG should use for SSO.

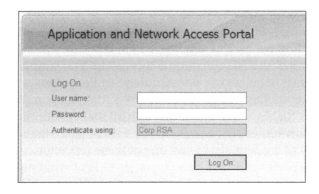

At this point you may be thinking to yourself: "OK, so if UAG is asking the user for an additional set of credentials in the middle of the session, then what's the advantage? Why bother configuring SSO if the end-user experience is not that of a single sign-on?" That's a great question, and here are the reasons why you may want to do this: first, it's not UAG's fault that you have configured a different repository for trunk authentication than the repository you configured for application SSO. Change that configuration to use the same repository and the user experience will be seamless.

Secondly, if you do have a good reason to have different repositories, having UAG perform authentication in the middle, between the browser and the backend application, is advantageous because this way you have the Edge device—UAG—perform authentication first, and only after the credentials are successfully validated, are user requests forwarded to your LAN. This is more secure, as the client does not interact with the backend server directly.

Furthermore, once UAG has collected a set of credentials for a specific repository, it will cache those for the duration of the session. So, if you have several backend applications for which you have configured UAG to use the same repository for SSO, UAG will only prompt the user for credentials to that repository once. After caching the credentials for the first time when SSO is needed, UAG will reuse the credentials to perform SSO to all other backend applications. Another advantage is that you might not want to collect a second set of credentials in the login page because the application that needs it might be rarely used, thus easing the user experience.

Last but not least, using this feature, you can request "step-up authentication" for certain applications from those you published in your trunk. This means that you require one level of authentication at the "trunk entrance"—the logon page, and this allows access to the portal homepage and some of the applications, but in order to access some other applications (more sensitive ones, perhaps?), users will be prompted for a secondary set of credentials, such as requiring them to enter their RSA SecurID passcode, if that is what you have configured (by the way, the same can also be achieved by using the **authorization** feature that we will discuss later).

We have covered the way UAG decides which credentials it needs to use in order to perform SSO. Let's now discuss the methods UAG can utilize in order to supply these credentials to backend applications. Any configuration you decide to use here must match the way the backend application requests the credentials to be sent to it. We'll start first with the options found under the **Select an authentication method** label.

The **401 request** method refers to standard HTTP authentication methods such as **Basic** and **NTLM**. If this is the way your backend application server accepts credentials, then whenever it receives an HTTP request from a not yet authenticated client, in this case UAG, the application will respond with an *HTTP 401 (Unauthorized)* status. According to the HTTP RFC, at least one *WWW-Authenticate* header exists within the response headers, which informs the requesting client what is or are the authentication methods accepted by the server. Since this exchange of requests and responses is standard, is it fairly easy for UAG to implement a solution to support it. Specifically, when the **401 request** method is selected for an application, UAG expects to receive the 401 response from the backend application and within it, the information whether *Basic* or *NTLM* is required in order to authenticate. If both are supported, UAG will always select NTLM, since it is considered a more secure method of transporting credentials over a network. Then, UAG will send the same HTTP request again, this time adding the user's credentials, in the format requested by the backend application.

Handling form based authentication to backend applications

When the **HTML form** option is selected as a method of providing credentials to a backend application, UAG has much more work to do. Since the application uses an HTML form, there is no standard that regulates how such a form might look, what fields it may contain, where the information should be submitted to, and so on. Therefore, in order for UAG to be able to handle such forms, UAG must have a configuration which is specific to each application and its own logon form. Indeed, UAG comes pre-configured to handle quite a few of these forms, for the most common applications it supports. This default configuration can be found in a file named `FormLogin.xml`, located in the `...\von\Conf\WizardDefaults\FormLogin` folder of any UAG server. You can even "teach" UAG how to handle additional form configurations that it are not pre-programmed to be able to respond, to match whatever kind of web application you may need to publish. This is another type of customization that UAG can perform, though we will not cover this in detail, as this is beyond the scope of this book. You can read more about this here: `http://blogs. technet.com/b/ben/archive/2010/09/02/uag-custom-form-login.aspx`.

The flow of HTTP requests and responses between UAG and the web application in the backend, when form based authentication is involved, differs than the flow that occurs when the authentication method is a standard HTTP 401 response status. Not only that, but when using form based authentication, UAG involves the client browser too. Here is a schematic representation of this flow:

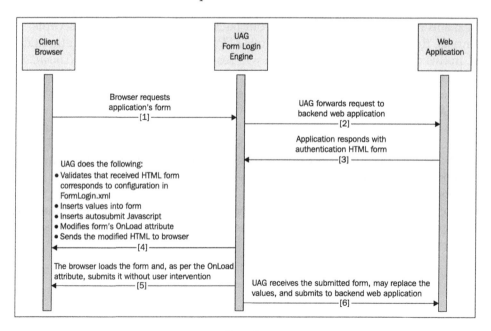

As you can see, when UAG receives the HTML form from the backend application, it does not simply fill it with credentials and submits it to the application, contrary to what you might expect. Instead, UAG fills the form with values, which could be the real user credentials but could also be just some dummy values (according to the configuration in the `FormLogin.xml` file), and then sends this form to the browser. Therefore you should not be surprised if you and your users will see this form rendered in the browser. Depending on the browser's internet connection speed, this might be just a quick flicker, or it may linger on screen for a bit. In any case, the user is not required to take any action, since as soon as the form is completely loaded in the browser, it will be automatically submitted back to UAG. This is due to additional code that UAG adds to the form, consisting of an `OnLoad` HTML attribute which invokes a **JavaScript function** which triggers the submit button. If the form was filled with dummy values in Step 4 shown above, when these form values reach UAG again, they are replaced by UAG with the real credentials for this user (stored in the repository) and then sent to the backend application. If these credentials are successfully validated by the application, the HTTP flow continues normally.

Kerberos constrained delegation

An additional method for UAG to authenticate backend web applications on behalf of the user is to use **Kerberos constrained delegation (KCD)**. By using KCD, you can configure the trunk to authenticate using any one of its authentication methods and then UAG will perform the SSO to the web application by means of a **Kerberos ticket**. One of the biggest advantages of using KCD is that UAG does not have to know the user's password in order to achieve SSO, or in order to request and obtain a Kerberos ticket from Active Directory. Therefore, one of the most common scenarios when KCD is used is for the types of trunk authentication where UAG does not receive the user's password, like **Client Certificate** or **smartcard authentication**.

In order to be able to successfully use KCD, there are a number of prerequisites and requirements that you need to take care of:

- The UAG server must be domain joined
- The UAG server and the web application server must be members of the same domain
- The Active Directory must be set to a domain functional level which is at least Windows Server 2003
- The users for which UAG should perform SSO to the application must be members of the same domain as the UAG and the application servers, or of a domain with bi-directional trust to UAG's domain
- The backend application must be able to consume Kerberos tickets as a means of user authentication

To configure UAG to perform KCD-based SSO to an application, check the **Use single sign-on to send credentials to published applications** setting in the **Application Properties** window, on the **Authentication** tab, and then select the **Use Kerberos constrained delegation for single sign-on** option. Below this option you need to enter the **Application SPN (Service Principal Name)**. The field is showing, by default, a wildcard **SPN: http/*** . This is actually a more convenient way to define your SPN, as it will match any application host name. However, this wildcard SPN can only be used if you defined your application addresses, on the **Web Servers** tab, by using host names or FQDNs. If, however, you used IP addresses to define your application address, you cannot take advantage of a wildcard SPN and must manually enter the specific SPN for your backend web server here.

There are some special behaviors and nuances here that need to be explained:

With the current UAG version, for most of the UAG application templates, when you select the **Use Kerberos constrained delegation for single sign-on** option, the **Select authentication servers** the list becomes grayed out. This makes sense, since when using KCD, the authentication is done based on the repository that was used for trunk authentication, by UAG performing protocol transition from whatever that repository is (for example, Active Directory or RADIUS), and obtaining a Kerberos ticket on behalf of the user. However, for SharePoint applications, the **Select authentication servers** list is not grayed out when selecting to use KCD for SSO to this application.

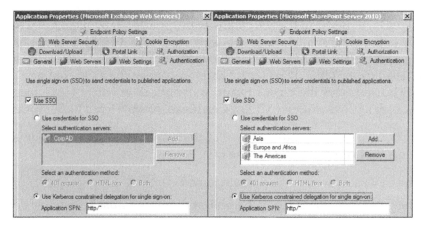

In either case, whether the **Select authentication servers** list becomes grayed out or not, whatever repositories were included in that list will change, once you close the **Application Properties** window. The UAG Management console will automatically replace any and all repositories there with **the first repository** appearing in the **Select authentication servers** list of the trunk (as seen in the **Advanced Trunk Configuration** window, on the **Authentication** tab). Here is an example—this is how the **Authentication** tab of the **Application Properties** window looks when KCD is just being configured for this application:

Here is how the same tab looks, after closing the **Application Properties** window and opening it again. As you can see, the very first repository in the **Select authentication servers** list of the trunk (on the left of the screenshot) has replaced all the repositories appearing in the **Select authentication servers** list of the application (on the right of the screenshot)

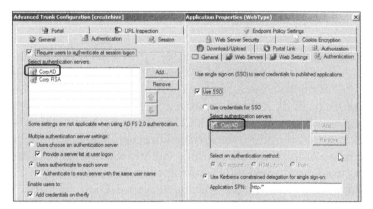

Another setting that you need to be paying attention to is how to indicate to UAG which Active Directory it should use in order to obtain a Kerberos ticket for the user. This is a "no-brainer" for UAG, in the case that your trunk front end authentication is done against a repository of type *Active Directory*. However, one of the nice use cases for KCD is authenticating users at the trunk scope with a repository which is not AD, for example RADIUS or SecurID, and the performing "protocol transition" to Kerberos. This transition involves UAG accessing an AD, but the question is: which one? The answer lies in the setting that exists on any UAG repository, labeled **Use a different server for portal application authorization**. Yes, we know—the label is a bit confusing, as here we are not talking about authorization. The reason that this is the text next to this option is historical: the option's initial purpose was indeed authorization, and only later in the product life, in IAG 2007 Service Pack 2, to be more specific, the usage of this option was extended also for the KCD scenario, but the UI text was not changed to reflect this.

But we're digressing. The point we're trying to make is that, when you are configuring UAG to use a non-AD repository for trunk authentication, if you plan to also use KCD in order to achieve single sign-on to some of the backend applications of this trunk, you need to enable the **Use a different server for portal application authorization** setting. Then, from the Select server drop-down list, choose the relevant Active Directory repository.

Once you have completed the settings discussed previously, you will also need to configure your Active Directory to enable delegation and to trust the UAG server for this task. UAG offers two methods of exporting the required Active Directory configuration settings. Both of these are available from the **Admin** menu of the UAG Management console, using the **Export KCD Settings to Active Directory...** option. When you click this menu option, the **Active Directory Delegation** window opens and displays a recap of the required settings, mainly the applications server's SPNs. Note that if you used a wildcard SPN in the application properties' KCD definition, UAG will automatically generate the specific SPNs based on the application servers' host names or FQDNs. In this window you can choose whether to **Export settings to an LDIF file** or **Export settings to a text file**. If you wonder what the difference is between the two, an **LDIF** file, or **LDAP Data Interchange Format** file, can be used to automatically configure the AD settings required for UAG delegation, by using the **LDIFDE** utility. However, many Active Directory administrators are anxious about running such automated tools on their AD server, and probably rightfully so. For these chaps, the second option, where KCD settings are exported from UAG to a plain text file might be the preferable solution. The text file can serve as an "aide-memoire", so you can manually perform the required configuration.

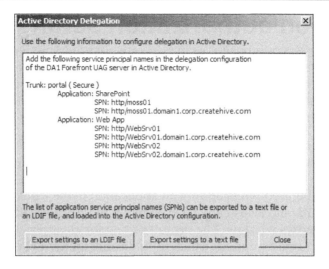

If the delegation configuration is performed manually on the AD, then the settings required are these: on the UAG server computer **Properties** window, on the Delegation tab, the setting **Trust this computer for delegation to specified services only** must be selected, as well as the **Use any authentication protocol** option. The list of Services to which this account can present delegated credentials must include all the application servers that UAG will use KCD for (as can be seen in the **Active Directory Delegation** window of the UAG console). Here is an example of such a configuration:

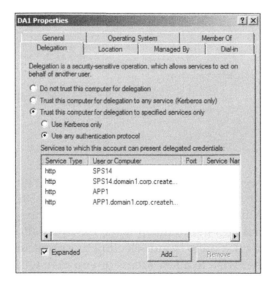

Application authorization settings

Authentication servers or repositories in UAG are not used only for performing front end authentication (meaning the trunk logon process) or backend authentication (meaning the process of UAG providing credentials to backend applications on behalf of the user). Another usage for repositories is the ability to configure authorization settings per application.

For any application published through a UAG trunk, you have the option of deciding which users can gain access to the application. This is true for all trunk applications, of all categories—built-in services, web, client/server, and so on. These settings can be configured while adding an application to the trunk through the **Add Application Wizard**, and also at any later point, on the **Authorization** tab of the **Application Properties** window. The default setting for all applications is **Authorize all users**, with only one exception, which is publishing the UAG **Web Monitor** as a built-in service. The Web Monitor is the only application where the **Authorize all users** setting is not enabled by default and it is up to you to select it, or to specify which users and groups you wish to allow access to this application. What does **Authorize all users** mean? It does not mean that anyone with a browser and an internet connection can gain access to this specific application via UAG, of course. This setting means that any user that can gain access to the UAG trunk itself, can also access this application. So, in the vast majority of cases, since trunks are using authentication, the **Authorize all users** setting can be interpreted as to authorize all authenticated trunk users.

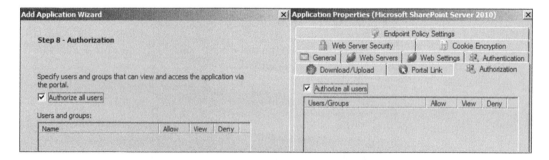

Assuming that at least for some of the trunk's applications you would want to be more specific with regards to who is allowed to access some applications and who is not, you will have to un-check the **Authorize all users** setting. This will enable the **Users and groups** list and the buttons under it and the **Add** button. This is exactly the button that you need to click on to begin selecting those specific users or groups of users to which you either wish to allow access or you may wish to specifically deny access.

When you click the **Add** button, the **Select users and Groups** window opens. Here, the first selection you need to make is in the **Look in** drop-down list, which contains all the repositories that are defined on the UAG server, as well as an additional resource named **Local Groups**, which we will discuss a bit later.

From this list you should select the repository which contains the specific users or groups you are interested in. If the repository is of type Active Directory, the list in the **Users and Groups in Repositories** section of the window will be populated with well, users and groups that UAG was able to find on that specific server.

From here on, you just need to dig in through the different folders, groups and individual users that are shown in this list, and select the ones you wish to add.

 Note that you can also use the **Search** text box in the middle of the window with the adjacent search button (it has a picture of a magnifier and a person), to quickly find a security group or user.

Once you locate what you need, just click on the **Add** button to add this user or group to the **Selected Users and Groups** on the lower part of the window. Note that you can mix and match users and groups from different repositories.

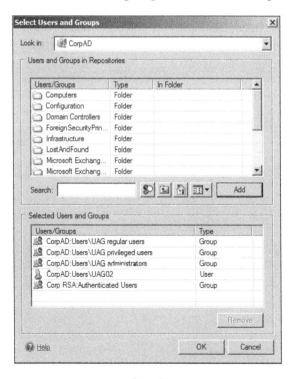

Before we close this window with **OK** and return to the **Authorization** tab or wizard step (depending on where you started from), let's discuss what happens when your users are authenticating against a repository that is not an Active Directory or RADIUS (UAG cannot extract any group and user information from other types of repositories).

You have two options for these kinds of repositories: the first one is the straightforward option—all UAG repositories have an implicit group named **Authenticated Users**. This group includes any user that is currently logged on to a UAG trunk and who has authenticated successfully against this repository.

However, what if you wish to be more restrictive and only allow access to *some* users? In this case you can choose the second option: for those repositories that do not have groups or UAG cannot extract group and user information from, you can define the **Use a different server for portal application authorization** option. By doing this, when you select such a repository for authorization in the **Select users and Groups** window, UAG displays the users and groups it extracts from the *different server* you defined and you can choose from those. For example, let's say that your trunk authentication is performed against an RSA SecurID authentication server. If you configure this repository to use an AD repository for authorization, when you select the SecurID server from the **Look in** drop-down list of the **Select users and Groups** window, you will actually receive the AD users and groups in the **Users and Groups in Repositories** section of the window. Obviously, in order for UAG to be able to match the user's SecurID credentials and his Active Directory account, the username must be the same in both the SecurID and the AD repositories.

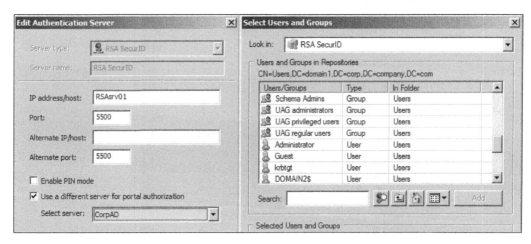

Once you have selected the desired users and groups and they are displayed on the **Authorization** tab or the **Application Properties** window, you can now proceed to set the authorization rules for these users. There are three options that you can choose from:

- **Allow** — probably quite self explanatory: The user or group is allowed access to the application. This option automatically includes the "*View*" right.

- **Deny** — just as self explanatory: The user or group is not allowed access to the application. The application link will not be displayed to this user or group on the UAG portal homepage

- **View** — if you decide to assign to some of the portal users the "*View*" right, they will only be able to view the application link displayed in the portal homepage but they are not allowed access to this application. This is not done just to spite your users. When these users click on the application link or launch it from the portal's toolbar *Run Application* button, they will be presented with the *on-the-fly login* page, asking them for some credentials to one of the repositories you have used in the Authorization settings of this application, so that they can gain access to the application. The logic is that some users may log on to the trunk with less privileged credentials, which allow them access to only a subset of the published applications, but they may provide another set of credentials in order to be allowed to access all portal applications. This logic can also be applied to achieve "*step-up authentication*" with UAG. For example, users log on to the trunk with AD credentials and are allowed access to some applications but, when clicking on the link to the more sensitive applications, due to the authorization settings on those, they will be presented with the on-the-fly login page so that they can provide their RSA one-time password.

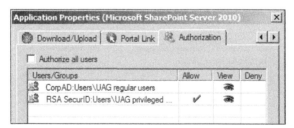

Local groups

Local groups, as the name indicates, are just a UAG grouping of users and groups, meant to provide you an easy way to apply the same authorization settings to multiple applications. Since authorization is performed per application, if you have a rather long list of users and groups you need to authorize, you have to repeat the selection of all these for each application. Instead of doing that you can just perform the selection once, save it as a *local group* and then use this group in each application authorization settings. You can create a *local group* by clicking the **Save As Local Group** button in the **Authorization** tab of an **Application Properties** window, after you have already populated the list of user and groups in that window. Pay attention though to the fact that a *local group* does not store the **Allow**, **View**, and **Deny** authorization settings. A *local group* only stores the users and groups in the original selection as one single entity, which you can then reuse, and to which you can apply a single **Allow**, **View**, or **Deny** authorization settings.

Another method to create a local group is to launch the **Local Groups** window from the UAG Management console's **Admin** menu, at the **Portal Application Authorization** option. Here you can also edit existing local groups.

Note that you can embed existing local groups in the definition of new local groups, and obviously, mix and match local groups with "real" (domain) groups and users. By default, any entry in the **Add Local Group** or **Edit Local Group** (which is the same window, just titled differently) list is included in the group. If, for whatever reason, you wish to exclude an entry from the group without actually removing it, you can click on the entry, in the **Include/Exclude** column, and toggle between its **Include** and **Exclude** status.

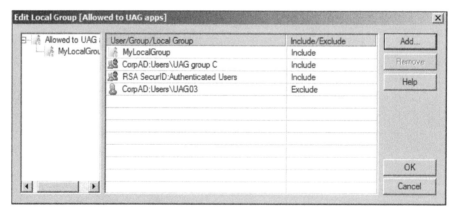

AD FS 2.0

Service Pack 1 for UAG adds an important feature to the authentication options available in UAG – support for Active Directory Federation Services version 2.0 (AD FS 2.0). We will not explain here what AD FS is and how it should be used, since this is an extensive topic which could easily justify an entire book. If you're planning to use AD FS authentication with UAG, you probably already have at least *some* knowledge of AD FS, and if not, we recommend you get acquainted with it. For those of you who are not familiar with Active Directory Federation Services, we'll briefly mention that AD FS is an identity federation solution in Windows Server. Originally introduced in Windows Server 2003, AD FS has been improved and extended in Windows Server 2008, and just recently AD FS v2.0 has been released, which adds even more functionality, now supporting the **WS-Trust**, **WS-Federation** and the **Security Assertion Markup Language (SAML)** federation protocols. AD FS provides single-sign-on to web applications by means of sharing **claims**, which are digital identity and entitlement rights. The great benefit of AD FS is the ability to share these claims, and therefore achieve SSO, across security and enterprise boundaries. This effectively allows seamless authentication and access to web applications for users that are members of, and may be located in completely different networks and organizations other than the organization hosting the application. In AD FS terminology, the organization owning and maintaining the users' accounts is referred to as the **account organization**, while the organization (typically, another company or organization) owning the resources accessed over the Internet is the **resource organization**. In a federated environment, two or more organizations can each manage their own user accounts and identities, without the need to replicate them by creating shadow accounts, in order to allow access to each other's resources over the internet. For more information about AD FS 2.0, visit the following link: `http://technet.microsoft.com/en-us/library/adfs2(WS.10).aspx`.

Requirements and limitations for AD FS 2.0 in UAG

Before you embark on the AD FS implementation journey, you should take note of the following requirements:

- It probably goes without saying, but you need an AD FS 2.0 server in your organization. This may be a dedicated server, or it can be installed on any AD server in your organization.
- AD FS 2.0 can be used only on HTTPS trunks, not on HTTP trunks.

- A single AD FS 2.0 server can be used only by one single UAG trunk. If you have a need to use AD FS 2.0 authentication on more than one trunk, you need to use additional AD FS 2.0 servers.

- In some scenarios, some shadow accounts must be created. To be precise, this is required when you need UAG to perform SSO to backend web applications which are not "claims-aware", therefore requiring UAG to use Kerberos constrained delegation or NTLM.

- In the most common scenarios, UAG and AD FS are used to allow access to so-called "partner-employees", meaning users of the account organization, to resources residing within your organization (the *resource organization*). In such scenarios, the partner organization too needs to implement a federation server, which must support SAML 2.0 tokens.

- A federation trust relationship must be established between the two federation servers, in the two organizations. Your AD FS 2.0 server must be added as a **relying party** (which means a web application or service that consumes Security Tokens issued by a **Security Token Service**.) on the federation server of the partner organization, while the partner federation server must be added as a **trusted claims provider** on your own AD FS 2.0 server.

- The domain suffix in the UAG portal trunk's public host name (for example, *createhive.com is the suffix for portal.createhive.com*) must be the same as the domain suffix defined for your AD FS 2.0 server (for example, *sts.createhive.com*), and the common name in the certificates used by both servers must match too. In addition, the public host name of the AD FS 2.0 application defined on the UAG server must be identical to the Federation Server name defined on the AD FS 2.0 server.

- Here are some limitations that you should be aware of when using AD FS:

- When using AD FS 2.0 for trunk or application authentication, this must be the only authentication method for the trunk or application. You cannot use other authentication methods in combination with AD FS 2.0

- You cannot use an HTTP to HTTPS Redirect trunk for a trunk that uses AD FS 2.0 authentication – it has to be "pure" HTTPS.

- It is not supported to publish web applications residing on the AD FS 2.0 server itself (but then again, why would you host a web application on your AD FS server, which may very well also be your AD server?)

- UAG only supports the *WS-Federation Passive* protocol, also referred to as *Web (passive) Requestors*, meaning web browsers.

Configuring the AD FS 2.0 authentication server in UAG

Adding an AD FS 2.0 authentication repository to your trunk is an easy task, comprised of just a few wizard-led steps. From the **Admin** menu, launch **the Authentication and Authorization Servers** dialog, and click **Add** in order to create a new authentication repository for your UAG box or array. In the **Add Authentication Server** window, select AD FS 2.0 as the **Server type** and give this repository a name of your choice. Next, in the **Federation Metadata** section of the window, you need to configure UAG from where to obtain the federation metadata of your organization's AD FS 2.0 server. You can select to either provide a URL which points to this XML file (residing on the AD FS 2.0 server itself), or you may have copied this file to the UAG server, and can import it directly.

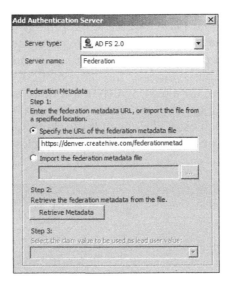

The next step is to click the **Retrieve Metadata** button, which will cause UAG to read the configuration from the XML file. If you are importing it from a URL, it will typically be an HTTPS URL, so make sure it is trusted by UAG. If it's not, you will receive an error like this:

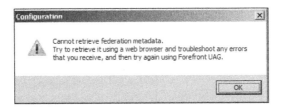

Unlike a browser, you cannot set UAG to ignore certificate issues with this URL, so just make sure it's nice and tight with regards to the usual certificate trust parameters (CN, CRL, trust chain, and so on)

Assuming that the SSL certificate used by the AD FS 2.0 server is trusted, clicking on the *Retrieve Metadata* button might generate another error:

This error refers to another certificate—the one used by the AD FS 2.0 server to sign the federation metadata file. You can either fix this issue, or choose to continue, which means that UAG should now be able to read the metadata file. Once the file has been read by UAG, the **Select the claim value to be used as lead user value** drop-down list should get populated with the values found in the metadata file. You need to select one of these values as the value that UAG will look for in the federation claims it receives for a user, which it will then use as the *"user name"* in the UAG Web Monitor. Your most obvious choice here would probably be something that uniquely identifies each user, like one of these claim types: "Name", "UPN", or "E-Mail Address". Make your selection and click OK to close the *Add Authentication Server* window.

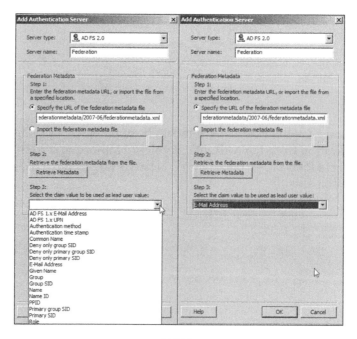

Once you configure a new trunk to use an AD FS 2.0 authentication repository, you should observe a few immediate changes on the trunk: the trunk's list of published applications will now show an application named *AD FS 2.0 - <repository name>* with an application type of *Active Directory Federation Services 2.0*. Another change which you may see (well, that is if you're curious enough to open the Advanced Trunk Configuration and take a peek at the Authentication tab) is that most of the options on the left side of this tab are now grayed out, and the **Realm** and **Federation Metadata** read-only fields at the bottom, in the **Federation Service** section, now show the actual URLs where this information can be found (usually they are grayed-out). Note that both of these resources are located on the UAG server, as we are now talking about the federation metadata of the UAG server.

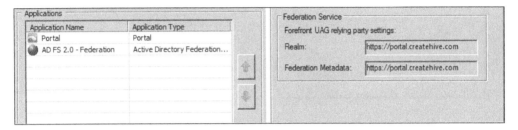

You are probably wondering, and rightfully so we might add, what this AD FS 2.0 application that has been *automagically* added to your trunk is. This is probably the place to explain the difference between how AD FS 2.0 authentication works with UAG, and all other authentication methods. As we have already explained, with any other authentication method except AD FS 2.0, UAG is the device that prompts the end-user for credentials, verifies them against the configured authentication repository, and if they are valid, then UAG allows the traffic to continue to backend resources. This does not apply to AD FS 2.0! In this case, UAG functions as an **AD FS proxy** server, but UAG does not validate the end-users' credentials, or the end-users' claims (for the "partner scenario", where partners are authenticated by a partner organization's federation server and then are supplied with federation claims which they present, through UAG, to your own organization's AD FS 2.0 server), by itself. In the case of AD FS 2.0 authentication, UAG relies on the existing AD FS infrastructure, meaning on the AD FS 2.0 server within your organization, in order to perform the authentication process and to provide the required claims required for SSO to backend claims-aware applications. Therefore, in order for UAG to be able to proxy the AD FS traffic between the client and the AD FS server, this AD FS 2.0 application is created in every trunk that utilizes AD FS 2.0.

The application's properties are created based on the information that UAG has received from the AD FS 2.0 federation metadata, including the federation's server's hostname, its address, paths, etc. Another automatic setting for this application is **Allow unauthenticated access to web server** (meaning to the AD FS 2.0 server), as seen on the **Authentication** tab of the Application Properties window.

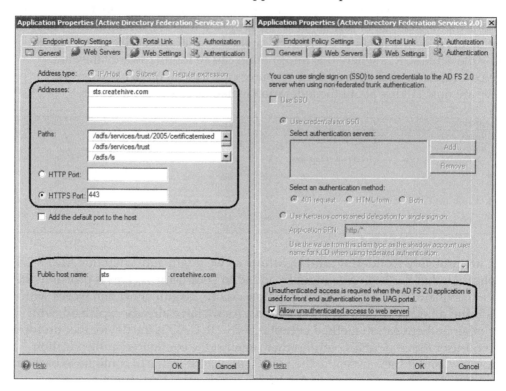

So how does UAG ensure that the AD FS 2.0 server has successfully authenticated the user? Glad you asked that! Let's discuss the flow of requests and responses in an AD FS scenario: the session starts by the end-user launching a browser and typing the URL of the UAG portal. Since UAG is configured for AD FS 2.0 authentication, it redirects the browser to the public host name of the AD FS 2.0 application (the one that was automatically added to the portal), in order for the AD FS server to authenticate the user. When the user reaches this server, they are presented with the **home realm discovery page**, where the user is asked to which organization they belong (remember that federation exists in order to allow users from multiple, different organizations, to authenticate just once, using their respective organization credentials, and then to access another organization's resources). Here, if the user selects a partner organization, they will be redirected to the partner federation server, a.k.a. **account federation server**, where they will have to pass authentication, be provided with a security token and then be redirected back to the AD FS 2.0 server (a.k.a. **resource federation server**). On the other hand, if the user is not a partner, but instead one of your organization's employees, they will select your own organization on the *home realm discovery page*, and then be requested to provide their domain credentials. Depending on the authentication method used by the AD FS 2.0 server, users may be transparently authenticated without any prompts, if the client machine is domain joined and the user is logged on with their domain account.

A note about the home realm discovery page: as soon as the AD FS 2.0 server accepts the end-user's authentication attempt, it sends a persistent cookie named **MSISIPSelectionPersistent** to the browser which stores the name of the domain that the end-user selected to authenticate to. Thus, on subsequent connection attempts, the AD FS 2.0 server **will not display the home realm discovery page** and instead will redirect the browser directly to the domain stored in the cookie. This cookie is stored by the browser for a certain amount of time, which can be configured in the `web.config` file found in the ...\adfs\ls folder on the AD FS 2.0 server, in an attribute named `lifetimeInDays`.

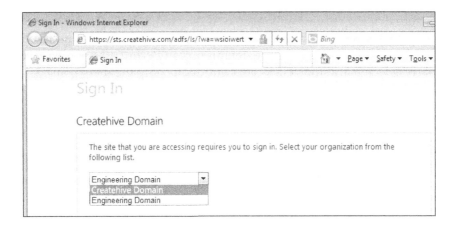

Once the user has successfully authenticated to his own domain, your own AD FS 2.0 server will now redirect the browser back to the UAG portal trunk, since the portal is the "entity" that initially redirected the browser to the AD FS 2.0 server. Here another federation trust relationship comes into play—the UAG server must be declared as a **relying party** on the AD FS 2.0 server. This will cause the AD FS 2.0 server to issue a security token for the UAG server, which will serve as proof to the UAG authentication mechanism that the user has successfully authenticated. Once that conclusion is reached, it can finally redirect the browser to the portal home page, or to whatever was the initial URL that started the session.

Additional configuration steps on the AD FS 2.0 server

As we just explained, one of the requirements for a successful AD FS 2.0 authentication is for the UAG server to be configured as a relying party on the AD FS 2.0 server. In order to do this, access the **AD FS 2. 0 Management** console on the AD FS 2.0 server, then, on the left side tree-view, open **AD FS 2.0 \ Trust Relationships** and right-click on **Relying Party Trusts** and select **Add Relying Party Trust** from the pop-up menu. In the **Add Relying Party Wizard**, on the **Select Data Source** step, choose **Import data about the relying party from a file** and enter the path to the UAG federation metadata XML file. This file resides on the UAG server, in the ...\`Microsoft Forefront Unified Access Gateway\von\InternalSite\ ADFSv2Sites\<trunk_name>\FederationMetadata\2007-06` folder. Alternatively, you can use **the Import data about the relying party published online or on a local network** and enter the URL which points to the same file. You can find the URL on the UAG portal trunk's Advanced Configuration window, on the Authentication tab, in the **Federation Metadata** field we mentioned earlier. However, note that this URL is built using the portal's public host name, which is not reachable from inside the network, where your AD FS 2.0 server is located. Therefore, if you want to use it, you need to ensure that the request will reach UAG's external NIC. Click Next to move to the next wizard step, enter a **Display name** of your choice as well as any **Notes**, if you desire. Click Next again, leave the default option **Permit all users to access this relying party** selected and then click Next until you complete the wizard.

An additional set of AD FS 2.0 server settings that you need to configure is to ensure that claim types and claim values that you are interested in will be passed by the AD FS 2.0 server to the UAG portal. Remember that, when configuring the AD FS 2.0 repository in the UAG Management console, you select a specific claim type (the UI refers to it as "claim value", but this is actually a *claim type*) whose value will be used by UAG as the session lead user. Therefore, you need to instruct the AD FS 2.0 server to look for this claim type in the information it receives either in claims issued by partners' federation servers, or in your organization's own AD (when authenticating your own users), and to pass over this information in the claims that this AD FS server will issue for UAG's consumption. An additional benefit that you can get from these rules is that you can filter out specific claims, as well as certain information specific claim values, so that they will not be sent onward by your AD FS 2.0 server in its own claims. You configure all of this in the AD FS 2.0 Management console, by right-clicking the UAG entry you just created in the *Relying Party Trusts* lists, and selecting Edit Claim Rules. Also remember to configure your **Active Directory** object, found in the **Claims Provider** trusts, to send the specific information that you wish to be included in claims.

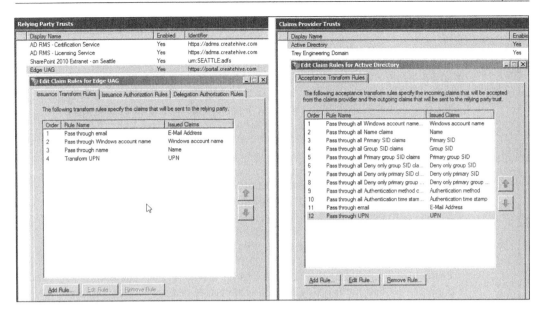

You can follow the AD FS 2.0 and the UAG TechNet documentation to configure rules that either **Transform an incoming claim** and rules that **Pass through or filter an incoming claim**. This is discussed in the following article: `http://technet.microsoft.com/en-us/library/gg274295.aspx`.

If UAG fails to receive the claim you have configured in the AD FS 2.0 repository as the lead user value, end users will receive a **Request cannot be completed. User details are missing** error in their browser. An entry will also be added to the UAG Web Monitor, describing which claim was not found. In such a case, revisit the claim rules on your AD FS 2.0 server, and on your partner's federation server, since the claim might not be sent by that server.

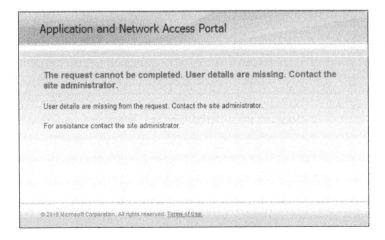

Finally, a tip for you: when using AD FS 2.0 through UAG SP1 and attempting to authenticate your own organization's users, the authentication may constantly fail. This can happen even though you are sure that the credentials provided are correct and that the user account is not locked. In such a case, here is what you should check: open *IIS Manager* on the AD FS 2.0 server, and on the tree view, navigate to the `Default Web Site\adfs\ls` folder. Here, double-click the **Authentication** icon, and then, if the **Windows Authentication** entry in the list of supported authentication methods is enabled, right-click it and open **Advanced Settings**. If **Extended Protection** is turned on, that is either **Accept** or **Required**, change it to **Off**. Restart IIS on the AD FS 2.0 server to ensure the new setting is applied, and then attempt to log on again from a client machine, through an AD FS 2.0 enabled UAG portal trunk. Our bet is that this time you will be successful. The reason for the failure has nothing to do with AD FS or with UAG. When **Extended Protection** is turned on, by default, this IIS feature checks the SSL connection Channel Binding Token, which does not work over reverse-proxies, as in the case of using UAG between the client browser and the IIS site on the AD FS 2.0 server.

Summary

Hopefully, by now, you have a better understanding of the great authentication, authorization, and single sign-on capabilities built into UAG. We realize that these are quite complex to grasp at the beginning, but if you start by using the most straightforward configuration settings, and then build on top of them more advanced requirements, we're confident you'll find the best setup that fits your organization's needs and requirements. In the next chapter, we will discuss the UAG client components and how to configure and customize them to your advantage.

7
Configuring UAG Clients

Until now, we have talked almost exclusively about UAG from the server's perspective, but UAG's client components are not less important. The client components are what the end-user sees, and they control the user's access to the portal and applications, so it's important to understand how they work, and what they can and cannot do.

What are the client components?

The UAG client components are a group of programs that are automatically installed on computer clients that connects to the UAG portal. The client components serve three major functions:

- They perform **endpoint detection**, so that the endpoint policies can be enforced
- They contain the **SSL tunneling components**, which allow **non-web applications** to work, as well as the **Network Connector**
- They contain the **Endpoint Session Cleanup component**, which cleans up the user's system after a session has ended

The various components are managed by the **Component Manager**. It is the first component that is installed, and it is in charge of downloading, installing, and managing all the others.

Endpoint detection

Endpoint detection is probably the most important security feature of UAG, and the client components are vital for it to work. When the user accesses the UAG portal, even before logging in, the client components are initialized, and perform a scan of the user's system. The scan collects a large amount of information about the computer, and compiles a table of values. This table is then sent to the server, which evaluates the **Endpoint Policies** set for the trunk, the portal and the applications, to determine the access level that will be provided for the user.

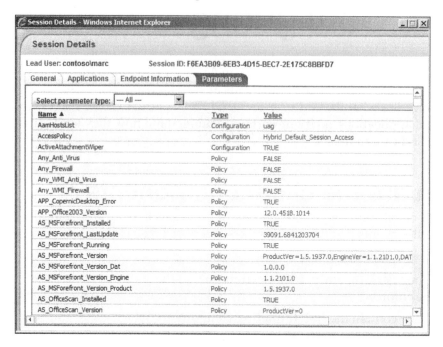

We will discuss endpoint policies in *Chapter 8*, but to put it briefly, access policies contain a list of conditions that are evaluated, and conclude with a logical "True" or "False". For example, a policy may say **McAfee anti-virus is installed and running and the computer is running Windows XP Professional**. The actual policy text uses Boolean logic keywords such as **AND** and **OR**, as well as parentheses, to allow us to build complex policies that accommodate for various conditions; so in this case, the policy will actually look like this:

```
((((System_OS_WinXPPro))) AND (((AV_McAfee_Installed AND
AV_McAfee_Running)))))
```

Why so many parentheses, you ask? Well, the above policy was automatically generated, and designed to accommodate other checks (for the Windows Service Pack level, as well as the AV's update status), so the original expression is longer and requires some more Boolean logic. You can see the full policy in the following screenshot:

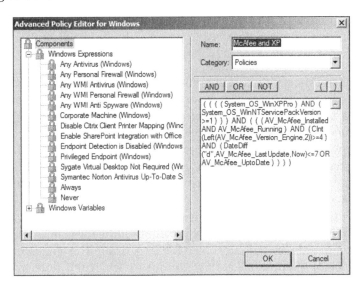

The policies are applied at three levels:

- The Trunk level
- The Portal level
- The Application level

Policies applied at the Trunk level will be enforced before the user logs on, and if the computer does not meet them, the user will not even reach the login page. The Portal level policy may prevent a user from visiting the portal after login, and the application-level policies may block access to some or all of the applications themselves.

Depending on which policies are set at each level, they may affect not only the ability to access, but also to perform functions. For applications, for example, there is a separate policy setting for **access**, **download**, and **upload**. The benefit of this is that the organization can have a certain policy to grant or prevent launching and using an application, but have a stricter policy for "upload", to make sure that a user from a less-secure system is unable to upload potentially dangerous files.

SSL Application Tunneling component

The SSL Application Tunneling component was known simply as the **SSL Wrapper** with UAGs predecessors. This component is the component in charge of establishing the tunnel between the client machine and the UAG server. This tunnel is established within the context of an authenticated UAG session, ensuring that only authenticated clients can take advantage of the SSL VPN tunnel. When the UAG session terminates, for whatever reason (for example, session timeout due to inactivity), the SSL VPN tunnel is terminated as well.

A second responsibility of this component is to download, via the tunnel, the specific tunneling settings for the Client/Server or browser-embedded application for which it is being launched. These settings configure the SSL Application Tunneling to operate in one of several modes it supports (more about this soon), as well as inform the component which client-side executable should it launch (for example: MSTSC.exe, for remote desktop connection) and what, if any, run-time configuration changes should the component perform in order to cause the client application to send its traffic into the SSL Application Tunneling listener. The run-time configuration settings that the SSL Application Tunneling might need to perform could be a **HOSTS** file change, a **registry** setting modification, an INI file edit, or launching the client-side executable, batch file or script with some **command line arguments**. Which of the possible configurations to perform is determined based on the client application that is being published. Whatever method is used, the reason is the same mentioned above: have the client application use the SSL Application Tunneling's listener.

Another responsibility of this component is to establish a **listener** on the client machine. This listener serves as the "entrance" into the SSL VPN tunnel. Once traffic is received, the SSL Application Tunneling **encrypts** it using SSL and sends it through the tunnel to the UAG server. The listener will use a loopback address (in the range of 127.0.0.X) and a port that depends on the method under which the SSL Application Tunneling is functioning. These modes are:

- **Simple relay**: In this mode, the listener is established on a random **loopback** address, and the **port** on which the SSL Application Tunneling listens is generally the same port the real application server listens on. For example, if you publish **Telnet** using SSL Application Tunneling, where the backend Telnet server uses port 23, then the SSL Application Tunneling's listener is established on a random loopback IP address, such as 127.0.0.116, and the listener's port is 23.

- **HTTP Proxy**: If the client application supports the use of an HTTP proxy, the SSL Application Tunneling component configures the client dynamically, at run-time, to use the SSL Application Tunneling listener as its HTTP proxy. This is preferable to using the simple relay method, since this allows the SSL Application Tunneling to support applications that *change* their traffic from one port to another during their session. The SSL Application Tunneling listener, in this configuration, is established on the 127.0.0.1:10081 IP / port combination.

- **SOCKS Proxy**: This method is similar to HTTP proxy, and is used for those clients that are capable to utilize such a type of proxy. In this configuration, the SSL Application Tunneling listener is established on the 127.0.0.1:1081 IP / port combination.

With UAG's predecessors, in the days where the predominant client Operating Systems were **Windows XP** and older systems, the SSL Application Tunneling component was used to achieve tunneling for quite a large number of applications. However, starting with **Windows Vista**, and continuing on to **Windows 7**, the SSL Application Tunneling component's ability to make changes to HOSTS file and to the Windows Registry on client computers is greatly reduced (in fact, it's very rarely possible for it to make these changes, so we can pretty-much consider this to be irrelevant from any practical perspective), due to the introduction of the browser's **Integrity levels**. As a result, the SSL Application Tunneling is not used anymore as a stand-alone tunneling component on Windows with Internet Explorer, and instead tunneling is achieved by using both the SSL Application Tunneling and the Socket Forwarding component, which we will discuss next.

The SSL Application Tunneling component is available both as an **ActiveX** based component and as a **Java-based** component, so it can be used on multiple platforms. We'll have more about that later.

Socket Forwarding

The Socket Forwarding component is an add-on, functioning *together* with the SSL Application Tunneling component. The Socket Forwarding component comprises two Windows Winsock modules: the **Layered Service Provider (LSP)** and the **Namespace Service Provider (NSP).** Once installed on a client machine, these two modules work together, transparent both to the end-user and to the application itself, by intercepting the traffic generated by the client application and redirecting it to the SSL Application Tunneling listener. This means that instead of the SSL Application Tunneling component reconfiguring the system to make the application send traffic to it, the Socket Forwarder "grabs" the traffic, and forwards it to the listener.

Note that the SSL Application Tunneling component is still responsible for establishing and maintaining the SSLVPN tunnel, for launching the client application, for SSL encrypting the traffic that reaches its listener and then sending it through the tunnel to the UAG server, and receiving the returning traffic from it. The SSL Application Tunneling is using its SOCKS proxy mode when working in combination with the Socket Forwarding component.

When using the Socket Forwarding component, the SSL Application Tunneling component is relieved of the need to make any configuration changes to connecting client applications. The client application "believes" it is communicating with its server, while in fact the UAG NSP performs a **dummy name resolution** of the server name, and the UAG LSP intercepts the traffic and directs it to the SSL Application Tunneling listener. Therefore, the current logged on user on the client machine does not require any special rights in order to be able to use Socket Forwarding (however, "power user" rights are necessary in order to install the Socket Forwarding component). Another advantage of this method is that it allows using a much wider range of applications, even those that use multiple servers, or where the servers are defined by IP address, etc. As mentioned before, for Windows Vista and newer client operating systems, the vast majority of UAG applications are using Socket Forwarding. The only exception to these is the **legacy TS Client Tunneling (Windows Vista/Windows XP)** application template, which still uses the SSL Application Tunneling component only, because it's easy to configure the Remote Desktop client to send traffic directly to the SSL Application Tunneling component, with no need to make problematic changes to the operating system itself.

Socket Forwarding is only available as an ActiveX control, and there is no Java counterpart currently, which means that applications that require it cannot operate on non-IE browsers or non-Windows platforms.

SSL Network Tunneling component

UAG's Application Tunneling achieves full **VPN**-like connectivity by using its SSL Network Tunneling capability. As described in chapter 5, there are actually two distinct methods used for this, depending on the client OS: for Windows 7 clients, UAG introduces the use of **SSTP**, while for Windows Vista and previous operating systems, the legacy **Network Connector (NC)** is used. In either case, the basic tunneling component—**the SSL Application Tunneling**—is still used. The SSL Application Tunneling component makes the decision, based on the client OS, whether to launch the Windows 7 built-in SSTP connection component, or to launch UAG's Network Connector.

In the context of this chapter, which discusses UAG components downloaded, installed and launched on client machines in order to achieve SSL VPN tunneling, SSL Network Tunneling refers to UAG's legacy Network Connector. On the client machine, the Network Connector SSL Network Tunneling components are comprised of a Windows service and a **virtual network device**. When the NC application is launched from the UAG portal homepage, a **virtual NIC** is created on the client machine and it is assigned an IP address from the pool of IP addresses configured on the server side. The SSL Network Tunneling then modifies the client machine's routing table so that all corporate destinations traffic (if the Network Connector Server is configured for **split tunneling**) or all traffic (if the configuration is for **non-split tunneling**) will be routed to the virtual NIC's IP address. Once traffic is received by the virtual NIC, it is sent to the SSL Application Tunneling listener, which, similarly to the other tunneling methods, overlays it with SSL and sends it through the tunnel to the UAG server.

Endpoint Session Cleanup component

The Endpoint Session Cleanup component enhances security by cleaning up files that have been downloaded by the user during a UAG session. If, for example, a user opened a document from a UAG-protected site, we wouldn't want it to be cached locally and available to others who may access the computer later. To this end, the endpoint session cleanup components goes through the browser's cache at the end of a session, and looks for files that have been cached during the session. If it finds any, it deletes them securely (in a manner that does not allow the files to be recovered with standard file recovery techniques). The cleanup component can also be configured to wipe out saved (cached) passwords and browser history, as well as other, specific folders, if needed. It is even designed to perform this cleanup in extreme situations, to provide better security. For example, even if the user forcibly "killed" the browser, or even pulled the computer's power plug, the cleanup will do its job as soon as it can, upon the next reboot.

Supported platforms

To accommodate multiple operating systems and clients, the client components are available in two versions. One is based on ActiveX technology, and the other on Java. This allows UAG to support Windows platforms running Internet Explorer, but also the Firefox and Safari browsers running on Windows, and Firefox and Safari running on Macintosh, Linux 32 bit releases (**Red Hat**, **Fedora**, **Debian**, and **Ubuntu**). UAG can accept connections from additional platforms, such as mobile phones, but the client components are not supported for them.

For Windows-based systems, the client components support both 32 bit systems, as well as 64 bit Vista and Windows 7 systems, although for 64 bit systems, there are some limitations. The limitation is that for 64 bit systems, only 32 bit applications are supported. Wait—What!??! Well, that's how this works. This means that you can use SSL tunneling, but only for 32 bit code running in the WOW64 32-bit emulation system that 64 bit Windows systems have. In reality, this may mean you need to take special steps to enjoy the benefits. For example, if you want to use SSL Tunneling with Telnet on a 64 bit machine, then you will discover that it can't communicate, because the Windows Telnet client on 64 bit systems is 64 bit too. If, however, you download a 32 bit Telnet client, such as PuTTy, it can be used with SSL Tunneling flawlessly.

The complete support matrix for the various platforms and abilities is large and may change over time, so to verify compatibility with your requirements, visit the following link: `http://technet.microsoft.com/en-us/library/dd920232.aspx`.

If a client that does not support all the portal applications connects to the portal, some applications may appear greyed out, while others may be completely hidden. For example, applications that are based on the SSL Application Tunneling component will be greyed out if the portal is accessed from a non-supported operating system, such as a mobile phone.

Installing and uninstalling the client components

A great feature of UAG is the automatic installation of the client components. Once a client launches the portal URL, the server detects if the current version of the client components is installed, and installs them, or upgrades them to the current version. Changes to the client components may require the browser to be restarted, and if this is the first time the components are installed, the user's computer may have to be restarted as well.

Three important facts to keep in mind about the client component installation are:

- When connecting to the portal, only the *basic* set of client components are installed, and these do not include the SSL Application and Network Tunneling components. This means that if the user launches an application that requires one of these components, only then will it be installed. The additional installation may also require the browser or the computer to be restarted.

- The installation procedure registers several executables on the computer, and since this is initialized from inside the browser, this requires administrative privileges. If your users normally log-on as non-administrative users, then the client installation cannot succeed, and may end up with a corrupt installation. In case your users are indeed non-admins, make sure the installation is performed by an Administrator when initially accessing the portal. If that is not possible for some reason, you may be able to overcome this by some manual installation techniques that are discussed later.

An administrator can configure the UAG server to always install the additional components automatically on every client, as part of the default installation. This procedure is considered to be a customization, and is beyond the scope of this book. It is not currently documented as part of UAGs official documentation, but it is described for UAGs predecessor, IAG, at the following link: `http://technet.microsoft.com/en-us/library/dd277980.aspx`.

The procedure for UAG is identical.

Once installed, the client components can remain installed indefinitely, and they pose no threat to the system, nor do they impact performance. When fully installed, the client components occupy about 2.5 MB of disk space, so that should not be a problem either. If, for some reason, the components need to be removed, this can be done from the **Add/Remove programs** | **Control Panel** item, or from the System Information page that can be called by pressing the appropriate icon on the UAG toolbar.

It can also be done using an automation script by locating the uninstall string in the registry's uninstall branch:

`HKLM\SOFTWARE\Microsoft\Windows\CurrentVersion\Uninstall`

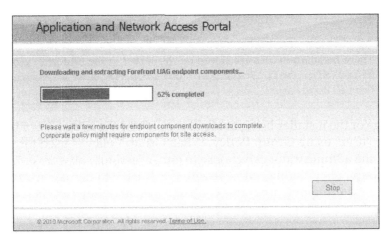

Preemptive installation of the components

Some organizations need to deploy the client components **pre-emptively**. One reason for this might be that the organization's users are not administrative users on their own computer, which would prevent them from installing the client components upon entering the portal. A different reason might be that the organization prefers that the client has all the components installed, rather than have the users be required to wait for the installation process when additional components are required.

Regardless of the reasons, UAG includes a pre-packaged version of the client components in the form of an **MSI** file. In fact, there are no less than five different versions of the pre-packaged installer:

- Basic
- Network Connector
- Network Connector Only
- Socket Forwarder
- All

The basic version is similar to the one that's automatically installed when a user first accesses the portal. The Network Connector is similar to the Basic, but also includes the Network Connector component. The Network Connector Only does not have any components other than the Network Connector, and the Socket Forwarder version has the basic components and the Socket Forwarder. Typically, when there is a need to install the components pre-emptively, it would be best to install the All version, which guarantees a hassle free experience for the user, with no future need to install additional pieces. Each of these installation files are similarly sized at approximately 3 MBs.

 These installation files are stored on the server in the folder: `C:\Program Files\Microsoft Forefront Unified Access Gateway\von\ PortalHomePage`

An advantage of the installer being available as an MSI file is that it can be distributed to users using **Group Policy**. When Group Policy is used for software distribution, the administrator can choose to either "assign" software or "Publish" software. Group Policy "Published" software is available to domain users through the **Windows Add/Remove programs** control panel, and they can choose to install it with the click of a button, without the trouble of trying to locate an installation source. Group Policy "assigned" software is automatically installed on a computer that logs on to the domain. The process of using Group Policy to distribute software is detailed here: `http://support.microsoft.com/kb/816102`.

An additional advantage of using MSI is that the installation (and un-installation) can be launched in "Silent" mode, without user intervention, or even without user knowledge, if that is desired. However, since UAG users are typically home users, connecting from their personal computers, Group Policy distribution may not be possible, unless these computers are domain-joined and the users employ some VPN technology. We are sure you wouldn't want all your users bringing in their virus-laden antiques from home, right?

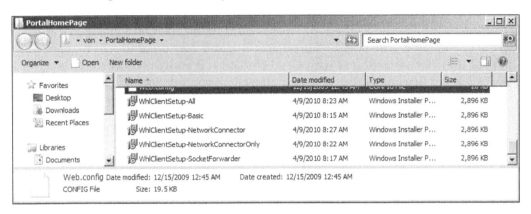

Checking the client components version

Sometimes, it is useful to know exactly which of the endpoint components are installed on a computer, and what version any of them is at. To do so, the UAG toolbar has a **system information** button, which shows this information as well as some of the information detected by the components. This information includes:

- The Anti Virus that has been detected, its version and update status.
- The Personal Firewall detected and its version.
- The operating system, version and service-pack level
- The browser version and the full user-agent string
- The Java Runtime version
- The computer's domain membership
- An indication of whether the computer is a certified and privileged endpoint

On a daily basis, this information is not particularly useful, but in case of a failed detection (which would typically lead to a user not receiving the level of access he is supposed to), it could be very significant.

Another useful part of the information screen is the three action buttons on the top-right. The left-most button allows you to delete the user-defined **trusted sites list** (more about this soon). The middle button allows the components settings to be reset, and the right button uninstalls the client components.

When the Socket Forwarding component is installed on a client, it will show two additional buttons next to it, which allow it to be temporarily disabled or enabled, and also uninstalled.

The following image shows the components that are installed on a client computer, and the version that is installed. This reflects an older version of the components (4.0.1152.100) that are included with UAG Update 1. If your server is running Update 2 or Service Pack 1, the version of the client components will be different.

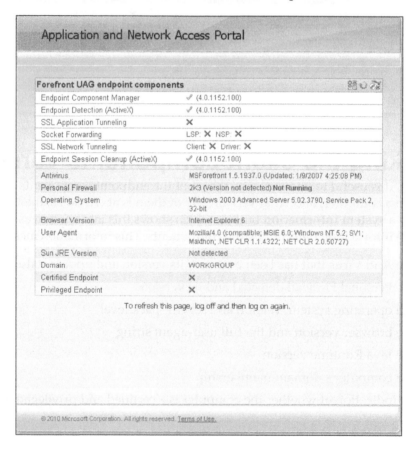

The trusted sites list

For security purposes, the UAG client detection component will not trust just any website that tries to launch it. This design is intended to prevent a potentially malicious website from launching the client components, and try to abuse them. When a user connects to a site, and the site launches the client components, the components check the list of trusted sites (which is *unrelated* to the list of trusted sites that Internet Explorer has), and if the site is not on the list, will warn the user and ask him whether to trust the site.

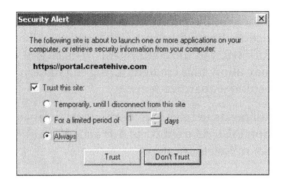

Unless the user has selected to trust the site, the detection component will not run. The user has the option of clearing the list of trusted sites using a button on the information screen that we discussed earlier.

 The settings are stored in the client computer's registry in this location: HKEY_CURRENT_USER\Software\WhaleCom\Client\CheckSite

An administrator can use the above registry key to automatically configure the user's computers to trust the organization's UAG site by creating a script that modifies the registry on the client's computers using Group Policy, a domain login script, or other automation techniques. Another aspect of managing this key is that it can be configured to set it to trust certain sites, but not prompt the user at all for others.

Don't need the Client components?

Some organizations will prefer to avoid using the client components altogether. There could be several possible reasons for this. For example, some organizations have policies that do not allow the installation of software, and can't or won't have the client components installed because of them. Other organizations allow the general public to access their sites, and prefer not to burden their visitors with installations. UAG can work fine without the client components, but disabling them brings about some limitations that need to be considered. In fact, when prompted to install the client components, the client can elect to not have them installed, and will still be able to use some of the portal's functionality. However, without the components, some functionality will be lost. For example, SSL Tunneling based applications cannot work without the components. The lack of the Endpoint Session Cleanup component may allow files created during the session to remain on the client machine, which could jeopardize security.

If your organization still needs to have the components disabled, this is done from the **Trunk Configuration** (also referred to as **Advanced Trunk Configuration**). To disable the components, follow these steps:

1. Open the **Advanced Trunk Configuration** window.
2. Switch to the **Session** tab.
3. Check **Disable component installation and activation**.

Once you check this option, a warning about the effects of disabling the components is shown:

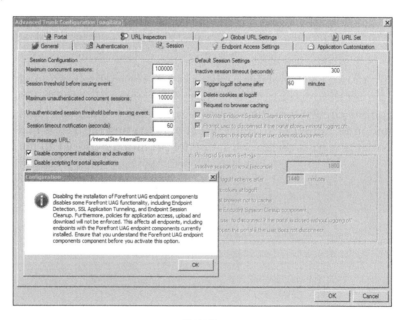

Summary

In this chapter, we talked about installing and uninstalling the client components, what components they contain and what does each component do. We also discussed compatibility of the clients and what can be achieved on various platforms. In the next chapter, we will go into details about the endpoint detection policy, and how it works together with the client components discussed here.

8
Endpoint Policies

Endpoint policies are touted as one of UAG's most important features. Indeed, the ability to enforce certain requirements and restrictions on endpoints can provide great protection from many threats for an organization's network. Furthermore, UAGs endpoint mechanism allows an incredibly detailed level of control, from simple operating system service pack level checks to custom scripts that can do almost anything. This chapter will discuss configuring policies.

What endpoint policies can do and how they work?

Endpoint policies in the UAG world are settings that an administrator can apply to UAG trunks, to published applications, and to the UAG portal (which is an application too, actually). These policies are a set of conditions that have to be met by the connecting client, in order to gain access to the object that is protected by the policy. The ultimate purpose of this is, of course, security, although this mechanism can also be used to enforce policies with other intentions, like compatibility verification.

The endpoint policies are configured on the UAG server, and are enforced by the endpoint detection component, which is part of the UAG client components. We discussed the detection component back in *Chapter 7*, and now it's time to understand how it works.

How it works?

When a client first accesses a UAG portal, the site redirects to an ASP page called `InstallAndDetect.asp`. This page launches `DMSERVICE`, which is the component manager of the client components. Assuming the client components are already installed, the **detection component** is launched. The detection component scans the user's computer and collects a long list of parameters, which are then sent back to the server. The list contains around 300 parameters, including the operating system version, the browser version, the name of the computer, the name of any antivirus and personal firewall software that it is running and much more.

When the server receives the parameter table, it reads the various endpoint policies that have been assigned to the UAG trunk and applications, and populates them with the appropriate values it collected. These values could be text strings, numbers, dates, or even blank data. The populated policy is then evaluated using Boolean logic, which returns a result of either **TRUE** or **FALSE** (Boolean 1 or 0). If the result is a TRUE, the policy is considered "passed", and the user is allowed access to the trunk. Otherwise, the user is shown an access denied page:

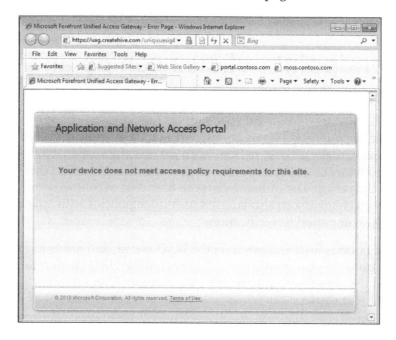

If the user has passed the trunk policy, he is redirected to the trunk login page. If the user logs in successfully (that is, has managed to remember his username and password), the server will grant him access to the portal (which is, as we said before, just another type of application from UAG's perspective), or whatever application is set as the **initial application**, based on the policies that have been evaluated earlier.

If the initial application is the portal, then the assigned policies can also affect the way it looks. According to the administrator's preference, some applications may be set to show as greyed-out if their policy is not met, and others may be set to be completely hidden if it isn't.

Why the three separate levels, you ask? Well, each of these three levels (trunk, portal, and application) may be assigned a different policy. Some organizations prefer blocking all policy-violators even before logging in ("trunk" level). Others prefer to be rather lax and allow access to the portal without any restrictions (other than a need for authentication, of course), but allow access to certain applications only to computers that meet certain guidelines. We always root for the extremely paranoid, of course, and recommend setting strict policies at every level, but your organization might have other considerations.

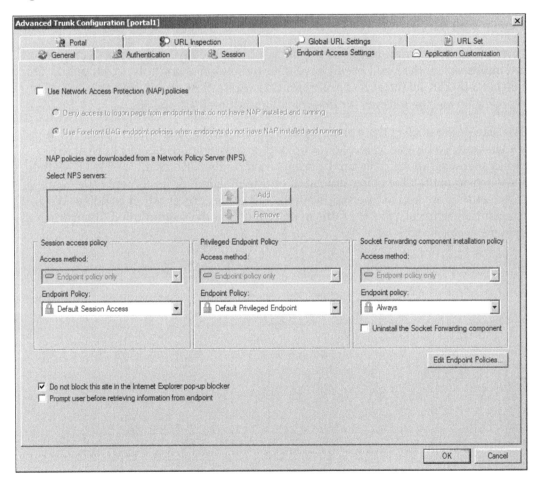

Endpoint policies access type

An endpoint policy is mostly used for controlling access—who can log in to the portal, and what applications users can launch, but it also can be used for more granular control. In addition to simply blocking a user's access to an application, applications that are published using the Web Application family of templates also allow an administrator to assign a policy for **download** and **upload** (a separate policy for each!). The idea is that downloading or uploading a file during a UAG session has more risks associated with it, and may require tighter security. For example, some organizations feel that it's OK for remote users to read their corporate e-mail using **Outlook Web Access (OWA)**, but opening **attachments** from their emails is not OK, because the users may save the files locally and thus expose the company to a data-leak. Other organizations feel that letting their users attach files to outgoing messages (which is a type of upload) is risky, as those files may contain malware.

In addition to the trunk-level access policy settings we saw earlier, applications that are published on the UAG portal have their own tab that controls access policy. On this tab, you can set the access policy for this application, and in case this is a Web App, it also has the settings for the upload and download policies.

The way policies affect the uploading and downloading is actually a bit tricky to understand. To be able to block and upload or download, UAG has to be able to detect such operations. This can be done based on the URL itself, the HTTP Method, the extension of the file being uploaded or downloaded, or its content type. Some of these settings are applied per-application, and some configuration is global. We will discuss the technical aspects of this in more detail in the section titled *Configuring upload and download settings*.

An additional access-level is the **Restricted-Zone policy**, which is designed to assign different (tighter, usually) access control to certain parts of an application. This can be used to enforce tighter security on an endpoint as a condition to allow it to access more sensitive parts of an application. For example, an administrator may want to let his users use some web application and only require that they run SOME antivirus program, but in order to access the part of the application that allows them to set options or change their password, their endpoint needs to be more secure by running a specific version of a specific antivirus product. In order to set this, the administrator needs to define which URLs would be considered "more sensitive", and we will discuss this in the section titled *Configuring restricted zone settings*.

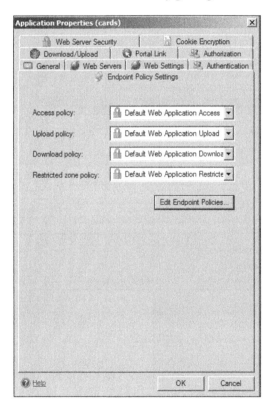

Platform specific policies

UAG supports clients running on multiple platforms, as you already know. In this spirit of open-arms, an administrator can even designate specific policies to each platform. This is particularly useful because other operating systems have different protection software, so the detection process needs to be relevant. Each endpoint policy is comprised of 4 sub-policies—for **Windows**, **MACs**, **Linux**, and **other**, which refers to anything else, including **cell phones**. We will discuss creating and editing the separate policies in more detail soon.

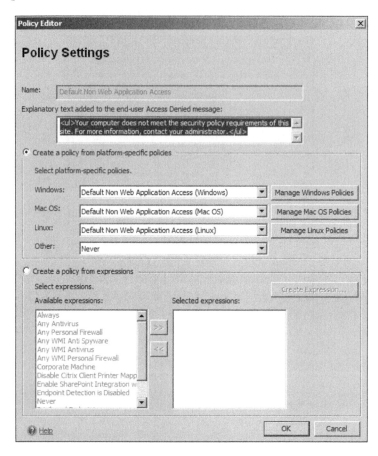

Assigning endpoint policies

Assigning endpoint policies is rather simple. Each application has an **Endpoint Policy Settings** tab, which can be configured during the **application-publishing wizard**, or edited later. On this tab, you select which of the available **Top-Level policies** you want to assign to **Access**, **Upload**, **Download**, and **Restricted Zone** (for the application types that have them). This tab also has a link to the **policy editor**, though UAG comes with a comprehensive set of built-in policies. At any point, you can edit the existing policies, create new ones, and change the assignment for each application. The trunk also has a policy setting tab, which is a little different. For a trunk, you assign only an access policy, but for three "levels":

- Session Access
- Privileged Endpoint
- Socket forwarding component installation

The **Session Access** is simple enough—users who do not meet the policy set there will be denied access as soon as the endpoint detection phase is complete upon launching the portal URL (this happens before the user has even a chance to login, but after the client component installation). The **Privileged Endpoint** policy is evaluated in addition to the Session Access policy. If a connecting computer passes both, it will be given higher privileges. If, however, it passes only the Privileged Endpoint policy, but not the access policy, it won't do it any good, and it will still be rejected from the portal.

> Privileged Endpoints are endpoints that receive 'special' treatment. No, UAG will not change the tires on your car for you, but privileged endpoints have separate session parameters that can be configured by the administrator. The idea here is that the privileged endpoint policy is more rigorous, and endpoints that comply with it would be secure, and so we can grant them longer time-outs, for example. More about this in *Chapter 10*!

Endpoints that meet the **Socket Forwarding Component installation policy** will be allowed to have that client component installed on them, if it is requested. If you remember from *Chapter 7*, by default, connecting clients only have the basic set of client components installed on them, but if the user launches an application that requires the **Socket Forwarding component**, UAG will automatically ask the component manager service to install it. The component manager will check if the client meets the policy set here before installing it. Why? Well, the socket forwarder integrates into the Windows networking components in a way that may conflict with other applications (this is known as an LSP or NPS conflict).

When this happens, the conflict can interrupt the traffic, and so the administrator may choose to avoid this risk by using this policy.

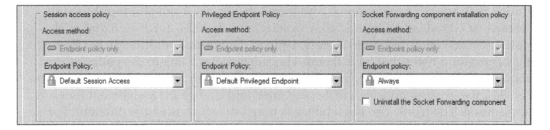

Built-in policies

Creating your own policy with UAG is not tough, as you will see soon, but nonetheless, the server comes with a nice and dandy set of policies that you can start using right away. The most common one is "**Default Web Application Access**", which is the one offered by default when publishing new web applications. On the application publishing wizard, it is offered with its accompanying sisters "**Default Web Application Upload**", "**Default Web Application Download**" and "**Default Web Application Restricted Zone Access**". What do these policies do? Let's pop the hood and take a peek!

1. On your main trunk, click on **Configure** next to **Configure Trunk Settings**.

2. Switch to the **Endpoint Access Settings** tab.

3. Click **Edit Endpoint Policies**.

4. Click on any policy (doesn't matter which).

 It doesn't matter, because after Step 5, you reach the **Manage Windows Policies and Expressions**, which shows *all* the policies the server has for Windows, no matter what you selected in Step 2.

5. Click **Manage Windows Policies**

6. Double-click on **Default Web Application Access (Windows).** The screen should look like this:

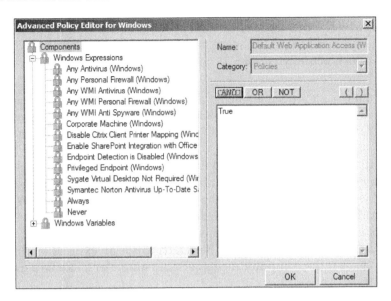

Do you see the word **True**? This is the policy! What this means, really, is that this policy doesn't ENFORCE anything. A policy, as we mentioned before, goes through a logic evaluation that ends up with either a "true" (which means the policy has passed) or "false" (which means it has failed). This policy always ends up the same, and so it will not deny access to anybody. If this scares you somewhat, keep in mind that this policy is an endpoint policy, not an authentication mechanism, users will <u>still</u> have to authenticate with a valid username and password to get into your portal. This just means that your users will not be required to run any specific Antivirus or firewall product, or meet any other conditions that an endpoint policy might include.

Let's have a look at something more challenging. Repeat the procedure above, but this time, open **Default Web Application Download (Windows)**. This should look like this:

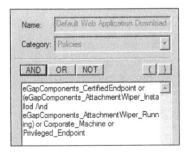

This is a bit more complicated. You can see how this policy uses variables, parenthesis, as well as the Boolean OR and AND operators to accommodate for multiple options. The expressions themselves are written without spaces, and they refer to **eGap**, which is the name of the first product in this line, predating UAG by a few years. Don't mind that — it's just a name that's been left here for compatibility. What all this says is actually simple:

> If this is a 'Certified Endpoint', or has the Attachment Wiper installed and running, or this is a 'Corporate Machine', or this client has passed the 'Privileged Endpoint' policy, then this client complies with this policy.

We have not discussed what a **Certified Endpoint** is, and we will soon, but for now, suffice it to say that it is a computer that has a **digital certificate** installed by your organization, which serves to validate the computer. The **Attachment Wiper** is what we referred earlier to as the **Endpoint Session Cleanup client component**, which has to be *installed*, but also *running* for this policy to pass. We will also go into detail as to what is a **Corporate Machine**, but basically, this is an expression that you can customize to check if the computer meets certain parameters, like be a member of a certain domain.

We will not go into the full details of each of the available policies and its variations, but it's important to know that many of them are simply set to "true". One of the more useful policies is **Default Web Application Upload**, which checks the endpoint for an Anti Virus product, and will pass if any such program is found that is both *updated* and *running*. It would be a good idea to go over the list of available policies, and get acquainted with them, before we go on and learn how to create them on your own:

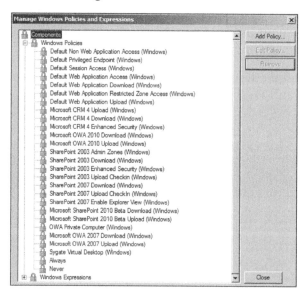

Choosing or designing the appropriate policies for your organization

As you have seen above, the built-in policies that ship with UAG are simple, but which one should you use? Well, there's no definite catch-all answer, of course, but here are some things that you should take under consideration:

- Whatever policy you choose, remember that it only controls the endpoint computer. An endpoint policy can enhance security, but it's not a replacement for proper user and access control.

- If your users typically use their home computers, remember that they may run whatever they want on them, including things that may be harmful, such as a file-sharing application or a comprehensive collection of worms and spyware.

- Despite the above, beware of choosing or creating policies that will torture your users. An organization may have preference to certain endpoint security products, but requiring everyone to use a specific product may be considered to be crossing the line. This may also have legal implications in your country or region.

- Before making your choice, it may be a good idea to conduct a survey of what type of endpoint security products your users are running, and use that data to help base your decision.

- If your organization is keen on security, consider purchasing a group-license of protection software, and providing it to your users for free, or at a subsidized price. This is a win-win: you get better security, your organization gets a tax write-off, and your employees get a benefit!

- Remember that even with the best security software, a secure operating system goes a long way. Consider, for example, encouraging your users to upgrade to a more modern OS, or even subsidizing it for them. Windows 7, for example, is one of the most secure systems out there, and even has a built-in personal firewall at no extra charge.

Many of UAG's customers are perfectly OK with setting their access policy to the default ones. If you plan on using the default policies, it might be a good idea to duplicate them, and then use the duplicates, so that if the policies change with a future update of the product, you won't find yourself facing unexpected behaviour. Some prefer enforcing an Antivirus and/or personal firewall product for access, and quite a few even create their own custom policies. Next, we will learn how to do this.

Creating policies using the policy editor

The endpoint policy editor may seem confusing at first, because the double-level editing may make it seem as if your server has billions of policies. In reality, the policy editing process is not that hard:

1. You create OS-level policies for the 4 OS groups (PC, Mac, Linux and Other)
2. You assign these to a top-level policy
3. You assign the top-level policy to an application and/or to a trunk

You can edit an existing policy, but the built-in policies are all built as a **script** (so you can only edit them in script-mode), which may be tricky for some administrators. It is very sensitive to syntax errors, so it's probably best to start with the **GUI-based** editor, and create a new policy. To do so, follow these steps:

1. Enter the endpoint policy editor by clicking **Edit Endpoint Policies**. This button is available in multiple places:
   - The **Select Endpoint Policies** page of the application publishing wizard
   - Through clicking on **Configure** next to **Configure Trunk Settings** on the main trunk-view page and switching to the **Endpoint Access Settings** tab.
   - On the **Endpoint Policies** step of the **Create Trunk Wizard**
   - On the **Endpoint Policy Settings** tab of the **Application Properties** window
2. Click **Add Policy**.
3. Type a name for your top-level policy, and specify an explanatory text, if you like. If you add text, it will be displayed to users when their computer fails to comply with this policy. For example, **Contact the IT group at (425) 555-3825**.
4. Click **Manage Windows Policies**.
5. Click **Add Policy** (*This is to get to the OS level policy, where the actual policy is created!).
6. Type a name for your OS-level policy.
7. Click on any of the component groups to your liking.
8. Click **Enable Group**.
9. Check one or more of the components that you want included in the policy.
10. If relevant, edit the **Version number** permitted and **Last Updated** value. If you set a blank value, then the field is ignored.

11. Select and configure additional groups to your liking.

12. Click **OK**.

13. Click **Close**.

14. From the **Windows** drop-down, select the new policy you created.

15. Click on **Manage Mac OS Policies**, if you need to create a policy specifically for Macintosh computers, and follow steps 5-15 to create it. You have to select SOME policy, so even if you don't want one, you should select one like **Always** or **Never** in the drop-down list.

16. If needed, repeat for **Linux**.

17. Select a policy for **Other**.

18. Click **OK**.

19. Click **Close**.

That's it! Your policy is now ready to be assigned to an application or a trunk. Remember that any changes to the UAG's configuration requires **activation**, so whether you just created and assigned a new policy, edited an existing one, or changed policy assignment, do activate for the changes to take effect. You can always go back into the policy editor, as described in Step 1, and edit one of your policies or sub-policies, if needed.

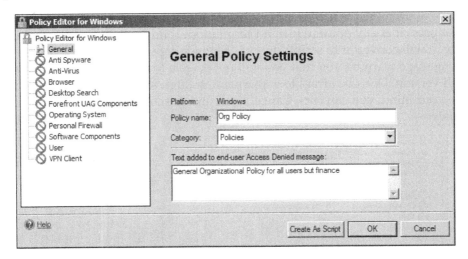

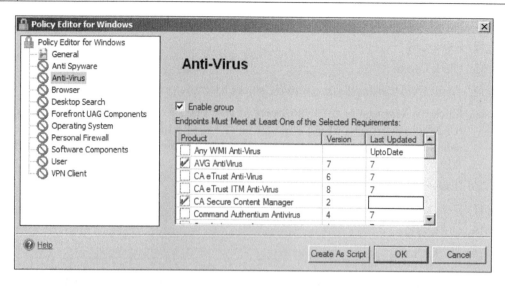

Editing policies in script mode

Creating or editing a policy in script mode is the advanced way to do this, but it requires close attention to detail, as even a small typo can not only invalidate a policy, but could also cause a nasty error message to be presented to your users. You may have noticed, on the GUI policy editor, a button that says **Create As Script**? You can press it at any point to turn on script mode, and if you have already built a policy, it will convert it to script for you. When doing so, you will be presented with a message warning you that you will not be able to convert the script back to the GUI version. Don't be afraid to experiment, though—if you click OK and then change your mind, you can click **Cancel** later, and the change will not be applied to the policy.

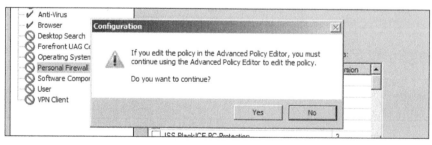

We have already seen an example of a policy script earlier, and now it's time to delve a bit deeper. As we said, a policy is an expression that is evaluated logically, resulting in a *pass* or *fail*. When doing this, UAG populates the expressions by values retrieved from the client (the "**parameter list**"), and performs the evaluation. These parameters are collected by the **endpoint detection component**, and you can use most of them in your policies. Let's look at some examples.

To see these mysterious parameters, we use one of UAG's monitoring tools—**the Web Monitor**. We will cover this tool in high detail on the next chapter, but for now, here's how to view the parameters detected for a specific session:

1. Open the UAG console, and click on the Graph icon.
2. Click on **Active Sessions.**
3. Click on one of the sessions.
4. Click **Parameters.**
5. Use the Excel button to export the list to an Excel file, so you can view them at your leisure.

The endpoint detection component looks for **Antivirus**, **Anti Spyware**, and **Personal Firewall** software on the client computer. It checks for most known brands of these software products, and for each, whether it is INSTALLED and if it is RUNNING. It also checks which version of the product is installed, and when was it updated. In the following clip, we can see **AS_MSForefront_Installed** is set to **TRUE**. This means that the component has detected that the **Microsoft Anti Spyware product (you might recognize it by the name Forefront Client Security)** is installed on the client. In the full table, you will see a long list of values starting with **AS**, **AV**, and **PF**, can you guess what these stand for?

AS_MSForefront_Installed	Policy	TRUE
AS_MSForefront_LastUpdate	Policy	39091.6841203704
AS_MSForefront_Running	Policy	TRUE
AS_MSForefront_Version	Policy	ProductVer=1.5.1937.0,EngineVer=1.1.2101.0,DAT
AS_MSForefront_Version_Dat	Policy	1.0.0.0
AS_MSForefront_Version_Engine	Policy	1.1.2101.0
AS_MSForefront_Version_Product	Policy	1.5.1937.0

You can also see above that the product is running, and its last update date, presented as a decimal value. The evaluation code actually converts the *current* date into a similar decimal number, and calculates the difference, which represents how many days have passed since the product was last updated.

Some products, including most Antivirus programs, actually integrate with Windows' **Action Center** (in **Vista** and **XP**, it is referred to as **The Security Center**), which has its own mechanism for tracking these products and their update status. In this case, the values are a bit different:

AV_MSForefront_Installed	Policy	TRUE
AV_MSForefront_LastUpdate	Policy	39091.6841203704
AV_MSForefront_Running	Policy	TRUE
AV_MSForefront_UptoDate	Policy	False

Above, you can see that there is a simple **UptoDate** field, which is set to FALSE. In this case, the Action Center knows that the AV product has not been updated recently, and UAG uses the **WMI (Windows Management Instrumentation) API** to query the Action Center and obtain this information. Action Center is a feature introduced starting with **Windows XP SP2**, as a better way to secure client operating systems. When you install an Anti-Virus or Personal Firewall product on a client computer, the product registers "WMI providers", which were written by the product vendor specifically for the Action Center to use. These "providers" are software pieces that the Action Center knows how to query, to get the info it needs (Microsoft told all security software vendors how to write them...and they did, so almost all current products support that).

To put all this to use, all you have to do is write an expression that checks for this data, using Boolean logic. If all you want is to check for something like an Antivirus or Anti Spyware, the GUI policy editor is good enough, but by taking advantage of other info that is detected, you can create elaborate policies, and the sky's the limit. For example, one of the parameters that UAG detects is the **domain the client computer is joined to**. The policy variable storing this parameter is called Network_Domains_NetBios, which is populated during the detection with the client computer's Domain. You could include that in a policy as a means of checking if the computer used has been joined to your domain. The expression would be:

```
Network_Domains_NetBios="createhive.com"
```

Naturally, you can combine this with something else, to make things even tighter. For example, you may want your client computers to be members of your domain, and running the Zone Alarm Personal Firewall—so your expression could be:

```
(AV_ZoneAlarm_Running and Network_Domains_NetBios="createhive.com")
```

This can be as elaborate and convoluted as you want—you can, for example, create a policy that will evaluate to true only if the computer is running version X of a certain Personal Firewall, and the browser (**System_Browser**) is IE4 and the operating system is Windows Vista Home (**System_OS_WinVistaHome**) and the display resolution is lower than 800x600 (**System_ScreenResolution_Height** and **System_ScreenResolution_Width**) and so forth. You could even set it so that if the user (**System_WindowsLoggedOnUser_UserName**) is that annoying auditor from HQ, he will be denied access randomly (the script runs in VB, so you can use most VB commands, for example you can check the system time).

Whatever you do, make sure you test your policy with a group of clients, and not just with your own computer. You need to account for multiple variations in OS, security products, browsers and more. Also, the value names and their results are case sensitive, so if you slip up and type **Network_Domains_Netbios**, it won't work, and we've seen people pulling their hair out over such things. OK, I'll admit—I did some hair pulling myself too now and then. Another thing that can ruin your day is keeping track of Boolean logic—ANDs, ORs, Numerical expressions and parenthesis can be hard to keep up with, especially with the policy editor's small text-field. If things don't work, try copy/pasting the expression to a text editor of your choice, replacing the variable names with values and walking through them one-by-one.

Now it's time to go back to that Detection Parameters Excel file you collected earlier, and going through the values you can use, you may find fantastic treasures in there! Keep in mind, though, that the only values you can actually use in a policy are the ones labeled as **Policy** in the **Type** column.

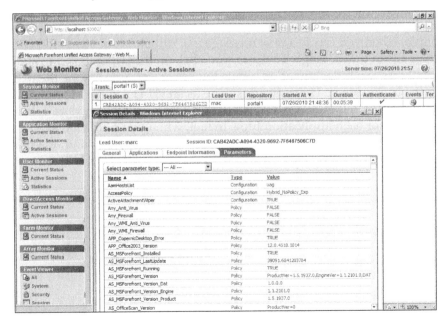

Configuring upload and download settings

The download and upload policies may seem straight-forward to configure, but surprisingly, they confuse an alarmingly high number of people. To configure this correctly, one needs to understand the logic behind the mechanism.

Configuring an upload and download enforcement has two parts. First, the administrators need to define to UAG what IS an upload, and what IS a download. Then, the policy is used to tell the server what to do with an upload and download.

What UAG does is inspect each and every request that a user does, and checks if that request constitutes an upload or download. If it is, then the server checks if the policy that is set for that application has evaluated as "passed" or "failed" at session logon, and based on that, will either allow the action, or deny it.

For the first part of this, UAG analyzes the requests sent by the user. This happens whenever the user's browser (or application) tries to request a URL from UAG. This happens when the user clicks a link on a page of a published app, but also can happen when the user submits a form, clicks somewhere on the screen—anything goes. Some applications are even designed to perform requests in the background. For example, when you open a page on a SharePoint server, the page "calls" for various graphics files and supporting scripts, and all is done in the background. Each request has several characteristics that UAG "sees", and can use to determine if it is just a regular request, or if it is an upload or download, based on configuration done by the administrator.

For example, when you create a new message in Outlook Web Access (OWA), you can attach a file to the message. To do so, you click on the paperclip icon, and select a file. You then see a little animation, while your browser uploads the file to the server in the background. This upload is done as an HTTP "**POST**" to a certain URL. UAG can be configured with a global list of URLs that are identified as uploads and downloads for each application type. In fact, when you publish OWA, it automatically adds the URLs that identify OWA-related uploads and downloads, to these lists of URL, named the Upload URLs and the Download URLs:

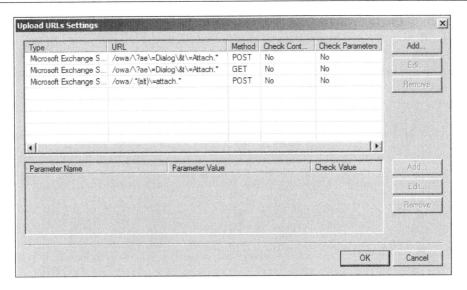

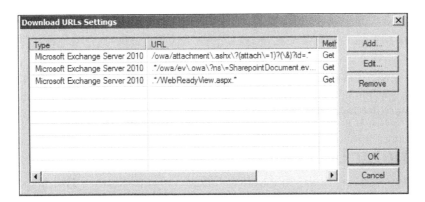

To see these settings on your own server, simply publish an **Exchange 2010 OWA** server (even if you don't really have one, you can just fill-in a made-up server name, and force the wizard to ignore the errors and finish). Then, click on **Configure** next to **Configure Trunk Settings** on the main trunk-view page and switch to the **Global URL Settings** tab. Then, click on **Configure** next to **Download URLs** and **Upload URLs**.

The pattern of the URL shown above is using **Regular Expression (RegEx)**, which allows UAG to find a pattern in URLs that are different for every upload. For example, the actual URL of an attached file may look something like:

```
https://uag.createhive.com/owa/?ae=Dialog&t=AttachFileHost
```

UAG receives the request from a user, and matches it with the RegEx pattern of the first upload rule you see in the previous screenshot, and BINGO! This request has been flagged as an upload. Now, UAG checks what the upload policy set for this application evaluated to at session logon. If it evaluated to "False", UAG will block the request and instead display a message about the block:

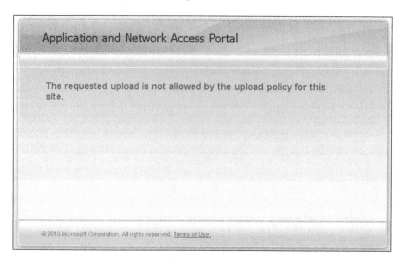

This, however, is just ONE of the ways for UAG to flag uploads and downloads. In addition to this, each Web application has a Download/Upload tab with additional settings. These settings are:

Identify by URL

This checkbox actually refers to what we talked about until now. This is turned on by default for both uploads and downloads for every application, but if you want, you can un-check either and then UAG will not try to match incoming requests with the patterns defined in the global upload and download URLs.

Identify by extension

Enabling this will scan the file extension of each incoming request, and try to match it against the list defined here. For example, if the URL in the HTTP request that UAG receives is for a file with the extension of PDF (`/folder/sub-folder/file.pdf`), UAG will see if the list says anything about PDF files, and act accordingly. Here, you can choose to either enable or disable "identify by extension", and define a list of extensions. You can set your list to either "include" or "exclude". If, for example, you have input the extension PDF with the setting on "include", then only requests for PDF files will be flagged as a download or upload. If you have set it to exclude, then any request OTHER than to a PDF will be considered an upload or download. Here's a riddle: if you define a list of extensions for download, set to exclude, and select the extensions as in the screenshot next, what would happen?

If you guessed "Armageddon", you were right. This will flag the web pages of the application itself as download, because we forgot to exclude HTML and ASP files (and other common web app extensions). If the Download policy selected for this application evaluates to "false", they will all be blocked and your server suddenly becomes a decorative and noisy sculpture.

Identify by size

When this is set, UAG will simply recognize files of size equal or larger than the number you specified (in KB) as uploads or downloads, and will apply the policy to them. This can be useful if, for example, your users decide to upload their home movies to your **SharePoint** site thereby annihilating your bandwidth.

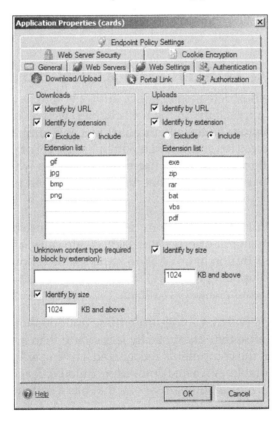

As you can see in the screenshot, the extensions are specified as-is, without a dot or a wild-card pattern.

Now that you have educated your server in what a download and upload IS, all you have to do is select which policy to apply to these. This is also a bit tricky, because the approach when designing this is often the *opposite* of choosing an access policy for an application or trunk. With a regular access policy, you want users who have something (such as an AV product) to pass the policy and get into the trunk or application. With an upload, you want to make sure that users who do NOT have something are blocked. This is somewhat of a mind-bender, because the fundamental logic of the policies is the same, but to get the results you expect, you have to plan this carefully. For example, what if you want to set it so that users will always be prevented from any uploads? The answer is to select the **NEVER** policy, though some people may think for a minute that selecting the **ALWAYS** policy is suitable. What if you want to make sure that people who do not have an Anti Virus cannot attach files to emails sent using OWA? In that case, selecting **Identify by URL** is enough, and a policy that requires an antivirus, like the built-in **Default_Web_ Application_Upload** policy, should be selected.

Configuring restricted zone settings

As we said earlier, the Restricted-Zone policy allows you to have a tighter security for certain parts of an application. In the next chapter, we will discuss the access rules that you can configure on the advanced trunk configuration, which allow you to completely block access to certain URLs with a high level of granularity, but using the restricted-zone feature can be more useful for situations where an application has certain areas that perform actions that may be considered to be more invasive or dangerous.

For example, when using Outlook Web Access, users may use the **Options** button to configure things like an out-of-office message, create rules, and change their password. Clicking this button in OWA 2010 requests the following URL, which shows the options pop-up: `https://mail.createhive.com/owa/ev.owa?oeh=1&ns =Options&ev=GetOptsMnu&canary=10a8f50e34f8492487b8e7dbc74cef90`.

An administrator might feel that configuring these options should not be done from an **internet kiosk**, because they are typically less secure than a user's own personal computer. If, however, the computer is recognized as a trusted one, then doing this may be perfectly acceptable. A trusted computer could be, for instance, one that is a member of the organization's domain or one that has a certain file or registry key configured on it.

To do this, you need to "teach" your server that this specific URL (or any other) is considered to be a restricted zone. This is done from the Restricted Zone URLs Settings on the **Advanced Trunk Configuration** (below the global Download and Upload URL settings we described in the previous section). All you have to do is add a URL, and specify the correct parameters:

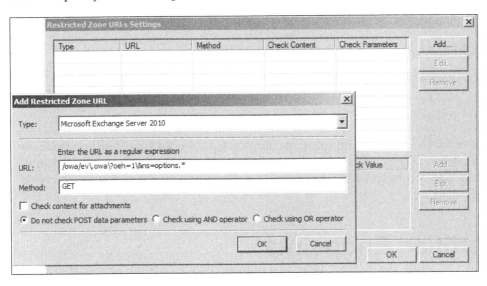

The preceeding screenshot shows the application-type that is selected, the method, and the URL. You may notice that the URL doesn't look exactly like the "real" one, but that's OK—we have used Regular Expression (RegEx) to define a pattern that UAG can identify, as the actual URL changes between users.

How does one know which URLs need to be restricted, or how to build a proper RegEx expression, you ask? Well, these are considered to be advanced configuration options, and some of them take some experience. It's important to know and understand the application that you are publishing. You may not "own" it, and therefore not be sure, but if so, perhaps your organization has someone who is versed in its structure. If this is a commercial product, you may be able to learn this from the product's support group, or from third party implementation consultants. Another way to learn more about an application is by recording its activity using a special tool. Several tools exist that can help. My personal favorite is **HTTPWatch** by **SimTec Ltd** from the UK. This tool integrates into Internet Explorer, and records vast amounts of information about each HTTP request and response that goes through the browser. Another tool is **Fiddler**, written by **Eric Lawrence** from Microsoft. Fiddler is a proxy, so it can do what HTTPWatch does, but also keep track of other applications, and not just Internet Explorer.

Another tool that's even more powerful is **Network Monitor** (**NetMon**), which is another Microsoft tool. NetMon can record much more data, and is a fantastic tool for forensics, analysis and troubleshooting. However, it captures so much detail that it takes significant experience and time to read and understand it.

To create a RegEx expression from the URL you are observing, read *Appendix A*, which provides an overview of RegEx.

Here are links to get the tools mentioned previously:

- `http://www.httpwatch.com/`
- `http://www.fiddler2.com/`
- `http://support.microsoft.com/kb/933741`

After creating the URL configuration, don't forget to set an appropriate policy in the **Restricted-Zone** setting of your application. Keep in mind, though, that the default web access restricted-zone policy is "True", so it won't provide you with much security.

Certified Endpoints

As we have seen so far, UAG has several mechanisms to validate a user and the user's computer. We can check for a password, certain software products that are installed, and even the computer's domain membership—but is it SAFE? Well, real paranoids have no limits, and it's our job as information security specialists to be at least somewhat paranoid, right?

You probably know that a computer's domain membership can be faked rather easily, and a getting a user to cough out his password is also not very hard, mostly. However, unless you walk around with a tin-foil hat, you will probably agree that a digital certificate is one of the most solid ways to verify a computer's identity. For this, UAG supports **Certified Endpoints**, which means Endpoints that have a digital certificate. By issuing an individual digital certificate to every client by a corporate **Certificate Authority** server, we can be sure that an incoming client machine is really who it says it is. To be clear, this is different than Certificate Authentication that we discussed in *Chapter 6*—Certificate Authentication checks the user's certificate (either a soft certificate, installed in the user's Personal Certificate Store, or a hard-certificate in the form of a FOB or SmartCard), while Certified Endpoint validation is about a computer's certificate.

Configuring an organizational certificate policy is no small feat, and for this book, we will have to assume that you already are familiar with the concepts of **PKI** and how to use a CA server to issue certificates to your users' computers.

One of the challenges for using this feature is getting the certificates to the users' computers. You may be lucky and have all your users bring their computers into the corporate network, but if your users are mostly home-based, it could be challenging. A common approach is to create an application on the trunk that will publish the Certificate Authority server, but not require the certificate. This way, the users can login and request a certificate, and once the administrator approves their request, they will be able to launch the other applications, which have been configured with the appropriate access policy. Naturally we would recommend that in this scenario, you should avoid an automatic enrolment procedure, as that basically negates the entire purpose of requiring a certificate. If an attacker can hack a user's details, the automation will allow him to get a certificate, and then access the main trunk with it.

To configure a trunk to request a client's certificate, all you have to do is check the option **Use Certified Endpoints** in the **Session** tab of the **Advanced Trunk Configuration**, and then activate your configuration. Following this, UAG will request a certificate and verify it. If it passes verification, it will be granted access to the applications which have been configured with a policy that requires the client to be a certified endpoint.

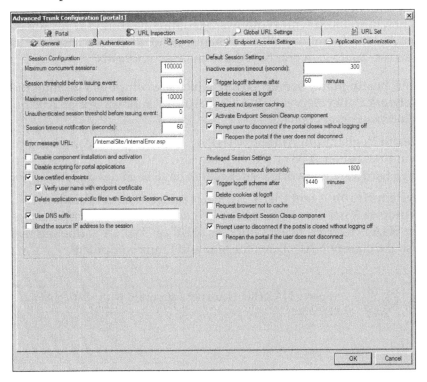

You can also check the option **Verify user name with endpoint certificate**, which will have UAG check if the authenticated user matches the name on the certificate.

This is a good opportunity to mention that having a client certificate does not mean that it can be used to authenticate to applications. Another thing that's important to know is that UAG has to trust the Certificate Authority that issued the certificates in order to be able to consider the certificate to be valid. Assuming the certificate is issued by an internal CA server, the usual certificate trust aspects need to be taken care of. This usually entails installing the CA server's **root certificate** on the UAG, or the trust-chain certificates, as well as making sure the CRLs are available for UAG to read.

Integration with Network Access Protection

Network Access Protection (NAP) is a relatively-new technology from Microsoft that can be used independently of UAG to provide better network security by ensuring that clients are in good "health". The well-known cure for computer-sniffles is an Antivirus, of course, and organizations throughout the world have been looking for creative ways to keep their computers safe.

NAP was first introduced with **Windows 2008**, and one could say it's somewhat similar to UAG's endpoint detection mechanism, though it's also used for local Network access. To do its work, NAP has 3 main components:

1. NAP **health policy servers (HPS),** which are computers running the **Network Policy Server** (NPS) service on a Windows Server 2008 or Windows Server 2008 R2.

2. **Health Registration Authority (HRA),** which can be a computers running Windows Server 2008 or 2008 R2, but also a **VPN** server, a **DHCP** server or even hardware **Network Switches** that have been designed to support NAP.

3. **System Health Agent (SHA),** which is integrated into **Windows 7** and **Windows Vista** clients, as well as **Windows XP SP3**. On a Windows system, the SHA is referred to as "Windows SHA" or "WSHA", although there are also third party NAP clients for Mac and Linux computers.

 3rd party NAP clients are not supported with UAG NAP integration

Many organizations elect to use NAP because it allows them to enforce certain security policies on all their computers, not just those that connect remotely. An organization that has a NAP infrastructure deployed can take advantage of it, and configure UAG to rely on the same infrastructure to check its own clients, instead of the built-in endpoint detection. NAP is not necessarily "better", but from an administrative perspective, it may be easier to manage one set of policies rather than two. UAG does provide endpoint detection for clients older than XP SP3, so it might still be handy to use both for some organizations.

How does NAP work?

The endpoint component of NAP is called the **System Health** Agent (**SHA**), and is included with XP SP3, Vista, and Windows 7. The client is running in the background, and monitors the status of the system all the time. The client agent periodically generates a **Statement of Health (SOH),** which includes information about the client's status, and sends it to the **Health Registration Authority (HRA).** The HRA sends this to the NAP **Health Policy Server (HPS),** which evaluates it and decides if the client is healthy or not, based on the specific **System Health Validator (SHV)** .

If the client is compliant with the policy (Healthy), the health policy server (HPS) tells the Health Registration Authority (HRA) so by issuing a "Health Certificate" for this specific client. The HRA then allows the client access to the network.

If the client is unhealthy, the HPS may issue remediation instructions, if configured to do so, and those are relayed to the client via the HRA. The client can then contact specially designated remediation servers that may offer the organization's Antivirus software of choice, or an update to it, and so forth.

At any point, a healthy client may become unhealthy, or vice-versa. For example, a user may return with his laptop from a long trip in which he was never online. At that point, his AV software is not updated, so he will be denied access. Within minutes, his software will be updated via the remediation servers, making him healthy. The reverse can occur – a client, while connected, may decide to uninstall or stop his antivirus, turning his computer non-compliant. For this reason, NAP Statement Of Health reports have to be re-sent every time a computer reboots, every 4 hours while the computer is working, every time a client makes changes to his security settings, and on some other occasions.

To learn more about NAP and how it works in more detail, refer to this link:
`http://technet.microsoft.com/en-us/network/bb545879.aspx`.

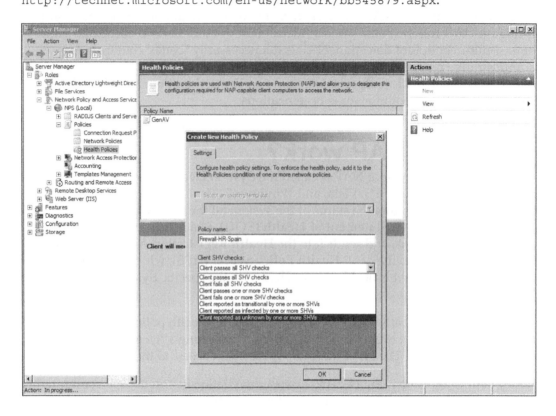

Configuring UAG to use NAP

To configure UAG to integrate NAP into its endpoint policies, the first step is to configure it as a Health Registration Authority (HRA). This is done on one of the organization's NAP health policy servers (HPS), in which UAG is configured as a **RADIUS** client. The term "client" may be confusing here, because UAG is a SERVER, but RADIUS terminology is such. A HPS server is the "server", and the HRAs are "clients". Hopefully, you can either hold your acronyms well, or have the patience to re-read this multiple times.

Once UAG has been defined as an HRA, you need to configure it to know who its health policy servers are (can be one or more), and finally, edit the endpoint policy settings to make UAG check the regular policies, or NAP policies, or both.

Installing a NAP HPS and creating a health policy is beyond the scope of this book, so if your organization has a person who owns the NAP service, consult him or her with regards to that, and also with regards to configuring the UAG server as a RADIUS client on the NAP Server. To configure the UAG-side of this, follow these steps:

1. In the UAG management console, open the **Admin** menu, and click **Network Policy Server (NPS)**.

2. Click **Add**.

3. Type a name for this NPS server to your liking.

4. Type the IP or host-name of the NAP health policy servers (HPS) for your organization, and the port it uses to communicate.

5. Type the Shared Secret that has been configured for this pairing on the HPS.

6. Click **OK** and **close**.

7. Activate the UAG configuration.

The next step is to configure, or re-configure the trunk's endpoint policies settings. If you have not created your trunk yet, the following configuration can be done in step 5 and 6 of the **Create New Trunk wizard**. For trunks that are already configured, follow these steps:

1. In the UAG management console, open the **Advanced Trunk Configuration** and switch to the **Endpoint Access Settings** tab.

2. Check the option **Use Network Access Protection (NAP) policies**.

3. Select whether to use the traditional Endpoint policies for clients who do not have NAP installed and running.

4. Click **Add**, and select your NAP server.

5. For the Session Access Policy, Privileged Endpoint Policy and Socket Forwarding component installation policy, select one of the three options as the access method:

   ° **Endpoint policy only**

   ° **NAP only**

   ° **Both endpoint policy and NAP**

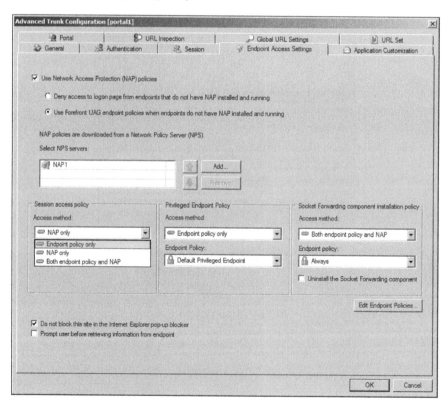

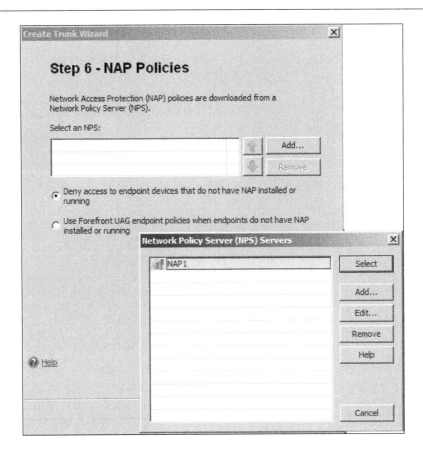

Summary

It may be hard to grasp just how powerful UAG's endpoint policies can be until you start digging into the policy editor and seeing how many things can be configured in there. The possibilities are endless, and with some creativity, this can make for an exceptionally secure access method—far greater than any other VPN product on the market. We also strongly recommend further reading of appendices A and B, which can help fine-tune the rules and take it to the next level. In the next chapter, we will discuss maintaining your server and keeping it in top shape using monitoring tools.

9
Server Maintenance and Upkeep

Once you have finished configuring the server, trunks, and applications, you might be lucky enough and get to let your UAG server tick-away in the server room and forget about it. If things go off-course, UAG includes some powerful monitoring and troubleshooting mechanisms, which might come in handy at some point. This chapter will discuss these tools and how to use them, as well as additional important functionality such as Backup and Restore and applying product updates and patches.

Who needs monitoring?

The current version of UAG has only been out for a few months at the time of this writing, but indeed we are aware of quite a few servers running previous versions that have been working for many years. In fact, some have been running smoothly for so long that when an issue comes up, no one within the entire organization even knows how the server LOOKS. We are not kidding... we have actually seen cases where a customer calls in and asks us what is that black box that's suddenly started ticking.

Beyond that, monitoring is not only good for solving problems. It allows the administrator to learn about the traffic patterns of his users, and to keep an eye on the server's performance over time. Usually, usage will increase, requiring a server upgrade at some point in the future and tracking activity is very important to be ahead in this game. Some people prefer to wait for the angry phone calls before starting to investigate the process and costs of an upgrade, but we'd like to think of you as being better than that. Another advantage of doing routine monitoring is being aware of any malicious activities done or attempted against your server. UAG is a very secure product, but given enough time, a determined cracker will eventually be able to guess a user/password combination. If you keep your eye on ball, you might be able to detect such attempts and be more proactive in preventing the break in.

The UAG activation monitor

We have already mentioned the **UAG activation monitor** back in *Chapter 2*, as it is used mostly to keep track of the activation process. This is a very important tool to be aware of, mostly for users who have used UAG's predecessors and want to test changes they made as soon as possible. This tool is even more important when dealing with Arrays, as the process of pushing configuration changes to other array members can take a significant amount of time, and testing configuration changes before they have been propagated to all members is futile.

Other than staring at the X (on the left-hand side of the activation monitor) and waiting for it to become a checkmark, there's very little to configure or do with the Activation Monitor, but one thing is good to know. All the tool does is performing a '**pulse-check'**—it polls the servers for status, and so the servers may actually finish activation a short time before the tool shows it. The Activation Monitor is configured, by default, to poll the servers every 20 seconds, but by clicking **Options** you can reduce that poll interval down to 10 seconds, and thus get a faster update.

Lastly, the tool shows a lot of debug information about what's going on during the activation. Any errors will be shown by the UAG management console activation pop-up, but the activation monitor will also show other relevant information, which can help identify possible problems. For example, the following screenshot shows information about some of the files UAG creates during activation, various IPs and ports that are being opened and some registry changes:

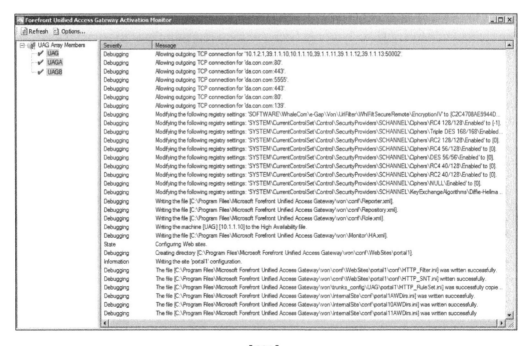

The UAG Web Monitor

The UAG Web Monitor is THE tool for monitoring your precious server. It is the absolute winner in every "what's up" category in the book. Some of the things you can see with the Web Monitor are:

- Active sessions, sorted by trunk, user, or application
- Session statistics
- Graphics information for the above
- Server status (In array configurations)
- System, Security, Session, and Application specific event info
- Detailed reports filtered by trunk, date/time, category, severity, and type
- Detailed session info, including endpoint information, full parameter list

To open the Web Monitor; open the Admin menu, and select **Web Monitor**, or click on the icon that looks like a graph on the UAG management console toolbar. You can also launch it from UAG's folder on the start menu.

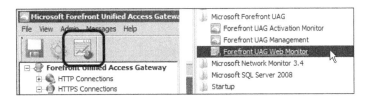

The Web Monitor is actually a web-site published on the local UAG IIS Server, and launching it simply opens a browser window pointing to `http://localhost:50002`. If you have just installed UAG, then upon opening the Web Monitor, you will be informed that the page uses **Java**, and to view it, you will need the **Java Runtime Environment (JRE).** The Web Monitor indeed uses Java, but only for displaying charts. You can take full advantage of the monitor without it, but if you want the full experience, visit Oracle's Java download page, and download the 16 MB installer: `http://java.com/download`

Alternatively, if you prefer to avoid installing JRE on your server, you can publish the Web Monitor itself as an application, and then access it from a remote computer that you don't mind installing it on.

Monitoring sessions

The first group of Web Monitor functions allows you to view information about existing sessions, such as the number of **authenticated** and **unauthenticated** sessions, both in a list view and as a chart. The "current status" shows this number, broken down per **trunk**. Unauthenticated sessions are sessions that have had an initial connection from the client, but the client has not logged in. Normally, you would have no unauthenticated sessions, or just a small number of them, because a user that enters the portal would log-in, causing his unauthenticated session to be replaced by an authenticated one pretty fast. One thing that could cause unauthenticated sessions to appear other than users who delve into their coffee and forget to log in, of course, is access by automated software. For example, if a search engine tried to "spider" the UAG URL, it might create such sessions. Smart-phones attempting to perform **ActiveSync** without being properly configured might also create such sessions regularly.

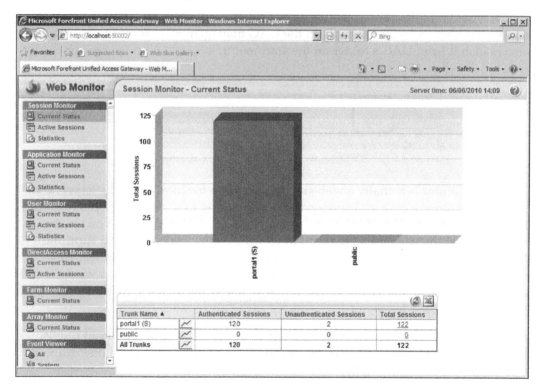

The **Active Sessions** tab shows all the sessions with more detail. It shows the ID for each, as well as the logged-in user, his or her **repository**, when the session started, what its duration is and whether or not it is an authenticated session. It also shows two action buttons—one takes you to a page with a list of events associated with this session, and another to terminate the session.

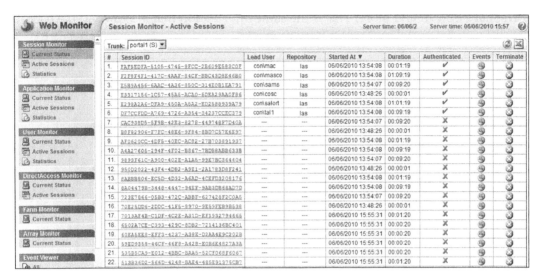

On the **Active Session** list, the **Session ID** is also a clickable item, which shows more detailed session info. It is divided into four pages:

General

The **General** tab shows the session time and duration, as well as the user and repository. It also shows you whether this session is **privileged**.

Applications

The **Application** tab shows a list of all applications configured on the trunk, including "Portal" (the Portal itself is considered to be an application). For each of them, the table shows whether the user has permissions to launch it, and whether or not he has launched it during this session.

Endpoint Information

The **Endpoint Information** tab shows a lot of information about the connecting computer or device, which is very useful for troubleshooting. It shows which of the UAG client components have been installed, and what version they are-of. It also shows details about the computer's **Operating System**, **Browser Version**, **Antivirus**, **Personal Firewall** and more. This is the same information that is shown to the user if he clicks on the portal toolbar's information icon.

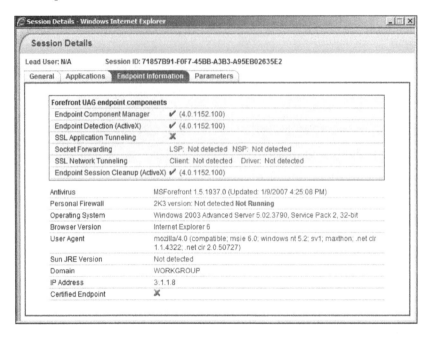

Parameters

The **Parameters** tab is the holy grail of troubleshooting client detection issues, as it shows the raw list of all **parameters** detected by the **client components** on the client computer. By inspecting the table, you can see what the UAG sees, and can use that to determine the root cause of many problems that may occur. For example, a user that is being denied access to the portal may insist that he has the proper Antivirus product installed, but the Parameter table may reveal that the product is indeed installed, but is not currently running (as you probably know, some AV products slow down the computer, so certain users turn them off because it's more important to them that their games open up faster than the risk of losing all their files to some worm). Another common scenario is that the AV product is indeed installed and running, but hasn't been updated for a while because the user has been on some vacation. We will discuss how to use this information specifically in the *Client detection troubleshooting* section in *Chapter 12*.

Session Statistics

The **Session Statistics** page in the Session Monitor group allows you to perform queries against the current active sessions. The information displayed is pretty-much the same as that shown by the **Active Sesson** page, but will be easier to use at times when the server is very busy and has a lot of data. For example, if you have 300 logged-in users at a single point of time, but you know that a specific user is having a problem accessing an application, using the query engine will allow you to locate that user's session without manually scrolling through hundreds of lines.

When creating a query, you can specify that the report will include one trunk, or several, and span a time-duration of anywhere between an hour and the entire duration since installing the server. The report will show a chart, which can be in the form of a **peak chart** or a **sample chart**. A sample chart shows the number of concurrent sessions sampled at the end of an interval, while a peak chart shows the highest number of sessions that were open during the interval period. Under the chart, a table will show statistics about concurrent sessions, session duration average and session duration maximum

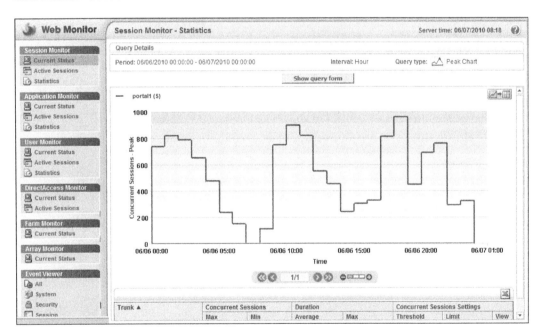

Monitoring applications and users

The second and third groups of Web Monitor functions allow a different view of the same data, but broken up by **applications** or **users**. It is useful when you need to analyze the usage pattern from that perspective. For example, you might use this to gather data for a *quarterly* or *annual* server usage report—the kind that upper-management likes to see. These two page groups offer the same style—a Current Status page, an **Active Sessions** page and a Statistics page.

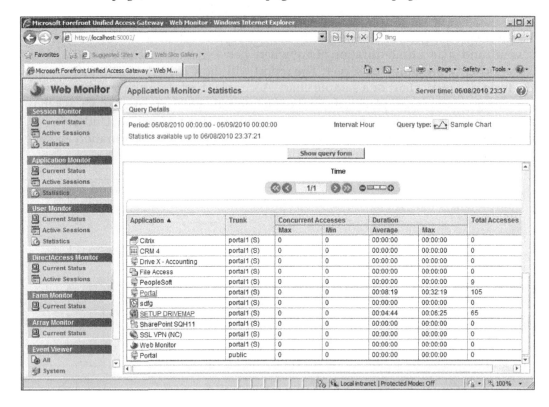

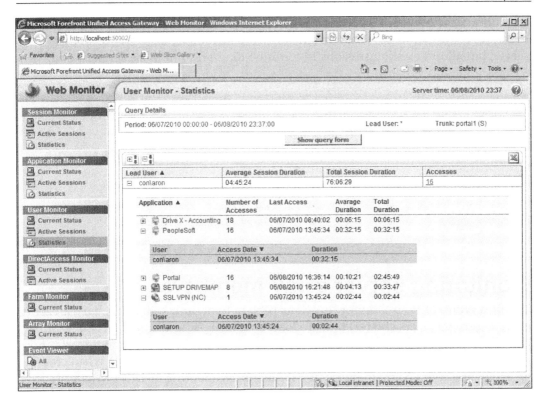

Monitoring server farms

The fourth group of Web Monitor functions comes into play when you have published applications on the UAG server that use a back-end server farm. We have already discussed how to configure server farms as part of several application types in *Chapter 4*, and this part of the Web Monitor allows you to keep an eye on these farms. This page shows a list of all configured server farms within the various applications, and their status. It also allows you to **Stop** and **Start** a farm, as well as **Drain Stop**.

The difference between a Stop and a Drain Stop is that Stop *immediately* blocks access to this server for all users, while Drain Stop does not route new sessions to this server, but allows existing sessions to continue to use it until those sessions end.

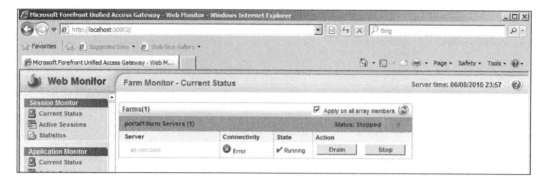

Monitoring server array members

The fifth group of Web Monitor functions pertain to organizations that have an **array** of UAG servers (a.k.a. **cluster**) that are load-balanced using **Windows NLB**. In this case, the Array monitor allows you to view the status of all the array members, and manage them. Other than starting the members, which you need to do when creating an array, this could come-in handy for some troubleshooting tasks. For example, you may run into trouble making some applications work, or get reports of a problem from your users, and you might not know for sure which array member is affected, or perhaps even causing the problem. In this situation, you can use the Array monitor to narrow down the symptoms by removing one or more members from the array.

The available commands that you can perform with the array monitor are:

- Start
- Stop
- Drain Stop
- Suspend
- Resume

To apply one of these actions to an array node, mark the node, select the action from the drop-down action menu and click **Apply**. Actions take a while to complete, so you can use the refresh button on the right until the "NLB status" column reflects the targeted value. The STOP command stops NLB on the array member, but the SUSPEND command also suspends all NLB cluster-control commands except RESUME and QUERY (if that makes no sense, keep in mind that NLB has many other commands that are not available through the web monitor). The specific purpose of the suspend command is to override any *remote control* commands that might be issued. For a full reference to NLB cluster-control commands:

`http://technet.microsoft.com/en-us/library/cc754596(WS.10).aspx`

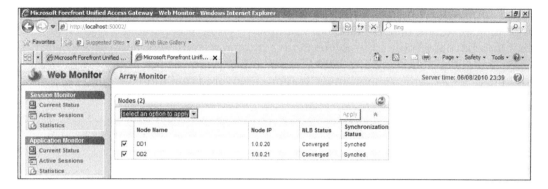

Event Viewer

The Event Viewer section of the Web Monitor shows various events recorded by the server, and is probably the most important part for troubleshooting. The Event Viewer records and shows events in four categories: **System**, **Security**, **Session**, and **Application**. You can also view the **All** page, which, well, shows all of the events. When you view all the events, the **Category** column will show to which category they belong to, and you can view the individual category logs to single these events out.

The System events would typically include information about changes to the server's configuration, configuration-activations and service starting and stopping. The Session log shows information about user sessions that start or end, as well as information about users joining or being removed from sessions. The application events show information about applications being launched or closed.

The Security log is probably the most useful, as it shows information about login success and failure, alerts about policy violation and password changes. This log will be informative in cases where a user is unable to login to the portal, is getting errors when trying to login or launch applications, or is being denied access to certain application resources.

Event Query

The event query allows you to view events related to any of the categories mentioned above, with *advanced filtering*. This is very useful when you are being informed of a certain problem that happened at a different time ("Yesterday, I was using the email application, when suddenly I could not attach any files to my messages") or repeating at certain times of day. For example, a certain company had users report that they have intermittent problems with a human resource application, and with the event query, it became apparent that the application was not responding during specific times at night. A short investigation discovered that this coincided with the application being backed-up.

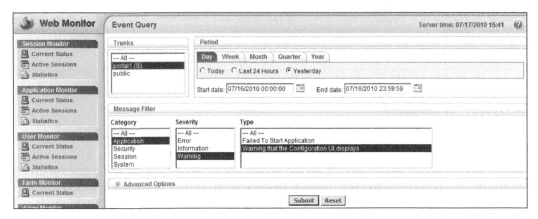

Configuring UAG event logging

In addition to using the built-in Web Monitor, you can also configure UAG to send events to three external resources—a RADIUS server, Email, and a Syslog server. These, as well as other logging parameters are configured through the **Admin/Event Logs Settings**. The settings you can configure through it are:

Queue and report size

The queue size parameter controls how many events are shown in the Event Viewer of the Web Monitor. The default is **50** messages. One reason that you might have for changing it is if you have a very busy server. If so, the server may generate so many messages that they might refresh too fast for you to track. Setting a larger number will allow you to see messages before they overflow off the display window.

The *Max Report Results* parameter controls how many events a query can display. This means that if you use the Event report to generate a report, it will not display more results than the number defined here (the default is 2000). You might also raise that number if your server is super active, but keep in mind that the report generator uses-up a lot of memory. If you set this number too high, generating reports may take a long time, and the server's performance may degrade during the report generation.

Built-in

The built-in log is a database of events collected by UAG, and it is used by the Web Monitor to show activity and query events, as we discussed earlier. By default, the built-in log is enabled, and this settings control to where these reports are saved. There should be no reason to disable this reporting...some users have done so in hopes of boosting performance, because they thought that the server may be wasting precious CPU power on the logging, but in fact, the impact is virtually unnoticeable. By default, the logs are stored in `C:\Program Files\Microsoft Unified Access Gateway\logs\Events`, but you may use this option to have the logs saved to somewhere else. For example, you may want to have the logs saved to another drive with more disk space, or to a network location that is easier for you to back-up.

RADIUS and Syslog

If your organization uses a **Syslog** or **RADIUS** server to manage logging, you can configure UAG to communicate with these servers and send them its events. The settings are quite self-explanatory — you set the host name or IP and port for both, and the secret key, if this is a RADIUS server.

Mail

Enabling Mail logging will have UAG send Email messages to pre-defined users, about events that occur on the server. This sounds very cool, but to make it really useful, you would need to configure exactly what events should trigger an Email. Configuring this requires editing an XML file on the server, but an easier method to achieve similar functionality is to use the System Event Log for this, which is described later. If you really want to mess around with the XMLs configuration, it is covered here: `http://technet.microsoft.com/en-us/library/ee428828.aspx`

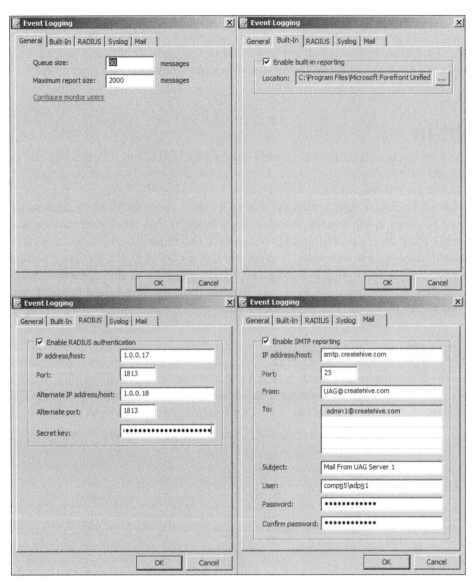

UAG services

When you install UAG, it adds a long list of services to the system, as well as a lot of dependencies between themselves and other system services. For example, without the TMG services running, UAG won't even let you open the configuration console, and the TMG services themselves depend on the *Secure Socket Tunneling Protocol Service*. A clear sign of something going wrong is an onscreen message that says some services could not be started, but if the server starts to behave strangely, begin by inspecting if all services that are set to "automatic" are indeed started. This can be seen in the **Services administrative** *tools*, which allows you to sort the list of services by startup-type.

Here is a list of services that are required to run for UAG to function properly, including services that depend on them:

- ISASTGCTRL
- Base filtering engine
- COM+ Event System
- Microsoft Forefront TMG Control
- Microsoft Forefront TMG Firewall
- Microsoft Forefront TMG Job Scheduler
- Microsoft Forefront TMG Managed Control
- Microsoft Forefront TMG Storage
- Microsoft Forefront UAG Configuration Manager
- Microsoft Forefront UAG File Sharing
- Microsoft Forefront UAG Log Server
- Microsoft Forefront UAG Monitoring Manager
- Microsoft Forefront UAG Quarantine Enforcement Server
- Microsoft Forefront UAG Session Manager
- Microsoft Forefront UAG SSL Network Tunneling Server
- Microsoft Forefront UAG Terminal Services RDP Data
- Microsoft Forefront UAG User Manager
- Microsoft Forefront UAG Watch Dog Service
- Network Policy Server
- Plug and Play
- Remote Access Connection Manager
- Remote Procedure Call (RPC)
- RPC/HTTP Load Balancing Service
- RPC/http load balancing service

- Secure Socket Tunneling Protocol Service
- SQL Server (ISARS)
- SQL Server (MSFW)
- SQL Server Reporting Services (ISARS)
- SQL Server VSS Writer
- Telephony
- Windows Firewall
- Windows Process Activation Service
- World Wide Web Publishing Service

 This list is different to the list of services added to the server with the installation of UAG that we saw in *Chapter 2*.

If you see a service that is supposed to be started, but is *not*, the next step would be to open its properties, and go to the **Dependencies** tab. The "This service depends on" list may give you some clue as to what's happening. Keep in mind that additional services may become necessary as you modify and add to your server's configuration. For example, the **Network Policy Server** service may become relevant if you actually use a Network Policy Server as part of your endpoint security.

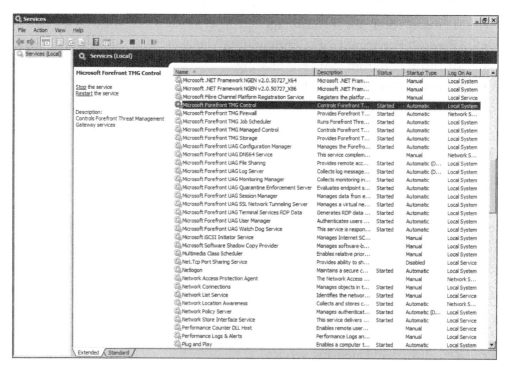

UAG and the System Event Log

Another important monitoring tool is the *System* Event Log (as opposed to the **UAG event log**). This essential system tool is critical to system management regardless of UAG, of course, and would often be one of the first to look at when trying to solve a problem. In fact, UAG is designed to send some of the events that you might see on UAG's own Web Monitor to the system event log, which is very convenient because you can configure the System event log to automatically send notifications when these events show up. For example, you might want to set your server to alert you via e-mail when the server detects a failed login attempt. This way, if there are multiple failed log-in attempts in a row, this could mean that an attacker is trying to brute-force his way into your portal (or, perhaps that one of your users has chubby fingers). If you have an e-mail-to-SMS gateway, you could use that to get alerts to your cell-phone, and demonstrate your dedication to your job by having messages from the server wake you up in ungodly hours. It's also possible, by the way, to configure UAG to send such alerts automatically, as noted earlier in this chapter, but then configuring which events to send is trickier and requires manual editing of XML files.

If you've managed servers for a while, then you probably know that sometimes servers generate messages that are pretty obtuse, quoting numbers that don't mean anything or really bizarre errors such as **Error: the operation completed successfully**. There is no magic trick to deciphering some of these, but whatever it is, it's likely that someone else had run into it in the past, and a quick search on the web might shed some light on it. If not, Microsoft's customer support group would also be able to help.

Even if there is no problem with the server, we strongly urge you to take an occasional look at the Event Viewer, especially if you have only recently installed the server, or if you decided to care less about our earlier suggestions and installed additional software on the UAG server. You can think of it as preventative medicine — a regular inspection of the logs may reveal something that's slowly developing under the surface, and allow you to catch it before it explodes. For example, hard drives sometimes start to go bad in stages, and the system would suddenly show messages about a bad disk block being detected. These can go on for months without any noticeable symptoms, and then suddenly cause the server's performance to degrade (I bought a Quad-core Xeon, darn it not a 486!). In worst-case scenarios, of course, the disk might just die on you, forcing you to spend hours reinstalling and reconfiguring the server just when you were planning to go to a concert or a romantic dinner with your significant other.

If you are using a professional storage device, such as a RAID array, it's important to monitor it as well, because a failed drive in an array might go out without a noticeable effect on the server itself...until another disk dies, taking it all with it. It is also important to keep in mind that the system normally generates a lot of routine messages, and it will serve you well to be able to recognize the normal patterns and exceptions to them.

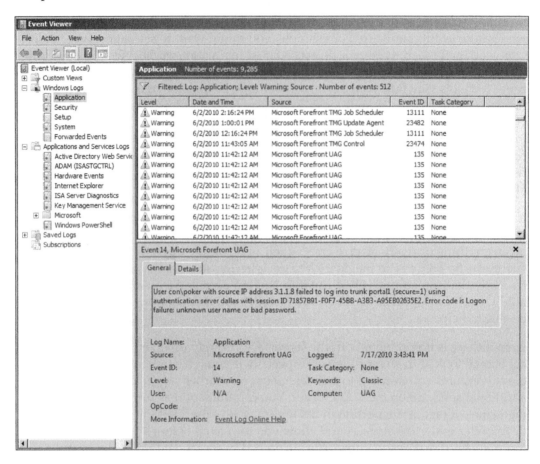

Publishing the UAG Web Monitor

A useful feature is to be able to view the UAG Web Monitor *remotely*. For example, if you are home or travelling, you may want to have a look and see how many users are currently online, or investigate a report of a problem with the server. To this end, UAG has a built-in template for this (we mentioned this in *Chapter 4*).

Publishing the Web Monitor on the portal is fairly easy — you select the **Web Monitor** template from the **Built-In** Services application group, using the publishing wizard, and select which users will be able to view it. Do make sure, though, that you make the Web Monitor available only to the *appropriate people*, as it shows a lot of data that may be sensitive.

Live Monitoring using TMG

Another useful tool that comes with your UAG server is the **TMG management console**. Those with a good memory will rise up and yell "But you told us not to touch it!" That is true, and you should never modify the configuration of TMG on a UAG server unless specifically instructed to by official Microsoft documentation or a Microsoft representative. However, for *monitoring purposes only*, it is perfectly acceptable to use the TMG console.

The TMG **Monitoring** tab in the TMG management console is very useful for seeing the traffic coming in and going out of the server, and can often pinpoint the source of a problem. For example, if you are attempting to configure the Network Connector, and notice that connecting clients are unable to communicate with servers on the internal network, the TMG monitor might reveal that TMG is blocking traffic for some reason (perhaps an invalid routing or IP configuration somewhere). It can also show that traffic is being received from the clients and correctly passed onward into the correct network, indicating that the UAG server is probably configured correctly, and the traffic is being blocked on the internal network (perhaps by an incorrectly configured internal firewall or router).

To use the TMG monitor, open the Forefront TMG management console, and click on **Logs & Reports**. By default, logging is on, but you won't see anything until you start a *query* by pressing **Start Query**. Once you do, the middle window will start showing any traffic that is received by TMG, including the **source, destination, protocol**, and much more. If you are running this on a server that is in production, the screen will fill up very quickly, making it hard to follow. To help you sort through this, you can define a filter to show just what you need. For example, if you are trying to understand if a certain internal server is being accessed, you can define a filter to show only traffic to/from that server's IP address.

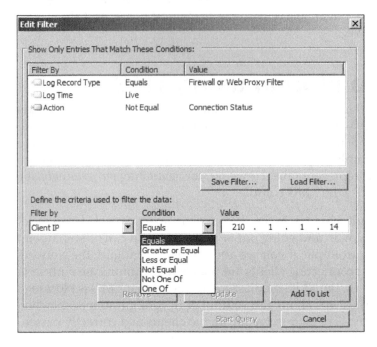

The log view also allows you to sort the data based on the various fields, and you can even export the captured data into another program for tracking or analysis purposes. For example, many people find **Excel** easier to use for analysing large amounts of data. To export the query result click **Copy All Results to Clipboard**. You can also select just some of the rows and click on **Copy Selected Results to Clipboard**.

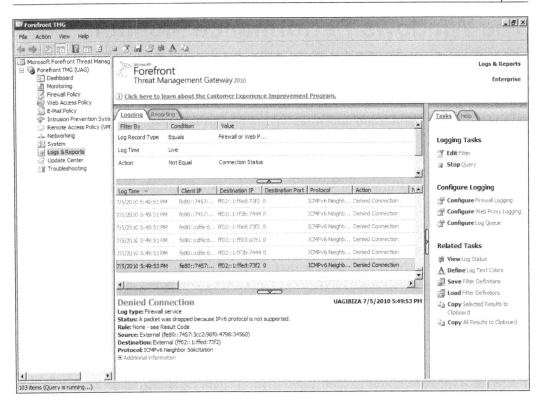

When observing the results of a query, notice the Rule column (the tenth column, which will require some scrolling to see), which indicates if an action is being blocked or allowed by a specific TMG **policy rule**. You should not tinker with the rules themselves, but merely noticing that a certain rule affects traffic may lead you close to finding the cause of a problem. For example, you may notice that an application is not working as expected, and the monitor query will lead you to the responsible rule, which may turn out to have been set to an incorrect IP address. This could be because you mistyped an address or IP when setting up the application or it could indicate a possible issue with name resolution.

The Windows Performance Monitor

One of the toughest challenges with any server deployment is accurately estimating the capacity of a certain server to service users. Some products provide very specific services that can be accurately calculated, but UAG, unfortunately, is not one of those products. The impact of each user on the server is incredibly varied, depending on the published application and what type of resources it uses, the UAG services in use (SSL, SSTP, NC, DA, applications, ActiveSync, RPC-over-HTTP proxy, and so on) and the way they are used by the users. Basically, the only way to know a specific server's abilities is to measure how it reacts to activity over time. An essential tool for this is the **Performance Monitor** (a.k.a. PerfMon), which is built into all versions of Windows.

By recording performance over time, analysis can be done, showing the relationship between the quantity of users who use the server and its ability to service their requests. The Performance Monitor is useful not only for an initial analysis, but also for ongoing performance monitoring that can tell you how the server is handling changes in usage patterns. Such changes include increase or decrease in the number of users who use the server, the number and type of applications published, changes to the infrastructure (Networking, backend servers, versions of published applications, software and hardware in use by clients, and so on) and more. Collecting this information regularly will allow you to be aware of the normal response of the server, and to clearly see when it changes, and prepare for the dreaded day in which your users or management (probably both) will threaten you with pogroms if the server is not upgraded.

The Performance Monitor is far from simple, and whole books have been written about the various parameters it measures. It is beyond the scope of this book to go into details about what things such as Commit Limit and Privileged Time mean, so we shall only suggest a few counters that are more relevant for performance tracking of a UAG server.

The technique for using the Performance Monitor is as follows. Using the tool, you create a "report", which includes the list of counters that need to be tracked, and the **sample interval** for the measurements (meaning, once per how-much-time should a reading be taken). Then, you activate the logging for a certain amount of time. Typically, either 24 hours, or one week of logging would provide a good pattern for analysis.

A "reading" like this should usually be taken as soon as the server is configured, to serve as a baseline of how the data looks when the server is idle (or as close to idle as possible), and again once a month from then onwards. Since UAG is mostly targeted at users working from home, most servers would show a performance drop (due to higher demand) after the end of a workday, and until the late hours of the night, so those periods need to be looked at closely. The graphs created by the performance monitor can be quite colourful, and have curves that might cause you to gasp, but don't rush into conclusions. For example, the **Packets/Sec** counter of the **Network Interface** object can show big spikes when many users access the server, but that does not indicate a problem or any reason for concern. If, however, you see a parameter that shows a certain graph usually and then suddenly looks much different than last month's reading, this would certainly be something to look into. In such a case, it would probably be a good idea to not wait another month, but take another reading as soon as possible, and see if the new pattern continues.

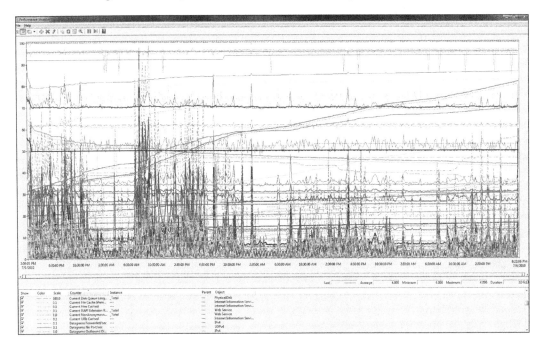

Here are some objects and counters that are good to keep an eye on:

- Internet Information Service Global
- IPv4
- Mcmory
- Network Interface
- Objects

- PhysicalDisk
- Processor
- System
- TCPv4
- UDPv4
- Web Service

Also, track the various counters for the following processes:

- `ActivationMonitor`
- `ConfigMgrCom`
- `Configuration`
- `inetinfo`
- `IsaManagedCtrl`
- `isastg`
- `MonitorMgrCom`
- `mspadmin`
- `ReportingServicesService`
- `SessionMgrCom`
- `ShareAccess`
- `sqlservr`
- `sqlwriter`
- `svchost_rras`
- `uagqessvc`
- `uagrdpsvc`
- `UserMgrCom`
- `w3prefch`
- `w3wp`
- `watchdog_service`
- `whlerrsrvd`
- `whlios`
- `wspsrv`

When creating your PerfMon report, be careful about setting the **sample interval**. The default is to take a sample every 15 seconds, which many administrators believe is not frequent enough. The opposite is true—a 15 second interval is OK if your log is for a few hours, but if you plan on logging for a full week, an internal of once a minute or even once every 5 minutes is perfectly fine. Under no circumstances should you use a lower setting than 15 seconds, as it would not only create huge logs (your computer may actually freeze when trying to display them), it could also reduce UAG's performance.

The tricky part about a PerfMon log is trying to actually understand what's going on from a colourful spread like the one you see in the screenshot above. To do so, select **All the counters**, right-click and choose **Hide selected counters**, which would blank out the display. Now, click on the **Show** checkbox next to an item to display just it, and observe the graph, as well as the **average**, **minimum**, and **maximum** values. Some values may show ups-and-downs, while others may be completely flat. There are no cardinal rules or easy-to-see symptoms, but two things that you should be on the lookout for are:

- Large spikes or drops in something
- A steady incline or decline

A spike or drop that goes back to normal is often not a big cause for alarm—it could be just a period where more users were connected (did anybody say National Holiday?), but it could also mean a connectivity drop that kicked-off many users. For example, an ISP maintenance or regional power outage could cause this. A steady decline or incline are usually more serious, as they may indicate a resource that is being depleted over time, like memory. Note that some PerfMon counters are meant to show a steady incline or decline, like the *Total Bytes Transferred* counter of the *Web Service* object, which shows the total number of bytes of data that have been sent and received by the WWW service since the service started. With so many counters that often have cryptic names, it's not always easy to see, which is why a baseline reading is so important—if you see a pattern that looks odd, compare it to the baseline, or other readings you took in the past. To find out the meaning of a specific counter, use the following links, which detail most of the counters offered above:

- http://technet.microsoft.com/en-us/library/cc776490(WS.10).aspx
- http://technet.microsoft.com/en-us/library/cc738536(WS.10).aspx
- http://technet.microsoft.com/en-us/library/cc786217(WS.10).aspx

Running a server trace

The ultimate monitoring tool is a **server trace**, which records in very high detail what the UAG server does, function by function. This procedure will be discussed in more detail in *Chapter 12*, but for now, we'll just say that this is one of the things professional support engineers at Microsoft use to troubleshoot some of the most complicated issues. The level of detail provided by a trace is extreme, and can produce thousands of lines of data per minute. The following screenshot, for example, represents the activity during a fraction of a second when the server retrieves a SharePoint file.

```
_layouts/1033/core.js?rev=F8pbQQxa4zefcW%2BW9E5g8w%3D%3D
[0]1468.17b4 06/30/2010-14:00:50.954 [whlfiltsecureremote ParserManager.h@89] Entering CParserManager
<CParserVBScript>::GetParser GetParser(ParserRequestHeader):
[0]1468.17b4 06/30/2010-14:00:50.954 [whlfiltsecureremote ParserManager.h@132] Exiting from CParserManager
<CParserVBScript>::GetParser GetParser(ParserRequestHeader, 0000000004F1EB20):
[0]1468.17b4 06/30/2010-14:00:50.954 [whlfiltsecureremote CParserBase::ProcessBuffer ParserBase.cpp@108]
Info:ProcessBuffer(ParserRequestHeader, 000000001EFCBAC0, 729, 0000000000047163A0)
[0]1468.17b4 06/30/2010-14:00:50.954 [whlfiltsecureremote CParserRequestHeader::DumpHeaderToTrace
ParserRequestHeader.cpp@3562] Info:ProcessBuffer(/_layouts/1033/core.js?rev=F8pbQQxa4zefcW%2BW9E5g8w%3D%3D)
StartConnection: Keep-Alive
Accept: */*
Accept-Encoding: identity
Accept-Language: en-us
Cookie:
uniquesig15CE8D1324F7E33497A3DA9E842AC735376CC02773171AC36F66B51C186194E8C76219FF6183F76521E7703645815B29
=PHOHIBBAMGMHMAKKNDPMCANJ; WSS_KeepSessionAuthenticated=91; MSOWebPartPage_AnonymousAccessCookie=91;
dwLastDetectionTimestamp=2010,6,1,9,0,49,0; WhlWinTitle=Home%20-%20Project-B%20Portal;
NLSessionCuagibiza=12T8VlC1mxq6D7Mery96R3stq4bNoYQI9k4KFYJba7zJ/TB2ZBSfArQkGyKSNsWh9h4FJ33G3hgEZIUsOtGFbFC4
YaqtUIV2swx319GNX807WxkgbuNd0mNpJjiC79M2
Host: uag
Referer: http://uag/default.aspx
User-Agent: Mozilla/4.0 (compatible; MSIE 6.0; Windows NT 5.2; SV1; .NET CLR 1.1.4322; .NET CLR 2.0.50727)
UA-CPU: x86

[0]1468.17b4 06/30/2010-14:00:50.954 [whlgenlib GetNextPathPosition url.cpp@23] Info:GetNextPathPosition
String[/_layouts/1033/core.js?rev=F8pbQQxa4zefcW%2BW9E5g8w%3D%3D] Offset [0] FirstPath [0]
[0]1468.17b4 06/30/2010-14:00:50.954 [whlgenlib GetNextPathPosition url.cpp@73] Info:GetNextPathPosition
String[/_layouts/1033/core.js?rev=F8pbQQxa4zefcW%2BW9E5g8w%3D%3D] FirstPath [0]
[0]1468.17b4 06/30/2010-14:00:50.954 [whlgenlib MultipleSearch_DFAImpl::SearchString StringFuncs.cpp@36]
Info:MultipleSearch_DFAImpl::SearchString() : [0000000000F867F0] - Found [1] string [/
_layouts/1033/core.js?rev=F8pbQQxa4zefcW%2BW9E5g8w%3D%3D] , offset [0] , size [1] , type [0]
[0]1468.17b4 06/30/2010-14:00:50.954 [whlgenlib GetNextPathPosition url.cpp@91] Info:GetNextPathPosition
```

Updating the server with Windows Updates

We discussed Windows Updates in *Chapter 2*, where we recommended updating the server with all available Windows Updates prior to installing UAG. Some organizations don't like to install newly released windows updates out of fear that the update may cause harm to the system. Microsoft does, of course, perform extensive testing of each update prior to releasing it, and we strongly recommend keeping the server fully updated at all times. Even though a faulty update may indeed creep through somehow, the risk of running an out-dated server should outweigh the risk of the server crashing and burning. Keep in mind that as soon as an update is publicly released, hackers world-wide reverse-engineer it, and start scanning the web for un-patched servers (hence the term **Exploit Wednesday**, which follows the more famous **patch Tuesday**). Having your server stop working because of an update is an extremely rare occurrence, but getting hit with a known vulnerability is pretty much guaranteed, it's only a matter of time. Naturally, keeping a good backup is always a good idea, and performing another one before applying patches is also recommended.

Assuming you are with us with regards to updating the server, the second consideration is whether to have it update automatically, or let you control this manually. Some administrators don't like their server rebooted without their knowledge or consent, but here comes the risk/gain once again. You probably know that since 2003, Microsoft has purposely released updates on the second Tuesday of every month, so for the most part; you can prepare in advance and notify your users of expected possible outage. Occasionally, high severity updates are released off this schedule, but the patching is done in the middle of the night, so should not affect many users (unless you have many workaholics in your company or many employees that are overseas). Even in case of the latter, we still recommend updating automatically, as you can imagine that if Microsoft elects to break the routine, there's good reason.

Updating the server with UAG updates

Fortunately, UAG updates are farther in-between than Windows updates, and they usually have lesser impact than system patches. As of writing of this book, several updates have been released for UAG, as well as Service Pack 1. UAG updates include not only bug fixes, but also new features, so they are a really good benefit to all. For example, Update 1 includes support for **Microsoft Office Forms Based Authentication (MSOFBA),** which we discussed in *Chapter 4* and enhances SharePoint functionality significantly. It also includes support for **SharePoint 2010**, which was only partially supported in the original UAG release. Update 2 adds support for UAG's Socket Forwarding endpoint component, which we discussed in *Chapter 7*, when running on Windows 7 64-bit client machines, as well as adds support for **Virtual Desktop Infrastructure (VDI)**. Update 2 also improves the publishing of Citrix applications and adds more granularity when configuring VPN access over SSTP. Service Pack 1 includes many changes to DirectAccess, which we will discuss in chapter 11, and it includes all previous updates, and installing it on all UAG servers is recommended both by Microsoft and by us. Further updates and service packs will be released over time, and we strongly suggest keeping on-top of any news on this topic, and consider installing the latest one wherever it's applicable and possible.

Updating UAG should be planned carefully, as the procedure may require a reboot, which will disconnect all current users, of course. Alternatively, it may require an activation, which disconnects SSL-VPN users. Planning is especially important if you are running multiple servers in an array, as it entails a specific procedure. The procedure changes slightly if UAG is used to publish applications, or used as a **DirectAccess** server, so consult the following KB article to learn the exact steps: `http://go.microsoft.com/fwlink/?LinkID=185074`.

The latest service pack (Service Pack 1) itself can be downloaded from here: `http://www.microsoft.com/downloads/en/details.aspx?FamilyID=980ff09f-2d5e-4299-9218-8b3cab8ef77a`

Other updates

In addition to Windows updates and UAG updates, other components of the server may require updating. For example, currently, TMG (which comes with UAG) has a Service Pack available for it, and it should be installed. In fact, installing UAG Service Pack 1 automatically installs TMG Service Pack 1. Usually, Microsoft recommends installing the latest updates to all products, so it would be a good idea to be vigilant about this, and keep an eye out for updates to TMG, as well as to the SQL server that is installed with it.

Antivirus on the server and other tools

We have mentioned countless times in this book (or so it seems) that you should *not* install anything on your UAG server, other than UAG itself. This, of course, raises the question of an Antivirus. Having good virus protection is very important, and the "do not install" statements are not referring to this, although it does require some additional considerations.

An Antivirus scanner, by design, may have to scan all system files on a server, and it may "hold" a file in use when it does so. UAG, TMG, IIS, and SQL running on the server may not appreciate this and behave strangely. To guarantee stable performance, you should exclude certain folders and files from the Antivirus scanning process.

Excluding paths and files is different for every Antvirus product, so consult your documentation on how to do this. The paths that need to be excluded are:

- `%ProgramFiles%\Microsoft Forefront Threat Management Gateway`
- `%ProgramFiles%\Microsoft SQL Server\MSSQL10.ISARS`
- `%ProgramFiles%\Microsoft SQL Server\MSSQL10.MSFW`
- `%ProgramFiles%\Microsoft Forefront Unified Access Gateway`

For more details about excluding paths from Antivirus scans, refer to the following guide: `http://technet.microsoft.com/en-us/library/cc707727.aspx`.

Sometimes, you may need to install additional software on the UAG server for administrative/technical reasons. One common example is device-specific software that some servers require, such as **RAID** array configuration software, or some hardware device's driver installation executable. Over the years, there has been more than one occasion where various software programs conflicted with UAG or its predecessors, so this is certainly something to be weary of, even though these software programs seem harmless. We cannot provide a list of software that is safe or not, so the general guidelines would be to avoid any installation that is not absolutely critical (who needs those fancy Gamma-correction options from the display driver anyway, right?) and delay the ones who *are* as much as possible, so you can establish a baseline for a fully functional server before any foreign influences. Then, install each piece of software independently, with at least some delay between them. This way, you will at least be able to isolate and determine if the software has any adverse effect on the server. In case you do find that such a piece of software causes a problem, it might be tough getting support for the situation. Microsoft support will most likely request that you first uninstall it, and the software's vendor may also decline to invest time in finding the cause of the conflict. If such a situation arises, you might find it more expedient to simply swap-out the hardware, or use UAG as a Virtual Machine (Microsoft does support the **Hyper-V integration services** software). For example, one of our customers discovered that a certain multi-port Network Card caused a blue-screen if you connected to the server with Remote-Desktop and ran intensive Batch files that refreshed the screen quickly. The card manufacturer refused to address it, forcing the company to replace all the cards for thousands of dollars.

Backing up UAG

The importance of backing up is something that goes without saying, right? Well, better safe than sorry, so we will say it anyway: backup your server as often as humanly possible! While doing that, there are certain important things to know about backing up this specific product.

The good news is that UAG can automatically create a backup each time you perform a configuration-activation, so even if you neglected or forgot to do a regular backup, there's a good chance that you have a bunch of usable backups at any point in time. The not-so-good news is that a backup doesn't backup quite everything.

The backup mechanism built into UAG creates an **XML** file containing the trunk and application configuration, but it does not include the local Network configuration or the computer's **certificates**. This means that if you neglect to back those up separately, a restore won't get you very far.

Don't worry, though—backing these up is not that difficult. A very useful and efficient way to back up the server is available if you are running UAG as a **virtual machine**. Saving a **Snapshot** every now-and-then would allow you a quick and easy restore in the event of a configuration corruption. You can also export the Virtual Machine and save it to another server or to removable media to protect against disk crashes or to have an off-site backup. If not, you might use some other disk-imaging utility to save everything in one neat package. If all these are not available or preferred, Windows 2008 R2, like all previous server products, contains very advanced backup software. In fact, the 2008 R2 version of the backup software even contains some new features, like advanced power-shell support that allows you to perform backups using scripts and schedules. You can read more about the built in backup utility here: `http://technet.microsoft.com/en-us/library/cc754097(WS.10).aspx`

Backing up UAG itself involves the following steps:

1. Open the UAG management console.
2. From the **File** menu, select **Export.**
3. Choose a name and location for the export.
4. Type in a password, which will be used to encrypt and secure your backup.

To do this even better, we recommend creating a batch or script, and scheduling the backup to occur automatically. Typically, UAG backups don't take a lot of space, so even if you store all and do a cleanup once every few months, drive space should not become a problem. The command-line configuration tool is called **configmgrutil** (it can do more than backup!), and is located at `C:\ Program Files\Microsoft Forefront Unified Access Gateway\utils\ConfigMgr`. This command accepts three parameters, in the following format:

configmgrutil export *filename password* [comment]

```
Administrator: Command Prompt                                           _ □ ×

C:\>"C:\Program Files\Microsoft Forefront Unified Access Gateway\utils\ConfigMgr
\ConfigMgrUtil.exe" export e:\backup\UAGBackup11Jul2010.xml P@$$w0rd "Backup11Ju
l10"
All configuration files were exported successfully.
C:\>
```

The backups that you create yourself can be stored anywhere you want, but the automatic ones that are created during activation are saved to `C:\ProgramData\ Microsoft\UAG\Autobackups`. It's important to know that this folder is hidden by default, so you might need to change your Explorer's View settings to see them. A backup takes longer to complete and occupies more disk space if you have more trunks and applications, but should not usually take more than a few minutes. Keep in mind that a local backup is great, but hard drives fail too, so be sure to copy or move the backups to another server, or at least another disk drive.

If you are experienced with IAG, UAG's predecessor, then another thing that's good to know is that you might run into a CAB file in the place where IAG used to keep its backups (the "backup" folder that's under the main UAG folder in Program Files). This file is part of UAG's array synchronization mechanism, so it may be very important if you use an array, but it is not a "real" backup, and you cannot perform a restore from it.

If you are not backing up the entire server using one of the options previously mentioned (VM snapshot or the built-in Windows backup utility), be sure to also backup the things UAG's backup does not store:

1. The computer's Network card configuration (IP, Subnet Mask, Default Gateway, DNS, and WINS)

2. The computer's domain configuration (the computer name, and to which domain it is joined, if you have more than one)

3. The computer's routing configuration, such as static routes

4. Any certificates installed on the computer for use with UAG

5. Log files generated by UAG (for the purpose of querying usage or generating reports)

6. Other third party configuration, such as two-factor authentication components

Restoring UAG (to itself, and to other servers)

Creating a backup is the easy part, of course. How lovely would it be if you could do the restore at your leisure-but that's never how it is, huh? Well, you can prepare for it by doing it at least once every few months for practice. To get a real sense of how it may look when you need to recover from a real crash, it would be best to perform the restore on a different server — perhaps you already have one in a test-environment, or on a Virtual machine.

The first important thing to keep in mind is that if your backup was created on a server with a certain update (or service pack, when those come out), the server should be brought to that same level of installation before attempting to restore. If this is impossible for some reason, you can force the server to accept a different-version backup by modifying the registry key: `HKEY_LOCAL_MACHINE\Software\WhaleCom\e-Gap\Configuration\`.

Create a DWORD (32-bit) value `ImportFromOtherVersion`, and set its value to `1`.

However, changes made to the product with updates or service packs can make the result unpredictable, so we recommend restoring to the same version whenever possible.

We already said that some things are not included in UAG's export, so to perform a restore follow these steps, in order:

1. Install the Windows 2008 R2 operating system on the server.

2. Restore or reconfigure the networking and routing.

3. Restore or reconfigure the computer's name and domain membership (if it is a domain member, of course).

4. Install available Windows updates.

5. Install UAG, as outlined in *Chapter 2*.

6. Restore UAG's log files, if required.

7. Import any certificates that you might need.

8. Install and configure any third party components.

9. If the backup you have was created on a server with an update, service pack, roll up and so on, install the updates.

10. Import the backed up UAG configuration.

11. Activate the UAG configuration.

12. You may need to reconfigure the trunk's certificate settings manually through the Trunk configuration page.

Restoring a backup to another server can be useful for a situation where you need to create a backup server for disaster recovery. Doing so is a valid approach, although using a Virtual Machine is a safer way, as it reduces the number of steps required, and eliminates most of the possible human-errors. If you do need to restore to another server from a regular backup, the procedure will be very similar to the one above. If the purpose is to have a hot-backup (one that is alive and ready to accept user connections if the primary site goes offline), there are several approaches to this, and this must be carefully planned with the help of a disaster recovery expert. Keep in mind that changing the IP address of a UAG server after it has been installed is not supported, so attention must be given as to the routing and DNS aspects of this.

Summary

In this chapter, we have discussed various techniques and tools to monitor and manage the server, as well as protecting it from disaster. These techniques and tools are important for the purpose of keeping the server ticking and cope with some problems and disasters. These tools will also be very useful when we look into troubleshooting and problem solving further down the road. In the next chapter, we will look into Advanced Trunk Configurations, and what it can do to enhance our security.

10
Advanced Configuration

The Trunk configuration is one place we have visited only briefly so far, but it contains some of the most important configuration features of UAG. Many of the options can drastically alter key features of UAG, such as the security rules and the access policy, as well as content handling. In this chapter we will look into all those things and what they can do for us.

Basic trunk configuration

The main trunk configuration screen is something we see constantly, so before moving forward, let's review some of the things we can do with it. This screen is the one that shows the trunk's public host name, IP, port, and more. We typically set these when using the **Create New Trunk Wizard**, and some of them can be changed here. You can type a new public host name for your trunk, or choose another IP from those configured on the computer, and if NLB is enabled, you can also select if the trunk will be using integrated or non-integrated NLB. You may be disappointed to learn that you cannot just select any TCP port, but are limited to port 443 for HTTPS trunks, and port 80 for HTTP trunks. The port selection option in the UAG console doesn't really do anything, but it exists there since with UAG's predecessors, you could actually choose any port you wanted to use.

Another important setting is the **Initial application**. The default setting for this is the Portal, which means that users who log in to the trunk will see the portal homepage which displays a list of applications. You can use this drop-down list to select some of the other applications configured. If you do change this setting, the **Use portal frame** option turns active, and by checking this option, you can make the portal completely hidden. It's important to understand, though, that if your plan is to have users go directly to an application, without going first through the portal, then you can also achieve this by publishing that application using one of the **application specific hostname** templates. For example, **SharePoint** and **Communicator Web Access** can do this, as well as generic web apps that use the **Web Publishing (Application Specific Hostname)** option.

The application list is something we have also mentioned before, but before we go on we should mention that beyond the **Add**, **Edit**, and **Remove** buttons, you can also have additional functionality via the use of the right-click button. These add the ability to duplicate existing applications, and also to disable active applications or re-enable disabled ones.

Another option that appears on the bottom-right is the ability to limit an application to certain subnets. This provides a general restriction, useful in case your UAG server is attached directly to your corporate network, and you'd rather that it didn't have access to all the network resources.

Lastly, the **Configure** button in the bottom middle opens up the **Advance Trunk Configuration** window, which is where the fun begins:

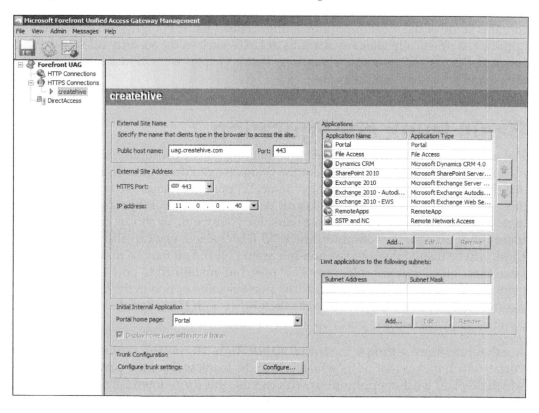

Advanced configuration overview

The advanced trunk configuration screen has nine tabs:

1. **General**: This tab controls some troubleshooting settings, but most importantly, the server **SSL certificate** (on HTTPS trunks only, of course) used by this trunk.

2. **Authentication:** This tab controls how UAG authenticates users who attempt to log into the trunk. It also controls the logon and logoff pages, the session termination timer and the setting which allows you to enable the OWA look and feel for the portal.

3. **Session:** This tab controls how UAG manages sessions, such as session timeout, the maximum number of concurrent sessions and the **session endpoint cleanup component**. It also controls the endpoint component use and **certified endpoint** use.

4. **Endpoint Access Settings:** This tab controls the **endpoint policies** applied to the trunk, including the use of **NAP** policies. We have already covered this in *Chapter 8*, so we won't cover it again here.

5. **Application Customization:** This tab controls how UAG customizes applications using the **Application Wrapper**.

6. **Portal:** This tab defines additional parameters, like the ability to skip parsing of certain HTTP requests and responses, and allows you to configure additional string replacements on certain URLs.

7. **URL Inspection:** This tab configures allowed HTTP methods, as well as allowed characters in URLs for the various applications.

8. **Global URL settings:** This tab controls various elements that pertain to UAG's interaction with URLs, such as global parameters in URLs, values that are to be rejected and patterns for identifying URLs as downloads, uploads and more.

9. **URL Set:** This tab controls the URL inspection engine, which allows you to block certain URL and parameter patterns.

We will now go into specific details about the above tabs, and how to configure them. This is not intended to be a dictionary listing each and every available option, but more to discuss the real-world implications of the significant ones. This also means we will be ignoring options that are self-explanatory. For example, the **maximum logon attempts** setting on the authentication page we don't feel takes a single additional word to understand what it means. Cool?

The General tab

The **General** tab has very few settings, the most important of which is the **Server Certificate**. Naturally, it only appears on HTTPS trunks, and shows the name of the certificate that is currently assigned to the trunk. As you already know, the certificate is selected when the trunk is created, but occasionally, you may need to change it. One such common occasion is when you decide to switch to a **wild-card certificate**, and another is when the certificate is expiring and you have renewed it. The certificate selection is a drop-down, which shows all the certificates from the "personal" folder of the **local computer certificate store**. Since the drop-down does not show the full details of the certificate, it can be confusing if you have more than one certificate with the same name (which can happen if you have purchased a new certificate to replace one that is expiring). In such a situation, you can use the **Certificate Hash**, also known as **Thumbprint**, to know which certificate you are looking at. To compare, open the local computer's certificate store on the UAG server, and check the thumbprints of your certificates. Then, compare it to what you see under **certificate hash** in the **Advanced Trunk Configuration** server certificate selection area.

To open the local computer's certificate store, follow these steps:

1. Click **Start**, and then click **Run**.
2. Type **MMC** and click **OK**.
3. Click **Console** in the new MMC you created, and then click **Add/Remove Snap-in**.
4. In the new window, click **Add**.
5. Highlight the Certificates snap-in, and then click **Add**.
6. Choose the **Computer** option and click **Next**.
7. Select **Local Computer** on the next screen, and then click **OK**.
8. Click **Close**, and then click **OK**.

You have now added the **Certificates snap-in**, which will allow you to work with any certificates in your computer's certificate store. You may want to save this MMC for later use.

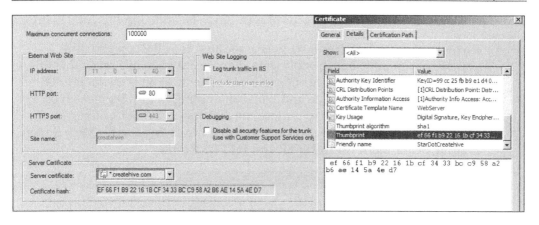

The setting at the top of the **General** tab controls the maximum number of concurrent connections to the UAG portal. Do not mistake this to mean that you can just push this number up to get more "bang for your buck" from your server. This setting defaults to 100,000, but that does not necessarily mean that your server can actually handle that many clients at once. The actual number depends on the server's hardware, and even more on the *type* of applications in use, and your user's *usage patterns*. The purpose of this setting is to be able to limit the number, in case you are running into performance issues.

For example, you might notice that, when reaching a certain number of concurrent connections, those angry phone calls start pouring in; complaining that the response time is unacceptably slow. In such a situation, you may choose to reduce the maximum number to something that is lower, so that even though some users will be completely denied access, the others will at least have a comfortable experience. The real solution to such a situation, of course, is to boost your hardware via a server upgrade or by adding an additional server and forming (or extending) a **server cluster** with **load-balancing**.

The setting for **Web Site Logging** actually turns on logging on **IIS** for the website associated with this trunk. This can serve as a rudimentary troubleshooting step in case you want to see which URLs the portal is serving, in case the browser shows a HTTP error that you want to get details for, or in case your organization requires logging to be enabled.

There are some words of caution/words of wisdom to be added to this little feature:

- If you have an HTTPS trunk with its associated **HTTP Redirect trunk**, you might run into some trouble should you want to enable or disable this setting, since **Web Site Logging** needs to be identical on both the HTTPS trunk and the redirect trunk, and when attempting to turn it on or off on one trunk, as soon as you try to close the Advanced Trunk Configuration window by clicking on OK, you will get an error saying **Enable Web Server logging is not identical in HTTP and HTTPS trunks**.

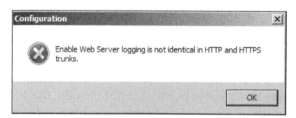

  Therefore, the only way to change the settings is to **disable** one of the trunks, typically the redirect one (by right-clicking on the trunk name in the left tree-view and choosing **Disable** from the pop-up menu), and then change the **Web Site Logging** setting on the other trunk, and then enable the first trunk back and change its **Web Site Logging** too.

- This setting actually configures IIS, so it has an equivalent option in the IIS Manager console. However, one should *never* use the IIS Manager console to turn on and off IIS logging, since when doing that, UAG is not aware of the setting made in the IIS console, and it gets "confused". This can lead to serious problems.

Debug mode is another troubleshooting mechanism, which basically disables all security features of the trunk, such as **URL inspection** and **endpoint policy enforcement**. Generally, this is not very useful, because almost all security issues can be understood well through the warnings displayed in the **Web Monitor**, but it can be used if you want a quick-and-dirty bypass of all of them just to run a quick check on something.

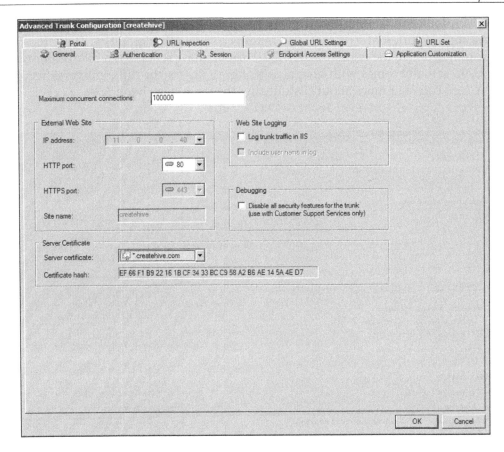

The Authentication tab

We have discussed most of the options of the authentication tab back in *Chapter 6*, except the setting for the **Outlook Web Access look and feel**. This checkbox configures UAG to change its default visual theme to one that resembles **Outlook Web Access**. It does not change the whole server—just the **Login** page, **Logoff** page, **System Information** page, and the **Error** page. The purpose is to give users a nicer user experience in case your organization wants to publish OWA as a primary (or only) application. Notice that when you check that checkbox, UAG automatically changes the parameters on the **User logon page** line from Login.asp to OWA/Login.asp.

The OWA look and feel simply switches UAG to a different set of ASP files, which have a slightly different structure, and reference some other graphics. These too can be customized, like the regular `Login.asp`. The naming scheme is a bit different, and UAG actually comes with several sets of graphics for the different versions of OWA. You can read more about customizing the login page here: `http://technet.microsoft.com/en-us/library/ff607319.aspx`.

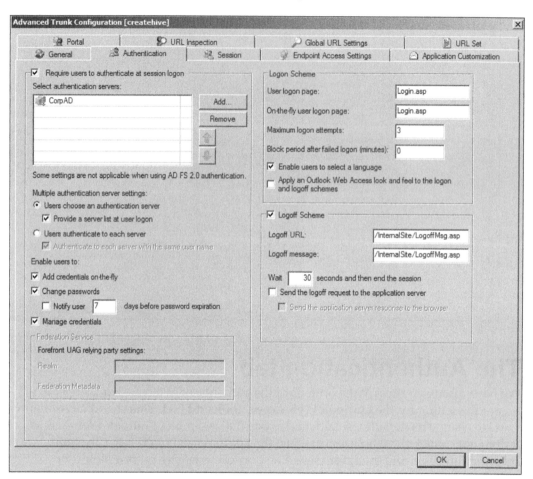

The Session tab

The **Session** tab is an important one, as it has a significant impact on the server's security and performance. The most visible piece is the **Default Session Settings**, on the right. These have a very noticeable impact on your users' experience with the portal, and you would probably want to tinker with them a bit.

Before going into detail, let's understand the difference between a **regular session** and a **Privileged session**. The idea with these two is that you might want to make the lives of some users easier, for example by letting their sessions be inactive for a longer duration, if they meet certain requirements. If you recall, we discussed this briefly in *Chapter 8*, where we saw how you can configure a trunk with a **Privileged Endpoint policy**. That policy would be typically different (usually stricter) than the regular access policy. For example, the regular policy could allow any endpoint in, but the privileged endpoint policy could check if the computer is a **corporate machine**. The logic behind such a move would be that a corporate machine is typically at a user's home or office, so it's not so terrible if the computer is left unattended for a few minutes and cleaning up after the session is not critical. If, though, the computer is unknown, it could be somebody else's computer, or some public computer, so we need to make sure that the computer is cleaned up after the session, and that the session gets terminated if it's unattended for even a short time.

The settings for the default sessions and privileged sessions are separate, but similar:

- Inactive Session Timeout: This controls the time after which a session is considered to be inactive and disconnected. UAG concludes that the user is inactive if no requests are received for that session for **Web applications**, or if there's no mouse and keyboard activity for other application types.

- Trigger logoff scheme after: This setting controls the maximum session length, after which a session logoff is triggered even if the user is active.

- Delete cookies at logoff: When this is enabled, logging off a session clears **cookies** that were received as part of the log-off request by overwriting their content with a blank value. This is very important for applications which use cookies to track their users. **SharePoint**, for example, is one such application that can go awry if the cookies are not cleared properly.

- Request no browser caching: Browsers are designed to automatically cache certain types of static files, like image files, HTML and others. This caching is done to speed up browsing, of course, and enabling this option causes UAG to add to each HTTP response it sends to the browser an instruction for the browser *not* to cache the file. This is a good security measure, because the cached files can have a potential security risk, as they could be harvested and become an information-leak issue.

- Activate Endpoint Session Cleanup component: If you want to *not* use the endpoint cleanup, this is the place to block it. However, it's important to remember that letting files remain behind can cause not only **information leak**, but may also affect the behaviour of some applications.

- Prompt user to disconnect if the portal closes without logging off: This is only relevant for applications that are **tunnelled (client/server applications** and **browser-embedded applications**, as well as **TS Client Tunneling** and **TS Web Client Tunneling**). When a user is using an **SSL-VPN** application and logs off the portal, the tunnel is also disconnected. However, if he just closes the browser, the tunnel can remain open. When this is enabled, and a user closes his browser while an SSL-VPN tunnel is running, he is prompted to disconnect the tunnel as well.

- Reopen the portal if the user does not disconnect: This complements the previous option, and is quite self-explanatory.

The configuration options on the top-left affect **global session settings**. The **Maximum Concurrent Sessions** is similar, but separate from the Connections settings we saw on the **General** tab. This is because a session can have several connections, but *not* the other way around. The unauthenticated sessions limit may be more useful, because in some circumstances, a large number of those might get created. For example, Smart phones performing **ActiveSync** are designed to keep the same session active all day long, but if the phone is not configured correctly, it might create a new, unauthenticated session every 15 minutes. Even a small number of phones can generate a large amount of renegade sessions.

The **Session threshold** settings (for both types of sessions) default to **0**, but it can be configured with an actual value that will trigger a message to the Web Monitor, so that you can get an active notification that the server is loaded. For example, if you already discovered that your server's capacity is 1000 concurrent sessions, but the normal usage is half that, you can set an alert at 900. This will let you know that your day is about to go down the drain, so you can at least get that lunch 'to go' and go check out what's up with the server.

The Error message URL setting points to the ASP page that shows various errors to the user. The purpose here is to allow for customization. By creating a custom file in the /InternalSite/CustomUpdate folder, you can have an error page with your own look and feel, or any other customization that is required.

Below the error page setting is a very important option: **Disable component installation and activation**. You don't need to read the entire book to know what this does, but it's important to consider the implications before setting this. Some UAG customers feel the whole component installation is unsavoury, especially when the user base is the general public. This is a valid perception, but before deciding to do away with the client components, keep in mind that they are not only about detection. We already talked about problems that can happen if you disable the Endpoint Cleanup component, but disabling the entire suite of client components also prevents the use of SSL-VPN tunneling, which makes many application types unusable. We are not saying this should never be done, just one decision that needs careful attention, planning, and testing.

Disabling scripting is a troubleshooting option that prevents an application from launching prerequisite applications, if any have been configured for it, as well as its **startup page**, if one was configured (this is a setting in the application's **Portal Link** tab). Selecting this setting also *disables* client/server applications.

The **DNS suffix** option is designed for a situation where you define a server for an application, where the server's name is a **short-name** (**NETBIOS name**) only. Keep in mind that if you don't set this, UAG will use its *own* DNS suffix by default. Also, remember that this is a *global* setting, and applies to *all* the backend servers on *all* the applications, so if your servers have multiple domain suffixes, you would be better off configuring your published applications with FQDN names for the servers.

Lastly, the option for **bind the source IP address to the session** is somewhat confusing. Contrary to what may appear obvious, it is NOT related to linking the client's source IP to its session, but to linking the UAG's internal IP address to sessions, when it communicates with internal web servers. This can be useful if you have multiple IP addresses defined on the internal NIC of your UAG server, and you want to control which IP address will be used by UAG to forward HTTP requests to the backend web servers. This is an advanced option which requires the creation of a custom script, and is beyond the scope of this book.

To learn more about this option, visit the following URL: `http://blogs.technet.com/b/edgeaccessblog/archive/2010/03/18/what-is-the-bind-the-source-ip-address-to-the-session-option.aspx`.

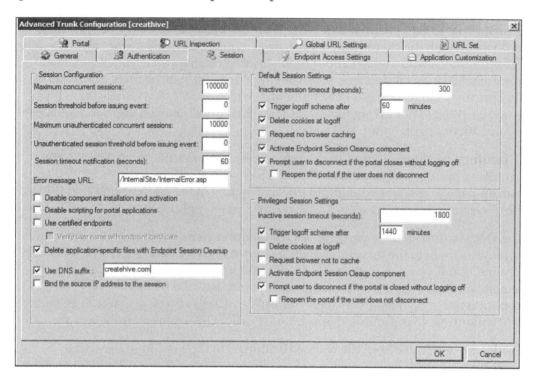

The Application Customization tab

The application customization is all about UAG's **content parsing**, part of which is the **Host Address Translation (HAT)** process. If you don't recall, this is the mechanism that iterates through web pages that UAG delivers to its users, looks for links and rewrites the URLs. This is done, of course, for every web application, but UAG also includes some specific templates for specific applications. For example, **Outlook Web Access** requires very specific changes to be made to the HTML code that is sent to the user and so do **SharePoint** and **Microsoft CRM 4**. In fact, you can take a look at this yourself by opening the file, `HTTPS_WhlFiltAppWrap_ForPortal.xml`, located in `C:\Program Files\Microsoft Forefront Unified Access Gateway\von\conf\WizardDefaults\AppWrapTemplates`.

Don't be tempted to change this file, though! You can create a custom file to perform your own changes to data coming from an application, but this is beyond the scope of this book. It is discussed with more detail here: `http://technet.microsoft.com/en-us/library/ff607339.aspx`.

By default, the use of application customization is *enabled*, and set to *Automatic*. The option to set it to manual is designed for customization of specific trunk types that no longer exist in UAG, so this option does not carry any usable functionality

The parsing engine is designed for **Web applications**, and so it is preset to do its work on text files – HTML, ASP, XML, JavaScript, and so on. You can, however, modify the list and add other content types, if required. This could be useful if you are trying to publish an application that uses text files, but carry a content-type header that is other than "text". For example, some applications may send pages marked with a content type of "multipart". In such a case, these pages will not be parsed by UAG, unless you add them here. To add a content type, click on **Add** and specify the content type using a **Regular Expression** (refer to Appendix A for an introduction to Regular Expressions). For our example, "multipart" has 14 different sub-types (http://www.iana.org/assignments/media-types/multipart/), so you could include all of them by adding the content type with a wildcard:

```
multipart/.*
```

You can also add just a few sub-types by using the following Regular Expression:

```
multipart/(form-data|header-set|mixed)
```

The question is, how would you know that your application requires a different content type, or what it is? This calls for some more detective work. A sign that something is wrong can be if you see that UAG is unable to sign links in your application. This is visible by some links not working, or only partially working. You can confirm this by recording your session with a tool like **HTTPWatch** or **Fiddler**, which we already mentioned in *Chapter 8*, and viewing the page's content. If, in the content, you find links to **internal server names**, and there are NO signed links at all, this might indicate such a situation (a situation where only some of the links are signed is something else, which we will discuss in *Chapter 12*). You can confirm this by viewing the file's **content type** in the HTTPWatch of Fiddler recording. If it is not one of the default content types (text/everything, application/javascript, and application/xml), then you may have found the culprit.

If you do need to configure additional content types, you need to also add it to a custom SRA template file. To do so, create a text file with the following format, and place it on the UAG server in the folder ...\Microsoft Forefront Unified Access Gateway\von\Conf\<trunk_name>\conf\CustomUpdate. If the folder does not exist, create it. Name the file WhlFiltSecureRemote_HTTP.xml if your trunk is an HTTP trunk, and name it WhlFiltSecureRemote_HTTPS.xml if this is a secure trunk. Note that the **Application Type** is based on the application type that is targeted by this customization, so adjust it based on your specific needs.

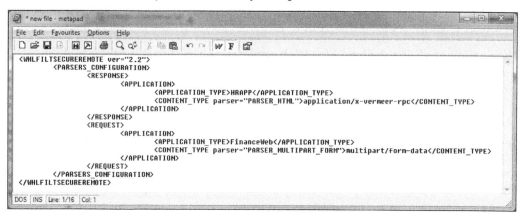

The last option on this page is **compression handling**. Sometimes, web servers send data in compressed form, which is useful for bandwidth conservation. Typically, you have little or no control over this, but that's OK, because UAG is designed to handle this. When UAG receives data from a backend server in a compressed form, it still has to be able to handle it, and this is what this setting is about. It comes pre-populated with most popular extensions, but you can remove or add others. If you are publishing an application that uses compression, and using file extensions that are not listed here, you should add these extensions. The default extension list is: exe, dll, aspx, php, html, htm, htc, css, js, xsl, xml, cgi, asp, jsp, no_ext, mspx, nsf, htt, stm, bas, c, etx, h, rtx, txt, uls, and vcf

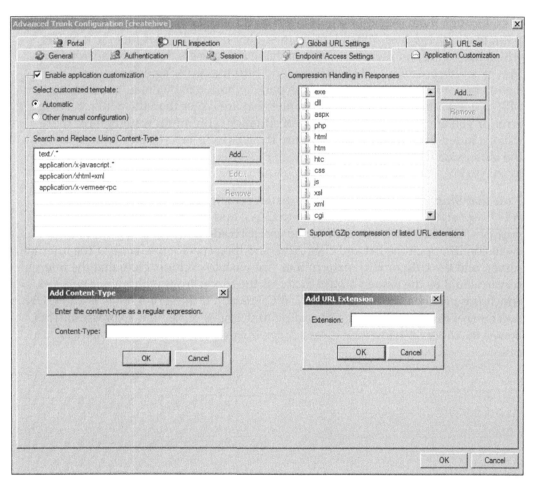

The Portal tab

The **Portal** tab is basically an extension to the **Application Customization** tab, adding some more configuration options related to UAGs parsing engine. The first part, **Skip Body Parsing**, allows you to configure specific servers and URLs on which UAG should *not* perform parsing on the body of the HTTP requests and/or HTTP responses, a.k.a. HTTP data. Note that UAG will always perform parsing on the HTTP headers. This could be useful if some responses contain files that have links in them, which you do not wish UAG to parse. For example, a server might hold documents that users are downloading, and these documents contain textual links that should remain as they are. By adding these URLs here, you can tell UAG not to go through them. Another scenario where this can be useful is when some URLs point to very large files. When UAG parses files, it accumulates them in a **buffer**, which uses up server memory, so if you have many users downloading very large files, it could consume a lot of memory and hurt the server's performance. This is a good opportunity to mention that the parsing buffer is, by default, limited to 10 MB, so users attempting to download files that are larger than this will receive an error. If you are running into this sort of situation, you might want to have these files excluded from parsing, or configure the UAG server's registry to increase the buffer size. This is discussed here: `http://blogs.technet.com/b/ben/archive/2010/03/25/parsian-gulf.aspx`

Note that **Skip Body Parsing** has two distinct configurations — the top one is for *HTTP requests* (data sent from the user to UAG) and the lower one is for *HTTP responses* (files sent back via UAG to the user). To add a Server and URL to the exclusion list, open the list and click **Add**, and then specify the name of the internal server, and the URL or URL pattern that you wish to exclude. Note that the internal server would be the name you use to access the server from within your network, which is typically a short-name (a NETBIOS name). If the server name is an **FQDN**, don't forget to adjust the string according to the rules of Regular Expression. This means that a server named `hr.createhive.com` would be configured here as `hr\.createhive\.com`.

URLs configured here should start with a slash, and also use Regular Expression, whether it's a single URL, or a pattern covering multiple URLs.

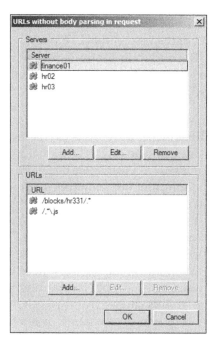

The settings for **Search and Replace Response Content** look similar to the **Skip Body Parsing** URL configuration list, but it is designed to specifically look for URLs in areas of the text that are usually not inspected. For example, sometimes a URL would appear in a page's text, and such links are normally not rewritten. By specifying such a URL here, you are forcing UAG to go through each and every link on the page, no matter where it is.

The **Manual URL Replacement** configuration is a last resort measure, if you will, for handling requests that cannot be handled by the engine automatically. This doesn't mean it's never used, in fact, when you publish an **Exchange** server, the template includes a configuration that is pushed here automatically, as you can see in the following screenshot. A manual configuration may be required, though, if you have some specific request that you want to manually handle. In this case, you specify the server name and details, and the source and destination URL. As always, the URL and Server name should be specified using Regular Expression.

The **replacement type** has two options — **Redirect** and **Reroute**. When you specify that the replace should be a redirect, UAG will issue it as an **HTTP 302** status response, instructing the browser to redirect to the specified URL. This is suitable for most applications. In some cases, though, a Reroute is needed, and UAG will then simply change the URL of the received HTTP request to whatever you have configured here as the To URL, and then continue processing this request, without involving the browser. This is suitable for applications that cannot handle a 302 redirect, such as **WebDav** applications.

This is a fallback mechanism for URLs that may not be signed (or as we like to refer to it, "not **HAT**-ed"), due to various reasons (dynamically built on client-side, embedded in Word or PDF files, and so on). A URL that is not signed might point to a totally different server than the UAG (for example: `http://sharepoint`). When that happens — this is not the solution, but sometimes, some URLs may still point back to the UAG public host name, just not include the HAT "signature". If this is the case, the browser will send such a request to UAG, but UAG may not know which backend server to send the request to, due to the missing HAT prefix. This is where this configuration comes into play. You can configure UAG to tell it what to do with a URL that is received by UAG without the HAT — where to send it to, whether to do it by redirecting the browser, or by simply forwarding it directly to that backend server (this is called "reroute" in this context), and whether to leave the URL as it was sent by the client (the most common scenario), or maybe to modify it (this is the optional value that can be entered in the To URL field).

UAG also allows you to configure **dynamic forwarding rules** by checking the option **Dynamic**. This, however, requires the creation of a dynamic hook, which we will not cover here. For more information about this, refer to this resource: `http://technet.microsoft.com/en-us/library/dd278056.aspx`.

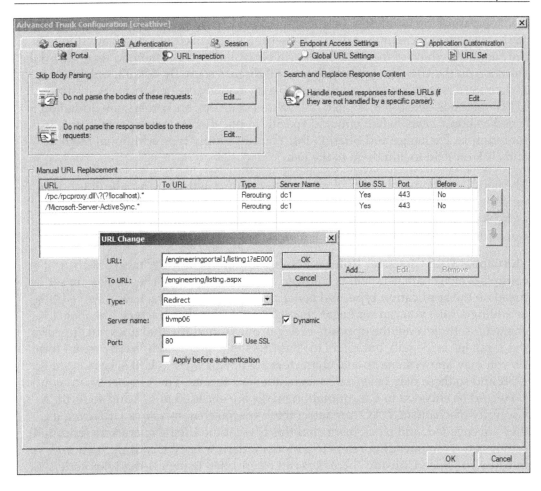

The URL Inspection tab

The **URL Inspection** tab is one of the most important ones, if security is high on your priority list. It controls the **HTTP methods** that UAG will allow, and the **characters** that will be permitted within URLs.

The top part of the tab shows, on the right, the currently available HTTP methods, or **verbs**, as they're sometimes called. This setting doesn't actually block anything—it only controls which of these methods will be available in the method drop-down list selection on the **URL Set** tab, which we will discuss soon. By default, only GET, POST, PUT, DELETE, TRACE, and HEAD are available on a newly created trunk. Some other HTTP methods, like OPTIONS, RPC_IN_DATA, PROPFIND, and others, are added on a "need-to-know basis" when you add specific applications to your portal trunk, like, for example, **Exchange** and **SharePoint**. You can simply type additional methods and click on **Add** to add them to the list.

The middle section of this tab allows you to define a maximum size limit for data uploaded by clients using HTTP requests with the POST and PUT methods, as well as to block the HTTP response headers **WWW-Authenticate: Negotiate:**. These two can protect against some types of **Denial of Service (DOS)** attacks.

The **Global URL Character Rules** is another important security mechanism, as it controls which characters will be allowed as part of requests. These rules are set based on the **application type**, and contain a list of Legal characters. When editing or adding a rule, you can set **Legal characters** *and* **Illegal characters**. The illegal character setting is not the opposite of 'legal' ones (anything that does not appear in the 'legal' list is illegal!), but refers to characters that are disallowed in *encoded* form. As you may know, some special characters are not allowed in URLs, because of RFC 1738, and so these may be encoded using the %xx format. The 'Greater Than' symbol (>) would be encoded to %3E, quotation marks are encoded to %22 and so forth. As a security mechanism, UAG can detect these special characters in a URL even if they are encoded, and block them, and this is what the **Illegal characters (encoded)** setting is for. **%u encoding** refers to a more modern way of encoding characters in URLs, in which **Unicode** characters can be encoded using a 4-digit hex code, preceded by %u. For example, a lowercase 'a' with the German Umlaut (ä) would be encoded as %u00E4. To learn more about character encoding in URLs, refer to RFC 1738: http://www.rfc-editor.org/rfc/rfc1738.txt.

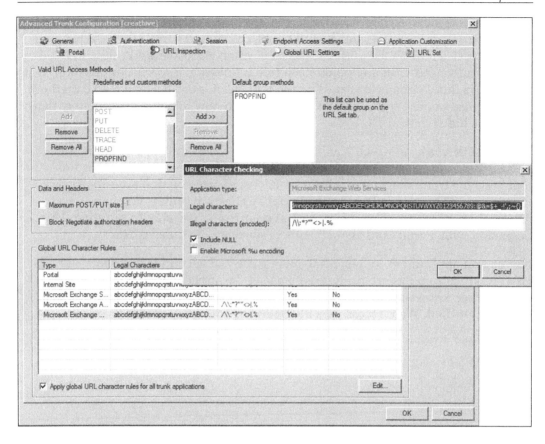

Global URL Settings and URL Set tabs

The **Global URL Settings** tab hosts additional configuration settings that pertain to the **URL Set**, and so it is time to introduce it. We will talk about the **URL Set** tab first, and then go back to the Global URL Settings.

The **URL Set**, also known as **URL List**, **Rule Set** or **Security Rules** is one of the most important security mechanisms within UAG. This is basically an engine that checks each web request that UAG receives from clients against a list of rules, and determines if it is to be allowed or denied. This engine is extremely powerful, as it allows the administrator to configure what is OK and what is not with a high level of granularity. We have already glimpsed at these rules earlier, in *Chapter 3*, and soon we will learn how to configure it.

The URL Set is a list of rules that define URL patterns (using our favourite mechanism: **Regular Expressions**), and how UAG should handle them. When you publish applications on the portal, some application templates add rules, and you can also add your own at any point. Each rule is linked to a specific application by its *type*, and includes options for handling the URL itself, as well as the **HTTP methods** that a request can use and specific configuration on how to handle **parameters** that may be included in the URL.

Even a blank trunk, on which you have not yet published any applications, has a few dozen rules pertaining to the **InternalSite** default website (this is the site that hosts the trunk's login and admin functions, in case you don't recall). Also, a freshly-created trunk would have the **Portal application** (unless you have removed it), and that adds more rules. If you look at your trunk, you should see about 12 rules beginning with 'Portal', and about 55 others starting with 'InternalSite'.

As you add applications to the portal, more rules will get added automatically. The UAG product team has pre-configured some of the application templates, based on their deep knowledge of how the applications they are intended for work. For example, **Outlook Web Access** uses the following folders as part of its operation:

- owa
- forms
- exchange
- exchweb

Therefore, OWA's template has been pre-configured with them, as well as with the URL parameters that it needs to accept. If you have already published Outlook Web Access 2010 on your portal, you should see a few dozen rules that pertain to it, though they might not make much sense to you yet.

When UAG receives a request from a user, it iterates through all the rules that pertain to the application type for which this URL is destined, from top to bottom, and looks for a rule that matches the requested URL. If it finds one that does, the rule may instruct UAG to accept or reject the request.

UAG also checks what HTTP method is used as part of the request, and if that method isn't included in the rule, it will be treated as a security violation.

If a request passes the URL and Method check and is *accepted*, the request parameters instruction is evaluated—it can instruct UAG to **handle**, **reject**, or **ignore** the parameters.

Request parameters are pieces of data that can be included in the request as instructions or data for the application. Parameters may be visible to the user as text that is appended to the URL following the ? sign, and separated by the ampersand or semicolon signs (& or ;). They might also be invisible, if they are sent using the POST HTTP method. For example, look at the following URL: `/owa/attachment.ashx?id =RgAAA&attcnt=1&attid0=BAAAAAAA&attcid0=image001.jpg`

This is a standard OWA 2010 request to fetch an email attachment. The request is for a piece of ASPX code, and it includes the parameters id, `attcnt`, `attid0`, and `attcid0`, which tell the code which file to actually fetch (`image001.jpg`)

A 'Reject' means that if the request has any parameters, it will be treated as a security violation, and rejected in its entirety. An 'ignore' means that the parameters will be passed on as is without any further checking. If, however, the setting on the rule is to *handle* the parameters, then the rule's parameter list will be processed. The parameter list can define, with high granularity, how to handle various parameters. For example, the first item on the Parameter list in the following screenshot is set to accept a parameter named 'dummy_repository', which can contain any characters except the characters /, \, *, ', ", ` and | and can be between 0 and 50 characters long. The value is specified using—as always—a Regular Expression, hence the use of the square brackets and asterisk. If that means nothing to you, we shall refer you once again to *Appendix A*, which reveals the mystery that is Regular Expressions.

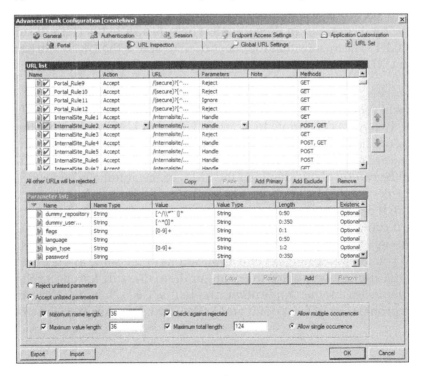

Any violation of the rules — wrong method, wrong parameters, or even a parameter that is too long or short will be answered with a firm error message, telling the user that he should be ashamed of himself. The same will happen if the request has not matched any of the rules. The actual error message is:

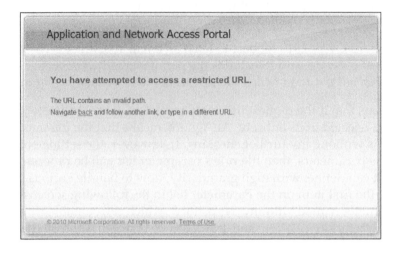

When this happens, UAG will log an error in its security log, providing more details. For example, the error could be **A request from source IP address 192.168.2.1 on trunk Portal1 for application Citrix XenApp of type CitrixXenApp5 failed. The URL /Citrix5final contains an illegal path. The rule applied is Default rule. The method is GET**. This means that the client tried to access the URL /Citrix5final, and none of the URL Set rules matched it, so it was rejected.

A little bit earlier, we mentioned that if UAG finds one rule that does match the request, it will process it. This also means that the rules have an order to them. Sometimes, two rules may apply to a certain URL, but UAG will follow the instructions on the first one it finds, ignoring the other. If you noticed, the URL list has two blue arrows on the right, and these allow you to move rules up and down. You should be careful about changing the order of the automated rules (InternalSite, Portal and rules created by applications), as that could have a devastating effect. Not only can it cause applications to quit working or spit out error messages in all directions, it could render the *Portal* itself inoperable, or even the trunk itself. Keep in mind, though, that the rule order can be an important troubleshooting step. For example, if you are publishing several applications of the same application type (as defined in the application publishing configuration), the rule for one application could interfere with another application, and in that case, changing the order can resolve the problem, or at least point you in the right direction as to the cause.

The HTTP methods that are allowed in each rule can be selected with a drop-down list, and this is where the URL Inspection tab settings that we discussed earlier come into play. The methods available on the drop-down list will be the ones you have seen in the list of **Predefined and custom methods**. UAG comes with a preconfigured set of methods, and you can edit your own, if you know your applications need them. Some of the preconfigured application publishing templates are designed to add methods to the list automatically, because their applications need them, so, as you publish more applications, the list will grow.

The **Parameter list** is where the Global URL Settings come in handy. That tab is where you can define global parameters that are processed in addition to the parameters you define within URL Set rules. For instance, you might be publishing a group of applications that are very similar, and many of their URLs have the parameter **clientos=windows7**. In such a case, instead of adding this parameter to each application's rule or rules, you can just add it as a global parameter. Can you think of another way of doing this? If not, read on.

If you remember, we mentioned a few chapters ago how important an application's *type* is. The importance is because the Rule Set is based on the application's type. If you have created multiple applications with the same type, then a rule pertaining to that type would affect all of these applications. This is a double-edged sword, because it can reduce your granularity on one hand, but save you effort on the other hand. This is also the answer to the question above – instead of creating a global parameter, you can create all the applications using the same type, and then create one URL Set rule that will apply to all of them.

The **Rejected Value** setting on the Global URL Settings tab is also a global list that is similar in the fact that it affects all applications, except that it is about parameters that need to be *rejected*. As always, it uses Regular Expressions (*Appendix A*, remember?) and if a URL is requested that includes a parameter with a value that matches one of the patterns you have defined, it will issue the usual **you have attempted to access a restricted URL** error.

Rule editing and modification

We already mentioned the risks of changing the rules order, but there are other considerations. As a general rule, we recommend against changing the default rules, but rather, duplicating them and editing the duplicates. The reason is that future updates to the product may overwrite your edits and ruin your day. It's also safer, in case you make some mistake. Because rules are processed in order, they don't contradict each other except if you need your rule to specifically reject a URL. In that case, you may have to move the rules up or down the list to make sure another rule is not approving the request before your rule is processed.

Another common mistake is forgetting to modify rules when customizing the portal. For example, if you customize the login page and replace JPG images with another type, you have to modify the relevant access rules to make sure they allow for the new type as part of the URL.

If you are getting unpredictable results, there are two things you can do:

1. Use the Web Monitor, which we discussed in *Chapter 8*, to view which rules are being violated and correct them.

2. Set the application to "Evaluate without enforcement" on the application's Web Settings tab to cause UAG to ignore the access rules for the application.

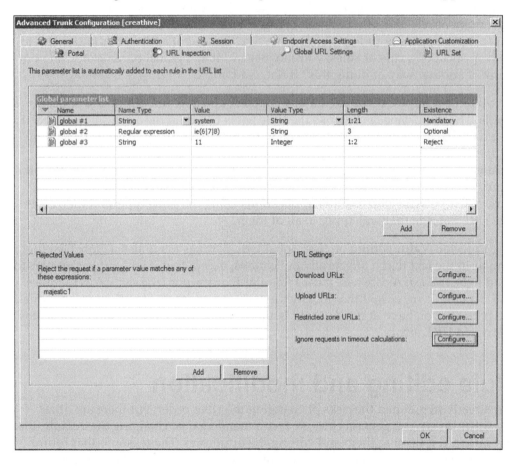

The **Global URL** Settings tab also hosts the URL pattern definition for **Download URLs**, **Upload URLs** and **Restricted zone URLs** that we addressed in *Chapter 8*, but also the settings for URLs that are to be ignored when UAG calculates **session timeouts**.

The purpose of this list is to prevent certain applications from 'fooling' UAG into thinking that the user is active, while in fact they are not. This trickery can happen if an application is designed to automatically send requests to the server without the user's intervention. For example, **Outlook Web Access** issues a periodic automatic request to: `/owa/ev.owa?oeh=1&ns=Notify&ev=ReminderPoll&UA=0`.

This happens even when the user does not touch the computer, so we need to make sure UAG doesn't think this is user activity, otherwise, the session will never time out even if the user falls off the face of the earth (don't we sometimes wish some of them would?). As always, the rules are configured using Regular Expressions, and some application templates already include a pre-configured set of them, like the Exchange template rules, seen in the screenshot below:

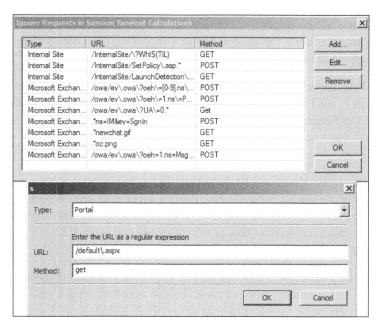

NLB and Arrays

Load Balancing (LB) is a very important feature for many organizations, because the number of users that the organization needs to service may be greater than what a single UAG server can handle. Once a single server has maxed out its **CPU** or **memory**, the only thing you can do is to distribute the load between two or more servers. Load balancing is done via a mechanism that intercepts a user's request, and redirects it to one of the servers configured as a load-balanced cluster. There are plenty of load-balancer devices on the market, such as **F5**'s Big-IP or a **Celestix** XLB device, and Windows itself also has a built-in mechanism to do the same thing.

Most load balancing services can also check the servers they are balancing for signs of life, and in case a server stops responding, re-distribute the load between the other members; so that users have as little interruption as possible (it's still interrupted, though—more about that later).

When servers are load balanced, they are represented by a single IP address, which is "shared" by all cluster members, referred to as **VIP (Virtual IP)**. With an external device, the load balancer hosts that single IP, and when a request comes in, it makes a decision to which server a request should go, and forwards it to that server. It then receives the response and forwards it to the client. When the **Windows load balancing** mechanism (known as **NLB**—short for **Network Load Balancing**) is in use, all cluster members are configured with the shared IP in addition to the regular, unique, IP address. When a request comes in, it is received by all cluster members, and the Windows NLB component on each server inspects the request, and decides whether it should handle it, or another cluster member. One member processes the request and responds to it, and all the others discard it.

Even though Windows has had NLB for many years, UAG's predecessor IAG did not support it, and the only way to load-balance IAG servers was via the use of an external load balancer, like the ones we mentioned earlier. With UAG, you can still do this, but you can also choose to employ Windows' NLB and save your organization some dough and yourself some effort (less 'items' to troubleshoot).

Since load balancing is designed to distribute incoming requests between two or more servers, you would typically want both servers to have an identical configuration. You can achieve this in two ways—either copy the configuration from one server to another manually (this is what people did with UAG's predecessors), or, better yet, take advantage of the **Array** feature of UAG.

An array is a group of servers that are linked together, *logically*. When creating a new array, you need to "promote" one server to be the array manager, and then configure all the other servers to be *members* of that array. This is configured using the **Array Management Wizard**, which you can launch on a freshly installed server as part of the **Getting Started Wizard**, or at a later time through the **Admin** menu. The following screenshot shows the path to the **Array Management Wizard** through the **Getting Started Wizard**:

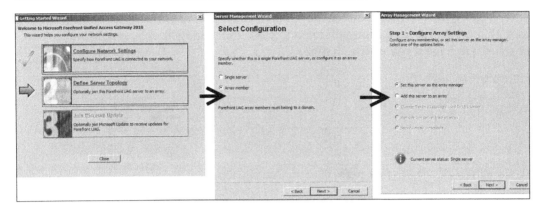

The **Array Management Wizard** allows you to:

- Configure a single server as an array manager
- Add a single server as a member to an existing array
- Move an array member from being managed by an array manager to be managed by another array manage.
- Remove a server from an array, converting it back to being a single server
- Change the array credentials, in case they have been changed on the array manager

Make sure that the **Set this server as the array manager** option is selected and then click **Next**. The array creation wizard will prompt you for the credentials that will be used by the array for intra-array communications, and it will then ask you to specify the name and IP of additional members that will be joining this array. This is the part that configures TMG to allow communications between the array manager and the members, so it is very important. If you need to add members to the array in the future, you have to go through the Array Manager *first*!

One thing to keep in mind is that a UAG array is limited to 8 members. Such a large array can handle a large number of users, but if, for some reason, you need a larger array, then your only option is to forgo the array feature, and use an external load balancer. Dedicated load balancers can work with a large number of servers, and some custom solutions can support even thousands of servers.

After adding the members and clicking **Next**, UAG prepares the array configuration, though after it's finished, you will need to close the management console and re-open it to have it reflect the change.

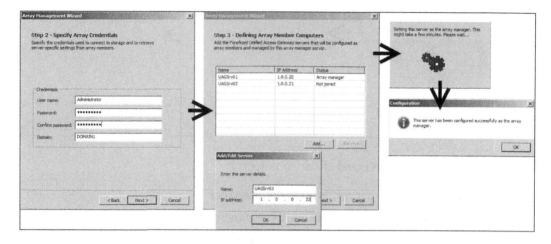

What does it reflect? Well, nothing, really. The configuration console will look almost identical, but if you launch the Array Management wizard again, it will show you that the status is now **Array manager**.

The next step is to add the other servers as members. Yes, even though you added the members to the list during the array creation wizard, you still need to let *them* know that they are now playing for a new band. This is also done using the **Array Management Wizard**, available through the **Getting Started Wizard**, or the **Admin** menu. The wizard will ask you for the FQDN or IP of the array manager, and the credentials. Then, after a bit of wheel-turning, you are done.

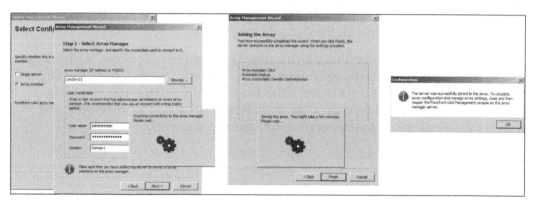

From now on, every time you perform a configuration **activation**, UAG will push the configuration to the other array members sequentially. You will be able to see this in the **Activation Monitor**—the servers will be listed on the left, and when each completes the activation, it will have a V next to it, or an X, if it was unsuccessful. Naturally, this will cause the activation process to take longer (because otherwise, it's refreshingly quick).

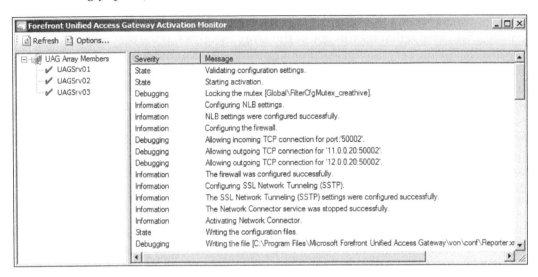

Now that you have an array running and active, you can always add more members (up to the limit of eight servers imposed by the product, of course) by launching the Array Management Wizard from the Admin menu. However, when you launch it, it will only show the option **Specify array credentials**. Don't worry—this is the right choice. Click **Next**, and then **Next** again (assuming you don't want to change the credentials at this time) and then add the new member, like you did before. Once that is complete, go to the new server and add it from its own Array Management Wizard. Removing a member is rather obvious – on the member, launch the UAG management console, which will tell you that you can only use the Array Management functions. Then, select **Remove this server from the array** and follow the wizard through. Once that is done, move over to the array manager and use the **Specify array credentials** option to remove the member from the list.

The same wizard can also be used in case the array manager fails. Assuming, of course, that you don't have a backup of it, or that you need the array to become operational ASAP with no time for repairs, you can use the array management wizard on one of the members to set *it* as the new array manager. It's important to note that even if the manager fails, the array still remains functional, but, without a working array manager, you will not be able to manage the array.

Adding load balancing into the mix

Now that you have an array, you can configure any third party load balancer to divvy up the load between your members. We have mentioned earlier that load balancing can distribute the incoming requests between users, and can also monitor the servers and redistribute in case a server goes down. It is important to know, though, that with UAG, this is *limited*, as UAG does not have a way of tracking sessions across servers. If a user has logged on to a UAG server array, the load balancer will assign that user to one of the array members. If the server crashes, the load balancing service will learn of it quickly and assign the next request from that user to another server in the array. However, the unique session that the user had on the original server will be gone, and the 'new' server will have to initiate the authentication all over again. Once the user re-authenticates, he will be redirected to the same URL he tried to reach, so depending on the design of the published web application, he will usually be able to resume his work immediately. If the user has been using an SSL-VPN connection, he will have to go back to the portal and re-launch the tunnel (either for a **tunnelled application**, an **SSTP connection**, or a **Network Connector** connection).

If you will be using a third party load balancer, then the exact procedure for configuring it differs among the various products on the market, so consult the balancer's documentation, or if you're lucky and it's owned by another person in your company, dump that task on him.

After you create an array, as described earlier, the main trunk configuration window will change slightly, and allow you to select whether you want to use **non-integrated NLB** (that's a third party load balancer) or **integrated NLB** (Windows' NLB). The default will be set to non-integrated, and you can now click on the IP column cells next to the server names, and choose which of the IPs configured on that server will be used as the public IP for trunk access.

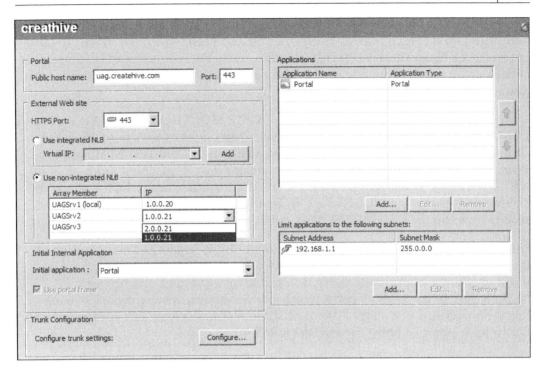

If your preference is to use Windows NLB, then we should point out that NLB is a complex technology, so we strongly recommend you read the following introduction to NLB in Windows 2008 R2 before proceeding: `http://technet.microsoft.com/en-us/library/cc725691.aspx`

The good part about UAG's NLB feature is that it's pretty simple to configure. Everything is integrated into one single interface - just configure NLB on the array manager and activate the configuration. What UAG does in this case is push the configuration you have set into TMG, which pushes the configuration to Windows' NLB across all array members.

The NLB configuration has several parameters that you need to consider. First, you can set the balancing to be on the **External network**, the **Internal network**, or *both*. Since we are publishing applications from inside your network to the outside world, you would typically *only* set NLB on the external interface. If you plan on using your server for **DirectAccess** (which we will discuss in the next chapter), Internal load balancing also needs to be configured, but for regular application publishing, it's irrelevant and *unsupported*. In fact, if you do configure load balancing on the internal network too, it will prevent the SSL Network Tunneling (a.k.a. Network Connector, which we discussed in *Chapter 5*) from working at all.

The second thing you need to consider is the IP assignment. Other than the IP addresses you set on your array members, you also need to assign a **shared IP** (also known as a **Virtual IP**, or **VIP**). This IP is the one that will be accessed by connecting clients, so the public hostname used by your portal also needs to resolve to it, so you also need to reconfigure the **DNS record**.

Lastly, NLB has three modes of operation—**IGMP MULTICAST**, **MULTICAST**, and **UNICAST**. The difference is the way the NIC's **MAC** addresses is used. With the Unicast method, all the servers are assigned an identical UNICAST MAC address. With the MULTICAST method, each server retains the original MAC address of the NIC, but the NIC is also assigned a MULTICAST MAC address, which is shared by all servers. When using MULTICAST, incoming client requests are sent to all the servers by using the MULTICAST MAC address.

Unfortunately, the shared MAC addresses on multiple hosts can cause flooding on the network. This happens because the network switch, which usually forwards traffic only to the appropriate ports, is forced to forward the UNICAST or MULTICAST traffic to all its ports, which effectively turns your clever switch into a dumb hub. Ideally, you should prefer MULTICAST to UNICAST, if your networking hardware supports it (most modern devices do).

However, MULTICAST can cause flooding just like UNICAST, unless you specifically configure the switch with static entries so that it will send the packets only to members of the NLB cluster and not all of its ports. What's even better is IGMP MULTICAST. It is similar to MULTICAST, except that it allows capable Network Switches to perform **IGMP snooping** on the traffic, and know on their own to which ports to forward the traffic. This makes the switch's life harder, but lets your network run better.

UNICAST appears first on the list, so it's more popular, but you should prefer IGMP MULTICAST, if your networking hardware supports it. If not, prefer regular MULTICAST, but make sure you configure your switches' static entries. If your switches do not support that either, UNICAST is your only option.

Putting it all together

To configure integrated NLB, open **Network Load Balancing** from the **Admin** menu. Then, click on **Add** and specify the **IP** and **subnet mask**. Keep in mind that you should be configuring the VIP for the external interface. After you click **OK**, select the **NLB mode** and click **OK**.

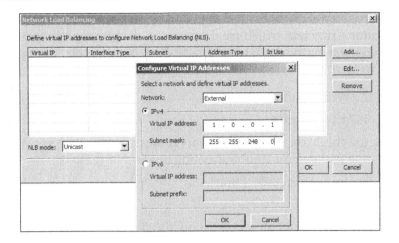

Once you have defined your Virtual IP, you can switch the main trunk configuration to Integrated NLB. If you have configured more than one VIP, you can use the drop-down to select the VIP you wish to use for this trunk. You can also click the **Add** button as a shortcut to the NLB configuration screen.

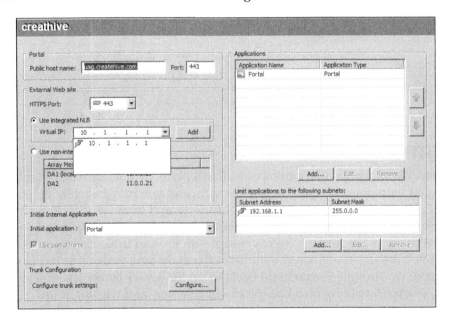

Note that if, after configuring integrated NLB, you go to the NLB configuration screen again, you will find that the "in use" column for that IP will now show "yes", and you will not be able to remove that VIP from the list. If you need to make a change, you can edit it, but if you want to remove it completely, you must first switch the trunk to use another NLB VIP or non-integrated NLB.

Now that you have an array with NLB at your disposal, you can manage it through the **Web Monitor Array tab**, which we discussed in the previous chapter. Until you actually go into the monitor and START the NLB on both servers, though, nothing will happen. To start NLB, follow these steps:

1. Open the Web Monitor.

2. Click on **Array Monitor.**

3. Check the checkbox next to all servers (unless, of course, you want to start only some of them, for troubleshooting or another reason).

4. From the drop-down, select **Start**.

5. Click **Apply.**

6. Refresh the page until all servers show the status as **Converged**.

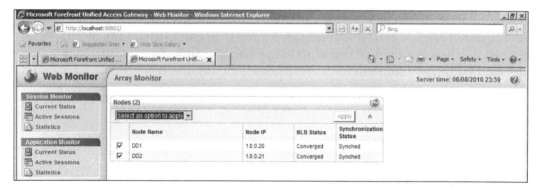

Summary

If your head is buzzing with options now, that's perfectly normal—this chapter has been loaded with new toys for you to play with, and you may be realizing now just how clever UAG is in protecting your applications, and how versatile it can be when configured correctly. Before we go on to the next chapter, we shall remind you once again that many of the settings we covered are tricky, and can cause unpredictable results if you are not experienced with them. To make sure your users' work is not interrupted, we strongly recommend backing up the server before making any changes, or experimenting on a non-production server (and backing it up too, why not).

11
DirectAccess

DirectAccess (DA) is a fantastic new type of remote connectivity technology that gives you everything that **VPN** does and more. It has been in the market for quite a while—it was introduced as a feature of Windows Server 2008 R2 to complement Windows 7, and companies all over the world implemented it with great success. However, as you will soon find out, together with UAG, the deployment experience is much smoother, and has some fantastic new features that make life easier and better.

What's in it for me?

Letting your employees access the corporate network remotely has been traditionally done with VPN. There have been many technologies and solutions along the way, but DA is by far the most user-friendly (to your users, not to you, that is). While all other solutions require the user to launch some kind of application or link, DA is "always on"—as soon as the user's computer departs his corporate network and connects to the public internet anywhere in the world, DA initiates the connection silently, without bothering the user with configurations or even a single mouse-click. From then on he is, for all intents and purposes, "still" connected to his corporate network. This is completely transparent, and unless there's some malfunction or specific blockage on the network the user is a guest on, he could have completely unrestricted access to all his corporate resources, just as if he was in the office.

That's not all, of course—the administrative overhead is also reduced. With other VPN technologies, the user, or his IT department, has to install client software, or configure the **VPN dialer**. With DA, there's no need for that. The components are already built into **Windows 7 Enterprise**, **Windows 7 Ultimate**, and Windows Server 2008 R2 and the configuration only has to be done on the server. Once done, it is assigned to the organization's users via **Group Policy**, and that's it!

Not hooked yet? Well, how about security? With DA, the only way to get connected is if the connecting computer is a member of your domain, is a member of the appropriate domain group, and has inherited the appropriate Group Policy. This serves as a **two-factor authentication** mechanism ("Who you are" – your username and password and "What you have"—a computer that is a domain member), which is very secure – much more so than remote connectivity that's based only on user/password authentication. Also, the connection itself is based on **IPSec** tunnels, which provides strong encryption for the traffic between client and server, providing a complementary security layer.

Naturally, DA has its down sides too. One limit is that only Windows 7 Enterprise, Ultimate and Windows 2008 Server R2 are supported as a client (if you missed that earlier), so all your older clients or non-Windows clients will have to use another technology, or come in to the office in the flesh. Someone might, at some point, develop DA client software for other operating systems or platforms, but that is not guaranteed, and even if it does happen, they might not be supported by Microsoft. Lastly, even though joining DA is very simple, it can only be done while connected to the corporate network, so to get on it initially, all users will have to come into the office with their computer at least once, or use another VPN technology to get their Group Policy straight. This also means that troubleshooting can be a bit daunting at times, because some fixes can only be done with the computer on the network.

A little bit of history

Back in October 2009, Microsoft released Windows Server 2008 R2, together with Windows 7. With these two concurrent releases, DirectAccess first became available. Naturally, quite a few organizations were already using pre-release versions of Windows Server 2008 R2 and Windows 7, and being early adopters of DA. Meanwhile, Microsoft was working on UAG, and decided early on to integrate it with DA, as it is Microsoft's main remote access product anyway.

With UAG, deploying DirectAccess is very simple. It integrates many of the configurations you need to make into a single, friendly wizard. It also incorporates IPv6 to IPv4 translation technologies, allowing you to deploy DirectAccess even if your network hasn't been fully migrated to **IPv6** (yes! You can deploy DA with virtually no knowledge of IPv6! Hooray!). Another advantage is **NAP** integration (we discussed NAP briefly in *Chapter 8*), which is available without UAG, but is much simpler to configure if UAG is in the picture. Lastly, it saves you time and effort by allowing you to take advantage of UAG's Array and Integrated-NLB functionality, so you don't have to configure those manually, or monitor your servers separately.

Of the above, the IPv6/IPv4 translation is probably the most important. Even though IPv6 has been around for many years, most organizations have only just started implementing it, and many haven't done so at all. If you were looking into using DA without UAG, you would have no choice but to go cold turkey on IPv4 and switch all your servers to IPv6 (or at least those you want your users to access from home). With UAG, however, you get the benefit of **DNS64** and **NAT64**, which are two components included with UAG. With these two, UAG lets your DA clients access IPv4 resources as well, so you can take your time and move over when you're really ready, but still have DA working like clockwork.

The reason why NAT64 and DNS64 are so important is because DA was designed to operate in an IPv6-only environment. In such an environment, there's no built in mechanism that allows the DA clients to communicate with resources that only support IPv4. This would not be a problem if all your servers and applications support IPv6, but some platforms and many applications do not support it yet.

How does DirectAccess work?

To put things very generally, DA works by creating an IPSec tunnel (actually, two tunnels, but more about that later) between the UAG server and the client, and encrypting the traffic that is destined for the internal network. UAG receives the traffic from the client and decrypts it, and sends it on its way to the internal servers. More specifically, the administrator creates a configuration using the UAG management console, and that configuration is added as a group policy object. Then, all clients are required to connect to the corporate network (either physically, or via other VPN technologies) and receive the group policy update. After the update, Windows is ready to automatically create the IPSec tunnels to the UAG server as soon as the computer leaves the corporate network and connects to the public internet somewhere else. Then, full corporate network connectivity ensues.

The tough part is creating the foundation for this, as it requires a fully functional domain, a **public key infrastructure** (**PKI**), and all that before even touching the UAG server itself. Configuring UAG is quite easy and, assuming everything else has been prepared correctly, can be done in just a few minutes. However, for larger scale deployments, more than one UAG server is required, which brings some more complex configurations into the mix — **array**, **NLB**, and usually some changes to the PKI.

IPSec and its tunnels

As we said, the traffic between the client and the DA server is encrypted using IPSec, and using two distinct **tunnels**. One tunnel is referred to as the **infrastructure** tunnel (also known as the "computer" tunnel), and it is established by Windows as soon as it detects the need to enable DA, even before a user has logged on to the computer. This tunnel can be used to access domain resources and management servers. For example, it can be used to resolve DNS queries, update group policy, download Antivirus or Windows updates from an internal **WSUS** server. The second tunnel is referred to as the **Intranet** tunnel (also known as the "user" tunnel). This is the tunnel that actually lets the user connect to the rest of the organizational network.

From a user's perspective, this is not visible, but it's important to understand for two reasons. First, it is up to you to choose whether you want to allow full intranet access, or just remote management. Full intranet access will establish the two tunnels and allow the clients access to your intranet's various resources (Servers, computers, printers etc) while Remote Management will configure the client to establish just the Infrastructure Tunnel. In Remote Management mode, your client will only be able to connect to infrastructure and management servers that you configure. This more restricted mode allows you to remotely manage these computers. For example, you can deploy updates to the system or application to these users without requiring them to go back to the office. The second reason this is important is because sometimes, when you configure full intranet access, only one of the tunnels comes up because the authentication was not completed or for some other problem. We will discuss this more later, as part of the troubleshooting section of this chapter.

IPv6—what's the big deal?

Many years ago, when the internet was conceived in the blazing minds of some **DARPA** engineers, they figured they needed to assign each computer a unique address, but they failed to anticipate just how popular the internet would become. The original paradigm for IP addressing, as you know, assigns each host an address composed of 4 numbers, each ranging from 0 to 255. In theory, this allows for a little over 4 billion different numbers, but even that large allocation turned out to be too small rather fast. Early on, many organizations were taking up blocks of 65,536 addresses, and some even grabbing blocks of 16,777,216 addresses, and life was nice and easy. However, as more and more users and organizations got connected, it became apparent that this resource wouldn't last long. At some point, organizations started using NAT to alleviate that, and this provides some more benefits from a security standpoint. However, even NAT has some limitations. Back in 1996, when many of us were still only learning of the existence of the internet, drafts were already published, describing a solution to this problem. Some estimated that the original IP ranges would be depleted very soon, but it's actually kind of amazing that it lasted as long as it did. We are getting close to the inevitable day where those who don't adopt IPv6 will have to find creative ways to have all their hosts still connected to the **World Wide Web**.

The basic concept behind IPv6 is that instead of using just 4,294,967,296 combinations as an IP address (that's what you get with 4 numbers ranging from 0 to 255 each: 256X256X256X256), we are actually using eight numbers, each ranging from 0 to 65535, to represent each host. An IPv4 address would typically be something like 192.168.2.1, but an IPv6 address would be something like 2001:0DB8:4137:9E76:207C: 30B3:9E81:8B1F.

The following screenshot shows a computer that has several Network interfaces which have IPv6 addresses:

Yup, my friends, the days of being able to remember your IP address by heart are over. If, however, all these letters are confusing, here's how it works. The actual address space for IPv6 is huge—it's more than ten to the power of 38, so to save you the trouble of having to write an IP address that's dozens of digits long, the powers that be who designed the whole thing decided to use **hexadecimal** notation, which allows us to represent such an IP address with "only" 32 characters. Whether saving 20% on the length is worth the price of having to contend with letters is a matter of opinion, but that's the way it is and we are all going to have to cope. Instead of the dots that used to separate the octets in IPv4, we use colons. Luckily for us, there's hardly any need to convert the hexadecimal notation to decimal, but if you do need to, it can be done with the calculator that's included with every Windows version.

Just switch it to "programmer" mode, and you can start converting away. Look at the bright side, at least they didn't go with Binary notation, that would make every IP no less than 128 digits long.

The good news is that as we go along, you will notice that some parts of the addresses repeat often so, with time, you will be able to "read" an address reasonably fast. More good news is when writing IPv6 addresses you can omit some zeroes, so there's less strain on your fingertips. For example, the address 2001:0252:0000:0001: 0000:0000:2008:0006:DB01 can be written as 2001:252:0:1::2008:6. Only the left zeroes in a number can be cut, so the 0252 is shortened to 252, but the 2008 has to stay as is. Also, the 0000:0000 in the middle is shortened directly into "::". The double colon can actually represent any number of zeroes, so the address 1080:0000:0000:0000:00 08:0800:200C:417A can be shortened to 1080:0:0:0:8:800:200C:417A, or even further to 1080::8:800:200C:417A. Unfortunately, though, you can use the double colon trick only once in an address. Sometimes, the IPv6 address will have a trailing percentage sign, followed by a number. This is a "zone index", which represents the interface number, and helps the system route traffic properly. All this is documented with more detail in RFC 1924 (`http://tools.ietf.org/html/rfc1924`). Having read all this, go ahead and have another look at the **IPCONFIG** output in the earlier screenshot, and see if the addresses you see make a bit more sense now.

More good news is that **subnetting** is easier with IPv6. Basically, An IPv6 address is split into two—the first 64 bit (or 4 groups of hex numbers) is the network ID, and the last 64 bits are the Host ID. The subnetting is usually standard at 48 bits, so most organizations will receive a fixed 48 bits prefix, and have another 16 bits for subnetting, and the last 64 bits for host IDs. Subnetting with 16 bits is still subnetting, but gives the organization enough breathing space to make things quite easy. This means that you can have over 60,000 subnets in your organization. The 8 hex number groups we mentioned earlier would be split like this: 3 groups for network ID, 1 group for subnet ID, 4 groups for host ID. Easy, huh?

Another advantage of IPv6 is that all the fiddling with **DHCP**, scopes, and IP conflicts is much less of a nightmare as well. There are 2^{64} possible **network IDs** and the same number of hosts in each network (that's about 18 million trillions), and with such a huge number of available addresses, we can have hosts automatically configure their own address, with virtually no chance of a conflict (DHCP is still preferred, but even that is much easier). The way this works is that an IPv6 capable computer sends out a multicast router solicitation request. If it is connected to a network that has an IPv6 capable router, the router responds with a router advertisement packet. The packet contains the configuration parameters that the host needs (Network layer information), and the **host ID** is chosen randomly. It's not completely random, actually, but if you want to know more about it, RFC 4862 can describe this with *only* 30 pages: `http://tools.ietf.org/html/rfc4862`.

If, until now, your organization has had nothing to do with IPv6, getting started may not be easy. You can configure and use DA with virtually no knowledge of IPv6, or no understanding of everything we just said. UAG has several components that let you get into it gradually. If you do want to get into it, and you're lucky, you may be lucky, and have a networking team to pin these duties on, but if not, you might consider reading up a little more about IPv6, or consulting your ISP or networking hardware vendor for suggestions and tips about going forward with this.

Hardware considerations

In *Chapter 1*, we discussed the hardware requirements for installing UAG. The same requirements stand for DA as well, but with a vengeance. DA is based on IPSec tunnels, and every packet that goes to and from each client has to be encrypted or decrypted. In addition to that, some clients will also require **SSL encryption** on top of that. All this is very CPU intensive work, so if you thought you can just grab some old machine and milk it to the bone, think again.

As always with regards to performance, it's not easy knowing for sure at what point the server will start to choke. Microsoft's official performance information suggests that a server with 2 **quad-core Xeon** processors running at 2.26 GHz, and with 16 GB of memory can sustain approximately 2300 users, each having a data transfer rate of 0.1 **Megabit per second** (**MBPS**). That does not mean that if you get this exact hardware configuration you can count on that number of users to be serviceable, because certain things can slow things down. For example, users can connect to DA using several mechanisms, like **Teredo** or **IP-HTTPS** (we will talk about these in more detail later), based on the networking environment on the client side. Depending on where your users are at (home, hotels, internet kiosks, partner networks), they may be using the more encryption-intensive IP-HTTPS, thereby impacting the server's performance even more. If the users are using Smartcard authentication, this also has a performance hit, and so does NAP integration and the inclusion of additional infrastructure servers.

If your target audience is a large number of users that is close to or over the number listed previously, you might benefit from load balancing your users by adding more UAG servers into the mix. We have discussed Arrays and NLB in the previous chapter, so if you skipped here straight from the installation guide in *Chapter 2*, now would be a good time to go back and educate yourself. If you have the option of installing stronger CPUs or additional servers, do keep in mind that more cores or an additional CPU doesn't have a linear effect on performance, and the same goes for most hardware upgrades as well. If you are working at an organization that has upwards of 2000 users, you probably can't afford too much guessing around, nor can you afford to tell your boss that this $20,000 server that you thought might be suitable turns out to be too weak. The proper way to handle this is in stages. Get a good server, and plan a multi-stage pilot for a group of a few dozen users, then a few hundred, and so forth. At each stage, keep a close eye on server performance (we discussed using the **PerfMon** in *Chapter 9*) and also measure your user's performance. As usage increases, you will notice a decrease in performance, and if you monitor it carefully, you can plot a load/performance graph that can help you estimate at what point you need more hardware.

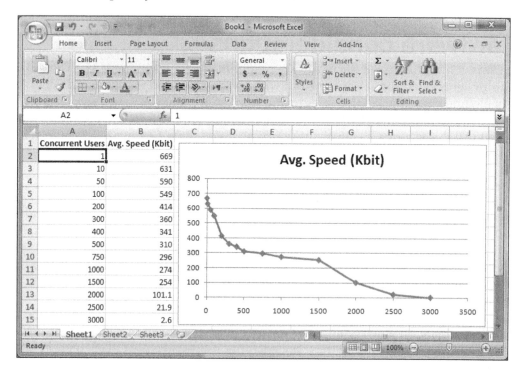

The preceding graph is fictitious, but your data should show similar patterns. As you can see, the performance drops as users are added, and flattens out at around 0.3 Mbps, but above 1500 concurrent users it suddenly takes a dive and at over 2000 users becomes what some organizations might find to be unacceptable (at 0.1 MBps, opening an average SharePoint document, for example, can take over a full minute).

For more details about the official benchmark for UAG DA performance, refer to the following link: `http://technet.microsoft.com/en-us/library/ff723731.aspx`.

Connecting your server to the Internet

Just like for **application publishing**, a DA server has to have at least two network interfaces. One will be facing the Internet and the other your internal network or **DMZ**. As we said in *Chapter 1*, UAG has **TMG** to act as its very own Firewall, but if you want additional protection, you can place UAG behind another firewall, and you can also place a firewall behind UAG, in between it and the corporate network. As always, make sure that the firewalls are configured to route traffic properly, and have the appropriate ports opened.

On the Internet side, there's an additional requirement. The external interface needs to have 2 IP addresses (those are IPv4 addresses), and they have to be *consecutive*. There are two reasons for this. One is that each one of the 2 DA IPSec tunnels needs to bind to a dedicated IP, so you need two. The second reason is for Teredo—Teredo needs to detect the type of **NAT** used on the Client side, because it cannot work with all types. We'll discuss the detection process in more detail later.

The two consecutive IPs must be public, so even if you are hosting UAG behind a firewall, you cannot use the 10.x.x.x, 192.168.x.x or 172.16.x.x ranges. If UAG is behind a firewall, then UAG still has to be configured with two IP addresses, and both have to be published by the firewall, and accessible on **UDP** port **3544** from the internet (otherwise, it will severely limit your client's ability to connect to DA – see 'client connection modes' later). For more information about how Teredo NAT detection works, and a lot more about Teredo itself, visit: `http://technet.microsoft.com/en-us/network/cc917486.aspx`

The Network Location Server

The **Network Location Server** (**NLS**) is an additional server, separate from UAG, which you will *have* to configure for DA. The function of the NLS is to allow your client computers to detect whether they are inside your organizational network or outside of it and, according to this, activate the DA connection. When an event triggers it (such as a reboot, or the network getting disconnected and reconnected), the computer tries to contact the designated NLS. If the connection is "successful", the computer determines that it is inside the organizational network, and DA stays off. If it is not accessible or the connection fails in some other way (more about that soon), then the client thinks it's on the internet, and enables DA.

The NLS is not that special—just some website listening for incoming HTTPS connections. You can use pretty much any plain old **IIS** server for that. All you have to do is setup a local HTTPS site, listening on some hostname to your liking, and with a **certificate** that corresponds to that hostname. The site doesn't actually have to have anything in it – just respond to the client with a valid certificate. Keep in mind that because the client "knows" it's on the public internet and not on the organizational network because the NLS is *not reachable*, you have to make sure the NLS is indeed *not reachable* on the *internet*.

The tricky part to setting up the NLS for many users is the certificate part. For a certificate to be "ok", the certificate has to meet *all* the following requirements:

- Match the **Fully Qualified Domain Name (FQDN)** that the client is trying to reach.

- Have a **Certificate Distribution Point (CDP)** that is accessible to the client.

- Have a valid **Certificate Revocation List** on the URL or URLs specified in the CDP.

Meeting the first requirement is easy, but do keep in mind that the NLS has to have a **Fully Qualified Domain Name (FQDN)**, and not a **short-name (NETBIOS name)**, and that the certificate has to match it. The CDP URL is included in certificates automatically when you create one for your NLS, but you do have to make sure the CDP URL points to a location that is accessible to the client. The CDP can be on the NLS itself but, to be reachable, you would have to put it in a folder that is accessible over HTTP. If the CDP is on some other server, do make sure it's accessible—you can do so by pasting the CDP URL in the client's browser, and see if you get prompted to download the CRL. The third requirement is usually not an issue, as the Certificate Server places the CRLs on the CDP URL, but if you have manually edited the CDP configuration, this might not be the case. Do check the CDP URLs and make sure there's a CRL on them, and that it is valid and gets updated properly.

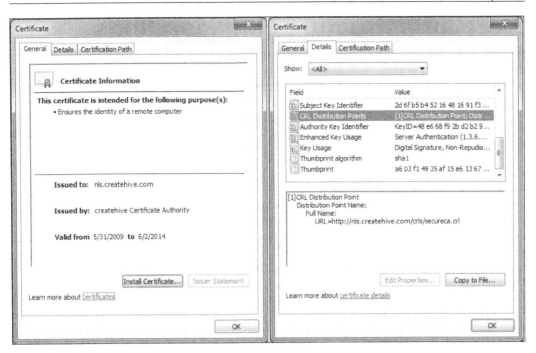

Another thing that is important to remember is that the NLS, despite being a simple website, is *critical*. If it is offline for some reason, corporate computers that have been configured to use DA will not know they are on the internal network and will activate DA. Can you spell NIGHTMARE? Yes, if this happens, these computers will not be able to connect to any corporate network resources until the NLS comes back to life (unless some other name-resolution technology is in use, like WINS). Conclusion? It might be a good idea to set up some kind of redundancy on the NLS. An **NLB cluster** is certainly warranted but, if not, at least make sure it's monitored routinely, backed up properly and that you, or your IT team, are well trained in restoring it back to health if it stops responding.

More infrastructure considerations

We already said that DA uses Group Policy to configure clients to use it. The way this works is that when you complete the configuration of the UAG server, it generates a script that creates the appropriate group policy objects that are required in the domain, and binds them to the organizational units automatically, as defined in the DA wizard. This implies that you do need a domain, based on **Windows 2003** or later, and have both the UAG server and clients joined to it. You will also need to create a user group for DA users, and add to it users who will be using DA. You would probably want to start with a pilot of just a few users and gain some confidence that connectivity works well for them, before moving on to larger scale deployment. Do keep in mind that the computers have to have full network access to have the group policy applied to them, so if these are mobile users, they will have to either come in to the office, or use another type of VPN. UAG supports **SSTP** VPN, and you can configure a trunk with the SSTP application on your UAG server as a way to do this. One important thing to remember with regards to that computer group is that the UAG server must not be a member of it. If it is, and becomes configured as a DA client, it won't be able to service "real" clients and nothing will work.

Another thing that is required is a PKI infrastructure—all client computers that need to use DA must have **machine-certificates** issued to them. You can do this manually, or as part of a global PKI deployment, but it is a must. You can do this with a Microsoft Windows Server Certificate Authority, or with any third party Certificate Authority, as long as the certificates are configured for Client Authentication or with IP Security IKE **Intermediate object identifier (OID)**.

Client connection modes

Before we go on about setting up the server, you need to understand the various client connection options, how they affect you (a LOT!) and how *you* can affect them (not so much).

As we said, DA is all about IPv6, but it's going to be quite a while before the Internet itself is ready for it. Virtually all the public internet is still using IPv4, and so several technologies have been developed to allow those steam-era machines to connect. Sure, your users are running spanking new copies of Windows 7 on their computers, but their home routers are still using IPv4, and their ISPs are too.

When a Windows 7 client that is configured to use DA loads, it attempts to use a technology called **6to4** to establish the IPv6 connection that it needs. 6to4 (which sounds a lot like '64' when said out loud) is a bridging mechanism, designed to encapsulate IPv6 traffic *inside* IPv4 traffic, thereby allowing the computer to use IPv6 on non-IPv6 networks. Once you have DA configured and enabled, and your clients have received the group policy update, they will try to initialize the 6to4 connection automatically as soon as they detect that they are on the public internet (by *not* being able to contact the NLS, as we described earlier). When the client attempts to use 6to4, it assigns itself an IPv6 IP address that starts with **2002**. The 6to4 component in Windows will then automatically encapsulate the IPv6 traffic inside IPv4 packets and send them out.

Unfortunately, the 6to4 mechanism is not compatible with private IPv4 ranges (10. x.x.x, 192.168.x.x or 172.16.x.x), and so it will not be usable if the computer is behind a NAT device, such as a home router or inside many organizational networks. In such a situation, the client will automatically fall back into another mechanism—Teredo, which we will discuss next. Another situation where 6to4 cannot be used is if **IP Protocol 41** is being blocked by the **ISP**—we have seen this with some **cellular networks**. If this is the case, the client will attempt to connect with IP-HTTPS, which we will also discuss shortly.

Teredo is also a bridging mechanism, designed to allow IPv6 traffic to be sent over an IPv4 network, but it works a little differently. If Teredo is called into action (because 6to4 has failed, or has been disabled for some reason), it will encapsulate the IPv6 traffic inside IPv4 UDP packets, sent over port 3544. When Teredo is activated on a client, it checks the Teredo server's public IPv4 addresses (it's those two consecutive IPs we talked about earlier), to see what type of NAT is in use. The possible types of NAT that it might detect are:

- **One-to-one NAT**, also known as **Full-cone NAT**
- **Address restricted cone NAT**
- **Port-restricted cone NAT**
- **Symmetric NAT**

The detection process starts with the Teredo client sending a **Router Solicitation (RS)** message to the Teredo server's IP address (the UAG server's 1st IP address). UAG then replies from the 2nd IP address. If the Teredo client receives the reply, it deduces that the NAT type is "Cone" (the first and second preceding option). If the client does not receive this reply, then it issues a *second* RS message, but this time, UAG will reply from its *first* IP, instead of the second. If the client gets this reply, it now knows that the NAT type is either Port-restricted cone (third option) or Symmetric (fourth option).

Now, the client sends a request to the UAG Server's *second* IP (which also acts as a Teredo server), and waits for another answer. When the answer comes, if it is from the same IP as the first, this signals to the client that the NAT type is Port-restricted cone (type 3). If they are *different*, this means that NAT is mapping the same internal address and port number to different external addresses and port numbers, which means that this is a Symmetric NAT (type 4).

When Teredo establishes a connection, it will assign itself an IPv6 address that starts with **2001:0000** (you can see such an address in the screenshot from a few pages ago), and will pack the IPv6 traffic inside UDP packets and send them out. More technical details about Teredo and its address assignment process can be found here: `http://technet.microsoft.com/en-us/library/bb457011.aspx`.

If the network blocks the UDP traffic on port 3354, Teredo will fail. The good news is that, as opposed to 6to4, here you might actually have some leverage—if a user's network is configured to block Teredo traffic, it might be 'convinced' to behave otherwise in some circumstances (such as changing settings on the router, or getting an organization to unblock port 3354). If not, then we also have IP-HTTPS at our service.

IP-HTTPS is the last fallback option for DA connections, if all the others fail. It is suitable for very restricted connections, where only HTTP and HTTPS are allowed, but the price is performance. If the client computer detects that all other options have failed, it will automatically enable IP-HTTPS, which encapsulates the IPv6 traffic in HTTPS IPv4 traffic. This means that the data will have to be encrypted with SSL, on top of the IPSec connection, and all that encryption is going to burden both the client CPU and the UAG Server's CPU. The result is that IP-HTTPS connections can be less effective from a performance point of view, depending on the capabilities of the client and server. If the client system has fallen back to IP-HTTPS, it will assign itself an IP address starting with **2002**.

We will talk more about these technologies later in the chapter, when we discuss troubleshooting, but for now, you need to keep in mind that these three technologies are here to *help you*. It's certainly not fun to have to understand so many technologies (still have a headache from the Teredo NAT explanation?), but you might find that in real life, you have little control over which client uses which technology. To make the best of it, you should strive to configure your server appropriately, so that all of them are available from a server perspective (for example, the appropriate server certificate for IP-HTTPS). If you are successful in this, then the majority or even all of your clients can use one of them, wherever they are.

Setting up the IP-HTTPS public site

The 6to4 and Teredo components don't require much work on your part, but IP-HTTPS is a bit more demanding to set up. When IP-HTTPS is in use, the traffic is encrypted with SSL, and that requires the UAG server to be configured with a certificate correctly.

When you run the DA setup wizard, it configures the UAG server as an IP-HTTPS server. Similarly to an NLS, this is just an IIS website, which does not need to host anything, but has to respond to HTTPS requests with some status code, and with a valid certificate. As opposed to the NLS, which needs to be accessible *inside* the corporate network, the IP-HTTPS site needs to be accessible on the *Internet*, and that may complicate things with regards to the certificate.

With the NLS, you could have used an internal **Certificate Authority** (**CA**) server, but for IP-HTTPS, this may be a problem. The reason is that for the client to be able to trust the certificate, it has to have a **Certificate Revocation List** (**CRL**) that is reachable on the public internet (because when the client needs to verify the certificate, it still hasn't established the IP-HTTPS connection, and has no access to a CRL that is published inside the organizational network). The best way to do this is to just get a public certificate from one of the leading certificate providers—all of them have their certificates configured with publicly accessible CRLs. If you decide to go with an internal CA, then make sure that the CRL of both the IP-HTTPS server and the issuing CA are published on a URL that is publicly available, publicly resolvable, and that the CDP in the certificate reflects the proper URL for the CRL, and no other locations. Essentially, you can use any web server that is published to the internet for that, but some organizations find it hard to locate such a resource.

Do keep in mind that you may need to tweak the configuration of your CA to make sure the certificate it generates has a CDP with the proper URL (otherwise, it would default to a CDP listing the CA's own URL for CRLs).

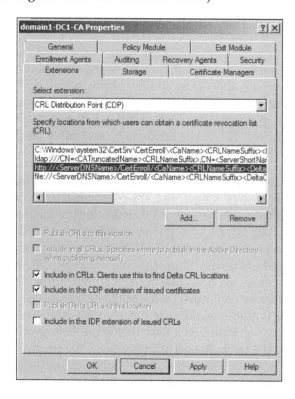

If you are using a Microsoft **Certificate Authority server**, information about configuring the CDP is available here: `http://technet.microsoft.com/en-us/library/cc773036(WS.10).aspx`.

Later on, after you have configured your UAG server with DA, do make sure you check its certificate, the certificate CDP and that the CDP URLs are reachable, and have a valid CRL to offer. Otherwise, IP-HTTPS will not work, and since it is the last straw for DA clients, without it, those clients will be out of luck.

The IP-HTTPS certificate has some additional required properties:

- For the Enhanced Key Usage field, the Server Authentication **object identifier (OID)**
- It must have a private key
- When installed on the UAG server, it has to be placed in the personal/certificate folder of the local computer certificate store.

DirectAccess name resolution

Well configured name resolution is very important for DA, and can be challenging to figure out. Assuming you have a domain configured in your network, you certainly have **DNS** setup, but for DA, it also has to support **AAAA** records so the DA clients can register themselves. There are plenty of DNS servers out there that support IPv6, such as **BIND 9**, but if you choose to go with Microsoft DNS, it's going to have to be version 2003 or later.

Another aspect of DNS with regards to DA is the matter of internal vs. external name resolution. Your DA clients will have to be able to correctly resolve the public hostname of your UAG server, or your server array. They will also need to be able to resolve the public URLs of the IP-HTTPS certificate CDP URLs on the internet. While connected to the corporate network, the clients will have to be able to resolve the NLS server, and when they establish the DA connection, resolve names of internal servers they need to contact.

If your organization is using the same DNS domain structure on the internal network and on the public internet, we refer to this as "**split-brains**" DNS, and it can be tricky, because you need to decide if you want DA users to access the published resources externally or internally. In such a case, you need to make sure that as clients move from using the internal DNS server on the corporate network to using the public DNS server that their ISP is hosting, they are still able to resolve all the appropriate URLs, and do so correctly. A problem could happen, for example, if there is a resource that is supposed to be accessible from *both* the internal network and the public one. Perhaps your **SharePoint** server is set up this way, or the company's public website may be. In such a situation, you have two options. One is to make a choice, and have that resource available either internally or externally (only to the DA users!). The other option is to configure the resource with an alternative internal name.

A very important part of the DNS resolution mechanism for DA clients is the **Name Resolution Policy Table (NRPT).** This table comes into play when a DA connection is alive and well, and is used to manage the way name resolution is done on the client. When DA is on, the client needs to be able to resolve internal corporate network names, but still resolve public hostnames on the internet. The public DNS it is configured with is still around, doing its job, and the UAG will be in charge of helping resolve internal hostnames. The NRPT simply tells the client for which URLs it should contact the UAG server, and for which it should not. The NRPT would typically contain two entries – one with the domain pattern (a.k.a. "Domain Suffix") for the organization, another for exclusion for the NLS server, and possibly for the IP-HTTPS FQDN name if it matches the domain pattern. If the organization has multiple internal domains, additional domain patterns may need to be defined. The domain pattern tells the client "for FQDN names that match that pattern, talk to your

UAG to get them resolved". The exclusion item tells the client "but for this specific FQDN, you're still asking your regular DNS, buddy".

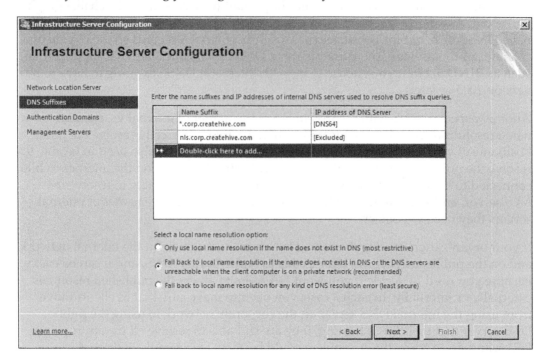

Why exclude the NLS? Well, since the NLS is located on the internal network, we want to make sure that the client still *cannot* resolve it when DA is on. If it could, it would think that it is actually on the internal network—and disconnect DA. The exclusion tells it to ask its own regular DNS (hosted by the user's ISP), which would fail to resolve it, and so, the client would still know that it's on the internet, and keep DA on.

Another situation where an NRPT exception may be needed is if your IP-HTTPS server, the IP-HTTPS certificate, or NLS certificate has a **CRL Distribution Point (CDP)** that is published on a URL that is based on your domain pattern. If you remember from earlier, the client has to be able to resolve those URLs on the public internet to establish an IP-HTTPS connection, but the domain pattern in the NRPT tells it not to use the public DNS server to resolve the URL. If the certificate is from a public provider, this should not be a problem, but if the CDP does point to a URL that matches your domain pattern, you need to add an exclusion entry for it as well.

Lastly, keep in mind that the clients have to be able to resolve the IP-HTTPS server's hostname on the public internet, so a public DNS host record is required. Make sure you have a public record that resolves the hostname specified in your IP-HTTPS certificate to the IP that's bound to the IP-HTTPS server.

ISATAP, DNS64, and NAT64

As we said before, many organizations are still using only IPv4 on their networks. It's somewhat ironic — the organizations that have moved to IPv6 are actually making it easier for others to stick to the old technology, in a weird twist on Game Theory. Anyway, one of the primary benefits of using DA with UAG is the fact that it includes several components that make using DA in a non-native IPv6 environment (meaning, a network that has little or no IPv6 hosts or devices) possible. The first of these is **Intra-Site Automatic Tunnel Addressing Protocol (ISATAP)**. ISATAP is a mechanism that allows IPv6 capable hosts to communicate with each other over a network that is based on IPv4. This is a similar *concept* to the connection mechanisms used by DA clients, but it is a different mechanism with a different *purpose*. It is designed to allow your DA clients to access IPv6 capable hosts (such as application servers, or other computers on the internal network) even though your infrastructure is incapable of routing IPv6 traffic. ISATAP is not part of UAG, but UAG installs and configures it automatically for you, when it detects that it's needed.

With ISATAP, the IPv6 data is encapsulated inside an IPv4 packet header, so the network infrastructure just passes it along, not knowing what's really inside. Hosts that are able to use ISATAP have a dual stack, meaning that they are configured with both an IPv4 IP address, and an IPv6 IP address that is *based* on the IPv4 address. That IP starts with a prefix that is set by the network administrator, followed by five address groupings, and then the IPv4 address. When you setup ISATAP as part of the setup wizard, you can specify that prefix. For example, if a host is configured with the IPv4 address of 10.0.0.3, its ISATAP address could be 2002:2f6b:1:1:0:5efe:10.0.0.3, as in the following screenshot:

If you are not yet ready to reconfigure your hosts for IPv6 or upgrade your routers and other network devices for it, you would go with ISATAP. For hosts on your network to be able to use ISATAP, they require the service of an ISATAP Router and, incidentally, UAG has this functionality built into it (we are not talking about a physical router — it's a software component, of course). During the setup of DA on the UAG server, UAG will automatically notice if it is not configured with an IPv6 address, and assume you want to enable its ISATAP router functionality. It will then provide IPv6 capable hosts (computers that are running Vista, Windows 7, Windows Server 2008 or Windows Server 2008 R2) with an IPv6 address based on their current IPv4 address.

One thing you do need to do beforehand is to enable ISATAP on your DNS servers, because they need to be able to provide clients with UAG's address as the ISATAP router. To do so, you need to manually create an A-record in the DNS zone for the host name ISATAP, pointing to UAG's internal IP address (if you are using an Array of UAG servers, add each server's internal address (both the dedicated IPs and Virtual IPs) to the A-record).

If you are running a Windows Server 2008 or 2008 R2 DNS server, there's one more step to perform, because Windows Server 2008 and 2008 R2 DNS servers are configured by default to not respond to queries for that name, even if an explicit record exists. To fix this, you need to edit the DNS Server's **Global Query Block List**, which is in the DNS Server's registry. To edit it, follow these steps:

1. Open the registry editor.
2. Navigate your way to `HKEY_LOCAL_MACHINE\SYSTEM\CurrentControlSet\Services\DNS\Parameters`.
3. Double-click the **GlobalQueryBlockList** value.
4. *Remove* the name **isatap** from the list (it's perfectly normal for it to contain nothing else, but it would probably have **wpad** as well, which you should leave alone)
5. Click **OK**, and exit the registry editor
6. Restart the DNS service, or reboot the DNS Server

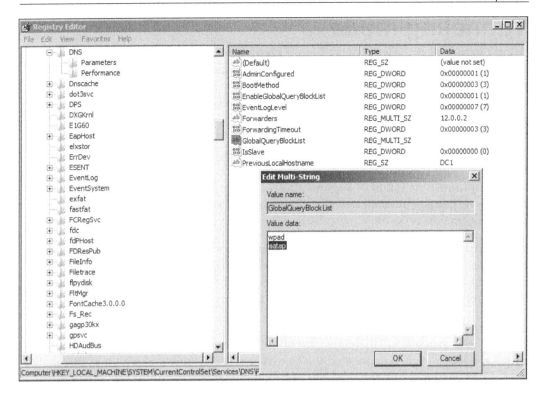

Well, we have ISATAP to take care of IPv6 capable hosts, but what if we want to access hosts that can't use ISATAP? Older operating systems, like Windows 2003, Windows XP, Windows 2000, and older are not able to use ISATAP—the component is not included in the operating system. This also pertains to most non-Microsoft platforms that you might be running. For them, UAG includes two additional services—DNS64 and NAT64 (pronounced DNS six-to-four and NAT six-to-four).

DNS64 and NAT64 act as a router for requests that your DA clients may send to IPv4 hosts that are not ISATAP capable. DNS64 resolves the IP addresses for them, and NAT64 accepts the IPv6 traffic from the DA client, and forwards it to the IPv4 host using IPv4 traffic. It then receives the IPv4 response from these hosts, and forwards it to the DA clients. These two are almost completely transparent to both you and your users—you just have to let UAG turn them on, as part of the DA setup wizard, and you're done.

Tunneling mode

Another choice you have to make before going through the last piece is whether to use split tunneling or forced tunneling. Split tunneling is a situation where the client computer sends traffic that is destined for the organizational network through the tunnel, but other traffic, such as browsing to public sites on the internet goes directly to the internet through the ISP's routers. Most VPN deployments go with that, and before SP1, UAG did not offer an option to select this mode through the configuration console. With SP1, you can choose to configure Forced Tunneling, which forces all traffic to go through the DA tunnel. This would be considered a stricter option—one taken by organizations that are concerned that split tunneling may jeopardize the internal network. As always, opinions about that differ, and the ultimate decision is yours.

Three important things to keep in mind, though, are that if you route all the "home" traffic through DA, you may be severely limiting your users' options, because unlike traditional VPN, they cannot just disconnect their DA. Secondly, by Forced Tunneling, you are increasing the load on your internal resources.

The last consideration is more of a technical nature. We talked earlier about NAT64 and DNS64, which UAG includes, and allow you to use IPv4 resources on your internal network when connected via DA. When using Forced Tunneling, there are additional considerations, because forcing the traffic through UAG poses some design challenges in routing IPv4 traffic. To learn more about this, read the public documentation for forced tunneling in UAG SP1.

DirectAccess Connectivity Assistant

To make life a little easier, DirectAccess includes a tool called the **DirectAccess Connectivity Assistant (DCA).** This tool can help the users solve certain connectivity problems, and can also collect information that can be used by the administrator to see what's wrong.

Once the DCA is installed on a client computer, it shows an icon on the user's system tray that indicates if DA has connected successfully, or if there's a problem that needs attention. If there is a problem, the tool generates a log, containing details about the problem, and the user can then email the log to you, or to the IT support group, to get help. This log contains the configuration details of the various DA-related components, like the computer's IP configuration, the state of the Teredo, 6to4 and IP-HTTPS interfaces, the firewall policies that are in effect, and even some details about the system, like the list of installed updates, hardware in use and more. The DCA can also show a link to a pre-designated web page to help your users deal with the situation.

DCA has some settings that you can configure as part of the DA configuration wizard that we will see shortly. The tool itself is the file `Microsoft_DirectAccess_Connectivity_Assistant.msi`, available on the UAG server, under the folder `\common\bin\da\dca\`. You can have your users install it manually, or deploy it to them in any way you see fit. DCA is generally considered to be an optional tool, and you can deploy DA without it. However, if you run into trouble, it will provide you with an invaluable mine of information, and save you and your users a lot of effort. In specific scenarios, like enabling strong authentication using OTP, it is mandatory, but we will not cover strong authentication in this book.

Putting it all together

Now that we have discussed the concepts, you are ready to start designing your deployment, and collecting the required data. Here are some questions you have to think about:

- Are you going to use multiple servers with load balancing? If so, you might consider starting with one server, and adding more only when you are sure you have a good understanding of DA, or have a solid working environment.

- Depending on how you manage your DNS, you may need some time to configure the public DNS entry for the UAG server's public URL.

- If your organization has security policies that govern the placement of the UAG server, or ports that can or cannot be open on the public or DMZ firewalls, these may need to be revised or pass some approval process

- If you need to purchase a public certificate for IP-HTTPS, you should plan this in advance, especially if you need to budget the process.

- You may need to purchase another server for the NLS role, or find a server that can host it.

- If you plan on deploying DA only for a pilot group, plan the list of users carefully. Keep in mind that some organizations take weeks to iron out the various kinks DA can introduce, so be careful not to put sensitive users in a position where they can't do their work, or have to run into the office frequently to get support for their DA issues.

- If your organization has a group or department that is in charge of Remote Access and domain management, you would need to ask them to create three group policy objects and grant you access to them.

- Are you going to use Forced Tunneling? If so, make sure your users are aware of this, because they need to know that stuff that they do in the privacy of their home is still going through the organizational network. That may have legal implications for them and for the organization (for example, if they have a taste for file sharing).

Something that almost all organizations who have deployed DA run into are certificate-related issues. DA requires a huge collection of those—IPSec, NLS, IP-HTTPS, machine-certificates for clients, and some have unique properties that make it a chore to work out. If you are unsure about your certificates, you might want to consult a PKI expert. More information is also available in the official DA documentation from Microsoft about designing PKI for DA: `http://technet.microsoft.com/en-us/library/ee406213.aspx`.

Before configuring the UAG server itself, here is a summary of the things you need to configure beforehand:

1. Configure the Array of UAG servers and NLB, if required.
2. Configure two public IP addresses on UAG's external interface (or VIPs, if NLB is in use).
3. If the UAG server is not a domain member, join it to your domain.
4. Create and install an IP-HTTPS certificate on the UAG server.
5. Locate a server to serve as the NLS, and configure it:
   a. Install IIS.
   b. Create an HTTPS site.
   c. Create and install an HTTPS certificate on it.
   d. Test the certificate and its CDP.
6. Create a domain group for DA users, and add the pilot group users to it.
7. If the UAG is behind a firewall, open the appropriate ports that it requires:
   a. UDP Port 3544, in both directions, for Teredo.
   b. TCP Port 443, in both directions, for IP-HTTPS.
   c. If there's a CDP on the UAG, you may need to open TCP port 80 as well, to make it publicly accessible.
   d. IP Protocol 41, in both directions, for 6to4 clients.

8. If the UAG is in a NATted network, you need to move it, so that its public IPs are public.

9. If the UAG has a firewall behind it (the UAG is on the DMZ, and the firewall is protecting the internal network), open the appropriate ports to provide DA clients with access to whatever servers you need them to access and enable UAG to authenticate the clients with the DC(s).

Once all of these have been taken care of, you are almost ready to configure the UAG server. One last step is collecting the following information, which you will have to provide during the UAG configuration wizard:

Parameter	Value	Explanation
DA client domain group		
1st Internet Facing IP address		The first of the two consecutive IPs you have defined on your UAG server's external NIC
Internal IPv4 IP address for ISATAP		Needed only if ISATAP is to be used by UAG
Internal IPv6 address		Needed if ISATAP is not to be used by UAG
Name of the certificate for IPSec verification		
Name of the certificate for IP-HTTPS		
FQDN of the NLS server		
The DNS suffix for your domain		Like `*.corp.createhive.com`
Names of infrastructure servers and names of all the domains of the users in a multi-domain environment		List of domains besides the domain to which UAG is joined.

Wizard Rime

With all the above configured, and all the information collected, you are now ready to start the DA wizard on UAG, and go through the steps. Keep in mind that until you generate the DA scripts in the final stage, anything can be changed, so don't be afraid to go back and forth within the steps. To start, open the UAG management console, and click on DirectAccess on the left. This will present you with the DA configuration screen, which is split into four parts:

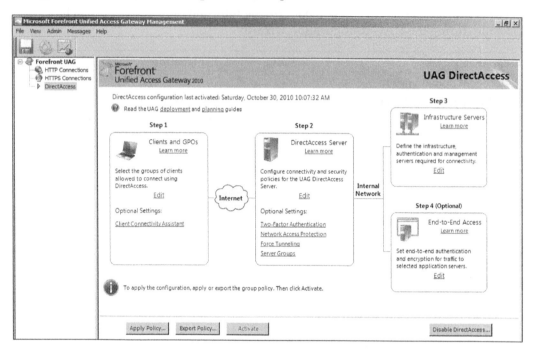

Your screen will actually show everything grayed out, until you click Enable DirectAccess. If you are not using an Array of servers, and have forgotten to configure your external NIC with two consecutive IP addresses, you will receive an error about this right away. If so, go ahead and fix that.

Client and GPO configuration

Start the DA configuration process by clicking on **Edit** under **Clients and GPOs**. The first steps asked you to decide whether to use full intranet access (**Allow DirectAccess clients to connect to internal networks**) or remote management only.

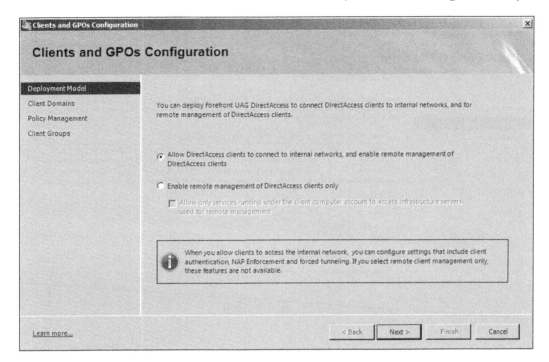

Next, you need to configure the domain or domains that the clients belong to. UAG will suggest the domain it detects, but you can click **Add** to specify additional domains.

The next screen configures whether UAG will generate new Group Policies, or apply settings to pre-existing GPOs. Some organizations prefer the second option, in case the UAG administrator does not have the permissions to apply changes to group policy directly. In this case, the policies can be created by someone else, and you can just name the policies that the Direct Access settings will be applied to.

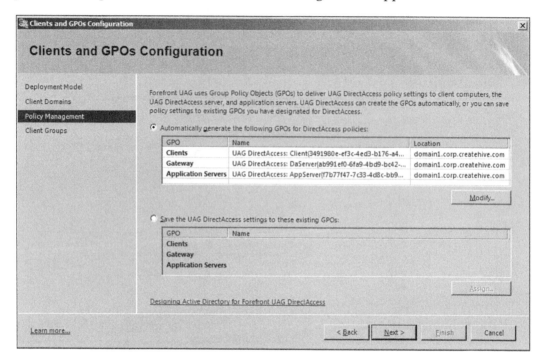

The last page in this step is about selecting the groups that the DA policy will apply to. This is a real no-brainer—just click **Add**, select the Domain group you have configured to host the users who will be using DA, and click **OK**. The only thing that you need to keep in mind here is that the DA servers themselves must not be part of these groups. If the DA policy is applied to the UAG server, nothing is going to work.

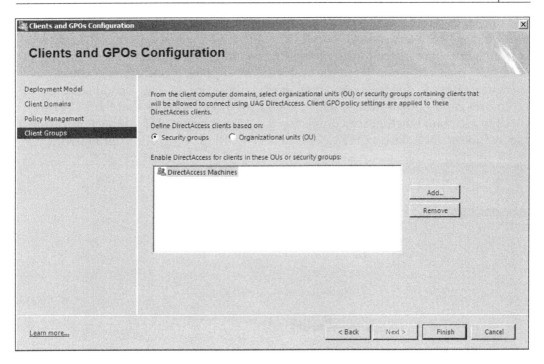

The DirectAccess Connectivity Assistant

The DirectAccess Connectivity Assistant, which we mentioned earlier, can be configured as part of this stage, by clicking **Client Connectivity Assistant** inside the Clients and GPOs box. This is an optional step, and does not install the client, but rather configures settings for it as part of DA group policy, which will be sent to clients to enhance DCA's abilities to help.

The first configuration screen is about turning on the settings for DCA. Even without turning those on, users can still install DCA and have it generate a report, in case of trouble. However, configuring the settings makes life a bit easier for them. For example, you can pre-configure the tool with the support group email address, so users don't have to guess who to email the diagnostic log to. The second screen configures connection verifiers, which are one or more locations that the DCA can check to ascertain whether the connection is working or not. The connection verifiers can include a UNC path, an HTTP or an HTTPS URL that's inside your network.

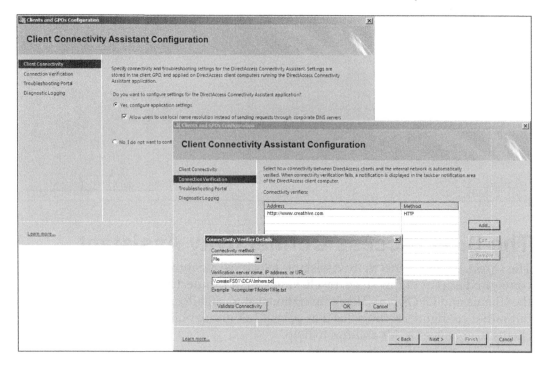

Next comes the troubleshooting portal URL. This is a link to a *public* web page that you can create to help your users cope with a DA failure. UAG does not actually create the website for you—you need to create one and populate it with the content you see fit (we recommend writing up some troubleshooting steps, and perhaps a link to "Relax" by Duran Duran). If you have a UAG portal configured on the server, you can choose it as the suggested link.

The next step allows you to configure an email address that DCA will use when the user clicks **Email Logs**. You can also specify a designated location for the log—otherwise, it is stored by default under `\AppData\Local\Microsoft\DCA`.

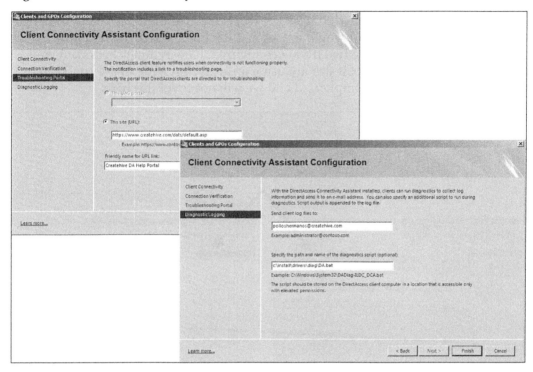

We will talk some more about DCA later, in the troubleshooting section of this chapter.

DirectAccess Server configuration

The next step is the DirectAccess Server Configuration. Click **Configure** under **DirectAccess Server**. This time, the wizard has either three or four steps. First, UAG checks if an Array is configured. If it isn't, it will check that the external interface has two consecutive IPs and warn you if it does not. If it has an array, it will perform a similar check, to make sure two IPs are configured. If everything checks out, you can continue to the next step. If you are using an array, but with an external **load balancer**, things get more complicated and we will not cover this here.

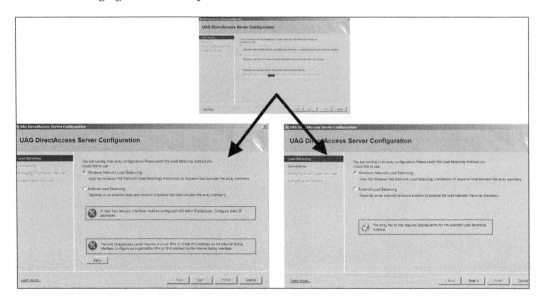

In case there's no Array, this step will be skipped, and it will take you directly to the **Connectivity** step. On the left side of the connectivity page, you have to select the IP address that will be used on the External interface, and UAG will automatically select the second one. The right side of the page asks you to select the IP for the internal interface.

For the internal interface, we have two options. If the NIC has been configured with an IPv6 address, UAG will assume that you have native IPv6 working on your network, and that you don't need the ISATAP functionality. In that case, you will be asked to select IPv6 IP from the bottom drop-down list. If you do not have one configured (IPv6 is disabled on the Internal NIC, or is set to automatically obtain an address), it will assume you *do* want ISATAP, and will prompt you to select the IPv4 address for the internal interface from the top drop-down list. It will also show a message reminding you to configure an A-record on your DNS, and remove ISATAP from the global block list (we discussed this a few pages ago—remember?).

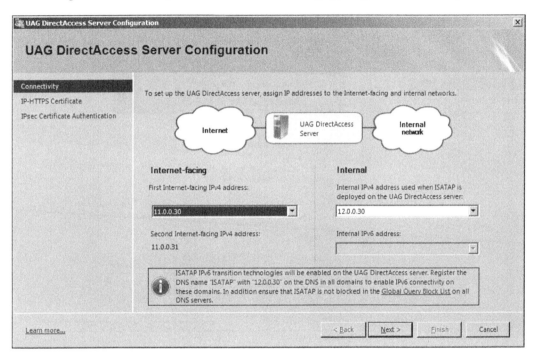

The next step is about choosing the certificate for IP-HTTPS client connections. This certificate is sent by the server to clients who attempt to connect using IP-HTTPS, and is very important. If you have not installed an IP-HTTPS certificate before now, you can take of this now, and continue with the wizard once you have it. Keep in mind that the certificate needs to be trusted by UAG itself, as well as by the clients. Ideally, this would be purchased from a third party certificate provider. If you chose to use an internal CA, make sure the trust-chain is configured on UAG and the clients, and that the CRL of both the certificate and the CA are accessible externally.

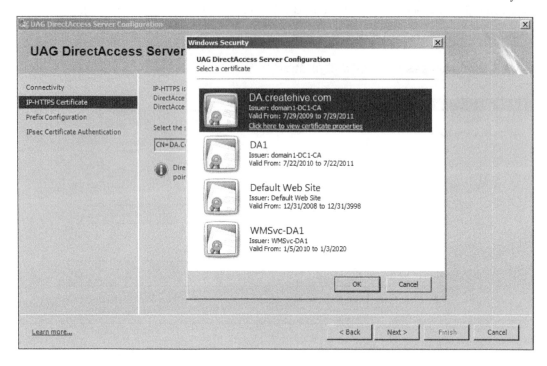

If, earlier, UAG discovered that your internal interface is configured with an IPv6 address, it will now show the IPv6 prefix configuration tab, in which you inform UAG of your organization's IPv6 configuration. Your IP Address block will typically be assigned to you by your ISP, but if your network is already using IPv6, you probably don't need us to tell you much about this page. If you're not sure, some more information is available here: `http://technet.microsoft.com/en-us/library/dd857387.aspx`.

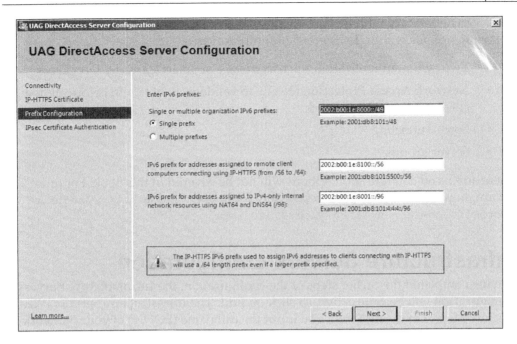

The next step is configuring the IPSec Certificate **authentication** option, which is the certificate used by UAG for IPSec. You can choose to use a certificate from a trusted root CA, or from an intermediate CA. This page also allows you to configure advanced IPSec options—the security methods for IPSec Key Exchange.

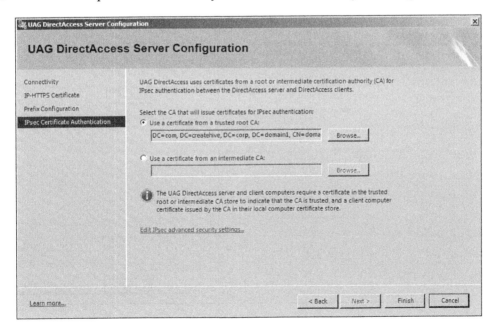

Before going forward with the next phase of the wizard, you can also configure the following options within the Server Configuration area:

- Two factor authentication, such as the use of Smart Cards by DA clients
- **Network Access Protection** (**NAP**), to validate client health before allowing a client to access the network
- Force Tunneling
- Server groups

These advanced configuration options will not be covered in this book. For more information, review the UAG DirectAccess deployment guide: `http://technet.microsoft.com/en-us/library/dd857320.aspx`.

Infrastructure Servers configuration

Having completed the earlier steps of the configuration, the **Infrastructure Servers configuration** will become active, so click on **Edit**. The Infrastructure Servers Wizard has four steps. On the first step, you input the full name (FQDN) of your **Network Location Server** (**NLS**), and click **Validate** to let UAG check it. UAG will connect to the NLS using HTTPS, and validate its certificate. If it goes well, you will receive a confirmation:

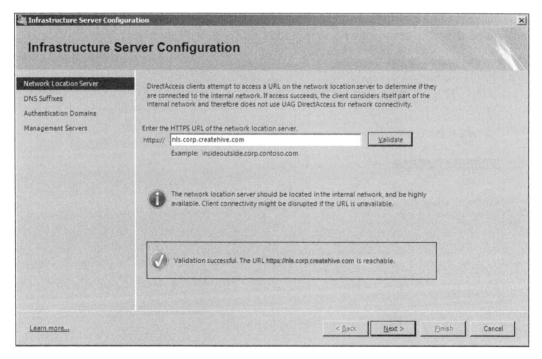

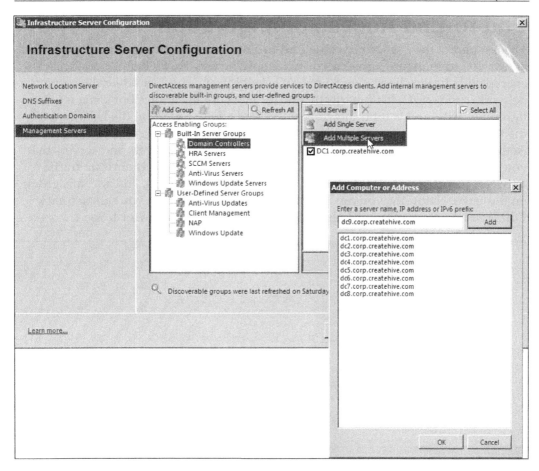

Keep in mind that the list of infrastructure servers can change over time, so you might need to revisit this part of the wizard again. This is perfectly normal and administrators make changes here all the time. Also, each server you add here complicates the IPSec policy that is generated, and that burdens UAG and affects performance to some degree (not a very high one—don't worry).

End-to-End Access configuration

The last part of the DA wizard is the **End-to-End Access Configuration** page, which allows you to configure tighter security for specific servers. By default, traffic is encrypted between clients ("end") to UAG ("edge"), and then sent over the corporate network *unencrypted*. This is perfectly fine for most organizations, but some require tighter security, and want traffic to be encrypted all the way from the DA client to the target computer ("end-to-end"). To do this, you will need to create a group in Active Directory, and populate it with the names of the computers and servers that you want this policy to apply to, and then enable the option **Authenticate traffic between DirectAccess clients and selected application servers**, and add this group on this page. Naturally, you can add more than one group, and you can also click **Edit IPSec cryptography settings...** to configure custom settings for IPSec.

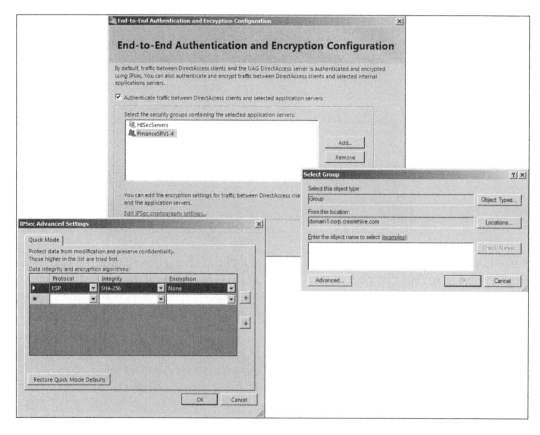

Once you are done with the End-to-End Access Configuration Wizard, the **Apply Policy** button lights up, and you are now ready to turn on DA. You can also click **Export Policy**, which opens a window with the option to save the script locally—this is useful for backup purposes, or if you want to view the script personally and try to understand what it does (good luck!). Exporting the script is also useful if you do not have administrative privileges on the GPOs. In this scenario, you may want to export the script and send it to another person who does have the appropriate permissions. In some scenarios, an organization's network administration team creates the GPOs ahead of this step and then asks a person such as yourself to use them. If so, you may have to make manual changes to the script. This is detailed here: `http://blogs.technet.com/b/edgeaccessblog/archive/2010/02/18/deep-dive-into-uag-directaccess-tweaking-the-gpos.aspx`.

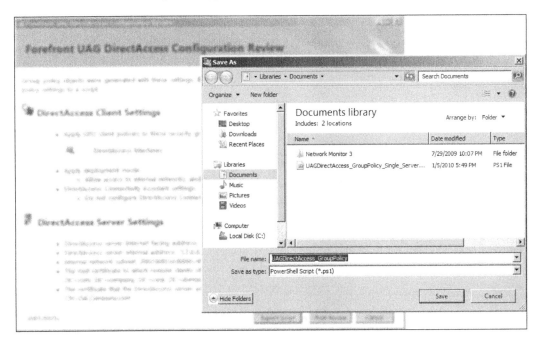

When you are ready to apply the policy, click **Apply Policy,** which will open up a new window with the summary of your settings. To apply, click **Apply Now** to run the script, which applies the new Group Policy to the domain. This process is usually quite fast, but if your configuration involves multiple domain sites, replication of the configuration to both the clients and the UAG machines may take longer. Once the script execution has completed, your DA setup is done, and you are ready to deploy it to your clients!!!

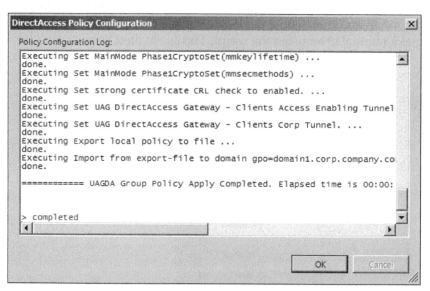

At this point, you can open the Group Policy editor for your domain, and observe the new policies that have been created. To do so, open **Administrative Tools** and open **Group Policy Management**. You should see the policies under your domain:

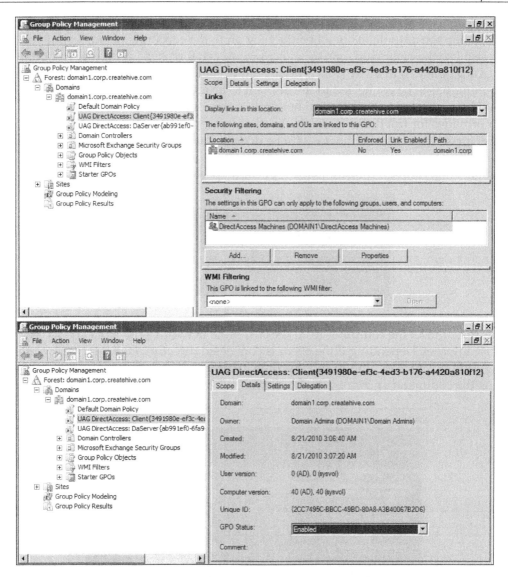

One last thing to do is to **Activate** the UAG configuration. Sure, the group policy is in place now, but you have to configure UAG itself to accept incoming connections, and also to configure other array members, if you have an array running.

To get clients to start using DA, they need to inherit the new Group Policy. This should happen automatically when they log on to the corporate network, but you can also use the command, gpupdate /force, which forces the computer to update its group policy right away (this is done on the client computer). Naturally, the client computer has to be connected to the domain to be able to receive GP updates—it could be connected to the physical network at the office, or use VPN technology that provides for full domain access. Another interesting point is that in multi DC site environments, even gpupdate /force doesn't guarantee the latest configuration, as the DC site the client is using may not have been updated with the latest configuration through the automatic replication process.

Now, disconnect the computer from the corporate network, and connect it to the public internet. Depending if the client is connected directly to the internet, or behind a NAT device, 6to4 or Teredo should come up. If 6to4 is up, you will be able to see it using the command ipconfig on the client:

```
Command Prompt
C:\Users\Administrator.DOMAIN1>ipconfig

Windows IP Configuration

Ethernet adapter Internet:

   Connection-specific DNS Suffix  . :
   Link-local IPv6 Address . . . . . : fe80::e959:149b:ad96:fe6a%14
   IPv4 Address. . . . . . . . . . . : 11.0.0.10
   Subnet Mask . . . . . . . . . . . : 255.0.0.0
   Default Gateway . . . . . . . . . : 11.0.0.1

Tunnel adapter Local Area Connection* 11:

   Media State . . . . . . . . . . . : Media disconnected
   Connection-specific DNS Suffix  . :

Tunnel adapter Local Area Connection* 12:

   Media State . . . . . . . . . . . : Media disconnected
   Connection-specific DNS Suffix  . :

Tunnel adapter isatap.{56CB6FDD-0BF5-4BCF-ADAD-B4FA628D7D8C}:

   Media State . . . . . . . . . . . : Media disconnected
   Connection-specific DNS Suffix  . :

Tunnel adapter 6TO4 Adapter:

   Connection-specific DNS Suffix  . :
   IPv6 Address. . . . . . . . . . . : 2002:b00:a::b00:a
   Default Gateway . . . . . . . . . : 2002:b00:1e::b00:1e

Tunnel adapter iphttpsinterface:

   Media State . . . . . . . . . . . : Media disconnected
   Connection-specific DNS Suffix  . :
```

In the previous screenshot, you can also see that the **isatap** interface, which is used inside the organizational network, is disconnected here, because the client is outside the network. The **iphttpsinterface** is also disconnected, because the computer was successful with 6to4, and there's no need for **Teredo** or **IP-HTTPS**.

If you try this from a computer that is behind a NAT device, such as a home router, 6to4 will not work, and the computer will fall back to Teredo, and your `ipconfig` output will look like this:

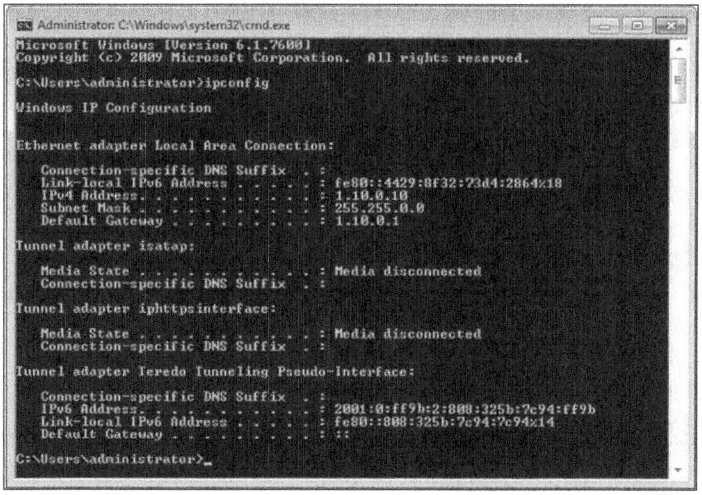

If Teredo hasn't been successful either (which can happen, if you recall, because UDP port 3354 is blocked on this network), then the system should fall back to IP-HTTPS, which will look like this:

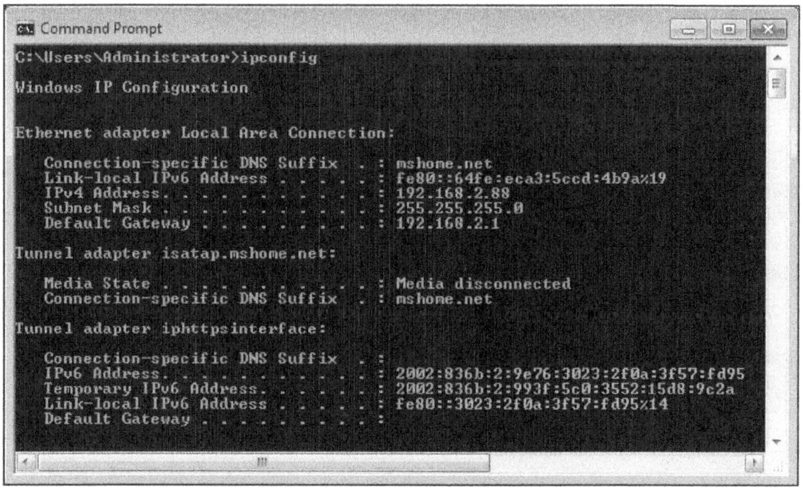

From the user's perspective, this should be completely transparent (although sometimes, as noted before, the IP-HTTPS connection might be less effective from a performance point of view, in certain circumstances). If one of the connections modes has succeeded, the client should have full corporate network accessibility (except to the NLS server, of course, because it's excluded). The client should be able to ping internal servers or other networked resources, connect to them using a browser or **UNC file-sharing** paths etc. Naturally, the performance of the DA connection is dependant not only on the type of connection (6to4, Teredo or IP-HTTPS) but also on the user's internet connection. This is more noticeable with non-symmetric connections like **ADSL**, and also with more traffic-intensive communication protocols like **SMB** (used for file transfers from network shares), or applications that are traffic intensive, like Microsoft Office applications. If all goes well, congratulations! You are now a proud DirectAccess user!

Keeping an eye on the server

Once you have DA configured and working, you will probably want to keep an eye on the server, and see who is using DA. Remember the Web Monitor we talked about in *Chapter 9*? Well, it has a special section for DirectAccess monitoring. It allows you to monitor the status of the server itself, so you can see if an array member is having a problem, and allows you to track active sessions.

The **Current Status** page shows you the list of servers in the array, and the status of the various components including DNS64, IP-HTTPS, Network Security, 6to4 Router, ISATAP Router, Teredo Server, and Teredo Relay

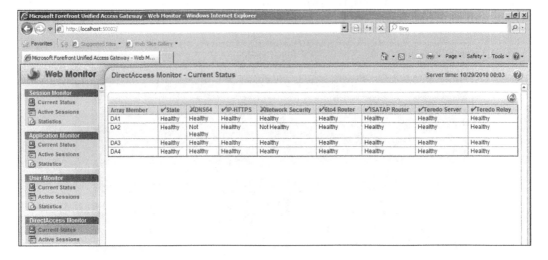

The **Active Sessions** page shows you a list of active sessions, and information about each, like the source IP, the computer account, the transition mode (connectivity type), the array member in use, and more. In a full scale deployment, the list may be long, so a filter is included to allow you to seek out a specific session by user name, computer name, IP, or certificate name.

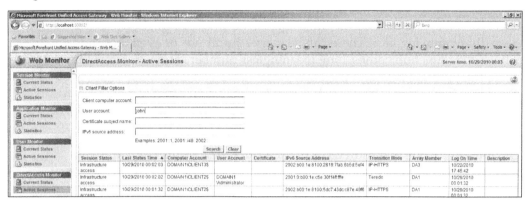

Another option you have to monitor your DA users is using the UAG DA monitoring PowerShell add-in. To do so, you need to add the snap in to PowerShell using the command Add-PSSnapin UAGDAUserMonitoring.

Once that is done, the command Get-DirectAccessUsers results in a list of current user and session info, which you can also filter using various filters. You can also pipe the output into a text file, and then use tools like Excel to manipulate the query of the data. The parameters accepted by Get-DirectAccessUsers are listed here: http://technet.microsoft.com/en-us/library/ff607407.aspx.

Trouble?

Well, since setting up DA was such a piece of cake, you can bet troubleshooting it is just going be to a ball of fun, right? Well, we are going to look at troubleshooting DA in 3 categories:

- Issues during setup, like errors or unexpected behavior
- Problems with the setup that are server-side (affecting all clients)
- Problems with clients that may prevent them from connecting on a singular basis

We will discuss specific issues that you might run into, as well as tools and techniques that can help you look for the reason you are having a problem. Naturally, for any problem we can discuss, there are thousands of variations (not including things that are unrelated to DA, but can still cause problems, like certain system services that are not starting, a non-functional virtual NIC, local networking problem etc), and we cannot cover all of them. When encountering a problem that is not solved by the troubleshooting steps we outline, you might need to do some deep diving into log files. These can be scary—hundreds or even thousands of lines with cryptic function names, long meaningless numbers and acronyms that boggle the mind, but with time and patience, you might be amazed at how good you can get at reading them. However, if push comes to shove, you can always try Microsoft's UAG support forum at: `http://social.technet.microsoft.com/Forums/en-US/forefrontedgeiag`.

Or, you can try one of hundreds of blogs written by various UAG and DA experts. If all else fails, Microsoft support services can surely resolve your issue: `http://support.microsoft.com/`.

Removing DirectAccess

We all know that, sometimes, the only way to solve a computer problem is with a reboot. With DA, a reboot will hardly solve anything, but sometimes you might want to just rip it all out and start from scratch. Keep in mind, though, that since DA configures **Active Directory**, just formatting your server doesn't solve much. If you need to completely remove DA, here's what you need to do:

1. In the UAG Management console, go to the DA Configuration page.
2. Click **Disable DirectAccess**
3. Activate the configuration
4. Open the Group Policy Management tool from your Administrative tools
5. Navigate to Forest\Domains\domain\Group Policy Objects.
6. Remove the following policies:
   a. UAG DirectAccess: AppServer
   b. UAG DirectAccess: DaServer
   c. UAG DirectAccess: Client

If you have removed DA and want to enable it back at this point, you can do so with no need to reconfigure everything—just click on **Enable**, recreate and run the script, and activate the configuration. If, however, you want to further "clean up" the server, you can do so now. Once DA has been disabled, you can also remove the NLB configuration, if you have one, and break your array. Start by removing the VIPs from the NLB configuration wizard, and then use the Array management wizard to remove the array members. If you also want to remove UAG itself from the server, make sure you perform the uninstallation only after removing NLB and breaking the array, so as to not leave the array members in limbo and the NLB configuration in place.

Setup and configuration errors

Naturally, you may encounter issues as early as the setup of UAG itself, but we will not address these here. We have discussed setup troubleshooting to some degree in *Chapter 1*, and will cover some more in *Chapter 12*. For now, we will assume you have a successfully set up server, and that you can successfully launch the UAG management console.

The first issue you might encounter is an error message about the **consecutive IP addresses**, which will be shown as soon as you enter the DirectAccess overview page, if you are using a single server (as opposed to an array). In this case, make sure that you have set up two consecutive IP addresses on the *external* interface. If you have, and the IPs are not accepted, make sure your **subnet mask** is appropriate, and try a different IP set. Keep in mind that addresses in the private ranges of 10.x.x.x, 172.16.x.x, and 192.168.x.x are not supported. Also, if you have assigned three IPs or more to the NIC, try removing all but two to verify there's no conflict. Lastly, make sure you have not configured the internal network with similar or identical networking parameters.

Another issue you might encounter during the setup wizard is in the **connectivity** page in the DirectAccess Server phase of the setup wizard. On the *right-hand side*, you need to select the IP of the internal interface and, sometimes, you see the IPv4 drop-down list enabled, when you expect the IPv6 one to be enabled, or vice versa. This selection is determined based on the IP configuration. If the Internal NIC on the server has been manually configured with an IPv6 address, the wizard will assume that you have fully deployed IPv6 on your network, and will only let you select that. This is all perfectly normal and expected.

In the **IPSec Certificate Authentication** page, you might not be able to see the intended certificate on the list of available ones. Keep in mind that the certificate needs to meet specific guidelines with its setup, so refer to that section earlier in this chapter. Also, make sure the appropriate certificates have been placed in the *Personal* folder of the *local computer* (not your user) store. If you receive a warning about the certificate, make sure that the Certificate Authority that issued it is trusted by the UAG server. For this to work, the CA's root certificate has to be imported into the trusted root certification authority folder of the local computer store, and if there are intermediate CAs, their certificates need to be imported into the intermediate certification authorities folder. Another thing to keep in mind is that DA clients will have to be able to trust these certificates as well, so make sure the certificates of the CAs that issued the certificates are installed on every client.

By the way, we mentioned this before, but the most common cause of DA issues is certificate problems. The most common problem with certificates is CDP/CRL issues, where the certificate itself is OK, but has a CDP that points to locations that are unreachable by the client for some reason. This in itself is often, when trying to put the CRLs on a server that is being used for something else, to conserve resources, and failing to setup up the name resolution, host-header or permissions properly, enough. If you suspect certificate problems, you can do basic verification of the certificate using a browser - open Internet Explorer on the UAG server, and connect to the URL that hosts the certificate. If you get any errors at this point, investigate them. Even if not, open the certificate's properties by double-clicking on the SSL Lock icon, and inspect the certificate properties. Things to consider as potential problems, beyond the obvious subject name, are:

- Validity date
- Certificate is not revoked on the CA
- Certificate trust chain (the server has to trust all the authorities that are in charge of the certificate, starting from the root authority and going through any intermediate ones)
- CRLs for all CAs need to be reachable
- Valid CDPs
- Valid CRL files located and downloadable from the locations specified in the certificate.

The difference between the third and fourth items is that a CDP can be invalid if it contains a location that is invalid by its very existence, like a UNC path that won't be reachable on the internet. A CDP can have valid addresses, but the addresses themselves may not be functional, because the actual CRL file is damaged, invalid, or missing.

The **DNS Suffixes Configuration** page can be confusing, especially if your domain configuration is complex, and even more so if you have split-brains DNS setup. Keep in mind that the page is supposed to have at least two entries – the **primary domain suffix**, and an **exclusion** for the NLS. Additional entries might be required if your domain structure has additional suffixes, if you have CRL URLs that are based on your domain structure, and if you need to exclude additional URLs in a split-brains DNS configuration (one where you share the same DNS structure internally and externally – we talked about this earlier).

Another issue you might run into is during the last stage, where the script is executed to create group policy objects. The script that UAG generates is fairly complex, and can take a while to complete. This process is sensitive to permissions and to timing. If the connection between UAG and the domain controllers is slow or not very solid, it can cause the script to fail, and script failure could result in damaged policies that may require cleaning up. If you have a complex network with multiple sites, inspect your site configuration to make sure that UAG communicates with a DC that is as close to it as possible. If you are configuring UAG with a user that is not an enterprise admin in your domain, make sure that the user has all the appropriate permissions to modify Active Directory. If you receive an error while running the script, do try to run it again – rerunning often rectifies the problem.

An additional issue that you might encounter is a cryptic error from IPSec when you enable DA. This may happen if you have disabled the IPv6 protocol on your external NIC on the DA server. Often, organizations disable IPv6 on the external interface, but IPSec requires that it be enabled.

Whose fault is it?

Well, yours, of course! Seriously, though, the very first step in troubleshooting is figuring out if the problem is a server-side issue, or a client side. Sometimes, your installation is only a temporary test in the lab, and you don't have a wide set of clients, and that could be challenging. You should strive to have at least two clients of each type (6to4, Teredo and IP-HTTPS), and make sure they are as clean as possible, to avoid the risk that some preinstalled software is causing a conflict. If you lack the hardware resources, a virtual machine hosting multiple clients may be an ideal solution for this. It might be hard to simulate a real-world situation in a lab or a test environment – especially the "public internet" part. Many organizations get a dedicated DSL line for this testing, and others use a **cellular modem** or a **tethered cell phone**. Keep in mind that some internet services are more limited than others – we already mentioned that some cellular networks block protocol 41, making 6to4 impossible to use. Speed may also be a factor, so a tethered phone connection might be too slow.

If, after successfully completing the configuration, you are unable to get clients connected, try the various connection types to ascertain if this is a general DA problem (no communication modes works), limited to all clients of a certain connection mode, or limited to a certain client machine. According to these findings, you can start the troubleshooting process.

DCA to the rescue

Your first line of defense against an evil computer which won't connect to DA is the DCA tool we mentioned earlier. Assuming you took care to have your users install it, they can easily use it to solve some problems, like internet connectivity issues, or generate a log that can help you determine the problem if it's more complicated. If DA is not working correctly, the DCA icon on the system tray will show an exclamation mark, and the user can right-click and choose **Advanced Diagnostics**. The Advanced Diagnostics screen has a link to start the troubleshooting process, but as soon as the user opens it, it starts to generate a log that is stored in the `\AppData\Local\Microsoft\DCA` folder by default, or at a location specified by you during the DA configuration wizard. The user can then click **Email Logs** to automatically create an email message addressed to the email you configured for that purpose in the DA configuration wizard. The wizard will also show a link to the help webpage you designated.

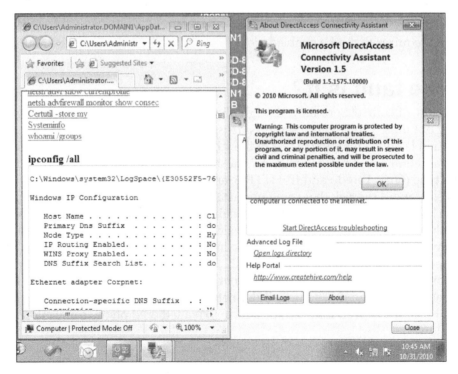

The log itself is an HTML file containing a plethora of information about the client. It shows the output of the following commands:

- `Ipconfig /all`
- `Netsh int teredo show state`
- `Netsh int httpstunnel show interfaces`
- `Netsh dns show state`
- `Netsh name show policy`
- `Netsh name show effective`
- `Netsh adv mon show mmsa`
- `Netsh nap client show state`
- `Webutil query -events Microsoft-Windows-NetworkAccessProtection/Operational /count:20 /format:text /rd: true`
- `Netsh int ipv6 show int level=verbose`
- `Netsh advf show currentprofile`
- `Netsh advfirewall monitor show consec`
- `Certutil -store my`
- `Systeminfo`
- `Whoami /groups`

These commands show information about the various interfaces and components that are related to DA. For example, the Certutil command shows the contents of the user's personal certificate store, which may reveal a problem with the certificate. This may be an expired certificate, or one that does not map to the user's account properly. A lot of what the log shows won't mean much to you at this point, but after finishing the chapter and observing the configuration of your users, you should be able to see common grounds, and learn what to expect from a "successful" output and a failed connection. These logs can may also be requested of you by Microsoft support engineers, in case you need their help with resolving a problem.

Server related issues

Even though most of the issues are happening on the server, most of the actual troubleshooting should be done on the client. As we said more than once before, certificates are the most common cause of problems, and unfortunately, they are not always visible to the naked eye. In fact, because DA has absolutely no user interaction on the client side (that is no dialler to launch), the user will not be shown any errors either, unless you deploy the **DCA**, which we have just discussed. The first step for seeing if DA even works on the client is to run an IPCONFIG and seeing if any of the 6to4, Teredo or IP-HTTPS interfaces are showing as connected and configured with a valid IPv6 address.

If one of the interfaces appears to be active, the next step is to ping a **Domain Controller**. If that works, then the next step is pinging another resource on the internal network, such as some internal server or another computer. If all that works fine, then you can try connecting to some local website, like a SharePoint server, using the browser. If that works, then the entire internal network should be available.

If things are not working out, and it appears to be a general issue affecting all clients, start by trying to access the IP of the DNS64 server (which is also the tunnel endpoint of the DA server or array). Naturally, we do this with PING, and for that we'll need to check this on UAG itself. To see that, look in the DCA log for the output of the command

```
netsh name show effective
```

You can also type this command in a CMD window to see the same result. Your output shows the content of the **Name Resolution Policy Table (NRPT)**, and will reflect the settings you configured on the DNS suffixes page of the infrastructure server configuration step of the DA wizard. You'll see the NLSs name as excluded, and then the IPv6 address of the UAG server. Now, try pinging that address. If you get a reply, it means that there's connectivity to the DA server *at least*.

If the results of the command are just blank, with the text **Note: DirectAccess settings would be turned off when computer is inside corporate network**, it means that your client hasn't been configured with DA at all. Typically, this is a Group Policy issue. It may have not been inherited to the client, or denied. You can verify this using this command:

```
Gpresult /f /h grouppolicyreport.htm
```

The `htm` file name is not specific—you can type any name you want. This will generate an HTML file that shows if the Group Policy has been applied, or not:

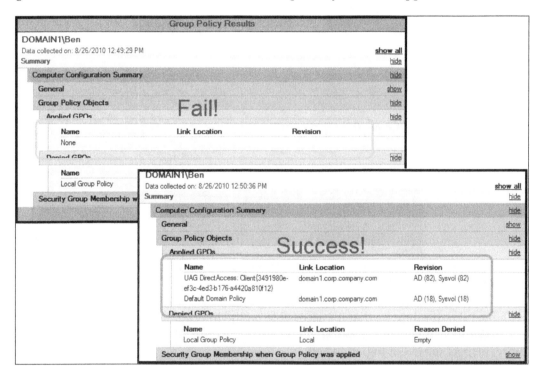

The result can vary—a policy could be "denied" as well, for reasons like permissions or accessibility. If so, the reason should appear under the "reason denied" column and shed some light on the cause. For example, the GPO didn't get the right users assigned.

Another common situation is that the client is not aware that it is outside the corporate network, therefore not activating the DA connection. The reverse also happens —it might be on the corporate network, but thinking it is outside. A simple way to check this is with the command (which is also part of the DCA log):

```
Netsh dns show state
```

The **machine location** (fourth item) will show where the client computer "thinks" it is:

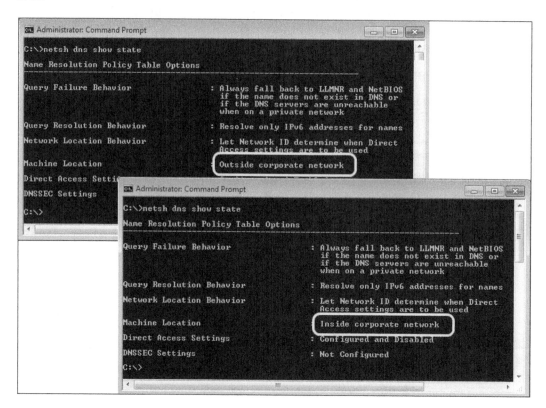

If the client is "wrong" about where it is, it's probably related to something wrong with the NLS. It might be that it's accessible on the internet for some reason, or that it's inaccessible inside the corporate network (bad certificate or server down?). To see more, inspect the event log on the client:

1. Open **Event Viewer** from **Administrative tools**.

2. Navigate to `Applications and Services Logs/Microsoft/Windows/NCSI`.

Inspect the events for information that might explain the problem and, naturally, inspect the NLS to verify that it is responding. Keep in mind that if the client thinks it's outside the corporate network while it is in fact inside it will prevent it from communicating with *anything* (unless an alternative name resolution method, like WINS, is used). You won't even be able to update the group policy settings, because the client will be trying to contact the domain controller through the DA tunnel, which isn't working. If you need to forcibly remove the group policy from the computer, you can do so by editing the registry:

1. Open the Registry Editor.

2. Navigate to `HKLM/Software/Policies/Microsoft`.

3. Delete all items under **Microsoft**.

4. Close the Registry Editor.

Once you do so, the policy affecting the computer is gone, and it should be able to communicate with resources on the corporate network successfully, but keep in mind that as a domain member, it will apply the policy back pretty fast.

As you've seen previously, an important tool for troubleshooting DA is the `NETSH` command, which is short for **Network Shell**, and is an important network configuration and analysis tool included with Windows. `NETSH` can be used to see detailed configuration information about the network and related components, and also to configure them. `NETSH` can be used directly, with certain parameters, but also can be launched as a "console" application. For highly detailed reference to `NETSH`, visit the following link: `http://technet.microsoft.com/en-us/library/cc725935(WS.10).aspx`.

Client side issues

The most common issue on the client-side is a problem with the Windows Firewall (also known by its short nickname **Windows Firewall with advanced security**). The firewall is there to protect the computer from attacks, but it's also the main engine behind the IPSec tunnels used for DA, so it has to be in perfect working condition for things to work.

Many organizations control the Windows Firewall through their own group policy, to make sure users don't turn it off because it's blocking their favorite game or something. Some organizations do the opposite—disable it, because they have their own preferred firewall product installed on every client. If your organization doesn't enforce it at all, or enforces it to be off, this might be the problem. For DA to work, the firewall must be on, but we have even seen cases where someone turned it off to troubleshoot DA, thereby exacerbating his problem! Not sure? To check, open the **Windows Firewall with advanced security** control panel, and click on **Connection Security Rules**. If no rules appear, it means that the firewall is off

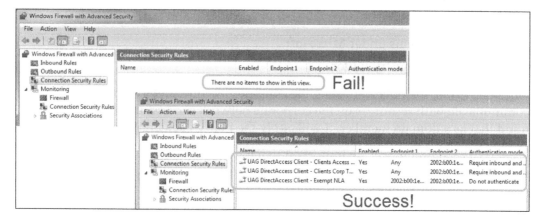

Transition technology issues

As you already know, DA clients have multiple methods of connecting to the DA server over the internet, and the one the DA client chooses to use depends on the infrastructure. A client that is connected to the internet directly will use 6to4, and if it is behind a NAT device, it will use Teredo. If Teredo cannot be used because the network is blocking UDP traffic (port 3354), the client will attempt to use IP-HTTPS. When troubleshooting clients, start by figuring out which of the above the client is using. To find that out, type `ipconfig /all` and see which of the adapters is connected:

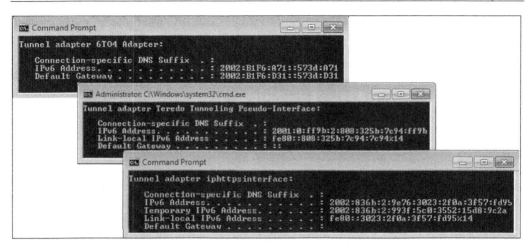

If you are using a client that is connected directly to the internet, and has a public IP (as opposed to a private NAT IP in the ranges of 10.x.x.x, 192.168.x.x, and 172.16.x.x), and it's unable to use 6to4, it would typically be because IP Protocol 41 is being blocked. We have already mentioned that some ISPs block it. Some do it because they block all non-critical traffic, and have not been given a good reason to allow protocol 41. Others do so because they know that since DA is always on, letting DA traffic through will put a load on their network. To figure out if it is indeed being blocked, you can use a network capture tool such as **Wireshark** or Microsoft's **Network Monitor**. If you see no Protocol 41 traffic coming *to* the client, then it is almost positively being blocked. For more information about troubleshooting 6to4 connections: `http://technet.microsoft.com/en-us/library/ee844172(WS.10).aspx`.

Statistically, few DA clients actually use 6to4, because of the prevalence of NAT on the internet. Even home users use routers with NAT pretty much ubiquitously. This means, of course, that Teredo is the most common connection method in use.

If your client is indeed behind a NAT device, but is falling back to IP-HTTPS instead of using Teredo, the first step is getting more details about the Teredo interface by inspecting the appropriate section in the DCA log, or by typing the command:

```
Netsh Int Teredo Show Stat
```

Here are several variations on the output of this. Naturally, the bottom one is the one we want:

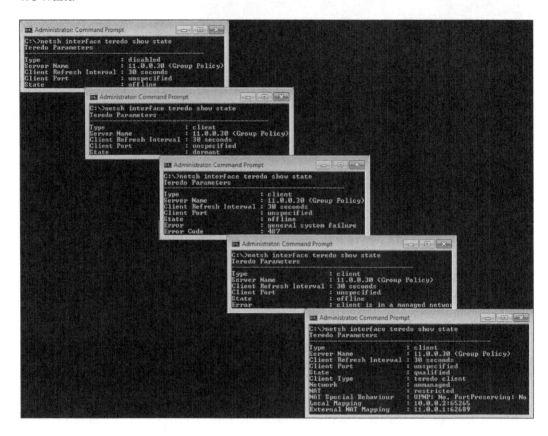

In the upper screenshot, you can see that the Teredo interface is *offline* because it is *disabled*. You can change the status of Teredo back to Client using the following command:

```
Netsh Int Teredo Set State Client
```

Or, if you need to disable it for some reason, use "disabled" instead of "client". If the state is not "**qualified**", DA will certainly not work, and it may show the reason as this error. For example, the fourth screenshot shows the error as "client is in a managed network", which means the client thinks it is inside the corporate network (probably a NLS issue—we talked about that plenty) or in a NATted network of a type it cannot traverse. Can you guess what the third preceding screenshot is about? If your guess was "bye bye web", you were right—a **general system failure** means that the network cable is unplugged. If the status is stuck on "**probe**" for a while, that means your internet connection is down (router? ISP? Virus?)

Beyond that, the next step is to turn on Teredo **tracing**, and inspect the trace. To do so, follow these steps:

1. Open the Registry Editor.

2. Navigate to `HKLM\SOFTWARE\Microsoft\Tracing\IpHlpSvc\`.

3. Edit the value **EnableFileTracing** and set it to 1.

4. Open the Service administrative tool.

5. Restart the **IP Helper** service.

6. Force Teredo to attempt a connection by running the command `netsh interface teredo show state`.

Don't forget to set the registry value back to 0 and restart the IP Helper service when done. The trace file will be located in the `%SystemRoot%\Tracing` folder, and it is going to be a text file, but may be tough to figure out, as trace files often are.

If you are OK with Teredo not working, because the client is indeed in a network that blocks it, then IP-HTTPS should come in handy. However, it may not work either. In this case, to see what's going on, inspect the IP-HTTPS part of the DCA log, or type the following command on the client:

```
netsh int httpstunnel show interface
```

The result we hope for would be the bottom one on this screenshot—0x0, IPHTTPS active:

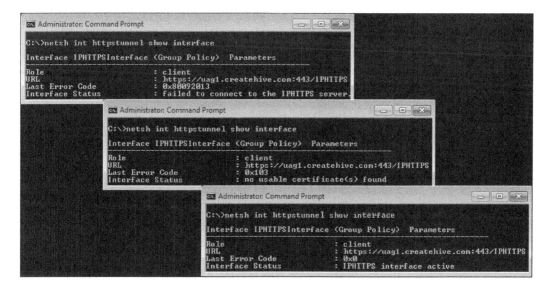

If, however, we see something else, the error number would usually indicate what the problem is. For example, the top screen from the preceding screenshot shows error no. **0x80092013**, which means **The revocation function was unable to check revocation because the revocation server was offline**. This is a classic issue that we have discussed earlier—a problem with the CRL of the IP-HTTPS server (the one you selected in the authentication options page of the DirectAccess Server Configuration Wizard step) or one of the CAs in the domain. You can see a list of IP-HTTPS possible errors here: `http://msdn.microsoft.com/en-us/library/dd542646(VS.85).aspx`

The error in the second screen from the preceding screenshot does not appear in this table, but is discussed in Tom Shinder's blog. Tom regularly writes about DA troubleshooting, and his blog is an excellent resource: `http://blogs.technet.com/b/tomshinder/archive/2010/03/30/troubleshooting-the-no-usable-certificate-s-ip-https-client-error.aspx`.

And here's another resource with specific details about troubleshooting various connectivity methods: `http://technet.microsoft.com/en-us/library/ee844100(WS.10).aspx`.

Advanced troubleshooting

The steps outlined previously are for some of the common issues but, sometimes, you might have to dig deeper. Since DA relies on IPSec, any one of multiple IPSec related issues can prevent your DA clients from connecting. Troubleshooting IPSec is quite difficult, and is beyond the scope of this book, but you can find more help about this here: `http://technet.microsoft.com/en-us/library/cc783041(WS.10).aspx`.

To go even deeper, if you dare, you can enable auditing for IPSec using the following command on a UAG DA client:

```
auditpol.exe /set /SubCategory:"IPsec Main Mode","IPsec Extended Mode" /
success:enable /failure:enable
```

Once you run this command, inspect your system *event viewer*, and look for events related to IPSec, to see what is causing them.

Additional resources

Being the complex technology that DA is, many things can go wrong, and if the previous steps and suggestions did not resolve your problem, you might have to consult additional resources. In addition to the forum we mentioned earlier, here are some additional resources that might be useful for troubleshootomg DA:

- `http://technet.microsoft.com/en-us/library/ee624056(WS.10).aspx`
- `http://blogs.technet.com/b/tomshinder/`
- `http://blogs.isaserver.org/shinder/`
- `http://blogs.technet.com/b/edgeaccessblog/`

Summary

As you can see, there's a reason we elected to put this chapter close to the end of the book. DirectAccess is certainly one of the tougher technologies to understand and configure, even with the help of UAG. However, with time and patience, we are sure you can conquer this too, and provide your users with the most convenient VPN solution in history!

12
Troubleshooting

They say that what goes up, must come down, and assuming this is not the first time you have used a computer, you probably know exactly what that means. Many organizations encounter many challenges when starting to use UAG for the first time, and we wouldn't be surprised to hear you purchased this book for the sole purpose of helping you solve some of them. If, however, you jumped to this chapter straight after installing UAG, we recommend you go back and read at least *Chapters 1* through *6*, because we will be referring to many keywords, acronyms, and abbreviations here that were explained earlier. Otherwise, good luck with your troubleshooting!

Whodunnit?

Unlike many other software products, the majority of the problems with UAG are related to the fact that it supports such a wide variety of products. With most other products, the software pops up an error, you look it up in the documentation or knowledge base, and follow the solution, but actually receiving an error message by UAG "itself" is relatively rare. The reason this is the way it is stems from what UAG does. The server has to authenticate the user, then authenticate on behalf of the user to one of dozens of possible backend servers with their authentication mechanism, and then fetch various types of data from that backend server, parse it, and present it to the user. This "data" is almost always a mix of graphics, text, binary objects, code in various languages and more. The content is also often encrypted or protected against tampering in one or more ways, and UAG has to go through all that for every web request and response. Add to that the fact that the user may be running one of dozens of browser types and versions on different platforms, and you begin to grasp the complexity of the tasks that UAG does. This is, of course, a very simplistic description, and UAG can and does so much more, but clearly, it's quite amazing that despite the infinite diversity and infinite combinations, UAG can still do so much and publish so many applications successfully.

We will divide this chapter into several sections:

1. Troubleshooting administrative errors: This will cover issues you might encounter while configuring the server—errors, oddities and things that may seem to make no sense.

2. Troubleshooting application issues: Here we will talk about common problems with specific applications, as well as general issues with applications that are published using the generic templates.

3. Troubleshooting client issues: Clients acting up? We'll review some "popular" issues your users might call up and scream about.

If you just finished installing the server, and ran into issues, keep in mind that we already discussed troubleshooting installation issues in *Chapter 2*. Also, if you are looking for help with your DirectAccess deployment, these issues were specifically addressed in the last third of *Chapter 11*.

Administrative errors

Most of the errors you might encounter while using UAG give a clear indication of what the problem is, assuming the concepts of how UAG works and what it does are clear. For example, a common error happens during activation, if the UAG server is unable to resolve the hostname of a server you have defined in an application. This error is quite verbose and usually makes sense and points you in the right direction. Troubleshooting it would involve basic networking skills—check if UAG can contact its DNS server, and if that DNS server responds to queries properly.

When thinking about administrative issues, one must understand the way UAG works and the intricate relationship it has with other components. The administrator configures settings in the UAG management console, and these are saved as an EGF file on the local hard drive. Only upon **activation** do these changes get applied to the actual configuration. When an activation is performed, UAG configures IIS by creating new sites or changing existing ones. It also creates or changes access rules and other configurations in TMG. TMG itself, in turn, configures other system components, like the RRAS service and **NLB** (**RRAS** is configured for **VPN** access, like **SSTP**). Other services that may be configured include NAP and RDG. All these steps are part of the reason activation takes so long, and why it is not just a simple and quick "apply" that other applications have .

File Access

A common administrative issue you may run into can occur when you try to configure the File Access application. Its configuration console requires you to select which domains, servers and shares you want to publish. Many users get errors when enumerating these domains, servers and shares, or get incomplete results. We already discussed this in *Chapter 5*, and explained that this tool relies on **NETBIOS** and the Browser function of Windows, and may require changes on internal routers and firewalls. For more information, re-read the section "Preparing to Publish File Access" in Chapter 5, which also includes verification steps. Another thing to keep in mind is that the File Access application does not support **DFS** shares, so if those do not show up, that's perfectly normal, and there's not much you can do about it.

SSL Network Tunneling

Another issue that some users have seen is a corruption of the **SSL Network Tunneling** (**Network Connector**) component, which could show an error during activation that says the Network Connector service could not be started. This can happen sometimes, but is fairly easy to resolve. The procedure includes uninstalling the service, and then reinstalling it:

1. Open a command prompt, and type the following command to *uninstall* the Network Connector:

   ```
   Regsvr32 -u whlvaw_srv.dll

   whlios.exe /Uninstall
   ```

2. Type the following command to *re-install* the Network Connector:

   ```
   Regsvr32 whlvaw_srv.dll

   whlios.exe /Install
   ```

Certificate problems during activation

Another issue that is sometimes seen is activation errors regarding the server's certificate, even though the certificate has not been changed. This could happen, for example, following the installation of an update or service pack. To resolve this, follow these steps:

1. Go to the advanced trunk configuration, and select *another* certificate under the **General** tab.

2. Click **OK**.

3. Go back to the advanced trunk configuration, and select the original certificate.

4. Click **OK**.

5. Activate the configuration again.

Backup and restore

Something else that you might run into is that you need to restore a backup, but you do not remember the password it was created with. Unfortunately, there's no official procedure or tool to crack a backup's password (be glad about that—it means your data is more secure, if a tape falls into the wrong hands).

Updating the server

Since UAG's release, Update 1, Update 2, and SP1 have been released, and if you need to update your server, you may encounter issues. The first thing to keep in mind is that a service pack is cumulative, meaning that it includes the service packs and updates that predate it, so there's no need to install Update 1 or 2 before installing Service Pack 1. That should save you some time already.

If you encounter a failure while installing an update or the service pack, the first step you should take is to verify that there are no "locked" files that the installer may be failing to access. A tool for that is **Handle**, which can be downloaded here: `http://technet.microsoft.com/en-us/sysinternals/bb896655.aspx`.

Put it on your UAG, and type the command:

`Handle.exe unified`

The word "unified" will filter the output to show just files in UAG's default folder. Normally, there should be some UAG processes that should be active (among them `watchdog_service.exe`, `ConfigMgrCom.exe`, `MonitorMgrCom.exe`, `uagqessvc.exe`, and `uagrdpsvc.exe`), but if you see anything else, that might be the problem. If you suspect a process is interfering, you can try to "kill" it using the command:

`TaskKill /f /pid <process id>`

Don't be too trigger happy about killing processes—it may destabilize the server and if you mistakenly kill a UAG or TMG process, may drop users or even cause it to become unresponsive. Some processes can even cause a blue screen when killed, so be sure you know what you are doing.

If this does not help, another step you may try is manually stopping the UAG, TMG and IIS services using the Service Management administrative tool. Naturally, stopping these will terminate all sessions, so be mindful about that as well.

If it is Service Pack 1 that you are installing, note that it also includes SP1 for TMG and update 1 for TMG SP1. In some cases, you may be able to overcome the failed installation problem by simply installing the TMG SP1 separately. It can be downloaded from here: `http://www.microsoft.com/downloads/details.aspx?FamilyID=f0fd5770-7360-4916-a5be-a88a0fd76c7c`.

If following these steps still does not resolve the problem, you may find additional clues in the setup log, which can be found at `C:\ProgramData\Microsoft\UAG\Logs`. You can also enable more extensive logging by running the installer with the following options:

```
msiexec /p  <update file> /L*v VerboseLog.txt
```

When reviewing the installation log, look for lines with "Value 3". The information surrounding this string would usually reveal more about the problem encountered.

Portal and Trunk issues

Some users run into a roadblock as soon as they turn on the server, you create a trunk or two, publish an application for the heck of it, but the thing won't come up in your browser. This frustrating start would typically happen due to networking issues. We discussed the importance of networking and routing back in the beginning of the book, so it might be a good idea to re-read it and draw a map of your network. Try to pretend you are a packet, and think to yourself "Where would I go?". This is not a joke—some networks are very simple, but in real-world networks, you may find that you defined your "external" network too wide, and traffic that's supposed to go to your Domain Controller is being routed out by UAG. Perhaps you defined a gateway on the internal interface instead of the external, and UAG is sending traffic into your network rather than out. Some users get confused by the UAG's getting started wizard, and end up with the wrong IP ranges defined as "internal", causing TMG to block traffic that's supposed to go through. This should not be too hard—just make sure all your IPs, subnet masks, default gateway, and static routes are correct, and then double check. If this still does not work, a good tool is the TMG monitoring console, which we discussed in *Chapter 9*. It can show you if your traffic is being received by the server at all, and if it is getting denied by TMG.

Application issues

Most UAG problems are derived from the fact that it can publish such a diverse range of applications. The diversity in application design and deployment is infinite, and now and then you may find an application that cannot tolerate being reverse-proxied. Some of them even forcibly resist being published by design. Many issues can be resolved with a deep understanding of how an application works, or by trying an alternative publishing method. For example, some applications can't handle the **HAT** process, and can only be published using their own hostname (using the "Other Web App (application-specific hostname)" template). Other web applications may not behave when contained within a browser frame, which is what the UAG portal homepage is. Such applications should be configured on UAG to open in their own browser window. Other applications may not work when published as a web app, because they have a non-web component, like an **ActiveX** control. In some cases, this might not be visible to you. Some applications may not work with no discernible error—just a blank page, or a button that does not respond, making it harder to know what's going on (It's like your significant other giving you the silent treatment).

Common application publishing mishaps

The most common causes for application publishing problems stem from misunderstanding of the application configuration dialog boxes. This applies mostly to the servers, paths and the portal URL definition in the UAG console. For example, many believe that the application path should include the full URL. Thing is, even if you realize later that it's wrong and change it, the URL Set rule doesn't get changed when you edit the application, unless you fix it yourself or recreate the application from scratch (which isn't such a big deal, really—right? Takes 2 minutes)

When defining a new application, the server needs to be listed as if you were browsing to it from within your organizational network, but without the protocol prefix. For example, if you typically go to `https://hrweb/hiringandfiring/firing.asp` when using the application from your computer at the office, then the server **addresses** would be `hrweb`, the **paths** would be `/hiringfiring/` and the **Application URL** would be `https://hrweb/hiringandfiring/firing.asp`. Note that when you reach the final page of the application publishing wizard, UAG will fill in the application URL as `https://hrweb/hiringfiring/`, because it cannot know the specific URL that's needed. Also, keep in mind that filling in the path is not always required. This depends on how the app works—many use the root folder on the server, which means you need to keep the path as "/". Additionally, most applications are configured to deliver some default document, so specifying just the folder is enough, but if your application fails, check and see if it requires the full URL to be specified.

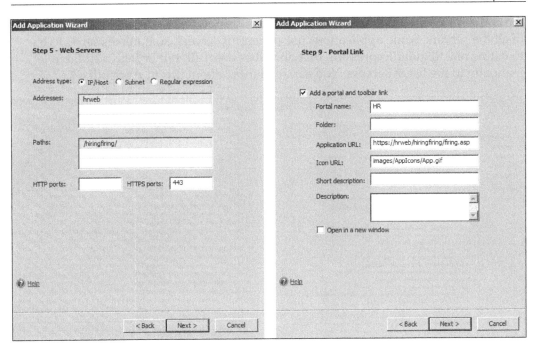

Also, notice that the Application URL is automatically prefixed with HTTPS in the above screenshot, because in the Web Servers step, we cleared the **HTTP ports** box, and left the **HTTPS ports** with 443. UAG cannot know, on its own, if the application is HTTP or HTTPS, so make sure you clear the irrelevant protocol box. Just to clear another common misconception: the HTTP vs. HTTPS selection refers to how the backend server is publishing the application, and it is unrelated to how we want UAG users to connect to the portal. If the internal applications server is configured for HTTP (as most internal applications are), then that is what you should configure, regardless of whether the UAG trunk is HTTP or HTTPS.

Another issue that surfaces for many applications occurs when you fail to fill in all the appropriate servers in the **addresses** list of the Web Servers tab. When you launch an application, you type one URL, but that doesn't mean the application doesn't also use other servers. If the application has links to other internal servers, UAG will not know them, and may leave the URLs unsigned (un-HATted). Another variation is when the server is defined with a name, but the application itself tries to contact it by IP. To address that, you will have to do some research and make a full list of all the internal servers that the application may "call", and add them to the addresses list. How to do this? Simple—use HTTPWatch, which we also mentioned in *Chapter 8*. Install it on a computer on the corporate network, start a recording and launch the application in question. Explore the application as widely and deeply as you can, and then inspect the HTTPWatch recording. You can also copy-paste the entire URL list into Excel, and use "remove duplicates" to quickly make a list of all the servers. Some applications use dozens of servers, so it makes sense to try to define one Regular Expression that describes them all, rather than add them all manually to the list of servers. You can read more about this in Appendix A.

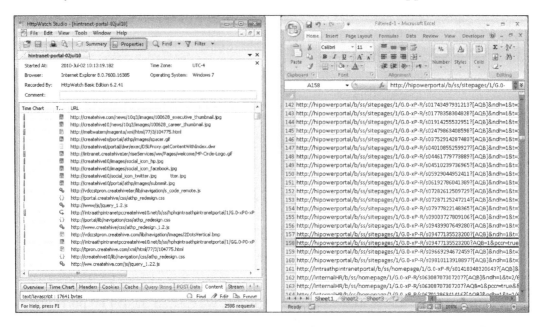

Blocking uploads and downloads

Upload/download blocking is an issue many users find hard to configure, but it's always because of misunderstanding of how it works. As we discussed in Chapter 8, just configuring a policy for an upload or download is not enough—the important part is to have UAG detect what is an upload or download, using a URL, a file extension or file size. Once UAG is able to correctly detect a request as an upload or download, it can apply the policy you have selected to it. Lastly, keep in mind that setting the policy to "always" doesn't mean "always block", but "always allow".

Sometimes, regardless of the application-specific upload/download configuration we just discussed, you may find yourself unable to upload or download a large file through UAG. If you are finding problems with files larger than 10 MB, it might be related to the default **buffer** size limit of UAG. When a user requests a file from UAG, then for certain file types, the server has to parse it, and rewrite links in it. For that, UAG has a buffer in memory, which is set to 10 MB by default. If the file is too large, it might not fit in the buffer, causing UAG to show a 500 error. You can read more about this in *Chapter 10*, in the section *The Portal tab*. The following screenshot shows such an error, but keep in mind that, by default, browsers are set to show "friendly" messages...which are quite meaningless for troubleshooting purposes. To change this, go to your Internet Options, go to the Advanced tab and uncheck "show friendly HTTP error messages".

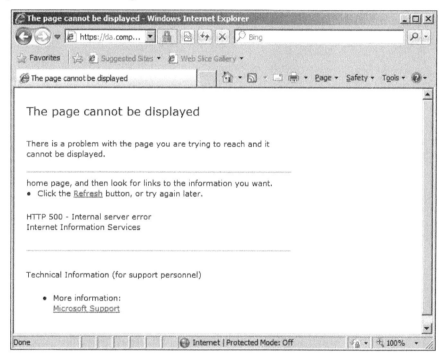

Sometimes, you might run into file size issues that are not related to UAG. For example, **SharePoint** is, by default, limited to a file size of 50 MB. Before calling the cops, test your application "directly" (connect to it from inside the corporate network, and not through UAG) to make sure it is not a preset limit or configuration issue. By the way, SharePoint also has limits on filename length and characters. To read more about that, visit: http://blogs.msdn.com/b/joelo/archive/2007/06/27/file-name-length-size-and-invalid-character-restrictions-and-recommendations.aspx.

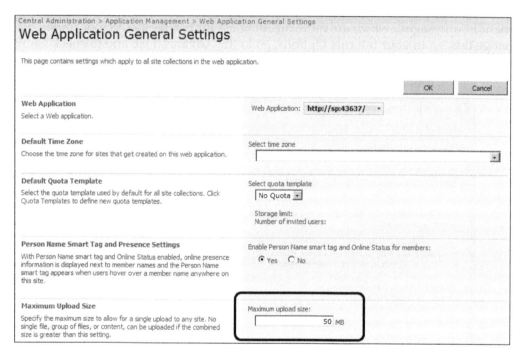

URL limits

Other than application-specific URL limits that we just mentioned about SharePoint, UAG has limits too. When publishing web applications using the generic templates, users often receive errors about security violations for certain URLs. These don't mean much to the user, but the corresponding event log message typically explains it pretty well. Often, these would be URL-Set issues—the server has received a request with a pattern that violates the URL set configured for that application type. In such a case, the blocked URL will be included with the error on the Web Monitor, and the specific rule that was violated will be listed by its name and number (so you can look it up and figure out what's wrong). It might also say "default rule", which means no rule was found to match that request. As you may recall, any request that has no rule to allow it will be blocked by default.

Actually, rule set violations could also happen with other templates. For example, the **Citrix** application comes preconfigured with a large number of rules, but often, the server would be configured with a different base URL that could invalidate many of the default UAG rules. For example, the Citrix app template is designed for a default site using the folder /Citrix/ but a Citrix server might have been installed in another folder on your server, making all these rules irrelevant, and ending up with plenty of access violations. To fix them, look at the URLs that have been blocked, and add or edit your rules (in Advanced Trunk Configuration/URL Set) accordingly. It might be tough at first, because you need to understand the intricacies of **Regular Expression** (**RegEx**) to be able to read the rules, but with time and practice, it should be a breeze.

Severity	Time ▼	ID	Type	Category	Trur	NodeName	Description
⚠ Warning	09/01/2010 14:32:30	67	URL Path Not Alllowed	Security	com (S)	DA1	A request from source IP address 11.0.0.20 on trunk genweb; Secure=1 for application test of type genweb failed. The URL /AppSite/default.asp contains an illegal path. The rule applied is Default rule. The method is GET.
⚠ Warning	09/01/2010 14:32:09	67	URL Path Not Alllowed	Security	com (S)	DA1	A request from source IP address 11.0.0.20 on trunk genweb; Secure=1 for application test of type genweb failed. The URL /po/face.asp contains an illegal path. The rule applied is Default rule. The method is GET.

Event Viewer - Security Events   Server time: 09/01/2010 14:32

Application and Network Access Portal

You have attempted to access a restricted URL.

The URL contains an invalid path.

A variation of this is when the URL character set rules are violated. We also mentioned this in *Chapter 10*—"other" web applications have a more restricted character set allowance by default, so if you rule out the rule set, inspect the character set for this application type in the **Advanced Trunk Configuration/URL Inspection** tab.

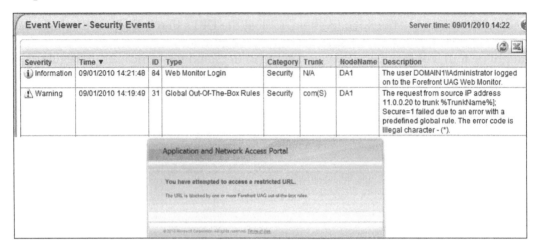

Did you notice how the client-side error message is slightly different (text-wise)?

Another violation could be when the **URL parameters** are violated. This could include a parameter in a URL where the rule is set to reject a parameter that is too long, too short, or has a string that is forbidden.

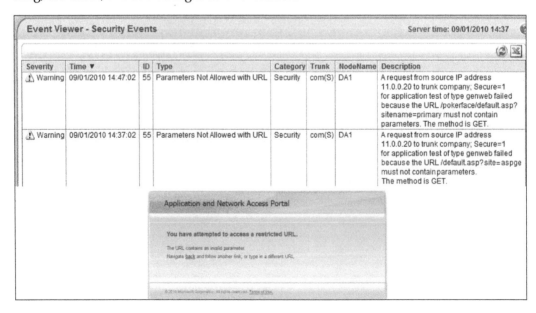

Once again, you may notice how the actual error shown to the user is textually different, making it easier for you to know what's up, even if your users have a hard time differentiating between a computer and a microwave.

A rare issue, but serious, can occur when trying to use UAG to publish applications running on non-Windows servers. Some such applications can generate very long URLs, and when UAG tries to publish those, they violate IIS's default security configuration. The policy dictates that a URL *segment* cannot be more than 255 characters (although the entire URL can be much longer). If this policy is violated, the IIS running on UAG will respond with a **400 Bad Request** error. One such application is **IBM's WebSphere** portal. To resolve this, all you have to do is edit the registry and instruct IIS to accept longer segments. This is documented here: `http://blogs.technet.com/b/ben/archive/2009/03/21/iis-link-parsing-wreaks-havoc-when-ibm-servers-are-involved.aspx`.

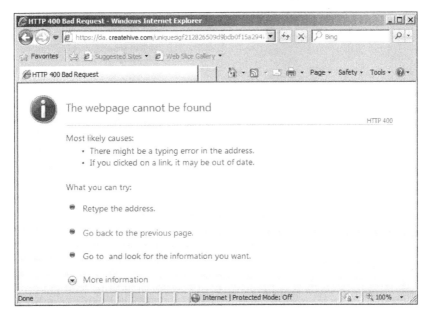

Another useful registry key to know is the one that controls the maximum size of **header** length. The length of headers is determined by the published application—most generate no more than a few hundred bytes, but some can be much larger. With UAG, the maximum header length is 8192 bytes (2K), and if it's longer, the server will show a 500 error to the user. To know what size you should set, record the application's traffic from an internal client (not through UAG) with a tool like **HTTPWatch**, and view the properties of the header. The registry value for the maximum length of headers is at:

```
HKEY_LOCAL_MACHINE\SOFTWARE\WhaleCom\e-Gap\Von\UrlFilter\
MaxAllHeadersLen
```

After modifying this value (or any value that affects IIS, for that matter), activate the configuration. You must also either reboot the server, or manually restart IIS and all dependent services (which include the UAG services).

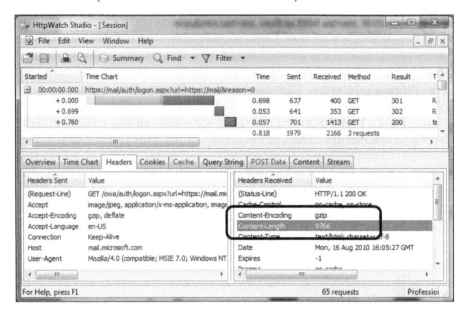

For information about additional registry keys that can be tweaked for UAG, refer to the following article: `http://technet.microsoft.com/en-us/library/ee809087.aspx`.

Server Performance

We have already said that it may be challenging to estimate in advance just how many users your server can service. Some applications are very "slim" in their design, or the usage pattern is very slow (users perform actions that generate requests infrequently), and even a relatively weak server can service thousands of users, while other applications generate dozens of sub-requests for every primary request (that is calling for supporting files, like graphics or script files), perform frequent automatic refreshes or perform activity in the background. Non-web apps can be even more resource intensive—Remote Desktop springs to mind, but not only that. If your organization is growing steadily, then it may be just a matter of time before demand on your UAG is such that it begins to slow down. At some point, it might even choke if the number of "connections" (which do not necessarily mean users, as often a single user has multiple connections) may grow so high that IIS itself cannot handle them, and chokes. To the users, this may look like it's taking a long time to complete a page, and in extreme cases, the time could be so long that the HTTP connection will time out and the user will see an error.

Generally, one cannot change the laws of physics (even Scotty can't), and if a server is overloaded, there might not be much you can do but upgrade it, or add another server to an array. However, before running to the store, it's important to try to understand what it is that's taking the hit. Using a tool like the **Performance Monitor**, which we discussed *Chapter 9*, you can see if it's a memory or CPU issue, and it could also be related to hard drive performance (not space), network card performance or most likely, the limits of IIS's ability to handle that many simultaneous connections. If you need more memory or a faster CPU, that's usually easy. If, however, this is not a hardware specific issue, you might have to move to a UAG array topology. There are no specific performance-related tune-ups or optimizations you can do within UAG itself, but you might be able to tune your application. Many web servers can be optimized for performance, and other aspects of applications may be as well. For example, if the application sets the headers for all of its files to "no-cache", and you can configure it to allow caching of graphic files, it may improve performance, as clients won't have to re-read all the files every time. This, however, may be negated by the UAG's session cleanup client component, or if you configure UAG to send "do not cache" directives to browsers, so this is not so simple. If an application has background processes that can be fine-tuned for frequency, or even eliminated, it could have an effect as well. For example, we have seen an application that contains very heavy animated Flash files that refresh very frequently and was causing a high load on not only UAG, but the network itself, and by reducing the animation files refresh rate, improved performance significantly. Here are some guides regarding server-specific tuning that might improve end results:

- **IIS**:
    - https://www.microsoft.com/technet/prodtechnol/
      WindowsServer2003/Library/IIS/e621190d-1015-40c2-a5ec-
      0dcb32c98286.mspx?mfr=true
    - http://technet.microsoft.com/en-us/magazine/2008.09.iis.
      aspx
    - http://technet.microsoft.com/en-us/library/
      cc770381(WS.10).aspx

 These suggestions are for backend servers running IIS. Making changes to the IIS configuration on the UAG server itself is unsupported and very risky.

- **SharePoint**:
  - ° http://download.microsoft.com/download/0/E/B/0EBA7263-A555-4279-B9DD-1720F0139A2E/SharePointOptimizationTWP.doc
  - ° http://technet.microsoft.com/en-us/library/cc263099(office.12).aspx

- **Microsoft Dynamics CRM**:
  - ° http://www.microsoft.com/midsizebusiness/businessvalue/crm-optimization.mspx
  - ° http://www.microsoft.com/downloads/details.aspx?FamilyID=ba826cee-eddf-4d6e-842d-27fd654ed893

- **Apache**:
  - ° http://httpd.apache.org/docs/2.2/misc/perf-tuning.html

- **Exchange**:
  - ° http://technet.microsoft.com/en-us/library/bb124129(EXCHG.65).aspx

Other optimizations

As we said, there is no fine-tuning or optimizing for UAG's performance, but there are factors that affect it. It's important to keep in mind that changing these does not "improve" the performance, because the speed boost may hit you from another direction, so proceed with extreme caution, and perform extensive testing before declaring a "win":

- Turning off client detection speeds up the time it takes to reach the login. The down side is, of course, no client detection, and no endpoint policies.

- Tweaking the body parsing settings (see *Chapter 10*) can free up some CPU time. The price can be missed links in the application, which could lead to loss of functionality or a bad user experience.

- Publishing your applications as HTTP, rather than HTTPS will make them run faster, although that has nothing to do with UAG—the HTTPS protocol requires encryption and decryption, and that's an overhead. Naturally, that can only be done if security is not a big deal to you, or if this is an application that does not necessitate it. If, for example, this is a public, unauthenticated application, using HTTPS may be redundant.

- Turning off authentication is another (though rather extreme) way of speeding things up. The actual application publishing performance won't be affected much, but the portal access will be really fast.

- Limiting the maximum number of concurrent sessions on the trunk or server will prevent the server from becoming overloaded, at the cost of alienating users who will be denied access once that limit has been reached.

- Reducing the timeout settings for inactive sessions and automatic logoff will clean up sessions faster, thereby freeing up resources. Naturally, the usability impact may be annoying to users, who may have to re-logon frequently.

You might also consider some general network optimization technologies, such as **SSL-Offloaders, WAN optimizers**, and, of course, LAN optimization devices such as smart switches and routers. By keeping your network as tidy as possible, reducing broadcasts and background traffic, you can protect your UAG server from having to process or discard irrelevant traffic, and thereby helping it become as efficient as possible.

SharePoint issues

SharePoint is one of Microsoft's most popular server products, and virtually all UAG customers need to publish at least one such server. The majority of problems with SharePoint publishing are a result of a mis-configuration of **AAM** (which is done on SharePoint itself), which often happens when the concept of AAM is unclear.

We discussed the concepts of AAM and how it works back in *Chapter 4*, so re-reading it may clear things up. The important part is to remember that with SharePoint, UAG does not perform the URL rewriting process (HAT) that we love so much, and instead, uses an "application-specific" hostname. SharePoint recognizes that the requests received from UAG are destined to be seen "from outside", and constructs the links accordingly, on its own. There are, of course, several scenarios for SharePoint publishing, so be sure to re-read Chapter 4 and make sure you understand which is the right one for you. Then, make sure you have an appropriate SSL server certificate, that you have configured the public DNS records correctly and that the AAM settings match everything.

If SharePoint is behaving "weirdly", the first thing to do is make sure you have all the current service packs and patches for your SharePoint server. This is especially true if you are publishing a SharePoint 2007, as there have been many updates for it. If you were hoping to publish SharePoint 2000, forget about it, as it is not supported. If you are getting errors with specific web-parts in SharePoint, make sure these web-parts support AAM. If a web-part hasn't been specifically programmed to work with the AAM component to translate its links, then these links will appear in the web-part as links to internal server names instead of the public names, and that will lead to various errors. For example, the **SQL Server Reporting Services (SSRS)** web-part in SharePoint 2007 has this problem. Unfortunately, if this is the case, there's not much you can do. Essentially, you may be able to reconfigure your server to always use an FQDN, but it may require a full rebuild of the server, which we would guess is not an option.

Another limit SharePoint presents us with is the limit of 5 **zones** in AAM. When you configure a publishing scenario with AAM, you use one of the zones to have the public URL. SharePoint has five zones: Default, Intranet, Internet, Custom, and Extranet. When you configure AAM, you can use any of them, except the Default (which is used for the 'internal' name), but if you need to publish multiple sites on the same server as separate UAG applications, then you can only do so for four sites before you run out of zones. Unfortunately, you cannot add zones to SharePoint, and in this situation, there's nothing you can do.

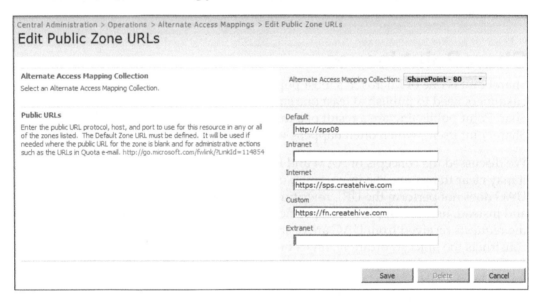

An issue encountered by many SharePoint users can happen when SharePoint has links to other servers. When those exist, UAG may need to be configured to recognize them, because if it doesn't, the links won't be HATted, and will lead to errors. The way to handle this is to go over your SharePoint server, and make a list of all the servers it links to, and then publish those as applications on UAG. You could usually include all the servers in a single app, and that app can even be set to not be shown on the portal homepage, if you are so inclined—as long as UAG is "aware" of these servers, it will be able to recognize the links and HAT them, and the rest should be fine.

One last thing you need to remember regarding SharePoint is that it has its own session tracking mechanism, which depends on cookies. This makes it very sensitive to customizations and tampering, so you need to be careful. For example, if you disable the UAG client installation and also customize the logoff process, the SharePoint session cookies get left behind when you log off a UAG session, which could cause users who log back on to experience weird behavior by the server. There are tons of things that can go wrong here, so our best advice is to plan carefully, and conduct exhaustive testing before declaring everything is ready-for-launch.

SSL tunneling

The SSL tunneling components serve multiple purposes on UAG—they are used as part of the Client/Server applications, Browser-embedded applications, SSL Network Tunneling (Network Connector) As well as TS Client Tunneling and TS Web Clint Tunneling. Their flexibility and power are astonishing, but they also fall pray to two common issues.

The top issue experienced by users is inexplicable disconnections. The symptoms are that while working on a tunneled app, or through an SSL Network Tunneling connection, the tunnel suddenly disconnects for no apparent reason. The actual reason for this is that the SSL Tunneling component is designed to disconnect if it senses a network interruption. Such an interruption may not be noticeable to a human being, but for a computer, even a tiny break-up can be very significant. The most common cause is wireless home networks. These networks are prone to disruptions of all sorts—sometimes it's electronic noise caused by your (or your neighbor's) microwave oven or cell phone. In other cases it's simply a matter of distance that degrades the signal, or a movement of the laptop computer that causes a short break-up. It could even be an overheating issue with the network card. Other causes of such small disruptions in connectivity are **Internet Service Providers** (**ISPs**). Many ISPs perform network maintenance and tweaks that cause small drops that are mostly unnoticeable to the typical user who is just browsing the web (you might feel it when some website stops loading for a few seconds, or some graphic file appears as an X in the page now and then). We've also seen cases where the local LAN infrastructure was causing these, when a network switch was performing port-speed negotiations at certain intervals, terminating most sessions at once.

The bottom line is that when the SSL-VPN component senses such a drop, it disconnects, and other than hardening the network, there's not much you can do. Hardening the network means getting closer to the wireless router, eliminating electronic interference sources or switching to an ISP or type of infrastructure that is more stable. If you are not sure, a good way to confirm this is by connecting a client to the UAG server without going through anything, or through the bare minimum. If the UAG is hosted as a virtual machine, this is easy—just install another VM with a client. If it's a physical server, attach a client directly to the UAG's NIC using a cross-over cable.

The second common issue is a misconfiguration of the application. The way the SSL tunneling component interacts with the Socket Forwarding components, and how both of these interact with applications may be tricky to understand, and it also requires that you understand really well how the application works. If your application refuses to work, claiming that the server does not respond (meaning the "backend" server, the app cannot communicate with it through the SSL tunnel), review your configuration, and consider the following:

1. The **Server Settings** tab needs to contain all the servers and ports that the client application needs to communicate with. You may not be aware of all of them, so you may need to consult with the app vendor, or use a tool such as Network Monitor to spy on the app's traffic and get the full list.

2. If the application uses multiple servers, or communicates with its servers using their IP (and not their host name), then you need to use the Socket Forwarder in addition to the SSL tunneling component. Make sure it's not set to **Disabled** on the application's **Client Settings** tab.

3. If your app needs to use the Socket Forwarder, make sure your client platform is supported (see *Chapter 7* for info on platform compatibility)

4. Some clients may suffer from an LSP/NSP or listener conflicts between the client components and other software that might be installed on the computer, so make sure you test on multiple clients and multiple platforms to confirm this is a server problem and not client or client-platform specific.

5. The client components can get corrupted in some circumstances, so if they are giving out error messages, even if those seem unrelated, narrow down your scope and focus by testing on multiple clients and multiple client-platforms.

SSTP

SSTP issues are rare, but if you run into one, keep in mind that it is not a component of UAG itself, but rather part of the **Routing and Remote Access Service** (**RRAS**) that's built into Windows Server. When you configure the SSTP settings in UAG, they are pushed into TMG which, in turn, configures RRAS appropriately. Here are some important things to keep in mind about SSTP:

- With UAG, SSTP can only be used with Windows 7. Even though Vista has an SSTP client, it cannot be used with UAG.

- While you can configure an SSTP dialer in Windows 7 and Vista directly, these cannot be used with UAG. Use only the portal link to launch it.

- SSTP relies on the trunk's certificate as part of the SSL process, so these need to be nice and tidy—make sure the Certification Chain is intact, the CDP is valid and the CRLs reachable to the client.

If you run into issues, the **Windows Event Log** on the client and server should provide you with information on the problem. You can also use the following resources for troubleshooting information:

- `http://support.microsoft.com/kb/947031/en-us`
- `http://blogs.technet.com/b/rrasblog/archive/2007/09/26/how-to-debug-sstp-specific-connection-failures.aspx`

Other server and application issues

A common issue that baffles many is the issue of **Single Sign-On** (**SSO**). This often appears as an authentication prompt when launching an application, or when visiting some link in the application:

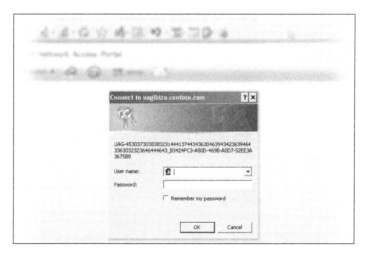

This is what we refer to as a **401 prompt**, because the browser automatically displays it when a server sends it a **401 HTTP status** message, also known as an **unauthorized**. You can simply type a username and password here, and UAG will transfer it to the backend server and the application should work fine, but ideally, UAG should use the cached credentials the user has supplied when logging in to the UAG portal itself and this authentication prompt should never reach the browser: that's what "single sign-on" is all about.

We have discussed authentication options throughout the book, but in case you missed this setting, it's in the Authentication page of an application. You can configure this when publishing an app, or at a later time by editing its properties. To have UAG perform SSO, the setting **Use single sign-on (SSO) to send credentials to published applications** should be active, and an authentication repository needs to be selected. Also, the appropriate method should be selected, depending on the application's configuration. Most organizational applications are configured by default for 401 authentication, and so the **401 request** option should be checked. Others may be set for **HTML form**, and you could also select **Both** to cover all your bases.

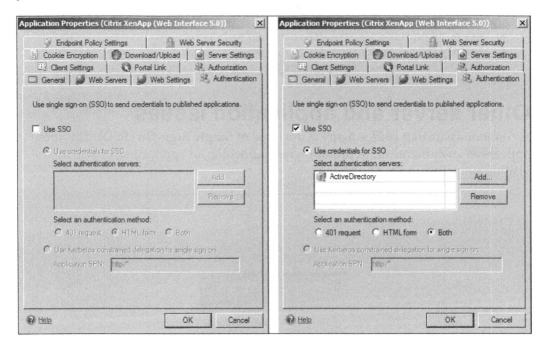

If SSO has been configured, but is still not working, it could be that your users are logging in using an incorrectly formatted user name. For example, they might be using their UPN instead of domain\username. If using a UPN is preferable to you, then you can configure UAG to support it, as is documented here: `http://technet.microsoft.com/en-us/library/ff607424.aspx`.

Another possibility is that the backend application is either configured incorrectly to participate in the 401 "conversation", or that it does not support it. In such a case, we would recommend contacting the application's vendor and asking them whether the application can be adjusted. HTML form authentication problems are a bit more prevalent, as there is no standard for HTML form authentication—every application has its own form, with many variations in the form-fields and form-submit mechanism. When a situation occurs where form login does not work, it may be possible to create a custom Form-login template to match the specific form and its structure. This is beyond the scope of this book, but you can read about it in the following blog posts:

- `http://blogs.technet.com/b/ben/archive/2010/01/23/custom-form-login-sso-how-to.aspx`
- `http://blogs.technet.com/b/ben/archive/2010/09/02/uag-custom-form-login.aspx`

Client issues

The most common problem with clients is detection, in which you have a client that supposedly meets a certain endpoint policy you have configured on your portal or application, but when that client tries to use your server, they get denied. As you may recall from *Chapter 8*, the policy enforcement is performed at several levels, so depending on your policy assignment, they might get into the portal without a hitch, and then be prevented from running, or even seeing some or all the applications.

The first step in solving access problems is to have a good understanding of what policies you have assigned at each level (to the trunk, to the portal application, to other applications, and to application functions like upload/download). The built-in policy names may not always make sense to you, so be sure to view their "inner" structure (in "script" mode) to understand what they are looking for. You will usually find that you simply selected the wrong policy, or that the specific client doesn't really meet the policy after all, because of some variation in the Personal-Firewall software, or because the AV is *installed*, but not *running* or not *updated*.

If you have determined that the configuration is intact and the client is still not getting what's rightfully his, the next step is to use the Web Monitor, which we discussed in *Chapter 9*, and getting the endpoint parameter table. By reading it carefully, you might find which aspect of the policy is not being met. For example, one thing that could happen is that the **Windows Security Center** (known as Action Center in Windows 7) is turned off or damaged, thus preventing the UAG client component from detecting the Anti Virus and Personal Firewall on the client, even though they appear to be functioning perfectly.

When you create your policies, it's up to you and your organization's policy to decide which security products are acceptable and which aren't. UAG comes preconfigured to support almost all major security product brands and versions, but occasionally, you might encounter one that isn't. If you need to support a product that does not appear on the list of available options, the solution is to use the "any WMI" element. This allows the UAG client to accept any security product that registers itself with Windows as part of the WMI infrastructure. Some customers find this option to be unacceptable, because selecting this policy element would allow ANY Anti Virus or firewall, and that net may be too wide for some organizations. In such a case, you have the option of creating a custom policy to detect it by other means, as detailed in chapter 8.

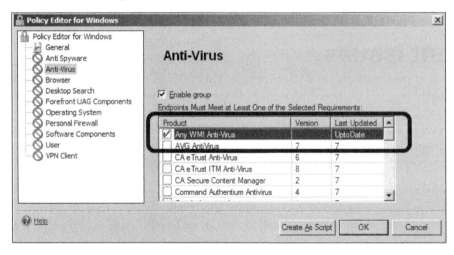

Client misbehavior

The UAG client components, as you may recall from *Chapter 7*, need to be installed by a user who is an administrator on the client machine. In a non-managed environment, this might become tricky, because various client settings and software may cause problems. If your users are connecting to the portal from their home on their own computers, it may be difficult to explain to them how to log on as an administrator or even finding out if they are an administrator or not. Sometimes, the computer is hardened in some way—there could be very strict settings in the **Security** or **Privacy** tab of Internet Explorer's configuration. Some users change these settings for various reasons, starting from "a friend told me it's the best" and up to extreme paranoids. Generally, we are less concerned about those that *lower* the security, even though that's not a good practice either. Generally, we like the settings to be at **Medium**, and keep in mind that the portal URL (as well as other hostnames used by other AAM and AAM-like applications such as SharePoint) need to be on the **Trusted sites** list. UAG adds itself to that list when installing the client components, but we've seen users remove it for no good reason.

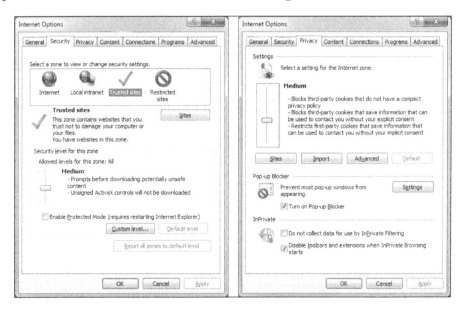

Other problems that are abundant are when security software on the client blocks the client components. Some may prevent the installation itself, such as Anti Virus software or state-protection software. Others may block its communications, as some personal firewalls do, so they may need to be configured appropriately. In fact, Internet Explorer itself tries to protect the user from the client components, as it detects the installation of an ActiveX as a potential threat. This presents itself to the user as an information bar:

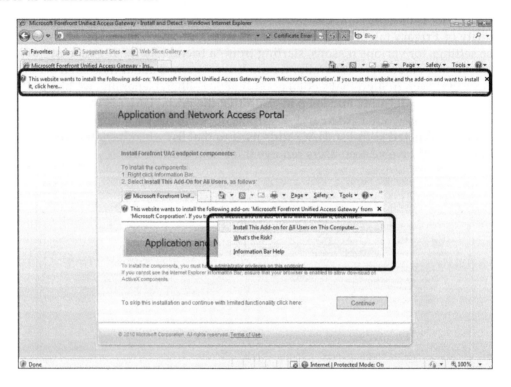

Naturally, the user needs to agree to install the add-on by clicking on **Install This Add-on for All Users on This Computer**. If you're experienced with user support, you probably know that most of them tend to be on the *less* careful side, and install anything that comes along the way, but if they are as paranoid as we would *like* them to be, they might need a nod from you to feel good about approving this add-on.

At any point in time, you can uninstall the client components from the Add/Remove programs control panel, and that would typically be a good starting point in case the client components are misbehaving. You can remove them as many times as you like, because they will be automatically installed as soon as the client connects to the UAG portal. If the automatic installation through the browser is not working out, you might try the manual installation using the **MSI** version of the client that is available on the server (see *Chapter 7, Pre-emptive installation of the components*).

Another thing that happens to many clients is where the browser needs an additional component. This could happen, for example, if the client has installed only the basic set of client components (which is perfectly normal), and then tries to launch an SSL-VPN based application. The client component manager will try to install the SSL-VPN component, which would be in a pop-up window, which could be a problem with pop-up blockers. The client components do try to add themselves to the built-in pop-up blocker in Internet Explorer, but if the user declined to approve it, removes them or uses another pop-up blocker, that could block the installation of the additional components.

A related issue may happen when a client launches a remote desktop application, which requires the remote desktop ActiveX to be installed. This would bring about the information bar warning in Internet Explorer again, but it's a little less conspicuous than the Client components bar (because the huge message in the middle of the screen that the client components show is not there). Naturally, the user has to agree to this as well for things to go smoothly.

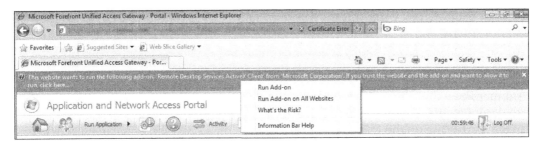

RDS client issues

The most common issue with RDS applications that use the «new» templates (see *Chapter 5*) is incompatibility with the client version. There are multiple versions of the client on different operating systems, and often, the user will see the following message:

The left message is on Vista, and the right is on XP. For both, we recommend you download version 7 of the Remote Desktop Client from here: `http://support.microsoft.com/kb/969084`

On XP, you also have to edit the registry, as follows:

1. Open the registry editor on the client computer.

2. Navigate to `HKEY_LOCAL_MACHINE\SYSTEM\CurrentControlSet\Control\Lsa`.

3. Modify the value **Security Packages** and add, under the existing items **tspkg**.

4. Navigate to `HKEY_LOCAL_MACHINE\SYSTEM\CurrentControlSet\Control\SecurityProviders`.

5. Modify the value **SecurityProviders** and add **credssp.dll** (separated by a comma).

6. Close the registry editor, and reboot the computer.

That's a lot of work to perform on each and every user's computer, so you might consider performing this with group policy, as described here: `http://support.microsoft.com/kb/951608/`.

You can also create a **VBScript** for this. This blog post describes how to do this: `http://blogs.technet.com/b/pfe-ireland/archive/2008/09/05/windows-server-2008-terminal-services-presentation-virtualisation-and-windows-xp-clients.aspx`.

Another issue that can happen with remote desktop publishing happens mostly in lab deployments, where we sometimes try to cut some corners and avoid installing an SSL certificate on the UAG server properly. With a browser, you can just click **Continue** and ignore an invalid certificate, but the Remote Desktop client won't let you, and shows the following message:

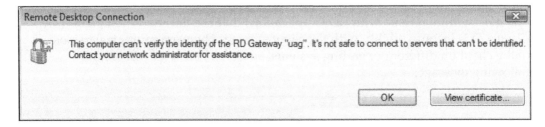

To get around that, simply configure the UAG server with a proper and valid **certificate**, and if it's one that was generated by an internal CA, make sure its root certificate (or other certificate chain certificates) is installed on the client, and that the **CRL Distribution Point (CDP)** is reachable by clients.

Another error that many users see, when trying to launch an RDP app is **Your computer does not meet the security policy requirements of this application**. This is a really confusing one, because it seems to indicate that the endpoint policy configured for the trunk or application is causing the problem. This error may have nothing to do with that. The Remote Desktop Client gives out this error for many different things—it basically means "I couldn't connect to the server, Yo!", without specifying the actual reason.

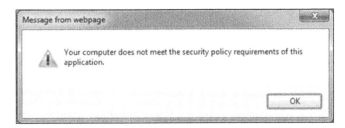

One possible reason is that the remote desktop server is indeed unreachable, though UAG should have told you that when you configured the application. If the server is up and reachable from the UAG server itself, then the application may be configured incorrectly. Some users try to define multiple servers using the subnet notation, so if you did that, make sure you formatted it correctly:

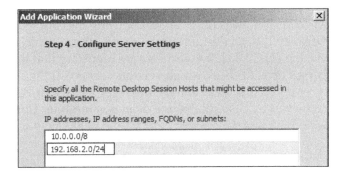

Misc client issues

An issue that is often misunderstood is **Drive Mapping**. This is a great application, but one must remember that it is not compatible with every operating system. Specifically, it only works with Windows XP and earlier operating systems, because of the way the **SMB** protocol is implemented with later systems. If your users are running Vista, Windows 7 (and of course, Macintosh and Linux), these applications will briefly open a DOS window, which will close with no drives being mapped.

Drive mapping may also fail on XP and earlier systems, if UAG has not been configured to let NETBIOS traffic through to the targeted server. Essentially, the Drive Mapping application opens an SSL-VPN tunnel to channel NETBIOS traffic, and then issues a NET USE command to perform the mapping. Like any other app, you should verify that you can achieve a similar action from the UAG itself before attempting to have clients use it. Also, if the share you are trying to map to is a **DFS** share, these are unsupported as well, unfortunately, because the DFS protocol uses a different communication mechanism than regular file shares.

Another topic of confusion in some circumstances is visiting the UAG portal on a cellular phone. As you may recall from *Chapter 1*, UAG includes two special versions of the portal for mobile phones. These versions, referred to as the "Premium" and "limited" portal, are delivered by UAG to clients that it recognizes as mobile phones. Phones that have a basic screen will receive the "limited" portal, which is text-based, and phones with large colorful screens get the "Premium" portal, which is graphic, but has only a small number of elements (compared to the "full" portal you see on a computer) that would make it more usable on a typical 3" screen of a phone.By default, applications are set to not allow access from a mobile phone browser, so you'll have to explicitly enable it on the application's Portal Link tab. Once enabled, UAG bases its decision on which portal to deliver to the client based on the **user-agent** string (also known as "Browser string") it receives from the browser, and with some phones, it may not be able to recognize that the client is indeed a phone.

It may also think a graphic phone is only capable of using the "limited" portal, or vice versa. It may even display the full desktop portal on the phone, which is unusable even on a large phone like the HTC HD2. If your users are reporting that they don't like what they see, the first step is to check which version they got. If the situation is indeed a mistaken identity, or if you just want to have them get a different version of the portal, this can be achieved by customizing the detection module. This is documented here: `http://technet.microsoft.com/en-us/library/ff607404.aspx`.

Customization issues

UAG's customizability is fantastic, and quite rare in our industry, but it can also lead to a lot of heartache. Editing ASP and HTML code takes a certain amount of expertise, and troubleshooting code issues is something that huge books have been written about, so there's little we can help with there. However, one common source of trouble is the misunderstanding of the fundamentals of the `CustomUpdate` process. A common mistake is copying a full file from the main folder or from the samples folder into the `CustomUpdate` folder, without modification. That rarely works, and will often lead to server errors (500 errors). This happens because UAG runs the code inside `CustomUpdate` in addition to the main code files, so this may cause various variable and function collisions or race condition. Also, the samples themselves often contain multiple examples in a single file, causing the code to do multiple things that may collide.

Another thing that may daunt you is the fact that not all files can be customized. Just by dropping a file into `CustomUpdate` doesn't determine that it will be executed. UAG's engine processes most files, but not all. If your changes seem to not get executed, you can use visual cues like the `response.write` command to prove that a certain function has been processed.

General errors

Other than the previous issues we discussed, most problems you may run into will most likely be published applications not working or misbehaving. As we said at the beginning of this chapter, this is quite common, and makes sense, considering the unique way each application is built. Problems you may see include JavaScript errors, 404 errors (page not found), 500 errors (server error), blank pages or popups, application-specific errors, or simply things not happening when they are supposed to (for example, clicking a button should open a dialog or save the data, but when you click, it's as if you haven't pressed it at all). Non-web apps may issue various errors related to communication problems with their servers, or even crash in inexplicable ways.

There's no one-size-fits-all way of solving such issues, we're afraid. In fact, some publishing issues can only be resolved with the help of Microsoft's **Customer Service and Support (CSS)**, **Microsoft's Consulting Services (MCS)**, Microsoft's **Premier Field Engineering (PFE)** or third party consultants. Some issues are so complex that even these teams can't help and have to contact the team that developed the product for assistance.

The first step in trying to troubleshoot such a situation is to consider if the application template you chose is the appropriate one. You need to understand how the application itself is built, at least to some degree, to be able to choose a template and configure it correctly. Next, make sure there is proper connectivity from the UAG server itself to the backend server, including all the ports that need to be open. It's usually a good idea to verify that the application is fully operational *from* UAG itself, if possible. Usually, if an application is not usable from UAG, it will not be usable from your clients through UAG either. Naturally, if this is a non-web app, you may not be able to install the application or a component that it needs on the UAG server, so this is just a generic diagnostic step that may not always apply or indicate a real problem.

If the application is showing a specific error, consult its documentation or a search engine to see if this is a known issue. Some applications need to be configured specifically to work with publishing products like UAG. Sometimes there's no getting around having to contact the application vendor to understand more about it. Some vendors have even published specific information about how to make their apps work with UAG, or similar publishing products.

If the error is a 404 (page not found), blank pages or pop-ups, JavaScript errors, or malfunctioning action elements (buttons, fields, forms, and so on), the first thing to check is that all URLs have been signed (HAT-ed) properly. This can be checked with a tool such as Fiddler or HTTPWatch, which we have mentioned several times in the book. Such an analysis begins with recording a session on the client computer, and then looking at the servers to which the requests are directed at. If it is for a server that is other than the UAG's public hostname (or application-specific hostname), then we have a problem. Next, look at the paths that are part of the URL. For portal-hostname applications, make sure the paths are signed. Also, make sure the requests are not for paths that are not included in the application's configuration, or blocked by the access rules. A request that appears as an error is also a bad sign, even if the erroneous file is completely invisible to the user. Here are some examples of such problems:

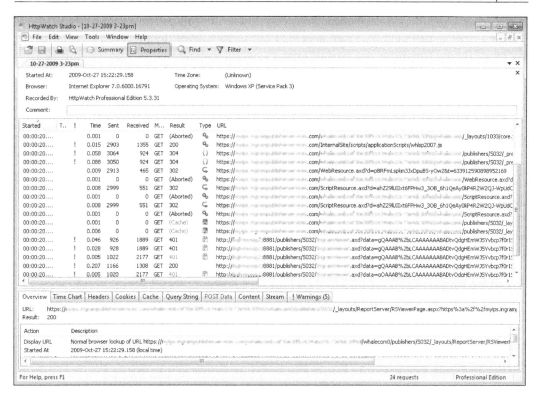

In the preceding screenshot, you can see how there are five unsigned (un-HAT-ed) requests at the bottom, and some of the requests at the top part are "aborted". The 3XX family of responses is usually OK—they are just redirects, which are normally not a problem, although if we have many of them, we should strive to learn why they are there. If you are feeling really adventurous, and have some experience of web technologies such as HTML and JavaScript, you might try having a look at the code that's behind these requests, and trying to figure out why it's going wrong.

The cause for the bad requests is not always easy to find. It may be something simple, like a server that you forgot to include in the application's configuration. The more frequent cause is that the request appears in the code in a way that UAG cannot understand, like a URL that's dynamically built with a JavaScript. Some applications can be configured to be "ready" for publishing (SharePoint's AAM can be configured to allow SharePoint to be published), so this is another situation where contacting the application's vendor is appropriate. If this is an app that was developed in your organization, this may be easy to resolve by changing the application itself.

If the errors are 500 (server error), things get even more hairy, and that's where **Tracing** comes into play. A Trace sets UAG to write a very detailed log of what it is doing. It logs functions, values and errors, which can sometimes be the only way to know what's really going on. For example, if there's a problem with a server's certificate, UAG may not be able to create a secure communication channel and may show a very generic error like "An unknown error occurred while processing the certificate". In this type of situation, a trace would be essential for understanding what the problem is.

The problem with traces is that they are hard to read for the inexperienced. In fact, the sheer volume of data in a trace can be overwhelming. A busy server may generate 700,000 lines of trace data in a single minute of activity! Add to that the fact that it contains application-developer level data, and you can see how this can be intimidating. Often, Microsoft support engineers will ask you to generate such a trace, as the only means to investigate a problem.

To collect a trace, we use a tool that comes with UAG. You can find it in the folder `\Program Files\Microsoft Forefront Unified Access Gateway\common\ bin\tracing`. In that folder, launch the file `LaunchHTA.vbs`. You must be an administrator to run this, or run it from an administrator command-prompt. The trace utility looks like this:

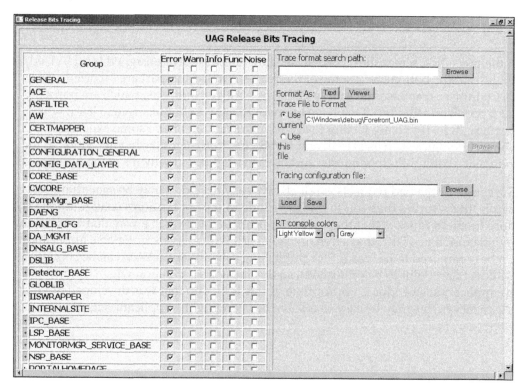

All these items on the long list on the left are names of various UAG components that you can trace. As you can see, by default, tracing is configured, but only at a basic level, so we'll need to set it to get more details. When you launch this utility, tracing will be ON, so we first need to turn it all off by scrolling all the way down and clicking **Stop**:

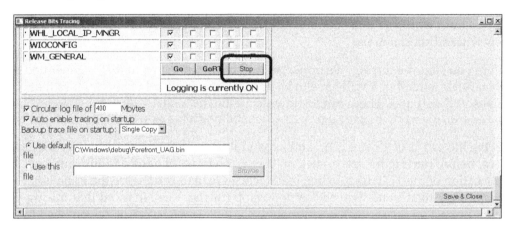

The next step is to check the appropriate boxes next to the components we want to trace. It may be tempting to check everything, but be careful—if you do so, the server will generate a huge amount of data that even seasoned Microsoft support engineers have a hard time reading. In fact, the end result could be a file that's so large, that it will be almost impossible to read. Here are some common troubleshooting scenarios, with the appropriate items to check:

Scenario	Components
General	INTERNALSITE and PORTALHOMEPAGE
Remote Desktop Gateway	UAGRDPSVC, WHLTSGAUTH, WHLTSGCONF, WHLFILT_CORE, WHLFILTSECUREREMOTE_BASE, WHL WHLGENLIB, and WHLGENLIB_GENERAL
Network Load Balancing (NLB)	CONFIGMGR_SERVICE and CONFIGURATION_GENERAL
SSTP	SSTP_ADMIN, WHLFILTSSLVPN_BASE, and SESSIONMGR_ SERVICE, WHLFILT_CORE
Authentication and Single Sign On (SSO)	INTERNALSITE, WHLFILTAUTHORIZATION_BASE, and SSLBOX_Base, WHLFILT_CORE
RPC-over-HTTP Exchange publishing	WHL_LOCAL_IP_MNGR, WHL_ASYNCCOMM_BASE, and WHLFILT_CORE

For each item, check all columns except **Noise**. After selecting the appropriate items, make sure you uncheck **Auto enable tracing on startup**. If you forget this, the server will restart the tracing when rebooted, and it will run and consume server resources without need. If you expect to need to gather a very long trace, you might want to uncheck the option **Circular log file of ___ Mbytes**, but keep in mind that even tracing everything, it would take a while to generate such a large trace file. Also, a 400 MB trace would actually contain millions of lines, making it almost impossible to view without special tools.

Before you start the tracing, it's important to know that the trace that is generated is binary, so to read it, it will have to be decrypted using a set of special files that Microsoft distributes. These can be downloaded here: `http://www.microsoft.com/downloads/details.aspx?FamilyID=FC052E67-2A04-4058-B326-9D92AA67B2C4`

Get the file `UAG_TMF_files.zip`, and expand it to some folder on your server's hard drive. Before starting the trace, click on **text** at the top of the trace utility, and specify the location of the TMF files. When ready, click **Go**, and reproduce the issue you want to investigate, and then click **stop** to stop tracing. Keep in mind that tracing has an impact on the server's performance, so don't leave it on unless you need to investigate something. Here's an example of what you can expect to find in a trace:

This is, of course, just a tiny piece and we won't be able to teach you everything about reading UAG logs here, but here is some info. The above piece depicts the start of a request from a UAG client to the UAG server. Each line has a time-stamp, down to the millisecond, followed by the component name (**whlfilter** in this example), and by the function name. Next comes the name of the source file and the line number of where the function is. You don't have access to the source so you can't read the full function, of course, but in many cases you could figure that out from the name. Then, after "info:" comes the data that this function recorded. At the top, you can see

the details of this request—the protocol (HTTPS), the HTTP method (GET), the URL and then more info, including the cookies, hostname of the server, user agent, and so on.

Below all this, you see the UAG filter starts processing the session info, so it can match the request to an existing user session (when there's a problem, it may fail to do so). On some of the lines you see a **PFC code**, which is a unique number assigned to this request, and allows you to track it along the trace. Later on, you can see the header encoding being handled and at the bottom of this snippet, the application that was identified for this request (Internal Site). Naturally, this is not the end, and this request goes on much longer—several dozen pages, and this is very normal.

Trying to understand all these functions and jargon can be frustrating, no doubt, but with time, you'll learn to recognize repeating patterns. You can also search the text for keywords like "Error" or "fail", if you are looking to troubleshoot a specific error. You can do a search for the expression "request from client to filter" to find a specific URL you are looking to troubleshoot. Generally, each request to UAG has 4 stages:

1. Request from client to filter (as the one seen above)
2. Request passed to the backend server ("Request sent from filter to web server")
3. Reply from the backend server to UAG ("Response from RWS to filter")
4. Reply from UAG back to the client ("Response from filter to client")

This means that, depending on where you see an error, it can indicate if the problem is with UAG itself, or perhaps with what the backend server is sending back in response to the request.

Tracing problems

Even tracing can have problems sometimes. A common issue is that the trace file has many or even all of the lines saying **No Format Information Found**:

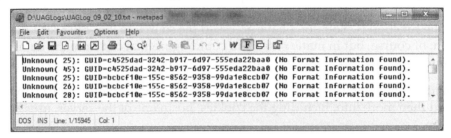

This typically happens because the decoder couldn't find the appropriate TMF files. This could happen if the file you downloaded is corrupted, did not open fully, or is for a version that's different from yours. The link we included above is for the latest version of the TMF files, and they are backward compatible, but do make sure you update your TMFs whenever you update the server. It's also possible that when specifying the path to the TMFs, you misspelled it.

The last thing to know is that a similar procedure can be performed on the client – the same utility is there, and the TMF files package includes data for client-side tracing. The trace utility is at C:\Program Files\Microsoft Forefront UAG\Endpoint Components\3.1.0\ LaunchHTA.vbs, and works the same as on the server.

What's next?

At this point, if even tracing hasn't revealed the cause, there's probably not much you can do on your own. Sometimes, capturing the Network traffic using a tool like **Network Monitor** or **Wireshark** can shed more light, but at this point you're likely to need assistance from professional UAG engineers. One thing that's good to keep in mind is that even though UAG is much more advanced than its predecessor IAG, they still share a lot in common, and many of the issues you might face may also be relevant for IAG, and have information in IAG forums, blogs or the original IAG documentation. Here are some resources that may be useful:

- IAG's user guide and advanced user guide:
    - http://download.microsoft.com/download/2/f/9/2f9d9113-b84b-4838-98a0-a3aefa6608e2/iag_userguide.pdf
    - http://download.microsoft.com/download/2/F/9/2F9D9113-B84B-4838-98A0-A3AEFA6608E2/IAG_AdvancedUserGuide.pdf

- Microsoft's UAG and IAG support forum:

  `http://social.technet.microsoft.com/Forums/en-US/fore-frontedgeiag`

- Microsoft's UAG Team blog site:

  `http://blogs.technet.com/edgeaccessblog`

- Additional support forums:
  - `http://forums.forefrontsecurity.org/`
  - `http://forums.isaserver.org/`

- Ben Ari's UAG and IAG blog:

  `http://blogs.technet.com/b/ben`

- Additional IAG and UAG blogs and resources:
  - `http://blogs.isaserver.org`
  - `http://microsoft-iag.blogspot.com`
  - `http://blogs.technet.com/b/yuridiogenes`
  - `http://blogs.ecreation.ch`
  - `http://blog.tiensivu.com`
  - `http://iag.elear.net`
  - `http://blog.concurrency.com/infrastructure`
  - `http://www.celestix.com/index.php?option=com_easyblog`
  - `http://www.nappliance.com/blogs/inder`
  - `http://uagengineer.wordpress.com/`
  - `http://isingh.spaces.live.com`
  - `http://blogs.technet.com/b/tomshinder`
  - `http://support.nappliance.com/index.php?_m=knowledgebase&_a=view`
  - `http://www.ssl-vpn.de`
  - `http://blog.msedge.org.uk`
  - `http://blog.msfirewall.org.uk`
  - `http://tmgblog.richardhicks.com`
  - `http://blogs.technet.com/b/fsl/`

Summary

We're sure quite a few of you have bought this book for the sole purpose of troubleshooting UAG, and we hope this book has shed some light on how this fantastic product works, and this chapter addressed your issue, or at least pointed you in the right direction. As you work with UAG more, you will find that it has much more in store. Starting from simple visual manipulations, up to advanced authentication customizations, it can do almost anything. To learn more, follow our public blogs, where we will be publishing information about things you can do with UAG, and addressing various issues. Have fun!

Introduction to RegEx RegEx

We have already mentioned a few times in this book the term RegEx RegEx, which is short for Regular Expressions. But the name is a bit misleading, as there is nothing "regular" in these expressions. On the other hand, don't despair either. Regular Expressions look more frightening than they actually are, and after gaining a little bit of experience, you too will be able to read and write your own regular expressions with no more difficulty than writing your own IPv6 address.

Why do I need this?

Regular expressions are used by UAG to describe patterns of information that would be inefficient or impossible to describe otherwise. For example, if you need to define multiple server names, as you commonly do when publishing applications, RegEx can save you a lot of work. You might have to include 20 servers in your application, but using RegEx, you might be able to describe all of them in one line of text, thus saving yourself a lot of typing, or mouse activity, or both. In other cases, such as when defining access rules for complex applications, it's virtually impossible to define the rules without using RegEx patterns. If you've been in the computer field for a while, you are probably familiar with describing DOS file names using patterns such as *.* or *.exe, and you will find that RegEx, although more complex, is not that much harder to understand.

What are Regular Expressions?

Regular Expressions are a formal, or syntactical, language, used to create strings of text, which define a search pattern. The writer of a regular expression has the choice to create a regular expression as specific or as relaxed as he wishes, meaning that it could match only a very specific piece of text, or it could possibly match many text strings, as long as all of them follow the same pattern described by the regular expression. Many programs and programming languages contain a RegEx processing engine, which allows the programmer to define patterns, rather than specifying exact strings for everything. A regular expression is a piece of text that contains regular characters, known as **literals**, and special characters, known as **non-literals**. You can think of non-literals as 'commands' that tell the engine to do something special. For example, the regular expression `tal[cekly]` means something that starts with tal and ends with either c, e, k, l or y. We are using just 10 characters to describe 5 distinct words!

The UAG RegEx RegEx syntax

In the world of computers, we are all very familiar with using wildcards to describe files and folders. RegEx is referred to, sometimes, as "wildcards on steroids". We will review here the basics of this syntax, with the help of which you will be able first to read and understand the regular expressions used by UAG, and then to modify those and even to craft new expressions, to match your specific needs. We will not cover every detail of the RegEx syntax, as there is enough of that to fill this entire book. We will, however, cover those you really need. It's important to know that there are many flavours of RegEx, and their syntax might change slightly from one to the other, but we will be referring only to the "RegEx++" syntax, since this is the library used by UAG.

Literals

It is probably obvious, but we'll still mention it: a RegEx may be formed of just plain letters, which do not have any special "RegEx meaning". These are called **literal characters**. Such a RegEx will simply match any string that includes the RegEx literals. For example: the RegEx `port`.

This RegEx will be matched by the following string: *port*. That's it! Just one single and very specific string will match. This is a slight difference in the usage of RegEx in UAG, compared to a regular RegEx search. In a regular RegEx search, as long as the pattern defined by the RegEx — in our example here `port` — appears anywhere in the searched text, that is considered a match. UAG, however, is more restrictive in that the RegEx pattern must match the entire string. We'll see soon how we can tweak our RegEx pattern to match more strings.

When creating RegEx, the English alphabet and numbers are considered to be literals, as well as some other characters.

Special characters

Special characters, also known as **non-literals** are characters that have a special meaning in the context of a regular expression. These are sometimes also referred to as **metacharacters**, and here they are:

- **The dot or period (.)**: The dot character **is** the quintessential wildcard of regular expressions. This special RegEx character will match any *single* character.

  For example the RegEx: `port.`

  - Strings that will match: `ports`, `portA`, `portC`, `portX`, `Port8`, and so on. Note that in UAG, RegEx is *not* case sensitive.

  - Strings that will *not match* the above RegEx: `portable`, `airport`, `port12`, and so on.

- **The asterisk or star (*)**: This metacharacter has the meaning of a *repetition* in RegEx, instructing the engine to match whatever was the previous character, *zero or more* times.

  For example the RegEx: `port*` (meaning the characters p, o, r, followed by t repeated zero times, or once, or multiple times)

  - Strings that will match: `por`, `port`, `portt`, `porttttt`

  - Strings that will not match: `portable`, `airport`, `port12`, and so on

The combination of the dot and the star is going to become a good friend of yours when you read and write RegExes. This combination means "any character" (the dot), repeated zero or more times (the star), which in effect means "anything"!

The RegEx: `port.*` (meaning the characters p, o, r, t, followed by "any character" repeated zero or more times)

  - Strings that will match: `port`, `ports`, `portable`, `Port-au-Prince`, `Port 80`, `portABC`, `portal`, `Portsmouth Football Club`, and so on

  - Strings that will not match: `airport`, `Freeport`, and so on

- **The plus sign (+)**: This is just like the star sign, except that the plus sign denotes a repetition of *at least once* or more times of the preceding character (unlike the star sign, which also allows no repetition at all).

  The RegEx: `server1+`

    ◦ Will match: `server1`, `server11`, `server111111`, and so on

    ◦ Will not match: `server1`, `server12`, `server7`, *and so on*

- **The question mark (?)**: This, too, is a repetition metacharacter, which allows for the preceding character to be repeated exactly *once or zero* times (meaning not at all).

  The RegEx: `appa?`

    ◦ Will match: `AppA`, `AppAA`,.and so on

    ◦ Will not match: `AppAAA`, `AppAB`, `App5`, and so on

- **The backslash (/)**: This is also known as "the escape character". Its task is to be placed in front of the special RegEx character when you want it to be treated by the RegEx engine as a *literal*, and not as a special character.

  The RegEx: `/images/logo\.gif` (meaning the dot before the string `gif` is a literal dot, not "any character")

    ◦ Will match: `/images/logo.gif`

    ◦ Will not match: `/images/logosgif`, and so on

Note that the repeat expressions we just discussed do not necessarily refer only to the preceding single character. They repeat the preceding "token", which means the preceding character or the preceding character set or sub-expression. Let's see what these are:

- **Character set**: As the name hints, this is a set of characters, where the RegEx engine can match any one of the characters in the set. A character set is delimited by the square brackets, which are both special characters.

  The RegEx: `potato[es]`

    ◦ Will match: `potatoe` and `potatos` (might come in handy when you need to cater for those who make spelling mistakes, like a certain VP back in 1992)

    ◦ Will not match: `potatoes`

- **A range of characters**: This is a special character set, which encompasses a full range of characters, for example, the letters from A to M, or the digits from 0 to 6. You do not need to specify all the characters in the range, instead you only specify the first one and the last one, divided by a dash (-). You can have more than one range in the set, and you can also mix-and-match between ranges and single characters in the same set. Note that the "-" character is a special character when found between square brackets, unless it is at the very beginning or very end of the set, which then makes it a literal.

  The RegEx: `server[a-f1-5]` (meaning "server", followed by *one* of the letters a to f, or the letters A to F, or the digits 1 to 5)

    ○ Will match: `serverD`, `serverF`, `server2`, `server5`, and so on

    ○ Will not match: `serverA1`, `serverAB`, `server05`, and so on.

  The RegEx: `/scripts/[a-z0-9_-]+\.vbs` (means `/scripts/`, followed by one of the letters a to z or the letters A to Z or the digits 0 to 9 or the underscore or dash, any of these repeated one or multiple times (due to the plus sign), followed by a literal period, and then by `vbs`)

    ○ Will match: `/scripts/mapdrives.vbs`, `/scripts/home_017.vbs`, and so on

    ○ Will not match: `/scriptsdrives.vbs`, `/scripts/test/run.vbs`, `/scripts/policy.cgi`, and so on

- **The excluding character set**: This is very similar to the character set, except that the characters specified in the set must *not* appear in the string. The excluding character set is defined by a caret (^) sign immediately following the opening square bracket.

  The RegEx: `server-[^br]ed` (meaning `server-`, followed by any single character except the letters b or r (as always, non case-sensitive), and then followed by `ed`)

    ○ Will match: `server-Ted`, `server-Med`, `server-8ED`, and so on

    ○ Will not match: `serverTed`, `server-Red`, `server-Bed`, and so on

- **Alternatives and sub-expressions**: Alternatives are more than one option that could result in a match. The options in a RegEx alternative are divided by the pipe symbol or vertical bar (|). The options can be single characters or groups of characters (for example: `green|yellow`), and they can also be grouped in a sub-expression, where the sub-expression delimiters are the opening and closing round parenthesis characters (`(` and `)`)

The RegEx: `/images/[a-z0-9_-]+\.(gif|jpg|jpeg)` (meaning `/images/`, followed by any letter, or digit, or underscore or dash, repeated one or more times, followed by a period and then by either `gif` or `jpg` or `jpeg`)

- ○ Will match: `/images/logo_small.gif`, `/images/corp17.jpeg`, `/images/87329.jpg`, and so on

- ○ Will not match: `/image/line.jpg`, `/logo.gif`, `/images/left(a).png`, and so on

Before we conclude, let's try to understand how this works in the real world. The last sample above shows an expression you might need. The default ruleset for the portal allows only JPG files to be used, and will block other file extensions. If you need to customize the appearance, and your design uses GIF files instead of JPG, you will have to change some of the portal rules using the pipe symbol to also accept GIF. Another example is when publishing major web applications, where we often need to specify many servers during the application-publishing wizard. Even using copy-and-paste, this is still a tedious and error-prone task, but RegEx allows us to reduce the risk and save time. Let's say that your organization uses a cluster of eight servers, named `HRWEB01` to `HRWEB08`. Instead of manually entering all their names, you can simply use the RegEx `HRWEB0[1-8]`. The tricky part is to choose the best combination of literals and non-literals so that we get the appropriate coverage for everything, but nothing (or, as little as possible) more. With time and practice, you will master this too. While experimenting, you might benefit from using a RegEx Evaluator, which can be a stand-alone software, or an online one. We cannot recommend a specific one here, but use your favourite search engine (Bing, we are guessing) to find one. Should you need, you can find more information about the UAG RegEx++ syntax here: `http://technet.microsoft.com/en-us/library/dd282903.aspx`.

B
Introduction to ASP

What?! I ain't no programmer! If that's what you are thinking right now, don't worry, because neither am I. This short introduction to ASP programming is not about to make you into a programmer. However, UAG has quite a bit of web-based user interface, and knowing a little about ASP and how it works will allow you to customize it to some degree. This could become very helpful even for small visual tweaks, but also for advanced customizations, such as custom detection scripts and integration of third party components into your environment.

What is ASP, and how does it work?

ASP (Active Server Pages) is actually not a programming language, but an engine for generating dynamic web pages on the server side. As you probably know, normal web pages are written using the **HTML** language, and these are referred to as "static" pages—they always look the same. As the web progressed, several technologies evolved to allow dynamic content. For example, **JavaScript** allows a web designer to include code inside the page, which creates dynamic content. JavaScript code usually runs on the CLIENT side, where it can manipulate content and appearance dynamically, but it's still "static" in a sense, because when it is sent from the server, it's always the same.

ASP pages are scripts that contain code that runs on the SERVER side. The code can make content and appearance changes to the page before it is sent to the user. Once it reaches the browser on the client's side, it appears to be static (though it may still contain JavaScript code that makes the page look more dynamic). With time, ASP itself was superseded by **ASP.NET** (pronounced ASP Dot Net), which offers advanced programming options. UAG includes code both in ASP and ASP.NET.

Creating ASP pages is really simple: these are just simple text files, which can contain regular HTML and/or client-side JavaScript code, but can also contain special ASP code. You can create these pages in a clever and advanced program such as **Visual Studio** or **SharePoint Designer**, but you can also create them using **Notepad**. Then, the file can be placed in a directory published by **IIS**, and named to have the extension `.asp`, and this causes IIS to process them when they are being requested by an end-user.

When IIS processes an ASP page, it looks for special tags that mark the start of the **server-side code**, and then runs the commands it finds in there. These commands can do a lot, starting from simple things like generating HTML code to alter appearance or content, and ending with very advanced code that can open databases, perform high level calculations and even emulate GUI-based programs (for example, most of the interface for **Outlook Web Access** is written this way).

The programming language used with ASP is usually **VBScript**, although it's somewhat limited. For example, with ASP, you cannot create GUI-based interaction like a VBscript can, but you can emulate some using other techniques. For example, it can build HTML tables and populate them with graphics and scripts and thus emulate a GUI based application. If needed, ASP can be configured to run commands in other languages too, such as JavaScript and **PerlScript**.

What can you do with it?

As we mentioned, parts of UAG are built using ASP, and understanding the language a bit will help you to understand how they work. If, with time, you become proficient enough in it, you could even manipulate them yourself. UAG offers a specific customization framework that allows you to influence the content of UAG pages, as well as different aspects of the flow of the authentication mechanism. You should not perform other ASP code changes that are outside of this framework, since if such a customization ends up breaking functionality, this is not supported and you are on your own.

Getting started with ASP

A typical ASP page looks very similar to an HTML page. Sometimes you might have to strain your eyes to even find the code in it. Within a page you often find a block of ASP code tucked away between HTML. The ASP portion starts with `<%` and ends with `%>`, and you should be able to see that it looks more like commands:

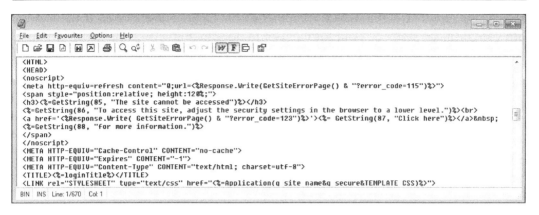

```
<HTML>
<HEAD>
<noscript>
<meta http-equiv=refresh content="0;url=<%Response.Write(GetSiteErrorPage() & "?error_code=115")%>">
<span style="position:relative; height:120%;">
<h3><%=GetString(85, "The site cannot be accessed")%></h3>
<%=GetString(86, "To access this site, adjust the security settings in the browser to a lower level.")%><br>
<a href='<%Response.Write( GetSiteErrorPage() & "?error_code=123")%>'><%= GetString(87, "Click here")%></a> 
<%=GetString(88, "for more information.")%>
</span>
</noscript>
<META HTTP-EQUIV="Cache-Control" CONTENT="no-cache">
<META HTTP-EQUIV="Expires" CONTENT="-1">
<META HTTP-EQUIV="Content-Type" CONTENT="text/html; charset=utf-8">
<TITLE><%=loginTitle%></TITLE>
<LINK rel="STYLESHEET" type="text/css" href="<%=Application(q site name&q secure&TEMPLATE CSS)%>">
```

The above script is a bit tough to understand at this point, of course, so don't get discouraged. As you can see, the first five lines are simple HTML, and the sixth line starts with the `<h3>` HTML tag, which sets the browser to display the text that follows it as a header. Then, the ASP script kicks in, and runs `GetString` with some parameters. This is what we refer to as a "function". You cannot see the function, which is located somewhere else, but what it does is open a language file with the various text messages UAG can show, and selects message no. 85, which reads, as you can guess, **The site cannot be accessed**. The advantage of using the `GetString` function is that the server can decide what language to return to the user, without touching the code or HTML pages. So the same `GetString` function, when the end-user decides to use the French language, will return: **Impossible d'accéder au site**, while for German it will return: **Auf die Site kann nicht zugegriffen werden**. As you can see, this function is used several more times in this script file and other parts of the UAG code, intermixed with the various HTML commands.

Putting the pieces together

Often, a program is comprised of several (sometimes hundreds or thousands) files that work together. This entails one file "calling" another, or redirecting to another. When a user enters the portal, for example, the file `InitParams.aspx` is read and executed, and it then redirects to the file `InstallAndDetect.asp`, which calls a bunch of JavaScript files like `LoginTimeout.js`, `install.js`, `detection.js` and more. Then, it redirects to `Login.asp`, which is the page in which the user has to feed in his authentication credentials. In the following examples, we see a script (left) that has four `include` commands, where each of the `.inc` files has more code that can be used by the primary script. By using `.inc` files, we can reuse the same code or content in multiple places. On the right piece of code, we see a script that ends with the command `response.redirect`, which tells the browser to request another file (`/InternalSite/Validate.asp`) and process it.

Depending on the way the code is written, this can be done automatically by the browser, or it can stop and wait for the user to do something (like the Login page).

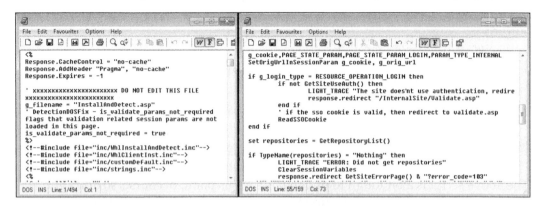

If you are wondering about the JavaScript files we mentioned previously, then this is also a very common practice with ASP. ASP code runs on the server, and the data that gets sent to the client is just static HTML. Often, we may want some code to run on the client side too, and that's where JavaScript complements ASP. For example, you already know that UAG installs **ActiveX** controls as part of the endpoint client installation. The process of ActiveX installation needs to be done on the client side, and for that, a JavaScript function is used—it's contained in the script file `Install.js`, which we mentioned previously, and looks like this:

```
Function WhlInstallComponentManager(compMgrInstallTag)
{
        index = 1;
        startProgress();
        var testObj,
                curver="4,0,1101,0",
                newver="4,0,1101,0";

        try
        {
                bExist=true;
                testObj = new ActiveXObject("ComponentManager.Installer.2");
                // Get this here, while in try/catch block, so if old client
exists, but doesn't support the Version
                // property, this would trigger an update as well
                curver = testObj.Version();
        }
```

Some more ASP principles

Other than linking files, the code can twist around in more ways. Generally, when an ASP page is processed by the server, it goes from top to bottom. Stuff that's not enclosed in `<% %>` gets sent to the client as is, with no processing, and the stuff that's inside the `<% %>` gets processed line-by-line. A lot of the action is about setting data into variables, which are just storage containers for data. A variable can contain a string of text, a number, or even a "collection" of numbers or text. The computer can also perform actions on the variables. For example, if we have two variables that have numbers in them, we can add their content, or perform other mathematical functions on them. For example, some code might put the date on which a file was created into a variable, and then subtract that from today's date, to calculate how old the file is. This is a way programs sometimes use to know if they need to get updated. It's worth noting that other programming languages are often stricter with regards to variables, and require you to define exactly what *type* of data the variable will contain.

If a variable contains text, it can be "added" to another by way of concatenation. The two texts are just linked together! For example, "Enter" + "prise" results in the string "Enterprise". Using the command `INSTR`, one can search within a string for another string, and then use the commands `LEN`, `LEFT`, `MID`, and `RIGHT` to cut out a piece of it. For example, UAG sometimes uses these to extract the protocol and server name from a URL:

In case you didn't guess, `LEN` checks the length of a string, `LEFT` returns a piece of a string, starting from the left of it, `RIGHT` does the opposite, and `MID` takes a piece from the middle.

To make the code easier to read, programmers try to give descriptive names to their variables, and usually start them with standard prefixes. A variable that starts with str will hold a string, and one that starts with int will hold an integer value (a number). You may also see the prefix bol, which stands for **Boolean** (a value of either **TRUE** or **FALSE**), and col, which is a collection of items. Some programmers use a shorter version of the prefixes — s, i, b, and c for str, int, bol, and col. Another thing programmers do to make things easier on everyone is include textual comments that describes what the code does. Such a comment starts with an apostrophe ('), to let the server know that it's supposed to ignore it. In the code sample above, you can see three such comments.

Two other very important things used in programs are **If-Then** statements, and loops. An If-Then statement is used to check if a certain situation is true, and act upon the results. For example, in the previous screenshot, we are checking if the variable strTempURL has the character "/"or the character "\" in it, and based on the results grab the piece of the string that's before that character. An If-Then statement starts with an IF, can have an ELSE and ELSEIF parts in the middle, if needed, and must end with an END IF.

Loops, on the other hand, come in several flavors. The classic is a **For-Next** loop, and another is a **Do-Loop**, which we can see in the previous screenshot as well. A loop is useful when we want to go through a lot of data and do something with it. The above script iterates through the characters of a URL, starting after the colon (:), and looks for the first character that's not a "/" or a "\", and then extracts the left part of the URL until that character...this returns the protocol part of the URL — HTTP://, HTTPS://, FTP://, and so on.

A For-Next loop will use a numerical (a.k.a. Integer) variable to perform something a certain number of times. For example, the loop would start with For i = 0 to 100, and end with Next. When performed, the commands inside the loop will be executed 101 times (If you know why 101 and not 100 — then you're a natural programmer!).

A Do-Loop will do something until a condition is met. The example in the above screenshot does it's shtick of incrementing the position counter (nPos = nPos + 1) until the character that's in that position is neither "/" nor "\". Once the condition is met, the loop ends and proceeds to the code that's after the ending-term Loop.

There are additional types of loops, like **For-Each** and **While-Wend**, but they are used less. You can read more about them here:http://msdn.microsoft.com/en-us/library/cbe735w2(VS.85).aspx.

No one likes to repeat himself

Just like in life, programmers don't like to repeat themselves when writing code, and we can cut down on that using the inc files that we described earlier, but also **functions** and **subroutines**. These are groups of commands that are given a name, and can be *called* from somewhere else within the program—like a tool that you can get from the toolbox when needed. Whenever there is something has to be repeated many times, programmers put it inside a function or a subroutine, and then just call it whenever needed. While normal code is parsed line-by-line, a function may be placed anywhere in the code (though most programmers like to put them either at the very top, or the very bottom of a file, or in a separate file altogether). A function starts with the word **Function**, and ends with **End Function**. A subroutine starts with **Sub**, and ends with **End Sub**.

When a function is called, the code can send data to it, and it can return a result. We mentioned an example of this earlier, with the `GetString` function. A sub, on the other hand, cannot— it just runs the code that's in it. When a function is called, the call includes the stuff we send to it in parentheses, and the result is usually assigned into a variable so we can do something with it. In the above function (left), we can see how the fifth line runs a function that reads a file, and its content is copied into the variable `str_source` (with complex programs, functions and subroutines are also often nested inside each other, as we see here). How do we know which of these commands are a call for a function and which are just commands? Well, that takes time and experience, and a good reference resource is quite important. This online reference, for example, is quite comprehensive: `http://msdn.microsoft.com/en-us/library/sx7b3k7y(v=VS.85).aspx`.

You will often find that a certain function needs to be used not only within a file, but also within a large number of files that work together. For this, we use things like the `INCLUDE` statement we saw earlier—we write the function in a separate file, and then call that file into other files using an include statement. The file extension doesn't matter—it can be anything, but it's customary to use "inc" to signify to the reader that this is a file that's included in another.

So, what's in it for me?

The bottom line is that the code that UAG runs is complicated. It was written and re-written over many years, and no one can be expected to just go through it in a day. The code, just like any other, goes around in loops, jumps from script to script and uses tons of variables and functions. We already mentioned the tool HTTPWatch back in Chapter 8 as a tool that can help us see what's going on. It shows the files that are being requested by the browser, and can help track them. It won't however show you files that are executed due to a server-side INCLUDE statement. Since this tool runs on the browser, it only shows the resulting HTML content after the server-side ASP code has been already executed, without the original VBScript code, but once you know which file leads to what file, it makes it clearer to track the code itself.

To really go anywhere with all this new knowledge you now possess, you need to figure out what you want to do. If you want to change some page that UAG shows to the user (assuming, of course, that the page is supported for customization), you first need to figure out which page this is (HTTPWatch can help) and start reading the code. Often, it will contain comments that indicate what it is doing and why. As you read, try to recognize what are functions and what are commands. Make a list of variables and try to figure out what they do and what kind of data they hold. Some people can do this in their heads, and others may need a piece of paper to keep tabs on everything. Professional programmers use a "debugger", which connects to a running program and allows you to step through different commands and "freeze" at a specific command, and shows what variables exist at that point in time, and what values they hold.

Naturally, you will need to understand a lot about HTML as well, and possibly JavaScript, to really know what's going on. The code will usually be used to manipulate HTML commands. For example, a set of loops can be used to create the <TR> and <TD> elements of a table and populate the table with data. By examining the resulting HTML code you recorded with HTTPWatch, and reading the original code in the ASP file and its comrades, you should be able to slowly understand what's going on, and with time, carefully change the code to do what you want it to do.

The road to being able to read UAG's code is long, and to being able to change it is even longer, but you can start with the official UAG customization guide, published by Microsoft: http://technet.microsoft.com/en-us/library/ee861168.aspx

Index

SharePoint publishing
  considerations 116, 118
  different external name 118-120
  different internal name 118-120
  same external FQDN name 120
  same external name 121
  same internal FQDN name 120
  same internal name 121
short name. *See* host name
Single Sign-On. *See* SSO
Single Sign On 190
smart card authentication 186, 187
SMB (server message block) 143
socket forwarding component,
        client components
  about 219, 220
  Layered Service Provider (LSP) 219
  Namespace Service Provider (NSP) 219
special characters 439-442
split-brains 349
SQL Server Reporting Services (SSRS) 413
SSL Application Tunneling component,
        client components
  about 218
  ActiveX based component 219
  Java based component 219
SSL Application Tunneling
  about 126
  ports 127
  the Port 127
SSL Application Tunneling component
        automatic disconnection 141
SSL Network Tunneling (Network
        Connector) component 399
SSL Network Tunneling component, client
        components
  Network Connector (NC) 220
SSL Network Tunneling. *See* Network Con-
        nector
SSL Tunneling 126
SSO 67
SSTP 431
SSTP (Secure Socket Tunneling Protocol)
        26
Statement of Health (SOH) 257
step-up authentication 179

Subject Alternative Name. *See* SAN
Subject Alternative Name certificate. *See*
        SAN certificate
subnetting 338
subroutines 449
System Health Agent (SHA) 257
System Health Validator (SHV) 257

T

TACACS 176
Teredo 339, 341, 345
The Dungeon 22
Thumbprint 300
TMG (Threat Management Gateway) 11
TMG management console
  about 281, 284
  used, for live monitoring 281-283
traffic filtering 146
troubleshooting
  administrative errors 398
  application issues 402
  client issues 419
  general errors 427
troubleshooting, DA
  about 379, 380
  additional resources 395
  advanced troubleshooting 394
  client side issues 389
  DA, removing 380
  server related issues 385-389
  setup and configuration errors 381-383
  transition technology issues 390-394
trunk
  about 63
  adding, post actions 90-93
  designing 73
  types 65
trunk, types
  ADFS 66
  Basic 65, 66
  HTTPS 65
  portal 66
  redirect 65
  Webmail 65
trunk-level authentication settings 176-182

About Packt Publishing

Packt, pronounced 'packed', published its first book "Mastering phpMyAdmin for Effective MySQL Management" in April 2004 and subsequently continued to specialize in publishing highly focused books on specific technologies and solutions.

Our books and publications share the experiences of your fellow IT professionals in adapting and customizing today's systems, applications, and frameworks. Our solution based books give you the knowledge and power to customize the software and technologies you're using to get the job done. Packt books are more specific and less general than the IT books you have seen in the past. Our unique business model allows us to bring you more focused information, giving you more of what you need to know, and less of what you don't.

Packt is a modern, yet unique publishing company, which focuses on producing quality, cutting-edge books for communities of developers, administrators, and newbies alike. For more information, please visit our website: www.packtpub.com.

About Packt Enterprise

In 2010, Packt launched two new brands, Packt Enterprise and Packt Open Source, in order to continue its focus on specialization. This book is part of the Packt Enterprise brand, home to books published on enterprise software – software created by major vendors, including (but not limited to) IBM, Microsoft and Oracle, often for use in other corporations. Its titles will offer information relevant to a range of users of this software, including administrators, developers, architects, and end users.

Writing for Packt

We welcome all inquiries from people who are interested in authoring. Book proposals should be sent to author@packtpub.com. If your book idea is still at an early stage and you would like to discuss it first before writing a formal book proposal, contact us; one of our commissioning editors will get in touch with you.

We're not just looking for published authors; if you have strong technical skills but no writing experience, our experienced editors can help you develop a writing career, or simply get some additional reward for your expertise.

Microsoft Windows Communication Foundation 4.0 Cookbook for Developing SOA Applications

ISBN: 978-1-849680-76-9   Paperback: 316 pages

Over 85 easy recipes for managing communication between applications

1. Master WCF concepts and implement them in real-world environments

2. An example-packed guide with clear explanations and screenshots to enable communication between applications and services and make robust SOA applications

3. Resolve frequently encountered issues effectively with simple and handy recipes

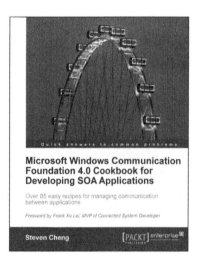

WCF 4.0 Multi-tier Services Development with LINQ to Entities

ISBN: 978-1-849681-14-8   Paperback: 348 pages

Build SOA applications on the Microsoft platform with this hands-on guide updated for VS2010

1. Master WCF and LINQ to Entities concepts by completing practical examples and applying them to your real-world assignments

2. The first and only book to combine WCF and LINQ to Entities in a multi-tier real-world WCF service

3. Ideal for beginners who want to build scalable, powerful, easy-to-maintain WCF services

Please check **www.PacktPub.com** for information on our titles

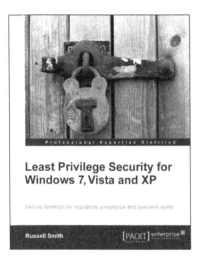

Least Privilege Security for Windows 7, Vista and XP

Secure desktops for regulatory compliance and business agility

Russell Smith   [PACKT] enterprise

Least Privilege Security for Windows 7, Vista and X

ISBN: 978-1-849680-04-2   Paperback: 464 pages

Secure desktops for regulatory compliance and business agility

1. Implement Least Privilege Security in Windows 7, Vista and XP to prevent unwanted system changes

2. Achieve a seamless user experience with the different components and compatibility features of Windows and Active Directory

3. Mitigate the problems and limitations many users may face when running legacy applications

Small Business Server 2008
Installation, Migration, and Configuration

Set up and run your small business server making it deliver big business impact

David Overton   [PACKT]

Small Business Server 2008 – Installation, Migration, and Configuration

ISBN: 978-1-847196-30-9   Paperback: 408 pages

Set up and run your small business server making it deliver big business impact

1. # Step-by-step guidance through the installation and configuration process with numerous pictures

2. Successfully install SBS 2008 into your business, either as a new installation or by migrating from SBS 2003

3. Configure hosted web sites for public and secure information exchange using Office Live for Small Business and Office Live Workspaces

Please check **www.PacktPub.com** for information on our titles

CPSIA information can be obtained at www.ICGtesting.com
Printed in the USA
LVOW03s1724150514

385952LV00011B/479/P